DENIM AND LEATHER

Michael Hann

Bazillion Points

PRAISE FOR *DENIM AND LEATHER*:

"Louder, faster, funnier...a number of lively vignettes... fascinating and entertaining" —*The Telegraph*

"Heavy metal fans will find much to enjoy."—*Independent*

"Entertaining and informative... In an extraordinary feat of structural engineering, *Denim and Leather* corrals the contributions of more than a hundred interviewees into a cohesive story of a movement that was at best disunified. The book is often funny, and even ribald. It is to Michael Hann's credit that [a] sense of poignancy...permeates almost every page. There's more than enough here to make this exhaustive labor of love the equal of other standard-bearing oral histories such as *Everyone Loves Our Town* and *Please Kill Me*." —*Kerrang!*

"*Denim and Leather* captures a moment in time and a genre of music that had a brief moment in the sun. The book is an honest portrayal, directly from the horse's mouth. The interesting thing is that it was people trying to discover their own identities, and the book sums it up by the people who experienced it." —Phil Collen, Def Leppard

"[An] entertaining and poignant oral history...part of the book's charm is Hann's rendering of local accents, even as his interviewees hold forth on their lurid flirtations with the dark side." —*Financial Times*

"Finally, a book about one of the most overlooked and unfairly derided movements in music history. There is so much in here, metal music that shaped everything that came afterwards, joy, pathos, humour and darkness. I learned so much; now excuse me while I go brush up on Witchfynde."—Frank Turner

"An exhaustively researched and entertaining book full of new interviews with most of the key players, offering genuine insights into a movement that changed the face of rock for the better." —*Louder Than War*

"There is a real tenderness to Michael Hann's perception of music, a perception that has balance of forthright investigation and humane intrigue. Hann's perspective on the New Wave of British Heavy Metal leads *Denim and Leather* to be what I want as a music fan: a revelation of the overlooked and a celebration of the underdog. Which is what the genre was all about in the first place! Magic."—Joe Talbot, Idles

"*Denim and Leather* acts both as the oral history its fans deserve and a deeply evocative primer for those of us who weren't paying attention at the time. With *Denim and Leather*, Michael Hann has masterfully interwoven dozens of disparate narratives to create a deeply evocative oral history of a hugely misunderstood chapter in British music history. *Denim and Leather* voyages beyond music history and into the realm of sociology to honor the importance of the misunderstood movement whose history it exists to tell—in the process creating a deeply evocative primer for both fans and the merely curious."
—Pete Paphides, *Broken Greek*

"Through interviews Hann presents a very comprehensive overview of the era. The amount of detail is incredible. The overall story is very familiar, stories about the various pubs, newsletters, magazines, radio shows, demo tapes, and quirky personalities that were a part of the early development of the scene. It was an exciting time and the stories provided by the people who were they, first hand, adds extra vibrancy and life to these tales."
—*Metal-Rules.com*

"Succeeds brilliantly in demonstrating why the NWOBHM is historically interesting. And the book also does something special: it makes the NWOBHM lovable."
—*The Quietus*

Steam rising from the crowd at the Monsters of Rock festival at Castle Donington, Leicestershire, August 22, 1981. GEORGE BODNAR ARCHIVE | ICONICPIX

For Tom and Daniel Kennish, and Ian Watts,
who first played me this music,
forty or so years ago

DENIM AND LEATHER

The Rise and Fall of the New Wave of British Heavy Metal

First U.S. printing, 2022

BAZILLION POINTS BOOKS

New York | United States

BAZILLIONPOINTS.COM

COVER: *Denim and Leather Man with Landscape, c.* 1982, by Max Siebel

BAZILLION THANKS TO Max Siebel, Tom Gabriel Fischer, George Chin, Steve Hammonds, Rob Halford, Neal Kay, Brian Tatler, Tom Noble, Tom Russ, Peter Paulson, Don Weeks, Geoff Barton and *Kerrang!*, Mike Smail, Satan, Omid Yamini, Jamie Walters, Area Records, Roman, Vivienne, and Dianna.

ISBN 978-1-935950-25-7

Printed in the United States

Library of Congress Control Number: 2022943416

Library of Congress Cataloging-in-Publication Data is available upon request.

Contents

Seven-inch singles, most of them self-released, were the NWOBHM's weapon of choice.

Introduction

The New Wave of British Heavy Metal was both a real thing and a confection. It did not form itself around a small group of people who hung around the same clubs, in the way the first waves of London and New York punk did. It was instead diffuse and regional. While it had its centers of gravity—the East End of London, Newcastle-upon-Tyne, the West Midlands (and, specifically, the small town of Stourbridge, which produced two of its greatest groups—Diamond Head and Witchfinder General)—it did not have a focal point.

Nor was it musically unified. The New Wave of British Heavy Metal (NWOBHM) encompassed everything from the pop-rock of Praying Mantis to the horrible noise of Venom, and all points in between. Many of the NWOBHM bands had been playing in one form or another for many years before the phrase "New Wave of British Heavy Metal" was coined. The late Paul Samson noted, mordantly, that he had been making the same music for an age but no one had cared until, to his surprise, he became one of the figureheads of NWOBHM. Other bands were kids, still in their teens, swept up in the new movement because they represented a generational change from the old guard of heavy rock. And they came from all over Britain—from Northern Ireland, Wales and Scotland, from provincial towns where the music industry never ventured. NWOBHM, truly, was democratic in a way the big-city scenes celebrated in the music papers never were. You didn't need to be hanging around the right club nights, or in possession of the right rare records, to be a NWOBHM musician. You just needed to play loud, and play heavy, and someone, somewhere would embrace you.

Yet NWOBHM was real—it was a self-fulfilling prophecy that proved to be a watershed in metal music. It was during the years 1978 to 1982 that metal as it came to be understood was codified: that the palm-muted chug of guitars took over from the vast open chords of Black Sabbath and Led Zeppelin, that the bands' uniforms of spandex, leather, denim and studs became commonplace, that the fans took to wearing "battle jackets" covered with patches. The bands of NWOBHM exerted a profound influence over future generations, notably through the direct inspiration they provided to the US thrash metal bands who emerged in their wake, and also in their role in fomenting the extreme metal of Scandinavia—Mercyful Fate were, to all intents and purposes, a NWOBHM band who happened to be Danish, while the Norwegian black metal bands who emerged in the late 1980s and early 1990s professed an explicit debt to Venom, even if the extremities of their behavior appalled Venom themselves. NWOBHM proved that metal could be a DIY enterprise, that heavy metal could thrive in the underground and did not need the bright lights of the biggest stages. Generations of extreme and underground metal musicians owe the bands of the late 1970s and early 1980s a debt.

This book is not a complete chronological history of NWOBHM. It could not be. There were simply too many bands with too short a lifespan to do that. There are important bands who are mentioned only in passing or not at all—Fist, White Spirit, Tank, More, Holocaust, Blitzkrieg and plenty of others. There are bands whose presence in this book does not reflect their status within metal—Iron Maiden and Samson, for example. Nor does this book provide a top-to-tail history of any single band. For that, there are official biographies and specialist books, in which you can find out what song was on which B side and who the bass player was on any given Tuesday night at the Marquee.

Instead, *Denim and Leather*—a title taken from the Saxon song that celebrated the metal explosion—tells a series of stories that together paint a picture of what NWOBHM was and what it meant, beginning with the night of May 8, 1979, when Iron Maiden, Samson and Angel Witch played Neal Kay's Heavy Metal Crusade gig at the Music Machine—now Koko—in Camden Town, London, and the subsequent *Sounds* review in which the six words "New Wave of British Heavy Metal" were first printed. Each chapter picks out a theme in the rise and fall of NWOBHM, be it the club circuit on which the bands

learned their trade, the major label signing spree of 1979, the obsession with the occult, or the launch of the world's first festival dedicated solely to heavy metal. Two bands get chapters devoted solely to them, as well as cropping up elsewhere—Diamond Head and Venom, both of whom left legacies that extended far beyond record sales—because their stories illustrate particular facets of the NWOBHM experience: the power of doing it yourself, and the perils of doing it yourself.

Writing *Denim and Leather* this way, though, has meant some of the most memorable interviewees—such as Thunderstick, the masked drummer of Samson—don't appear as frequently as their colorful recollections perhaps deserve. And my apologies to Mick Hopkins of Quartz, the only interviewee who didn't make it through to the final draft.

Because metal fans to this day dispute exactly what NWOBHM was, this book is necessarily incomplete, to some extent. While I include the bands formed from the ashes of Deep Purple—Rainbow, Whitesnake and Gillan—who found commercial success in the NWOBHM era, I don't include Black Sabbath, who were a crucial influence on the movement (and, arguably, were influenced themselves on the *Heaven and Hell* and *Mob Rules* albums). Nor, though they are mentioned several times, do I include Motörhead, who—like Sabbath—seemed to exist on their own planet entirely. Regrettably, the writer Geoff Barton did not respond to many emails asking for an interview, but he haunts these pages nevertheless, in the recollections of almost every one of my interviewees. Peter Mensch, who managed Def Leppard, and was mentioned again and again by musicians, told me to stop emailing him asking for an interview. Iron Maiden are represented only through the memories of former members and associates, because Phantom Management insist Maiden are not and never were a NWOBHM band, so they did not wish to put Steve Harris or Bruce Dickinson forward for interview (it appears that no band that found commercial success or left a deep and lasting legacy considers themselves to have been a NWOBHM band, even while they reaped the advantages of their associations with the movement at the time. Def Leppard, though equally adamant they are not and never were NWOBHM, participated happily, though).

The world depicted in *Denim and Leather* is one that has disappeared, one of stale cigarettes and flat beer in backstreet pubs. No longer do

young bands learn their trade by playing sets either side of the bingo in working men's clubs. Nor does any band with ambitions to end up with a major label dare exist entirely off the grid of the mainstream music industry until such time as the industry comes looking for them. Nowadays the bands who signed to Neat Records in Newcastle would have been flocking down to London at the earliest opportunity.

They would have publicists in place long before they reached any kind of public attention. But it's not just a lost world of the music industry, it's a lost world of white, working-class male culture: being a rock star was an aspiration in the same sense that being a footballer was: a rocket launch out of a humdrum existence. (One of the interviewees here, Rick Savage, had even tried being a footballer first, having trials at several clubs before switching to music.) NWOBHM was entirely apolitical (unless you count Us Against The Man anthems such as "Breaking the Law" by Judas Priest or "Strong Arm of the Law" by Saxon as political). It existed in a time before identity politics and where—for better or worse—the fact that it was almost entirely male and wholly white was completely unremarkable, though that has slowly changed as the years have passed and metal has become a worldwide genre. (In early 2019, in Bangalore, I saw a female-fronted death metal band from Nepal, on a bill that also featured the American band Suffocation, including the African-American guitarist Terrance Hobbs. Metal has been evolving for years now.)

The book is based almost entirely on hundreds of hours of interviews with participants in the New Wave of British Heavy Metal—musicians, managers, producers, those who worked for or ran record labels, writers, broadcasters and fans—conducted over the course of 2020. The vast majority of these interviews were conducted specifically for this book or for an oral history of NWOBHM I wrote for the *Guardian* in May 2019. The interviews with Ritchie Blackmore, Ian Gillan, Phil Mogg, Andy Parker, Michael Schenker, Robert Plant, Jimmy Page, Rob Halford, Scott Gorham and Brian Downey were conducted for other projects, but contained material relevant to this book. In a very few instances, my own interviews were supplemented with material from other writers. I am grateful to Dom Lawson for allowing me the use of the transcription of his interview with Cronos of Venom, for the *In Nomine Satanas* box set booklet, to supplement my own Cronos interview. Thanks also to David Fricke for allowing me to use material

from his book *Def Leppard: Animal Instinct*. All quotes from Peter Mensch, Cliff Burnstein, Mutt Lange, Rick Allen and Pete Willis come from David's book. I am indebted to Bauer Media and Wasted Talent Ltd for permission to quote from Geoff Barton's articles for *Sounds* and *Kerrang!* In the few instances where other writers' articles for *Sounds* or *Kerrang!* have been quoted, I tried to track down the writer to seek permission. My apologies to those writers I could not trace. The quotes from *Music Week* magazine are made with kind permission of Future Publishing.

Because the events described are now distant history, recollections differ. Sometimes dramatically. Where participants have differing memories of the same events, the contrasting accounts are presented. Sometimes that was impossible, sadly: Ritchie Blackmore's management did not respond to requests for a follow-up interview to give his version of his rivalry with David Coverdale, the events at Wembley Arena in 1980, or why support bands kept departing Rainbow tours early. Where the interviewees' memories differ from the historical record—in matters of chart positions, or magazine covers, or *Top of the Pops* appearances—I have noted the discrepancy in the text. It is all 40 years ago; no one should be expected to have an exact memory of what happened.

It is a measure of the passage of time that four of my interviewees died in the time between me interviewing them and this book being published: Judy Totton, Ian Ravendale, Jon Zazula, and Malcolm Dome. This book is dedicated, also, to their memories.

In the song that gave this book its name, Saxon's Biff Byford sang of the power of Denim and Leather, how it brought an entire generation of music fans together. He also pointed back at the crowd and said something that holds as true today as it did then: it was those fans who set the spirit free.

Who's Who

ABADDON (Tony Bray)—drums, Venom

PHIL ALEXANDER—fan, future *Kerrang!* editor

RICK ALLEN—drums, Def Leppard

TOM ALLOM—producer, Def Leppard and Judas Priest

PHIL ASTON—guitar, the Handsome Beasts

PHIL BANFIELD—manager, Gillan

GEOFF BARTON—writer, *Sounds* and *Kerrang!*

DAVID BATES—A&R at Phonogram for Def Leppard

PAUL BIRCH—founder, Heavy Metal Records

RITCHIE BLACKMORE—guitar, Deep Purple and Rainbow

GRAHAM BONNET—vocals, Rainbow

DANTE BONUTTO—writer, *Record Mirror* and *Kerrang!*

CLIFF BURNSTEIN—comanager, Def Leppard

BIFF BYFORD—vocals, Saxon

TIM CALDER—fan

MURRAY CHALMERS—publicist, Kate Bush

PHIL COLLEN—guitar, Girl and Def Leppard

PHIL COPE—guitar, Witchfinder General

ANDY COPPING—fan, Download booker/promoter

ANDRO COULTON—bass, Witchfynde

DAVID COVERDALE—vocals, Deep Purple and Whitesnake

JESS COX—vocals, Tygers of Pan Tang

CRONOS (Conrad Lant)—bass and vocals, Venom

STEVE DAWSON—bass, Saxon

JON DEVERILL—vocals, Persian Risk and Tygers of Pan Tang

PAUL DI'ANNO—vocals, Iron Maiden

DAVE DICKSON—writer, *Kerrang!*

MALCOLM DOME—writer, *Record Mirror* and *Kerrang!*

BRIAN DOWNEY—drums, Thin Lizzy

K.K. DOWNING—guitar, Judas Priest

DENISE DUFORT—drums, Girlschool

JOE ELLIOTT—vocals, Def Leppard

FENRIZ—fan, guitar and vocals, Darkthrone

PAUL FLOWER—fan

JOHN GALLAGHER—vocals and bass, Raven

ROBIN GEORGE—producer and engineer, Witchfinder General

IAN GILLAN—vocals, Deep Purple and Gillan

ASHLEY GOODALL—A&R at EMI for Iron Maiden

SCOTT GORHAM—guitar, Thin Lizzy

ROSS HALFIN—photographer, *Sounds* and *Kerrang!*

ROB HALFORD—vocals, Judas Priest

JENNIE HALSALL—publicist, Samson, Rainbow, and Monsters of Rock

STEVE HAMMONDS—fan, music catalog consultant

SEAN HARRIS—vocals, Diamond Head

MIKE HEDGES—producer, Diamond Head

DAVE HILL—vocals, Demon

PETE HINTON—A&R and in-house producer, Carrere Records

TERRY HOPKINSON—bass, Ethel the Frog

NIGEL HUTCHINGS—manager, Marquee

ALLAN JONES—writer, *Melody Maker*

KEITH KAHN-HARRIS—fan, sociologist, and writer

NEAL KAY—DJ, promoter, impresario

IAN KELLY—fan

ROBERT JOHN 'MUTT' LANGE—producer, Def Leppard

DAVE "LIGHTS" BEAZLEY—lighting technician, Iron Maiden

PAUL LOASBY—promoter, Monsters of Rock

KIM MCAULIFFE—vocals and guitar, Girlschool

JOHN MCCOY—bass, Gillan

MARK MANGOLD—keyboards, Touch

MANTAS (Jeffrey Dunn)—guitar, Venom

BERNIE MARSDEN—guitar, Whitesnake

PETER MENSCH—comanager, Def Leppard

PHIL MOGG—vocals, UFO

MONTALO—guitar, Witchfynde

NEIL MURRAY—bass, Whitesnake

TOM NOBLE—comanager, Tygers of Pan Tang

JIMMY PAGE—guitar, Led Zeppelin

ANDY PARKER—drums, UFO

ROBERT PLANT—vocals, Led Zeppelin

SIMON PORTER—publicist, Venom, Girlschool, and Motörhead

ANDY POWELL—guitar, Wishbone Ash

IAN RAVENDALE—writer, *Sounds*

KEVIN RIDDLES—bass, Angel Witch

DOUG SAMPSON—drums, Iron Maiden

RICK SAVAGE—bass, Def Leppard

MICHAEL SCHENKER—guitar, UFO

CLAIRE SCHOFIELD—fan

BRIAN SLAGEL—fan, founder of Metal Blade Records

DOUG SMITH—manager, Motörhead and Girlschool

DENNIS STRATTON—guitar, Iron Maiden

PHIL SUTCLIFFE—writer, *Sounds*

PAUL SUTER—writer, *Sounds* and *Kerrang!*

BRIAN TATLER—guitar, Diamond Head

STEVE THOMPSON—house producer, Neat Records

THUNDERSTICK (BARRY PURKIS)—drums, Samson

JUDY TOTTON—publicist, Monsters of Rock

TINO TROY—vocals and guitar, Praying Mantis

JODY TURNER—vocals and guitar, Rock Goddess

LARS ULRICH—fan, drums, Metallica

TOMMY VANCE—DJ, Radio 1 *Friday Rock Show*

BEN WARD—fan, vocals, Orange Goblin

TOM GABRIEL WARRIOR—fan, founder of Hellhammer, Celtic Frost, and Triptykon

PETE WATERMAN—impresario, producer, songwriter

ROBB WEIR—guitar, Tygers of Pan Tang

ENID WILLIAMS—bass and vocals, Girlschool

PETE WILLIS—guitar, Def Leppard

TONY WILSON—Producer, Radio 1 *Friday Rock Show*

PETE WINKELMAN—friend of Diamond Head, owner of Milton Keynes Dons Football Club

DAVID WOOD—founder, Neat Records

JONNY Z (JON ZAZULA)—record store owner, promoter, founder of Megaforce Records

STEVE ZODIAC—vocals and guitar, Vardis

1

"The Music Machine sounds hollow this Tuesday evening."

In May 1979, Neal Kay brings together Iron Maiden, Samson, and Angel Witch for a show at the Music Machine in London. *Sounds* magazine sends along Geoff Barton— and in his review the phrase "New Wave of British Heavy Metal" is used for the first time. A movement is brought to life.

JOE ELLIOTT (vocals, Def Leppard): The New Wave of British Heavy Metal—NWOBHM—was a phrase invented by *Sounds* magazine.

IAN RAVENDALE (writer, Sounds): NWOBHM was sort of invented by Geoff Barton. Well, no, it was invented by Alan Lewis [the editor of *Sounds*] for the subheading of the Music Machine gig review in May 1979.

NEAL KAY (DJ, promoter, impresario): It was Alan Lewis who coined the term. Everyone says Geoff Barton. But Alan Lewis is the man. And we must have that right. I never saw it as a movement until the press told me it was. I was just doing my work, doing my job. I was bringing bands down from all over the place. But not only bands, fans started coming in from everywhere too.

SOUNDS *Magazine Headline, MAY 19, 1979:* If you want blood (and flash bombs and dry ice and confetti) you've got it: The new wave of British Heavy Metal.

NEAL KAY: I'd been putting bands on at the Wagon [the Bandwagon, where Kay ran the Heavy Metal Soundhouse]. Paul Samson played the Wagon often. The band were good, just a three-piece, even though it was never going to fly. Paul had a manager called Alistair Primrose. The phone rang one day and it was Alistair. He said, "Look, I'd like to put together a university and college tour, two or three dates and then we go home, maybe around the burbs and then down to the south coast." He said, "I can get the bookings—would you be interested in coming with us as our Soundhouse man, our compère, DJ, link man?"

We did universities and technical colleges. But the big problem was that Samson had to headline every show. It was Alistair's arrangement, and over a period of a few weeks at the gigs, it was obvious that Iron Maiden were mullering everybody. Paul Samson was getting more and more upset, and he came to me and said, "If this is you doing this, and deliberately telling the audience not to applaud us, I'm not impressed." I said, "Paul, I wouldn't dream of doing it. It's just what you play and how you play it. Maiden are just better than you for the kids. You're still living in the past and we've got to look to the future, man, and you ain't doing that." In the end I got a phone call from Mick Parker, the manager of the Music Machine. He said, "Listen, Neal, I've been following this Heavy Metal Crusade you've been doing. Would you like to bring it to the Music Machine?"

KEVIN RIDDLES (bass, Angel Witch): It was one of those nights. Tuesday night at the Music Machine. The Music Machine wasn't a rock gig, by any stretch of the imagination. So to us, the Music Machine was quite a big gig. It wasn't one that was on our radar. We got there and went, "Jesus, look at this place!" I mean, it was clean! Somebody had swept the floor before we got there! What the hell?

It was something a bit different for all of us. The main thing was the size of the stage. I don't think any of us had played on a stage that size. A PA was provided—there was a huge PA, and a massive lighting rig. It wasn't a band lighting rig, it was a disco lighting rig. But what the hell, it was five thousand watts of lights. It seemed like a very big gig, a step up. I remember it being different. It felt like the sort of place we wanted to be playing.

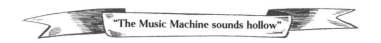

Camden High Street (Off Mornington Cresent Tube Station)
Telephone 01·387·0428 -9
MUSIC MACHINE
SAVE 50P
NORMAL ADMISSION £1·20
70s
ission
Heavy Metal Bonfire Night
Explosion Featuring
IRON MAIDEN, PLUS
ANGEL WITCH, PLUS
PRAYING MANTIS,
Plus DJ Neal Kay on
Monday 5th Nov.
Management Reserve The Right To Refuse ADMISSION.
Live Groups, Food, Bars, Dancing 8pm -2am.

The Music Machine's Monday night shows became a key part of the emerging NWOBHM movement—though headlining bands risked playing an empty venue.

GEOFF BARTON (writing in Sounds, May 19, 1979): The Music Machine sounds hollow this Tuesday evening. One or two punks loon about on the dance floor, a few more motley longhairs wearily occupy the sidelines and look on with suspicion. Whenever I've been to this venue before, it's always been jam-packed with a seething mass of humanity, hundreds of people piled right up to the rafters…therefore it's so strange to see it so deserted, stripped of its usual Bacchanalian atmosphere.

NEAL KAY: I phoned up Paul and said, "Do you want to do the Music Machine? Deal with me and Mick Parker will pay the fees. Are you going to do it or not? Are you going to be sulking forever?" And he said, "Fuck you, Kay, I'll do it." We did the gig, and Barton covered it, over two pages. It wasn't as full as I'd have wished it to be, because back then people didn't travel. It was during the week as well. If we wanted it full we'd have had to do a Saturday night, but Mick's Saturdays were full.

KEVIN RIDDLES: Ken [Heybourne, Angel Witch manager] got a phone call from Neal. Neal wanted to put us on. And we had a discussion: "Are we going to go out supporting a bloody DJ?" That was almost the limit of the discussion. The thought was that Neal Kay was the headliner, and that didn't sit particularly well with some of us. But we went off and did it, and we did worse: we supported the bloody Radio Caroline road show at one point, as well. But then in my cover-band days, I supported electronic hamster racing, so what the hell?

THUNDERSTICK (drums, Samson): It was strange. And the reason I say it was strange is that with the arrogance of youth, we looked at the size of the venue and said: "We belong here." Simple as that. Because we're in the music press every week we belong in a place like this. And we started filling it. The first time we played the Music Machine, John Lydon was there, Lemmy was there, Girlschool, all kinds of different people. So we were aware something was happening, but thought that because of the work we were putting in, that was how it should be. That we were there on merit.

DANTE BONUTTO (writer, Record Mirror and Kerrang!): There was a blues element to Samson, because Paul Samson had that in his playing. And the thing with them was their drummer Thunderstick, who was a masked drummer, often a caged and masked drummer, who I thought was amazing. I don't know if anyone ever commented on his drumming, but I loved his persona. He was often on the front cover of magazines on his own—he was a figurehead for NWOBHM because he had this hood with tassels. He looked quite menacing.

GEOFF BARTON (writing in Sounds, May 19, 1979): During Samson's performance you get dry ice, flash bombs, dry ice, showers of confetti, dry ice, fireworks, dry ice, clouds of multi-colored smoke and dry ice. Seriously, I don't think I've ever seen a band use so many effects so effectively or with such excellent timing—and, believe it or not, that includes Kiss. . . So while I feel less than enthusiastic about Samson's music, the band are deserving of a gold star for presentation alone. Simply, their stage show has got to be seen to be believed.

MALCOLM DOME (writer, Record Mirror and Kerrang!): Samson were not great that night. Paul Samson was convinced Iron Maiden sabotaged Samson's set because, Paul said, the labels were there to watch Samson not Maiden, and Maiden wanted to look good. No, I don't think they did. That's rubbish. Samson were just off-form that night.

THUNDERSTICK: We were still stuck in that blues-rock thing. With the benefit of hindsight, we should have done things differently. As a band we were making up for the material with huge amounts of pyro and special effects. Geoff Barton did a review and said we were using

ANGEL WITCH: "Black Sabbath through a cement mixer." GAB ARCHIVE | REDFERNS

more pyro than Kiss were at the time. Which was insanity. You can't win fans with smoke machines. The fundamental thing has to be the music.

MALCOLM DOME: Angel Witch were great. They always were. I was the only one that ever wrote positive things about Angel Witch in the mainstream media. Geoff hated them. He saw them as a third-rate Sabbath rip-off, which I thought was unfortunate and unfair, and everyone else who wrote about them dismissed them. I thought they were great, and they were a really strong, loyal band in terms of the following.

GEOFF BARTON (writing in Sounds, May 19, 1979): [Angel Witch] lurch into their first number, "Extermination Day," and it's instant time warp: to the sound of what can best be described as the first Black Sabbath album being played through a cement mixer, Angel Witch toss their long hair, stomp around, pout, pose, punch their fists into the air after each agonizing guitar solo…Angel Witch make

one hell of a noise, but their music is too fast (no need to be "punk conscious") cluttered and ill-refined, leaving you dazed or, in extreme circumstances, comatose.

DAVE LIGHTS (lighting technician, Iron Maiden): If I remember rightly, it was our first big show outside the East End. Girlschool were there as well. And Lemmy was there. There was quite a lot of people. It was exciting. The stage was quite high and it had a cave underneath it. It wasn't as high as the one at Glasgow Apollo. The one there was about 18 feet high, and they put it in for a Rolling Stones concert so people couldn't get onstage. The Music Machine was the first time I used a proper lighting rig. I didn't use mine, because they had proper PAR cans [parabolic aluminized reflector lights].

PAUL DI'ANNO (vocals, Iron Maiden): I was a bit awestruck going up there, thinking, "Cor, this is really massive." I used to go up to the Music Machine now and again; I always liked that place. I remember walking back from there a few times. I saw Samson that night, and I'd seen Angel Witch loads of times up the Ruskin. Paul Samson was a good bloke, but they were just a slightly better than average pub band. Angel Witch were good; they had a good following.

DOUG SAMPSON (drums, Iron Maiden): When Steve [Harris, Iron Maiden bassist] said we were doing this gig down the Music Machine, I just went, "Oh right." He said we'd be playing with Samson and Angel Witch. I hadn't seen Angel Witch, but I'd previously gone to see Judas Priest at Hammersmith Odeon, and I'd seen a lot of Angel Witch T-shirts, and that was my introduction to them. So when he said Angel Witch, I said, "They seem to be very popular." But to me it was just a gig, and it was only when we got down there and saw it that I realized, "This is something else." It was so much more professional—the sound, the crews, the dressing rooms. This was proper, you know. And it was brilliant on the stage.

GEOFF BARTON (writing in Sounds, May 19, 1979): Resplendent in tight-fitting leather trousers, Iron Maiden are poised, coolly confident, and their opening number "Rock Child" [*sic*] is as demented a rock "anthem" as I think I've ever heard…Unfortunately, though, it takes until the end of the set for the group to produce another number

of equal caliber…For "Phantom of the Opera," the band enjoy the ultimate accolade: a guy down front, playing a cardboard guitar, cut out to resemble the classic Flying V shape. He really enjoys himself and—uh—gets down.

DOUG SAMPSON: If I remember rightly, I didn't think we got the credit we deserved from the review.

PAUL DI'ANNO: We went up there and had Kate Bush up on stage with us, I remember that. I was seeing her at the time.

MURRAY CHALMERS (publicist, Kate Bush): Kate doesn't know that guy and has never been onstage at the Music Machine.

MALCOLM DOME: It didn't happen. I was there. It didn't happen. But I think he genuinely believes what he comes out with. He lives in a fantasy world, to some extent.

DAVE LIGHTS: Take everything Paul says with a pinch of salt.

NEAL KAY: Here's the thing: it was a successful night. The kids that came loved it. They were a mixture: it was the first time east London met west London, and south London came up because Angel Witch were on the bill. Let the fans meet each other—that was vital.

The next week the phone rings and Mick Parker was on the blower. He said, "Listen, would you like to do a regular show? You arrange all the bands, I'll pay them." He said, "You can DJ the night, or do it as you want, but I want you to do it as your own night promoting bands at the Music Machine." I said, "I'd love to." Here was an opportunity to put bands on a decent-sized stage.

KEVIN RIDDLES: The only drawback, which we found out on that first night, was the fact that it was right outside Mornington Crescent tube station, which seemed like a great idea at the time. Except the last train went at a quarter past twelve, and the last band went on at twelve. It didn't take very long to realize that the last thing you wanted to do was headline. After that first gig, which must have been half full—five or six hundred people, probably the biggest crowd we'd ever played to—at ten past twelve the place literally emptied. There was almost nobody there. That was a lesson for the future. The Music Machine

was known as one of the few late-night clubs, so that was their policy—the entertainment went on till two in the morning. So, consequently, doors didn't open till eight, first band on at nine, second at half ten, third band just before midnight. That's the way it ran, and it became obvious you had to work round that.

As far as the first one went, I know it was a huge success. Not just because Barton had turned up—it was almost under sufferance—he didn't have an excuse to get away from Neal's phone calls, as the Music Machine was just up the road from *Sounds*' offices. It was less than half a mile away. They didn't have the excuse that it was miles away in south London. And because, from the outside, it looked like it was a step up for all these bands, and for Neal, they had to cover it. From that point of view, we all knew there was something a bit different about the Music Machine, which is why we all did it, and we all did it for months afterwards.

MALCOLM DOME: The Music Machine shows were hugely important. They created a certain community. It was an extension of the Soundhouse, but it also created a situation where bands like Maiden, Angel Witch and Samson got a chance to play in front of decent audiences in a decent venue. So I think they really played a part in cementing together the whole scene.

Going down there on a Monday, we'd all meet, have a few drinks, see some bands. Neal would play the classics and some new tracks—it became an extension of what was going on at the Soundhouse. And because it had a good stage and it was a fair-sized venue, it gave an opportunity for bands to learn their craft a little bit. Let's not forget that's where Iron Maiden got signed. EMI created a huge controversy between Maiden and Samson, which I don't think was ever resolved. But that's where EMI first saw Maiden and thought: "We like them. We want to sign them." Fantastic times.

THUNDERSTICK: Our management had been talking to EMI. We were told we had got a deal and that was great. An album deal! It's done! Then we had a track they wanted to put out as a single. That was great—if we're going to be signing to them, that's wonderful, let's rush it through. So they did that. And I think they pressed about 2000, then the pressing plant went on strike. We were saying, "Excuse me,

what's happening with the deal with EMI? I thought we were going to be signed to EMI." It transpired it wasn't an album deal, it was a single deal with an option to take up for an album, depending on how the single went. We threw a hissy fit and said, "That's not what we were told. We're not interested."

We were really losing ground, because Maiden had got a nice promotion advertising budget behind them, and they had direction, whereas we…We laughed about our image, but at that time we should have really got our shit together but we hadn't. We were still floundering about, going are we this, are we that? Are we heavy metal or are we hard rock?

STEVE HAMMONDS (fan, music catalog consultant): Those Music Machine shows weren't massively attended, to be fair. It's like the Pistols at the Lesser Free Trade Hall—a lot of people said they were there but they weren't. They had the Monday night shows for quite a while, then the Marquee got in and did stuff, and the Lyceum used to do four- or five-band bills, which were always pretty good. And the Lyceum was easy to get to, and it had a curfew, which was good—the Music Machine didn't have a curfew, so if you stayed to the end you had to walk back. I used to have walk back to Victoria from Camden to get the train back to Crawley.

KEVIN RIDDLES: All of the frustration had built up in Geoff's head about being hassled about this new thing, this new genre, these new bands coming up at the same time—all he kept hearing was, "You've got to come and see my band!" And I wonder if his review was almost a reaction to that—"Even if I like these people, I can't say I like them, so I wonder if I can put them off? If I jump on the bandwagon, then I'm never going to hear the bloody last of it. If I'm a bit more lukewarm, perhaps they'll leave me alone for a bit, and I can go and do stuff I really want to do." I wonder whether that was the reaction.

I don't remember being disappointed, simply because, "Hold on a minute—that's a double-page spread in *Sounds*!" And the "Black Sabbath through a cement mixer" and the generic line that "I didn't particularly like Angel Witch, but the crowd absolutely loved them"— to us that was a great review. I genuinely didn't give a crap about one person not liking us. What I did give a crap about was five hundred

people liking us. So it was great having the name up there, it was great doing the gig, and the review afterwards, to me and to the rest of the band, was "We've got a double-page spread in *Sounds*!" That's what surprised us more than anything else, that it was that big. It almost didn't matter what they said about us. What we were interested in was the fact that he said five hundred people really enjoyed us. That's what we were going for. And the other bands, Maiden and Samson, had come up the same way—it was predicated on hard work and it was bloody obvious we were enjoying ourselves. I think that came across on stage and that's what a lot of people picked up on.

JOHN GALLAGHER (vocals and bass, Raven): I saw the article about the New Wave of Heavy Metal with Angel Witch and Iron Maiden and Samson. They were kindred spirits in terms of attitude, and that was the thing with all these bands. They were all people with the same approach. They were fed up that maybe they weren't hearing the music they wanted to hear, so they just went out and played it with loads of attitude and energy.

KEVIN RIDDLES: From that moment, we were taken more seriously by the people who were writing about music. Up to that point? Completely ignored. Even down to not having bad reviews. There were just none. It was almost impossible to get people to travel south of the river anyway, but Neal enabled bands to take that next step, and that's what he did with those Music Machine gigs.

With that one show, not only did Neal get the recognition he wanted for the Bandwagon, he also took his career further. He was then taken a bit more seriously as a promoter. It helped all of us. Without that, without Neal injecting that spark into the whole genre, it may have taken longer to happen. The result was an almost immediate increase in respect from journalists, and an immediate effect from just being in *Sounds*. It was very important at the time.

ALLAN JONES (writer, Melody Maker): Alan Lewis was a brilliantly sharp editor, and he was really quite ruthless. I remember him changing the direction of *Sounds* completely in late '76 and early '77. I remember Barbara Charone telling me she had just delivered an exclusive with Rod Stewart—which was still a big exclusive in those days—and went away on holiday. And when she came back, she found

out that Alan had decided to drop Rod Stewart from the cover and put the Damned on. He just threw everything into punk, in the same way he did with the New Wave of British Heavy Metal. He exploited that moment and the popularity of that music.

PAUL DI'ANNO: There's no way in hell you could say bands like Angel Witch and Saxon and Samson were New Wave of British Heavy Metal, because they wasn't. They'd been going before. All power to them, but they been going for years. When you're stuck and you can't describe a band, you stick them under that—New Wave of British Heavy Metal.

THUNDERSTICK: Obviously Geoff Barton was not aware of any kind of movement at that time. Nor were we, really. It was just: thank God we have the opportunity to play live again. We hadn't had the opportunity because punk bands had been dominating the scene for such a long time.

ROSS HALFIN (Photographer, Sounds and Kerrang!): NWOBHM was purely, one hundred percent Geoff Barton invented. And carried on and propelled by Geoff's own durability as a writer. And then it found a life of its own because the record companies started signing all these bands, because it was a new thing to latch on to.

MALCOLM DOME: There were very few people writing in the music press who had any interest in rock and metal. They thought it was played out, boring and dull. And there were lots of punk and new wave writers who didn't care about it and saw it as an extension of the dinosaur rock they hated. As far as they were concerned, what would you want to bother with that for? They didn't see what was going because they didn't want to see what was going on and certainly not write about it.

Until *Kerrang!* came along in '81, even in *Sounds* it was pretty much Geoff, unless you count Garry Bushell and Robbi Millar, who were also writing about this stuff. Even Garry and Robbi were writing about a very small niche. There was a guy called Ian Ravendale in the northeast, who wasn't liked by a lot of the northeast bands, who thought he was jumping on the bandwagon, but very little was going on because basically there was no one there who wanted it to go on. And

you had Des Moines [Nigel Burnham] writing in *Sounds*, who strangely didn't really like a lot of what was going on and then put together a compilation for Logo Records called *New Electric Warriors*. But it was literally just a case of no one seeing what was going on because no one wanted to see what was going on. Until, suddenly, Alan Lewis said, "Hang on a minute, you're writing about all these young British bands: why don't we put them under a collective umbrella? We'll call it the New Wave of British Heavy Metal," which is a dreadful name, but it stuck. NWOBHM. It just absolutely stuck, and these bands had been given a movement: there was a movement out there.

JOE ELLIOTT: Sometimes things just have a natural energy, and you can't say why it happened. We were all in the same headspace and had the same thought process going on. It's just that Maiden were doing it in London, we were doing it in Sheffield, Diamond Head were doing it in Birmingham, Tygers were doing it in Newcastle, Vardis were doing it in Wakefield, Saxon were doing it in Barnsley. What brought us together is the collective that was available to us: *Sounds*, Tommy Vance, *Top of the Pops*, *Whistle Test*.

THUNDERSTICK: *NME* hated it. They were snobbish. They would worship at the feet of Killing Joke and bands like that. They wouldn't have any time for hard rock or heavy metal. *Sounds* latched on to it and became our paper, our rag, specifically for us. There were some really good writers, even if some of them hated the image I had.

PHIL SUTCLIFFE (writer, Sounds): NWOBHM was *Sounds*' thing. Essentially, the other papers weren't interested, and the vibe was a bit scornful. It was definitely one of those moments when *Sounds* was striking out and connecting with a bunch of possibly existing readers and reinforcing their taste, but also dragging in new readers. I don't know if it showed up in the circulation.

My memory of the late '70s is that in the course of that period, whether it be with punk or the New Wave of British Metal, or some beautiful point when the effect of both combined, we did overtake the *NME* and get up to about a quarter of a million. It didn't last long, but I'm pretty sure we overtook them at one stage. We were certainly over two hundred thousand. So *Sounds* was really sailing along, and Alan's decisions were completely vindicated, commercially and culturally, and so were the tastes of individual writers.

SAXON, *newly signed to Carrere, pose in May 1979, with Steve Dawson far left and Biff Byford center.* FIN COSTELLO | REDFERNS/GETTY

MALCOLM DOME: Nineteen seventy-eight and the early part of '79 there were exciting young bands coming through, but there were always exciting young bands coming through. It was only after *Sounds* came up with the term the New Wave of British Heavy Metal that suddenly a diverse collection of young hopefuls became a movement. The name actually focused everyone: "Oh, that's what we are."

ROBB WEIR (guitar, Tygers of Pan Tang): After *Sounds* coined that phrase it became easier for new rock bands to get the recognition that they hoped for. And it also made all the major record companies look up and think, "Right, this is the next big thing, we will need to sign a New Wave of British Heavy Metal band."

So, in late '79, '80, that's when the companies went out and started to sign bands. Iron Maiden were signed to EMI, Leppard were signed to Phonogram, Saxon were signed to Carrere, we were signed to MCA. We were kind of the first four that sort of were talked about and reviewed and started it all off, and then other bands started to get signed after us.

STEVE DAWSON (bass, Saxon): We weren't really aware there were other bands. The only thing you'd be aware of is if you did a gig with

them. You opened up *Sounds* and there would be gig guides. You'd see Iron Maiden would have fifty-two shows back to back, and we'd only have twenty. And you'd think, "Why the fuck have they got all them gigs?" It were a rivalry.

We tended to cross paths with Iron Maiden quite a bit, because really Saxon were the first ones. We did a show somewhere in the London suburbs—Iron Maiden, Samson and us. Bruce Dickinson were called Bruce Bruce then. He was, we thought, a dickhead. With a fucking fencing foil. Mincing about the stage. I'll never forget that. Obviously, Bruce has gone on to do alright for himself. If you can afford an airplane you've done alright for yourself. I'm at the lowly heights of a Rover 75, diesel. We couldn't believe Samson. We just thought it were a joke. This twat in a fucking mask in a cage. Some bloke running about pretend fencing. It's not arty or anything. It's just stupid. Why would you cover yourself up? No one will ever know who you are. I suppose Kiss have made a good living out of it. I'm telling you the truth. I've got nowt against Samson or Thunderstick or anyone, but to a northern bloke, it reminds us of speciality acts in working men's clubs.

JOE ELLIOTT: We weren't aware this was happening in 1978/79. We were just doing our own thing, oblivious to the names Iron Maiden, Saxon, Vardis, Tygers of Pan Tang.

PAUL DI'ANNO: I heard about the other bands through *Sounds*. I used to get the music papers every week. I had boxes full of the bloody things. You'd start to read about these other bands, and this movement just sprang out of nowhere. At least, we thought it had sprung out of nowhere—it hadn't; it had been going on for some time, but we was unaware of it because you get caught up in your own little bubble.

DANTE BONUTTO: Because these bands were doing well, labels wanted to have one of them, so they all got record deals. Whether that would happen today I am not sure. But at that point, if you were an A&R man, you thought, "I have to have a NWOBHM band." That's why they all got major record deals. Which probably helped the whole thing, because there was money being pumped into it. Which meant there was money to send us to exotic places, and take ads in magazines, and make great records. And in those days they were made in proper studios with proper producers, like Martin Birch making the Maiden

records or Mutt Lange with Def Leppard. They were high-quality records. Perhaps not the early seven-inches, but they developed into great-sounding records made by great people in great studios with a great vision. It was a very exciting period and we're still feeling the waves of it today.

TOM GABRIEL WARRIOR (fan, founder of Hellhammer, Celtic Frost, and Triptykon): It is one hundred percent correct to say the NWOBHM is the starting point of modern heavy metal. I have no idea where modern heavy metal would be without the New Wave of British Heavy Metal because all the bands who have shaped modern metal are in turn directly influenced by the New Wave of British Heavy Metal. The most notable influence is on extreme metal, on thrash metal and black metal. Even the bands who kept the blues, they played it more precisely, more heavily, more extreme. They changed even that. The entire metal scene was influenced profoundly. One single or a track on a compilation, one single song could completely change the life of a musician and influence all their subsequent work. It didn't matter that it was a pub band who never made it.

In my case, for example, on the *Metal Explosion* compilation, there was a track by More and a track by Angel Witch, and on *Metal for Muthas* the track "Baphomet" by Angel Witch. These individual songs influenced everything I have done; even to this day all my long songs that I ever wrote are influenced by the song "Baphomet" by Angel Witch, forty years later. So it's wrong to underestimate bands because they were lo-fi and they had no money and no production values. Because they really influenced everything. Look at Metallica and so many other bands.

JOE ELLIOTT: If you sit down and did this as a college class, you'd be able to explain why the blues started disappearing from hard rock at this point, because bands weren't listening to the blues, they were listening to bands who had listened to the blues. There was a band called Vardis, and I remember the first time we heard them. They sounded like Status Quo. And that's all they did. Whereas Status Quo sounded like they'd been listening to the blues, Vardis sounded like a band that had been listening to Status Quo. We had our moments where we sounded like we'd been listening to Lizzy or Rush or Kiss. We sounded like we'd been listening to Thin Lizzy, who definitely grew up listening to the blues.

MORE

Impact in small doses: MORE publicity photo from WEA Italiana. According to Tom Gabriel Warrior, one single More song on the Metal Explosion *compilation album, "influenced everything I have done."*

I didn't know what the blues were. The blues, for me, was music other people listened to. It was music that influenced musicians, but nobody ever bought it first time round. Nobody knew who Son House was or Howlin' Wolf. These were people we only listened to once CDs came out and you could buy *The Ultimate Collection* for £6.99 in a petrol station and you'd think, "I'm going to give this a go, because I've read so many times about how without Robert Johnson there'd be no Eric Clapton." And I'm thinking, "I'm not a huge Clapton fan, but I love 'Layla.'" I didn't love Cream, I found them irritatingly ordinary, no matter how many times Brian May told me to listen to *Disraeli Gears*. I did, Brian. It's crap. Because I wasn't your age when I heard it: I've heard it since, and you're much better than Cream.

KEITH KAHN-HARRIS (fan, sociologist, and writer): The creation of heavy metal is a process rather than an individual event. It goes on through the seventies, and it's a process of expunging the blues. You can hear blues elements in Black Sabbath. You can certainly hear it in Deep Purple. In very early Judas Priest, you could hear bits of it. But you get to 1979 or 1980 and you don't hear it at all. If you listen to Saxon or Iron Maiden you just don't hear it at all. So, in a way, it accelerates that process, which is not in and of itself problematic. But what it signifies can be a little bit uncomfortable. It is a racialized process, but it wasn't necessarily a conscious process. You'll also hear

that in the transition from pub rock to punk—that's also a process of taking out the blues. That's why Dr. Feelgood is not a punk band, although Dr. Feelgood is part of that milieu that was one of the sources of punk. So it's a very similar sort of process that happens throughout rock genres by the late seventies.

PHIL ALEXANDER (fan, Kerrang! editor): [NWOBHM] was absolutely crucial to the development of metal, and we're still feeling the effects of it all these years later. It does two things. One, it's a shot in the arm for the genre and reinvents it for an audience that is younger and full of enthusiasm, and it is really, literally a second coming of the genre. But the other thing that's really brilliant about it is the sheer joy and naiveté that is included within it, which really informs a lot of what comes afterwards.

It's the spark of enthusiasm that lies at the heart of NWOBHM that is the most overarchingly important element of it to me. Because it kind of shapes an attitude at that time, that goes beyond the idea of just do it yourself, it's an attitude that says: these people are real, these people will be your heroes, you will identify that, and as a result of that you will also do things yourself. So it is a real spark, a real catalyst for things that come after it. The obvious things are thrash metal wouldn't exist without NWOBHM, so consequently the world would be a completely different-sounding place. The other thing is the impact on the media, based on the sheer demand from the audience. What you get off the back of NWOBHM is the creation of, for want of a better term, hard rock media, in a very, very real way. *Kerrang!* is a direct result of that.

TOM GABRIEL WARRIOR: For us young fans, we were also a new generation. This really matched. We all loved the existing bands—Rainbow and Black Sabbath and everything, we loved them—but there was a movement with people that were basically our generation and had our frame of mind and were looking to play more extreme. That totally appealed to us. You have to understand, I wasn't just a casual hard rock listener—I was a real fanatic. I grabbed anything I could. I heard the first Accept album and tons of underground bands from Scandinavia or the Benelux countries. So I really tried, with the means we had at the time, to be on the pulse of what was happening in the metal scene. But none of these bands could compete with what the New Wave of British Heavy Metal provided.

I know people in the British Isles are sometimes bewildered by how other people see the New Wave of British Heavy Metal. I've heard a lot of negative comments about the New Wave from my friends in the British Isles. They say, "Well it was just a few demo bands, a few pub bands, and it's completely overstated." And I'm always frustrated hearing this. Maybe they were just demo bands and they recorded tracks for a few pounds, and of course the sound quality is poor and the playing is deficient, but that doesn't matter. It's the content that matters, and the content was nothing short of a revolution.

LARS ULRICH (fan, drums, Metallica): The reason I wanted to be in a band was NWOBHM. Because if these guys could do it, I could do it. It was really that simple. I never wanted to be in a band because of Led Zeppelin, or to be as big as Deep Purple. I've spoken hundreds of thousands of times about how influential they were as a musical entity and part of my story, but I never sat there and thought: "Wow, I'm listening to 'Highway Star,' I could do that!" It was more, "Oh my God, this is great!" But at some point when I heard Trespass or Diamond Head and these other bands, I thought, "I can do that, and I wanna do that. And if these guys can do that, and make records and release them and play shows and get talked about in the press or have T-shirts and patches made with their name on them, or have pen pals or have people like myself who had pen-pal circles and write to other people that are like-minded that like this, I can do that."

BRIAN SLAGEL (fan, founder of Metal Blade Records): It felt like a fresh new sound. You could clearly tell there was a massive influence from all the seventies stuff, but it was new, it was different, it didn't sound exactly like anything else I had heard at that point. A lot of us would be doing something else if it wasn't for that scene. In the early eighties, it was a change of decade, it was a time of uncertainty, especially here in America things were changing. We had gone through the disco thing, which I hated, and this was kind of the anti-that, something fresh and new. Very independent, too. There were all these bands doing it on their own, or on small labels, and I loved that entrepreneurial spirit as well.

PHIL ALEXANDER: There is another thing that comes from NWOBHM: the creation of pure metal labels, and that is really significant. Because without Neat Records, does Brian Slagel actually

decide to launch Metal Blade? I very much doubt it. And that becomes the bastion of extremism. And generationally, we start looking at louder, harder, faster, and that's exactly what happens with thrash. It kind of crystallizes and spawns its own scene, and instead of the seven-inch its weapon of choice is the cassette, the demo. And the one thing I remember about NWOBHM is that I don't remember it being demo-driven—the band would self-release a single. Thrash takes that to the nth degree because you can copy a cassette and send it around the world. So you've suddenly got a totally different network, and it's faster in every sense of the word. What you would all do, though, is tape things for your mates—but you needed the originals to tape. It wasn't bands deciding to issue a cassette. The NWOBHM release was a seven-inch, and homemade.

MALCOLM DOME: What punk gave a lot of these bands was the inspiration to say, "We can go out there and do it." And they didn't need to be virtuosos. That's why some of these bands decided: "We're not going to do nine-minute songs, because we can't. But what we can do is a three-minute song: verse chorus verse chorus solo verse chorus get out." And that's what they were doing. And that appealed to a younger generation who were coming through, who didn't want to delve into massive conceptual pieces, even though later on they probably grew into them. But, yeah, in that respect punk did play its part.

So many bands were self-releasing. There were loads of bands who didn't bother going to independent labels, but just said, "Right, we'll put it out ourselves. We'll finance it ourselves." Hence Diamond Head's *White Album* [also known as *Lightning to the Nations*]. A lot of bands did that because they knew they were good—"It'll cost a few hundred quid and we'll do it"—and because they had seen punk bands do it. And the more NWOBHM bands did it, the more others thought, "Yes, that's what we should do. We can't get a deal, let's just get something out there and get noticed." And that made a big difference, because having something pressed up that you could hand to people or sell to people really was important for getting noticed. These bands didn't say, "We'll get around to doing it one day," they just went out and did it. And it gave them something to send to Tommy Vance and Tony Wilson at the *Friday Rock Show* and something to send to journalists as well. A record was better than sending a three-track cassette demo. It just seemed more significant. More like, "This is a proper band."

PHIL ALEXANDER: What you also have within this is a grassroots network of venues and artists that spreads across the country. So you really genuinely have local heroes. For me, growing up in south London, there were a whole bunch of people in two-bit bands who don't get anywhere—the band local to me is a band called Demon Pact, who no one really knows very much about any more. They released a single called "Eaten Alive," and it never went anywhere. But that didn't stop me painting their logo on my denim jacket in silver paint.

That's the key to the impact of NWOBHM as far as I am concerned. On the one hand, there is a musical impact. And on the other there's a cultural and ideological impact that changes the way in which the world evolves as far as hard rock is concerned. Extreme metal as a whole can be traced back to NWOBHM—two hundred percent it can be. What happens is the idea that everyone wants to go a little bit faster, a little bit heavier. They take the things that were there already and make it their own. That's as evident with Maiden as it is with Venom.

KEITH KAHN-HARRIS: Many of the foundational elements of metal culture as we understand it today were set by that movement. If you look at early metal bands before the new wave—Deep Purple or Black Sabbath—and their fans, they don't look metal as we understand it today. What the New Wave of British Heavy Metal did was to turn a fairly disparate movement into something quite specific and defined. Heavy metal existed before that, but to understand that as a distinctive kind of subculture was one of its major contributions.

JESS COX (vocals, Tygers of Pan Tang): Metal and punk, there weren't distinct lines between them. It was only a matter of what coat you had on sometimes. I remember going out, and we had straight pants on—I know this sounds ridiculous—not flares, and we had a fringe. In heavy metal you had hair parted in the middle and flares. I used to wear a blazer and tie on stage in the early days, and I had a fringe and straight drainpipe pants. It was half punk and half metal. And the songs were, too—the topics we sang about, like "Euthanasia." It was very punky influenced, with rat-at-at-at-at music. We had punks coming to the shows. It wasn't like it was one or the other. It was a melting pot, although NWOBHM got a uniform quite quickly with the badged jacket.

TOM GABRIEL WARRIOR: Before we had access to patches we did our own jackets. We didn't want it to look amateurish. We spent a lot of time. We would cut stencils out of cardboard and make really high-quality, detailed jackets with spray cans. We'd correct it to make it look really perfect and then of course we began to discover the patches. Everybody in our circle of friends had two or three full jackets with all kinds of bands. There were so many bands and to show off you really needed more than one jacket. I did my own sewing, amateurishly. My mother wasn't going to sew Witchfynde on my expensive jacket. She'd buy me a cheap jacket if she thought this was meant to last thirty years and I'm just going to put patches on it and ruin it. For her it was a waste of money.

KEITH KAHN-HARRIS: It's important to say that the NWOBHM look didn't spring out of nowhere. Like most things, it comes from various sources. And we shouldn't forget that metal's style also draws on underground gay culture as well, which is an extraordinary thing in many ways. I think there's a bit of a frisson there, or at least that was initially, given that relationship to gay culture. The idea of drawing on that sort of underground culture and perhaps in some way reclaiming it a bit for heterosexuality to a degree, while still retaining the elements of camp, was probably quite an exciting thing to do at the time.

At a basic level, to coalesce as a subculture at the time required developing some kind of dress code. What denim and leather does—denim and leather and studs—is bring together this sort of transgressive underground gay culture with blue-collar working-class culture in a quite unique and interesting way. Although if you look at what the bands on stage are wearing compared to what the audience is wearing, there's often quite a little bit of disjuncture. Spandex, for example, was very common onstage for bands at that time, particularly Maiden. I don't think that fans were wearing spandex or those skin-tight things. Why did spandex become stage gear but not audience gear?

BRIAN SLAGEL: We were so influenced by what was happening in the UK. Lars Ulrich went over to the UK and he would bring back stuff. And you'd see pictures of jackets covered with patches, and go, "Oh my God, I have to make that." But I never had one of those

because it was so hard to get the patches. So I just did the black leather jacket, with tons of wristbands and studded leather gear.

The way it occurs to me that I heard about them, is that back then people didn't have a lot of money and it was difficult for the bands to make shirts, so patches became a thing. And you could wear a jacket and have thirty of your favorite bands on it, as opposed to wearing just one shirt of one band. It became a way to show off all the bands. And then it became a competition: you had to have the coolest patches. Especially in LA, it was like, "Whoa, you got a Jaguar patch!" which would be so cool because nobody else had it.

PHIL ALEXANDER: The other thing to bear in mind, in terms of the appeal that comes from NWOBHM, is the visual aspect of it. People talk about it from the point of view of it being silly. But there's a reason Iron Maiden will always sell records to a bunch of fourteen-year-olds, much as they will sell records to people who are sixty and were there in 1979. The thing for that is the creation of that emblematic artwork: Eddie is absolutely crucial to the success of Iron Maiden. He's totally identifiable. I bet there are a bunch of people who have bought into Motörhead as a band based on the concept of the logo before they even heard the music. Just the power of that imagery.

It's easy to look back at some of that NWOBHM stuff and see it as absolutely comical. But by the same token, there is power in the naiveté that comes from that. And it launches a million and one terrible heavy metal sleeves. But Venom's logo is really significant, the way it looks, the way it feels. All of that artwork is.

KEITH KAHN-HARRIS: NWOBHM certainly lays the groundwork for sort of tape trading in the 1980s, which is absolutely vital to the development of extreme metal. You wouldn't have death metal without tape trading, for example, but tape trading and DIY culture do have earlier roots than is sometimes acknowledged. It also has roots in hippie culture and the underground press. Fanzines were not created by punk; they existed beforehand. The first fanzines were in sci-fi subculture, but the form they started to take in the late seventies was the form that was built on by underground metal in the eighties. A lot of the mainstream, quote unquote, infrastructure of metal also develops during the New Wave of British Heavy Metal.

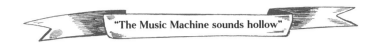

TOM GABRIEL WARRIOR: Tape trading was one of my interests at the time. Like all the other traders I had a multipage typewritten list of the demos that I was trading. I have to say, tape trading was really more effective with bands from America a couple of years later.

The tape traders I was in contact with, they didn't have so much New Wave of British Heavy Metal material. We got access to the music of the new wave by literally spending all our weekends travelling through Switzerland to obscure record stores, of which there were hundreds at the time. We would go to little villages where we knew there was a record store. Everybody would gather at the house of the one guy that had a car and we would drive for hours through the countryside to obscure record stores and find the odd New Wave of British Heavy Metal single, and then whoever bought it would tape it for all the others.

Tape trading was like YouTube is now, basically. You get these lists of people's tape collections and there would usually be a very short description: "short and heavy," something like that. You would go by that and the name of the band. I found out about the addresses of other tape traders, number one from friends who were also tape traders— we would also trade the addresses. And then the early photocopied fanzines arrived from Germany, the Netherlands. Those were really primitive homemade fanzines, but in there were the ads for tape traders, and I myself also placed ads, and that's how you networked.

STEVE HAMMONDS: There was a guy in Birmingham who used to tape every Diamond Head show. There were about thirty or forty big tape traders. It was a really important thing. Tape trading was huge with NWOBHM. The American fans couldn't get enough of NWOBHM, and the British fans couldn't get enough of American bands—the Godz live at the Agora in Cleveland, which was a radio broadcast. So all of that. The market for those high-speed tape dubbers was huge.

DANTE BONUTTO: When you look back on it, it was built on writing good songs. Everyone wanted to be at the top of their game and hone their craft. When you do something like that to create the best you can, the influence is always very wide-ranging. It felt very British. Sometimes with British music, you feel that though it's from here, it's very much underwritten by what's happening elsewhere, and I don't

think this was. Even though these bands liked a lot of American music, it was flying the flag for what we were doing here and for our tradition. It's been very influential and represents a halcyon period where something can come up and burn brightly without fizzling away. It's very exciting when something like that can happen.

MALCOLM DOME: Very little linked the NWOBHM bands. They all came from different backgrounds, and not just geographically but musically. You had Leppard who were inspired to some extent by Lizzy; Maiden came from a Priest style of music; Diamond Head were much more of a Zeppelin; Praying Mantis were much more an American approach; Angel Witch were Sabbath. They were all over the place in terms of where their influences came from. That's why no one connected them until the dots were connected by Alan, who just came up with this idea: "Let's start this movement and see where it takes us." And suddenly everyone jumped in. You had Girl who were more trashy and glam. Everyone came from a different approach, a different attitude. No one would have put them together had it not been for that. You could connect Leppard with Girl with Maiden with Saxon with Girlschool. And let's see where it goes.

LARS ULRICH: It's more of a movement than a musical style. Of the six letters in NWOBHM, I think the "B" is very significant. You really have to understand the British element of this, and how wide-ranging it was in terms of the role of the press, and how small the island is compared to the United States or continental Europe. The "B" is very, very significant. There were bands that were playing NWOBHM to a degree that weren't British, but that's already a contradiction. I think you could argue Metallica was a NWOBHM band, but obviously we're not British, so we're not a NWOBHM band. If you start going down the whole thing from Praying Mantis to Venom, that covers a lot of musical fucking ground, but the one thing all those guys have in common is the British element.

ROBB WEIR: I think NWOBHM has been the biggest of all the musical movements. You don't often hear people talk about Bay Area thrash or grindcore, but you do hear people talking about NWOBHM.

"We must have done a lot for Peru."

By 1979 the glam bands that had inspired many NWOBHM
groups were gone. The previous generation of heavy rock
heroes was stumbling. Punk brought swirling chaos, but
also signaled a way forward for a swathe of newcomers.

JOE ELLIOTT (vocals, Def Leppard): In October of 1971 I saw T.
Rex. My mum and dad let me go. I was twelve. I got in just after he
went on, he was already on the go, twenty seconds into "Jeepster,"
and I went through those swing doors at the Sheffield City Hall that
have got the portholes in them, and I just walked into a whole new
world that I had seen glimpses of in black and white on TV. But all of
a sudden I walk into this insane din of the sound coming offstage and
the audience screaming back. And all these kids—it wasn't just girls, it
was guys that all looked like they should have been at a Status Quo gig,
all denim and hair and dandruff and headbanging. There were people
on their knees playing air guitar and girls screaming. Standing there,
just inside the swing doors, not even at my seat, just underneath the
balcony and watching this insanely fantastic thing, like a church, was
just phenomenal.

I didn't go to the City Hall again till 1975, when I went to see Hunter
Ronson. From that moment till '79, I probably went four hundred
times. But when I walked on to the stage to sound check [when
Def Leppard first played there in 1980], I remember walking up to
where Marc Bolan was stood, and standing looking back at where I
was watching him from. That full circle connection of "Okay, nine
years on here I am" was the weirdest thing. It was so bizarre. When I

Tony Iommi of BLACK SABBATH, City Hall, Newcastle upon Tyne, circa 1980.

RIK WALTON / ARENAPAL

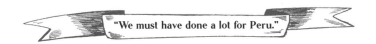

walked through those doors to see T. Rex, it was more like walking into something like an arena from the back. It felt massive. I was twelve and I'd never been in a room that big. I'd never even been to a football match. I'd never been in anything large, other than a park.

When I stood on the stage and looked back at where the twelve-year-old me was, I swear I could have spat that far. It was so tiny. We hadn't played any big gigs, but the event of the twelve-year-old watching T. Rex was so much bigger in my mind than the reality of it. One of those lifetime things you never forget.

STEVE ZODIAC (vocals and guitar, Vardis): Bolan had ambiguity—physically, musically. The escapism. Bowie were doing similar things, but with Bolan, because he's a guitar player—very underrated, his simplistic style was very much in the tradition of old blues players—the simple vibrato and the downbend instead of an upbend gave Bolan this unique sound. Of course, it's based on old school-blues playing, which nobody ever realized at the time. My God, when he performed those songs, and felt them, it came over. It connected. Very few bands really understand that. I think that feeling were there in the fifties, with the majority of performers and singers. And I think it went all the way through to the eighties with the majority of singers.

You couldn't move in the early seventies for rock music. You'd go in the record shop and every week you'd think, "Which one do I get?" You could buy a single for a few bob. You didn't have to spend money on albums. You could just get Rod and the Faces doing "Stay with Me" and rock out to it. It were incredible stuff.

There was one dandy in the underworld in Wakefield in them days. He was hard as nails. Frankie, his name were. He used to hang out in all the bars. He used to take some stick. But by God he could dish it out. But he were a sweetheart.

MANTAS (guitar, Venom): My musical growing-up was through the seventies, the glam rock era. I was born in '61 so by the time I was ten years old, '71, I'm getting into music, looking around at these bands. First favorite band ever was Slade. I was massively into T. Rex. *T. Rex* was the first album I ever bought, "Ride a White Swan," and then of course Alice Cooper comes along, which is slightly heavier. First single

I ever bought, seven-inch vinyl, was "Seven Seas of Rhye," Queen. But me and a friend I'd met at a taekwondo club—he was a few years older than me and he actually is the guy that I started Venom with— we found we had a similar love for music as well as martial arts. He was into Deep Purple so he introduced me to Purple, and he used to get tickets, we used to go and see anybody. There was another friend of mine who'd come—pubs, clubs, anything that was guitar-driven, any band. I seen Squeeze at the City Hall, I seen Japan, I seen Rory Gallagher. I was lucky enough to see all these people.

RICK SAVAGE (bass, Def Leppard): When Queen came along, it blew everything out of the water for me. All of a sudden I had found this band that could fit in the category with the heavy stuff, but were also pop—great production, great vocal sound, orchestrated guitars. That was happening with Sweet and T. Rex and the glam rock bands. They encompassed everything and more. That's when I started getting into it, to the point of thinking, "Crikey, it would be great to be able to do something like this." It started from there.

KIM MCAULIFFE (vocals and guitar, Girlschool): As a kid I loved all the glam stuff. David Bowie was the most incredible creature on earth. There was always music in the house. Mum and Dad used to listen to the Beatles and the Stones and all that. And the radio was on. There was *Top of the Pops*, which was the most exciting thing in the world ever, every Thursday evening. T. Rex, Sweet, Slade, David Bowie. Glam was more rock than pop. It was a segue into the heavier rock stuff. And it was exciting as well. Seeing Alice Cooper do "School's Out"—it was so exciting. And seeing David Bowie do "Starman," and Queen do "Seven Seas of Rhye" on *Top of the Pops*. It was so exciting because you never knew who was going to be on.

Then my cousin started getting into other stuff and said: "You have to listen to this!" And that was Black Sabbath, Deep Purple and Led Zeppelin. And I moved into that. The first two gigs I ever went to were Black Sabbath at the Hammersmith Odeon and Deep Purple when they did the *Burn* album at Hammersmith Odeon.

PHIL COLLEN (guitar, Girl and Def Leppard): I was into everything when I was a kid: Motown, reggae. I'm from London and it's a great place to absorb all this amazing stuff. I loved Bowie and T. Rex,

THE SWEET on the BBC TV music show Top Of The Pops *in 1974.*

MICHAEL PUTLAND | GETTY IMAGES

and my cousin told me: "You've got to check out progressive music and Zeppelin and Pink Floyd." And he got me into that. And I loved all of it. I still loved Stevie Wonder—he's still my favorite singer—but it was an amalgamation of everything.

JOE ELLIOTT: When I saw T. Rex do "Ride a White Swan" on *Top of the Pops*, all of a sudden I was like, "Hello." And then "Hot Love," and then "Get It On" and "Jeepster." And then "Starman." And then Slade. And then "Ballroom Blitz." And "Killer Queen." And "Virginia Plain." "This Town Ain't Big Enough for the Both of Us." All of a sudden, "I've got my stuff now. This is my music." It's not fair to lump all those bands together, just as I don't want us to be lumped in with NWOBHM, but the British glam rock scene of the early seventies made me want to be who I am. David Bowie and Steve Harley would turn in their graves, if they were both dead, at being thought of alongside Slade or Sweet, but the fact is they all made three-minute songs that were capable of going in the top twenty, alongside "Tie a Yellow Ribbon," with drums and guitars and huge, big football choruses, if you're talking Slade. If you're talking Bowie,

he was turning the sixties white blues even further on itself—"Jean Genie" was just a rewrite of a Yardbirds song, which was itself a rewrite of a Bo Diddley tune. Each generation takes it and hardens it up a bit more. Music was getting heavier, but when you think about the way pop music was in the seventies, things like "Devil Gate Drive" by Suzi Quatro, in comparison to what pop music is now, it was fucking heavy metal. Even "Dyna-mite" or "The Cat Crept In" by Mud, you could hear Mötley Crüe doing it in comparison to what's going on now. And you'd hear those songs all day long: if you didn't have a record player, you'd just wait for them to come on the radio.

When you have to go mining this stuff yourself, once you actually get it, it means so much. It's like getting a tattoo or something. We had to get a bus down to town in the rain, go into town to the nearest record store. You're doing four paper rounds so you can buy one record a week, but which one do you buy? There's brand new Rod Stewart, brand new T. Rex, brand new Bowie, brand new Elton. Which one do you buy? Thank God for second-hand ex-jukebox singles and things like that, where you had to buy the plastic inserts for the hole.

PHIL ALEXANDER (fan, Kerrang! editor): One hundred percent glam is significant, British glam. Glam is a precursor to punk—that's obvious. Glam is a precursor to British pop culture as a whole—short songs. The significance of Sweet is actually huge. There's a real crash-bang-wallop quality to what they do. You can play "Blockbuster" alongside "Paranoid." Of course you can. The same with Mott the Hoople. T. Rex is slightly different because that's a real pop game that Marc is playing, quite deliberately. A lot of people probably look at T. Rex and don't consider that to be a proper band. They're not a heads' band; they become that retrospectively, but when you think about where they are in 1974 to 1977 they're almost a kids' band, but that's the significance. It's the kids who take this. And what you get from that is the sense of: "Yeah, we can do this." It comes back down to that.

DENNIS STRATTON (guitar, Iron Maiden): I always loved playing with two guitars—because Wishbone Ash were my favorite band.

ANDY POWELL (guitar, Wishbone Ash): We got to a point with Wishbone Ash where I said, "Why don't we try doing something different with twin lead guitars?" The first song we wrote was a song

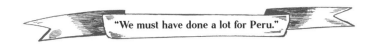

called "Blind Eye," which has a little riff in it, rather like a brass riff or a horn riff. We went, "This could be our sound." In the early seventies, every band had their own sound, whether it was Yes, Jethro Tull, and you needed that.

TINO TROY (vocals and guitar, Praying Mantis): I started listening to Thin Lizzy when we were jamming, and that's where we developed the twin-guitar thing from—and there was Wishbone Ash as well. That's where we got our vocal harmonies. We did a couple of Wishbone Ash covers—"Blowin' Free" and "Throw Down the Sword." Loved it. When I met Martin Turner I told him he was one of our influences. It seems weird that they weren't more celebrated, because a lot of the bands cited them as an influence, even though a lot of the music doesn't sound anything like them.

BIFF BYFORD (vocals, Saxon): Wishbone Ash invented twin harmony guitars in heavy rock. I used to go and see them when they played in Leeds or Sheffield or Barnsley—they were on the circuit a lot in the early seventies. I was a bass player then, and they had a great bass player with a good style, with really cool vocal harmonies. It felt groundbreaking—it was a big explosion of rock and Wishbone Ash were a pretty loud band. In Saxon we used the twin-guitar harmonies occasionally—we don't want to copy anybody, but it is a theme, it is in there.

ANDY POWELL: Twin lead guitars depend on tone. You've got to know what tone is. A lot of young players make the mistake of over-processing the sound. They think, "Oh man, this is sounding heavy." In point of fact, it ends up sounding less heavy, the more processing you put on it. And by that I mean distortion, that kind of thing. You've got to have a good understanding of how to get a tone out of really good-quality guitars and good-quality vintage amplifiers, and we got that right from the beginning. As soon as we started touring we would collect all these great instruments. These mid-fifties instruments were made by people that were casting an ear back to the forties. They were making amplifiers and guitars that could make a thick, juicy sound, with just a minimal amount of overdrive. We knew how to coax the best sound out of all the gear. Another thing that enhanced it was that by the time the third album came around, we went from eight-track recording

to sixteen-track recording, and I had the bright idea of double-tracking the guitars. We started off with really good guitar sounds, and just enhanced them even further, so it just commanded you to listen to the guitar lines.

A lot of people that joined bands like Judas Priest and Iron Maiden, they would have been five years behind us in terms of age. I came of age with Wishbone Ash in '69/70. I was born in 1950. Those NWOBHM guys would have been at our concerts, and they would have taken it on board as they were taking on board all the other things they were seeing. I think it took people three to five years to catch up. There were a couple of bands that were more our contemporaries, like Thin Lizzy. I got word from Scott Gorham that the first band they saw when they came over from Ireland, at the Lyceum, was Wishbone Ash, and Phil turned to the guys and said, "That's the fucking sound we want." You had the more contemporary groups who were saying, "That's a cool sound, let's grab a bit of that," and then you had the younger crowd, guys from Maiden and so on.

SCOTT GORHAM (guitar, Thin Lizzy): The twin guitars didn't come from Wishbone Ash. No, not at all. There's an argument for the Allman Brothers. Hell, even Fleetwood Mac were doing a little bit of the harmony guitars. I've had to correct a lot of people throughout the years. "Hey Scott, man, you guys invented harmony guitars!" No we didn't. What we did, that made it so different, is we put it into the rock form, and we played over the minor chord sequence, which gave it that different sound, and that's why there's a distinct difference in what we did compared to other people who were playing harmony guitars. But to say we invented it? Les Paul was doing harmony guitars back in the forties, for God's sakes!

PHIL COLLEN: By the late seventies, the big heavy-rock bands were losing their way. They definitely were. That's why punk happened. I remember seeing Zeppelin, and there'd be twenty-minute solos, and it was really hard work. There were bands like Bad Company, and there was no vibe there. There was no inspiration. It was really dull and boring. People who liked exciting rock were kind of left in the balcony, if you like.

ROBERT PLANT (vocals, Led Zeppelin): Time is a funny thing when you're onstage. It did leave me occasionally a little bit adrift. But I'm a Jimmy Page fan, so I like to hear where he goes. I can't remember too much about those days, except for I know the sets were long.

JIMMY PAGE (guitar, Led Zeppelin): Sure, the sets got longer, but it wasn't just necessarily because of extended solos, although that certainly would have helped, whether keyboard solos or guitar or whatever it was. The thing is, as each album came along, we would introduce some new material, and then the set would just get longer 'cause we didn't want to lose some of these numbers and by the time we got to *Houses of the Holy*, for example, we had quite a catalog there going on.

LARS ULRICH (fan, drums, Metallica): A lot of the rock stuff ended up as what the British press dubbed "dinosaur rock" and became very progressive and narcissistic and selfish and became very much about musicianship, became about ability. It became about crazy, extended, self-obsessed musical endeavors. And I don't mean that in a disrespectful way; I'm just trying to describe it.

And what was happening with punk rock in England, and in New York with, say, Ramones, that was an answer to the grandiosity of all of that. So when Ramones started turning in ninety-second songs, and the Sex Pistols and the Damned and all these great bands came out and made it about simplicity and attitude and energy and the idea that if you were a fan you could create your own band, you didn't have to go to music school or learn how to play the Hammond organ for twenty-two years or whatever the fuck it was—you just needed three chords and a bit of swagger. That do-it-yourself approach spilled over into a younger generation of kids that had one foot in Black Sabbath and Judas Priest and Rainbow and Thin Lizzy, but still wanted to keep it more punkish in attitude, and keep it edgier, keep it rebellious, keep it less grandiose and self-important, less contrived.

So there was an energy, there was a usefulness, and it just felt fresh compared to fifteen minutes of "Dazed and Confused" or whatever. I love Led Zeppelin, but at that moment, Led Zeppelin would put out these records that were full of sorcery, with pretentious covers. And here was Iron Maiden, and they were just five dudes, and it was a different thing. It felt fresh and young and vital and new.

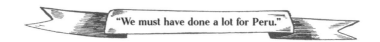

KEVIN RIDDLES (bass, Angel Witch): It did feel as though everything [in hard rock] had become a bit of a parody of itself. Other people with far better vision and foresight than me realized it, and that's why punk worked. That was a reaction to what had gone on. Ours was a reaction, but to a slightly lesser degree. We just wanted to take the genre, take what we were writing, and make it fresher and more exciting and punchier. And put back that zest and life that it seemed had been lost.

One of my favorite live albums is Emerson, Lake and Palmer live at Newcastle City Hall, *Pictures at an Exhibition*, one of the finest live albums, one of the finest pieces of music ever written. But when I listen to it now, I think, "Jesus, self-indulgent twaddle or what?" Because it just went on and on and on. I think the rot set in much earlier, with bands like Cream. I remember seeing their final concert at the Albert Hall, and the songs were just drowned. They were great songs, but they were drowned in self-indulgence. You didn't need a half-arsed Ginger Baker drum solo to make those songs great. You didn't need Clapton wailing away like nobody's business and Jack Bruce burbling away on bass that you couldn't hear—you could feel it, but you couldn't bloody hear it. You didn't need that to make those songs great. It was, literally, rock by numbers a lot of the time.

We were aware we could do something a bit different. We could make it fresher, and—it's a horrible word, I know—give it some pizzazz, give it some fun, give it some showbiz. Fortunately, we were allowed to, because I think crowds and fans and punters were ready for it. In that regard, the New Wave of British Heavy Metal did come along at exactly the right time. There was space for it. There was a niche for us to sit in. We were in the right place at the right time.

ROBB WEIR (guitar, Tygers of Pan Tang): The City Hall bar was rammed for the solos. We'd see Rainbow or Whitesnake, and when Jon Lord did his keyboard solo, we just wanted to hear songs. There was quite a collective in the bar. When the solo sections finished you'd down your pint and go back for the next song. When they recorded those songs they didn't have the solo sections.

NEIL MURRAY (bass, Whitesnake): Yes, you're aware on the one hand that some of the audience are groaning and sloping off to the bar when the solo comes along. But you're also aware that it seems to go

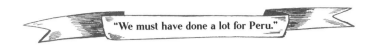
down an absolute storm, and it's such an accepted part of the set that you don't really question it. You don't really say to Jon Lord, "How about not doing a solo?" We would be bitching behind the scenes: "How much longer is he going to go on for?" And I've noticed over the years, with many, many different musicians, that if they are tired or hungover or not playing very well, if they are doing a solo it lasts much longer, because they keep on trying new things—"That didn't work, let me try something else." They don't have an internal clock telling them, "Look, leave them wanting more."

MALCOLM DOME (writer, Record Mirror and Kerrang!): You can look at it and say Deep Purple were over, dead. Sabbath were in chaos. Zeppelin were still around and still massive, but you got the feeling they had really done their best work

JOHN GALLAGHER (vocals and bass, Raven): You can look back at it now and see that, what it was, was the drugs. After a certain amount of time taking the drugs, they all fell apart, every single one of them. And all around the same time, around '78 or '79. You had Aerosmith fall apart, Zeppelin were falling apart. Even coming up to their height, UFO were barely hanging on. Michael Schenker was out of his mind and gone, and the rest of them were either drunk or on drugs all the time. That can only work for so long. So there was definitely an air of that. And around '78 or '79 they all started trying to play funk music, for some reason.

PHIL MOGG (vocals, UFO): We must have done a lot for Peru. It was a bit like when you used to go out and have a fun night at the weekend. Come Monday you'd have to straighten out and go to work. The thing with bands is that every night is like a party night, so you never have the chance to get over the hangover you had before, so you continue that cycle. I saw one of our date sheets from one of the older tours—in a month's work you'd have two days off. So there's no time for recuperating and there was no one there to say: "Don't you think it would be a good idea if you did this?"

   We were doing a concert with April Wine, and the following day we had another one with Fleetwood Mac in San Bernardino—this is the late seventies, just starting to kiss the eighties—and we'd run out of something or other. Our bus driver called another guy who was driving to the gig with April Wine. He said he had certain substances, and we should meet at the next truck stop. So we got there, and this guy comes along with a briefcase, chock-a-block with stuff. "Oh this is great," we said. And it was a bit like one of those movie scenes where they chop out a line that goes from here to next week. In our bravado, we were "Yeah!" But by the time we reached the gig no one could talk. We were absolutely rigid. Time to come on, and we couldn't move. We were onstage, absolutely stationary. It was a big open-air gig, and it was one of those where you think: "I ain't doing that again."

ANDY PARKER (drums, UFO): It's amazing we managed to show up for as many shows as we did, and do them. When we were opening for Ozzy Osbourne we were amazed at how messed up he would get, to the extent that he couldn't do some shows. Or he'd sing the first line and then collapse onstage. That really didn't happen with us. Phil suffered a bit here and there. As did Pete [Way, bassist]. For me it was a bit different. Being the drummer I wanted to be sure I kept things together, not that I was an angel. And there was a point where Michael [Schenker, guitarist] wasn't supposed to drink. He was on that drug they gave Keith Moon, for people who have alcohol problems, but he'd figured he could have so many beers without his face turning purple. He had his whole schedule written down.

Our drinking seems comical now. It was white wine for the sound check. Then beer. Then on to the hard stuff in the evening. That was the good thing about playing special guest slots: there was always booze left if you raided other people's dressing rooms. We were doing cocaine and weed; the really heavy stuff didn't come in till later, the really nasty stuff. I never dabbled in that. I did quite a bit of blow, but then you end up staring at the ceiling at three in the morning when you have to be up in three hours. It got a bit tired after a while.

MICHAEL SCHENKER (guitar, UFO): My biggest problem was stage fright. And to overcome that I had to drink, and the more often you drink, it becomes a vicious cycle. And you end up at a point where the body goes, "Hey, hey, hey, I can't take this any more." That's what happens to many, many people. That was the main horror.

When we had a hit with *Lights Out* I got a weird feeling: "Shit, I have to tour consistently now. And people expect me to write more of this."

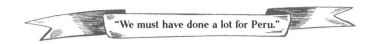

It was a snowball. I was seeing the snowball become an avalanche. I said to Gabi, my partner at the time: "I'm scared. It's going to become an obligation. The fun is out of the window. People are going to expect me to do more of the same. And I am going to have to drink around the clock now." Because I had had time when we didn't tour—I took that time to rest and stay away from alcohol. I had space and time. But now I saw no more chance for rest. It happens to many bands: the moment they made it big, they all collapse. And they get into a vicious cycle of being obnoxious and completely controlled by alcohol and drugs.

MALCOLM DOME: It's a story in itself how far Lizzy might have gone had it not been for the drugs.

SCOTT GORHAM: We'd always dabbled, but not in the super class-A stuff, the heroin and all that. It was a couple of lines of coke, everyone smoked a lot of weed, drank quite a bit. But it wasn't until we got to the *Black Rose* album [in 1979] and we were in Paris. We were in the hotel and [Thin Lizzy front man] Phil Lynott called me up and says, "Come on down to my room, I got something I want to show you." I had dabbled with heroin in California before I came, so England to me was saving me. I didn't know anyone who had it or was doing it, and I was really clean and felt great about life. I walked into Phil's room and he pulls out this package. He opens it up and I see the brown powder, and he says, "You know what this is?" And I went, "Yeah." "Have you ever done it before?" "Yeah." You want do some now? "Yeah." And that was the start of the whole thing. Drug dealers started beating down the doors of the studios and we just let 'em in. That was the real sad downfall of Thin Lizzy when all that shit hit our doors. That was the worst mistake that band ever made.

BRIAN DOWNEY (drums, Thin Lizzy): That whole period of heroin addiction was all a part of the downfall of the group. It certainly did not improve our look and really dragged the band down, and the guys with it. You go onstage wondering what the hell is going to happen tonight. Things started happening onstage that never happened previously. It was hair-raising, to say the least. Sloppy stuff was happening, and the band had had a reputation for being impeccable live. All that was disappearing in front of my eyes and it was so sad to see.

THIN LIZZY swinging twin harmony guitars in 1976. IAN DICKSON | ARENAPAL

I had to try it, because the conversations that were going on in the band were all about drugs. I got really inquisitive, especially about heroin. I'd tried everything else, I think, and heroin I had never tried because I was so scared about it. I'd heard so much about it—jazz musicians dying of a heroin overdose, and people in the early days of the rock scene—so I was scared off. But then when Phil and Scott started talking about it, I said to myself, "I have to try this if everybody is saying it's so great."

And when I did I was so out of it. The buzz was great, but the next day was the worst hangover I've ever had in my life, and we had to play a gig. I tried to play as best I could, but I discovered my muscles had seized up. I was really struggling on that gig. I just couldn't play. I had to say to the guys on stage: "Forget the drum solo on 'Sha La La,'" I couldn't play that. We had three or four days off after, and it took three or four days to get over the hangover. Looking back, it's the best thing that ever happened to me. I didn't get hooked. I only tried it once and that was it. But it didn't have that effect on Scott and Phil and they just continued on it until the end of the band.

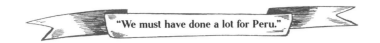
DANTE BONUTTO (writer, Record Mirror and Kerrang!): UFO and Lizzy were probably our two best melodic rock bands. The two who could write hits. And they were both in an awkward period.

JOE ELLIOTT: Me and my mates used to go to every gig in Sheffield. Every gig. We would go to the Top Rank, the Limit Club and the City Hall. The Limit was maybe five hundred. Top Rank is now the Academy, and that was maybe one thousand six hundred. The City Hall was two thousand two hundred. That was the big gig before we had the arena. Waiting to get into gigs there'd be somebody on the pavement selling fanzines. We had all the bands coming through—the Stranglers, Clash, Radiators from Space, Pink Fairies, Trapeze, AC/DC, Scorpions. We would go to see every single band.

A lot of bands would sell records on the T-shirt stall because they were independent. We were very aware of Cherry Red and Stiff Records fighting the big labels and giving artists like Elvis Costello and Nick Lowe a chance to get played side by side with things from Columbia or Atlantic on the John Peel show. When you hear the energy of the Undertones or Eddie and the Hot Rods, or the Clash and the Pistols and the Damned—you hear "New Rose," it's just insane energy that had been so lacking. When I heard "Get It On," "Metal Guru" or "Telegram Sam," that was the same thing, but four years later they just took it to another level. It went backwards musically, but it went forward with attitude, and that was a great balance. I thought it was great. I would see these bands live, and the odd ones who were brave enough to do *Top of the Pops* like Generation X, and the first thing I would say was: "I could fucking do that." But I wasn't saying it in a negative way, like on "Money for Nothing" by Dire Straits. It was just: "I could do that," and that's what happened.

BRIAN TATLER (guitar, Diamond Head): My first love was Led Zep, Deep Purple, Black Sabbath, the classic seventies bands. But I also liked Rush, Genesis, Pink Floyd a bit. I never got to see Floyd or Genesis, at least not with Gabriel. I had a real fondness for prog and some of it seeped in as an influence. And then in '77 punk happened, and I liked that as well. I used to listen to John Peel, and he'd be playing the Adverts and Ramones and stuff, and I thought it was great. And also I thought, "Ooh, I can play 'Pretty Vacant.'" So the fact that

I couldn't play prog—I didn't have a clue how to play anything by Genesis—but I could play punk rock. Brilliant. That spurred me on as well. I wanted to be onstage, really. I wanted to do my own thing, and I had this kind of dawning that I didn't have to become as good as Ritchie Blackmore, because I thought, "How am I going to get that good?" Practise forever or just go, get rocking.

STEVE ZODIAC: Punk gave the whole movement of rock music a shot in the arm, and in a way a lot of the Vardis attitude and some of the material, there's a lot of punk in it, and some of that could easily be a punk band. There's a fire that has to come out in the music sometimes.

DENISE DUFORT (drums, Girlschool): When we used to play, people didn't know if we were a punk band, a rock band or what. At one of the shows we were put on with Sham 69, and we were spat at because we weren't punk enough for that audience. We were too punk for the rock audience, and too rock for the punk audience. And that's where the New Wave of British Heavy Metal came into it all. We got lumped in that category.

PAUL DI'ANNO (vocals, Iron Maiden): When I first got bitten by the bug was when I first heard Ramones, and I went, "Cor blimey." You didn't think you could do anything, but when punk came around it seemed that anyone could have a go, and that's what did it for me. I would sit in my bedroom when I was a kid and copy everybody from Elvis to Bowie to Bolan. I could imitate the lot of them and I sounded just like them, but I didn't have a voice of my own until the punk thing came about and I started having a go at that. I liked bands like Zeppelin and Deep Purple, but I wasn't approaching it from that angle.

JOHN GALLAGHER: When the punk thing came along, it was, "Yeah, they've got a lot of energy, but talking loud and saying nothing. We've got more energy than that, but even at our stage we can actually play." So we weren't punk fans. You listen back to it now and hear the Sex Pistols and it's just a great rock 'n' roll band. They've got a swagger that none of the other bands had—they had a great feel. Some of the stuff was hilarious and great—Sham 69, I mean, you'd just die laughing at the lyrics. But at the time we thought, it's not serious, it's just bashing away on full barre chords with crappy guitar distortion. No thanks. Not interesting. In Newcastle it was the hairies versus the punks.

PAUL DI'ANNO: Steve [Harris, Iron Maiden founder] don't like punk whatsoever, but he had to tolerate me. We was in the same band, but from two different sides.

KEVIN RIDDLES: The whole ethos of punk was that even people who weren't rock stars, not talented musicians, could get up and play. That pissed off a few people, because a lot of people had spent a lot of time learning their craft. And here were these bloody upstarts who couldn't even hold the instrument the right way round, turning up and getting gigs. What the hell was that all about? We didn't realize the implications, but we realized why it had happened and why it was taking off—because of that dissatisfaction. It was the same dissatisfaction we'd felt, but punk had taken it the next stage further.

To all intents and purposes, punk was a shorter-lived phenomenon than the New Wave of British Heavy Metal. It was a very short, sharp, extreme and intense period. I have to say, it screwed a lot of us up, because of its intensity and because of its immediacy. It exploded, kicked a lot of people in the balls, then faded away fairly quickly. It

Long-haired punks MOTÖRHEAD, Hammersmith Odeon, November 26, 1980. LAURENS VAN HOUTEN

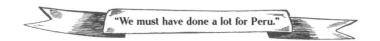

was a starburst. Bear in mind, our whole basis for being in bands wasn't making money or making records. It was playing live. That was the way that everybody felt was the way to get on. And all of a sudden, a lot of the pubs and clubs went from putting on rock nights to putting on punk nights. And ne'er the twain would meet.

Angel Witch had tours cancelled. There was a chain of clubs called Top Rank. Tuesday night would be bingo night, Wednesday would be a roller disco, Thursday would be a rock night. And that would be maybe fifteen or twenty clubs around the country. And overnight that became a Thursday night punk night. We could literally tour doing almost nothing but Top Rank clubs if we wanted to—Top Rank Reading one night, Top Rank Darlington the next night, Top Rank Middlesbrough the night after—and all of a sudden that disappeared. Because punk would draw the crowds.

There was that animosity between rock and punk, because we thought punk had nicked our gigs. They weren't better bands than us. They weren't writing better songs than us. They just happened to be a very short-lived fashion. The music business probably needed it, but we didn't see that at the time. All we saw was them nicking the bloody gigs. Bastards. That was the attitude: "Bastards!" We'd be supposed to be playing somewhere on a Thursday night and all of a sudden it would be cancelled because they'd decided to book a punk band instead. That was how punk affected us. It usurped a lot of our gigs and that pissed off a lot of people.

JOE ELLIOTT: Around 1979, nightclubs were starting to let bands play again after disco had shut it all down. So many punk bands had got live music banned from the little clubs around the UK, at the same time as disco was really kicking off. The people who ran these clubs found the easy way out in getting a DJ in. Cut to three years later, and it's softened. That happened to coincide with a bunch of kids who were sick of disco and a bit more musical than punk coming along with some of these bands and started making music and getting gigs. I'm saying this with the benefit of hindsight because we weren't aware this was happening in 1978/79.

KEVIN RIDDLES: To this day, Steve Harris won't mention the word punk. It was traumatic to a lot of people. The other thing is we couldn't

understand why, because it was shit. Musically it was absolutely crap compared to what we were doing, we thought. I'm sure Burt Bacharach thought we were crap, compared to what he was doing. We couldn't understand it. I think that was the other thing—this shock at what the hell was going on. It transpired that it was probably exactly what the music business needed. We didn't see that at the time.

MALCOLM DOME: I think the reason Steve is anti-punk is that a lot of labels in those days said, "Cut your hair, call yourself punk, and I'll sign you." And Steve quite rightly said, "Fuck off." But in terms of the DIY ethos, they got it from punk. Absolutely. Of course they did. The whole thing about putting out your own records, not having to sign to major labels. They definitely got those things from punk. Also, a lot of the energy and drive came from punk as well. Some bands took more than others and I'm not suggesting for a minute that musically Maiden or Leppard owed much to punk, but some bands did. Definitely. You can't just dismiss punk and say it didn't belong there, because it did.

KEITH KAHN-HARRIS (fan, sociologist, and writer): I think there's definitely a connection between NWOBHM and punk. But it obviously varies between the acts. I think one of the things that binds the two together is Motörhead. Motörhead is in some ways part of both and part of neither. You can hear Motörhead in later punk, certainly, and you can definitely hear it in New Wave of British Heavy Metal. In terms of the subcultural infrastructure that they built, there is definitely cross-fertilization, because the idea that you release your own records, you put on your own gigs, you release demo tapes and stuff like that— there's no question that is cross-fertilizing, usually from punk to metal rather the other way around—punk creates that precedent a couple of years before it really gets going in metal.

You do hear a punk influence in some bands. Usually not the bigger ones, but certainly some of the smaller ones—a band like Tank, for example, you can hear the punky, Motörhead-y influence. But once you get to America, those connections are made very explicit because early eighties thrash is influenced by American readings of punk and the New Wave of British Heavy Metal. They bring it together again. You can hear that in Exodus and Metallica. I think NWOBHM is probably more influenced by punk than it sometimes claims to be.

3

"Plumstead, for a few months at least, was the center of rock."

The NWOBHM bands take to stages in tiny clubs and pubs where patrons come to play bingo. Fighting to win over crowds, bands resort to drastic measures, lighting up gigs with gunpowder and fireworks with "hit or miss" results.

STEVE ZODIAC (vocals and guitar, Vardis): I left school at sixteen. I went to the careers officer. "What do you want to be?" I'd always loved sport, and I said I'd love to be a footballer one day. And that I'd love to be a professional guitar player. He looked at me, and he said, "Here we are then, thee can either go to Wakey Tech or be a carpenter or a motor mechanic." And he totally ignored it. Fair play, he probably heard it from every other young lad. I knew it were a long shot, but I was just being honest. I weren't saying it for a soft option.

DENISE DUFORT (drums, Girlschool): My brother used to be a professional rock musician. He played with lots of bands. He's thirteen years older than me, so when I was growing up I was watching him play and rehearse in my parents' living room with different bands. He's a rock drummer as well, so I watched everything he did as I was growing up. He used to sneak me into gigs to watch him play when I was about nine, actually. That's how I got into it.

The neighbors did used to complain. They used to get the police to come round sometimes when my brother was rehearsing with his band in the living room. I was about ten or twelve and I remember the cops coming round. So he had to start padding his drums. But they still used to rehearse. When I got old enough I started playing his drum kit and I

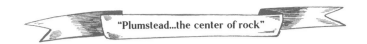

Axe-wielding boogie warriors VARDIS (from left: Alan Selway, Steve Zodiac, and Gary Pearson)

FIN COSTELLO | REDFERNS

realized, "Oh my God, this is what I want to do."

I wanted to be a drummer. I was about twelve when I could actually sit behind his kit and reach the foot pedals. When I could reach the bass drum I could actually play and it was amazing.

JOHN GALLAGHER (vocals and bass, Raven): My dad had a guitar. He'd never let us touch it and it was a source of fascination, sitting in the cupboard. I remember silly things like beating on biscuit tins when the Beatles were on *Ready Steady Go!*, and just soaking in music from the radio or *Top of the Pops* or wherever. It got to the stage where we were really into bands like Slade and Sweet and Status Quo. We'd get our friends and put the records on and jump around with tennis rackets.

We went on holiday to Spain in '72 maybe, and in the hotel restaurant, when we finished eating, there was a band playing. The guy was playing a Strat, and he had the coiled cord and the wah-wah pedal, and was playing behind his head and with his teeth, and it was amazing. We went out in Benidorm town, to another restaurant, and again they had a band playing. After that, we wanted a guitar. So my brother got a guitar, and we'd share it and fight over it.

DENIM AND LEATHER 65

Eventually one day he came in with Paul Bowden, the kid from down the street, and just said, "We're going to form a band, and you can play the bass." Which was fine by me, because I was spending half my time tuning down the guitar trying to play bass lines. We formed the band before we could play two or three notes. And before we had enough instruments. So we bugged our parents and got second-hand electrics for Christmas, and it was, "You're on your own from here on in."

We used to go round dumpsters and look for the old radiograms, which had a valve amplifier inside. If you fiddled with the wires and didn't get too much electric shocks, you could make it work as an amp. We'd go out on binges of car-washing to make up the money to save up to buy amplifiers. We made our own speaker cabinets. There was a family who had an electronics store down the street who would help out with stuff occasionally.

BRIAN TATLER (guitar, Diamond Head): My brother David is six years older than me. He had a guitar. My sister won £500 on "Spot the Ball" in 1968, when I was eight and Dave was fourteen, and with those winnings she bought him a guitar. He struggled for years to learn to play, but eventually he got okay and joined a band. A local band, doing covers. I started getting interested in music through him.

My brother liked the Beatles, and then he got into rock. He saw Sabbath in 1971, and Zeppelin, Genesis. He'd bring these albums home, and I'd listen to them with him. I got into the guitar through him. I would pick up his guitar and he would show me a chord or a simple riff. By fourteen, I decided I wanted to get good, I wanted to practise. There was a track by Deep Purple called "Highway Star," which had an incredible guitar solo by Ritchie Blackmore. Once I heard that—Purple and Zeppelin were my favorite bands—I thought, "If I'm going to play like that, I'm going to have to practise like a bastard, do hours and hours of practice every day."

I eventually overtook Dave. I didn't have proper lessons. I just listened to records, taped them, slowed them down, listened to little sections, tried to work them out. There was no YouTube, no nothing— it's so much easier to learn songs with YouTube. Dave had a thirty-watt Linear Conchord amp, and at one point I didn't have a speaker for it—I just borrowed his amp. I had a three-watt speaker I found, from an old record player. I figured out how to solder a jack plug into it, and put

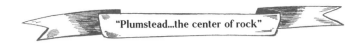

that in, and I didn't know about ohms and impedance and all that—just KERRANG! I thought it sounded great, distorted like hell. So that was my sound then. I would have been sixteen when I got that.

Then Dave bought a Gibson SG after watching Tony Iommi—he had a job, so he could afford it. I think it cost him a hundred and fifty quid. And so then I was able to play his old guitar, which had cost fourteen pounds, any time I liked. I didn't have to ask Dave or worry about breaking it. So that was it. I was away.

ROBB WEIR (guitar, Tygers of Pan Tang): I used to go to gigs from the age of fourteen—because I always had a moustache, I used to be able to get into the Newcastle Mayfair. I think I put one of my dad's tweed jackets on and my jeans, my flared Wrangler jeans, which you had to have in the day. So I was in there every Friday night, watching, and every Friday night, they had a name act on: it would be UFO, Uriah Heep, Baker Gurvitz Army, Alex Harvey Band, Sammy Hagar. I've seen everybody there, absolutely everybody. One of the crazy bands that made me think, "Oh my God, I really, really need to be doing this," was the first time Cheap Trick came into the country, and I saw them at the Mayfair. Rick Nielsen had Sound City 4 x 12s stacked two and two and two, so they were three high but two wide, and all the grilles were kind of mutilated, so it looked like a giant spider's lair, and you must have had ten Hamer guitars on stands, going right across the stage, and, well, my jaw was just on the floor for the whole thing. It wasn't the music: I was just completely in awe of the stage set-up. I thought, "One day, one day, I've got to have something like this."

PHIL COLLEN (guitar, Girl and Def Leppard): I went to see my first concert when I was fourteen. It was Deep Purple on the Machine Head tour, at Brixton Academy, which was then called the Brixton Sundown. That gig changed my life. It was, "Oh my God, I have to do this. Nothing else matters." That was the one. I wanted the dream of being a singer, guitarist, rock star or whatever, but that was the really profound moment. I went home to my mum and dad and said, "Right, I need a guitar." I kept on at them and got one for my sixteenth birthday, which is kind of late. I was obsessed with it and it took over my life.

DENIM AND LEATHER 67

PAUL DI'ANNO (vocals, Iron Maiden): There were all these great pub bands, like Stray, all coming out of the East End. Uriah Heep was from round our way, and before that we had Small Faces—Steve Marriott was a local legend. Later on, when I was just leaving school, we used to go down to Walthamstow Town Hall and I'd see bands like Cockney Rebel. Me and Phil Collen went to school together, in the same year. We used to go round each other's houses at night. He lived just opposite our school. We used to think his old man was the dog's bollocks because he drove one of those massive Attwood cranes. "Cor, your dad's got a really cool job!" Me and Phil used to spend all our pocket money on monster magazines, sit there reading them on doorsteps. Out of our little crew in Walthamstow, quite a few of us became musicians.

DENNIS STRATTON (guitar, Iron Maiden): The East End was fantastic. There was a band used to play at the Bridge House in Canning Town Tuesday, Thursday, Friday, Saturday and Sunday, which was Powerpack. They did everything from Deep Purple, Uriah Heep, right the way through to ballads. Spooky Tooth, things like that. Fantastic band. We used to go up there and watch the band. It was then, at sixteen, watching Terry Newman [of Powerpack], that I wanted to buy a guitar. Everyone in that area, we all grew up not being good enough for football so the idea was that we all bought instruments. Every night without fail I went up there and watched him, and 'cause I lived round the back of the Bridge House, in the old part of Canning Town—they were all bombed houses with no hot water—I used to get home and still have these tunes in my head. I'd sit on my bed with the guitar and just try and work out what I just seen him play, slowly. That's how I taught myself to play guitar.

STEVE DAWSON (bass, Saxon): My first band was called Blue Condition. First gig we ever played were in a pub in Swinton called the Canal Tavern. And it just went from there. We played anywhere we could. We didn't have a van or anything. We went on t'bus to the Canal Tavern gig. I can remember trying to get on t'bus outside my mum's house with a bass drum, and t'bus driver said, "You're not getting on with that." We went back in t'house, and my dad said, "Oh, I'll take you there on t'barrow." So we went and put t'bass drum and a few bits and pieces on the barrow, and went and did our first show. I think that were an early indication of the determination you need to succeed.

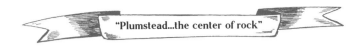

BIFF BYFORD (vocals, Saxon): I was in a band called Coast. We had an excellent guitarist. I played bass and sang. The guitarist that was in Coast had mild agoraphobia and he couldn't handle a lot of people around, so we didn't really get a lot of gigs.

KEVIN RIDDLES (bass, Angel Witch): Our gigs started off with twenty people, mates and that sort of stuff. And quite quickly it grew and swelled. There was quite an undercurrent in southeast London, certainly. It went from twenty mates to, within three or four months, two hundred in the Green Man and it was packed. It became a regular monthly rock night, so it was Angel Witch "and"—so there would be another band on, or more usually a rock DJ. So it grew organically. We built a little audience in southeast London and took it from there.

Compared to everything else that was going around, it was out there. The in-thing at the time was Judas Priest—great songs, but heavy regular rock songs. They were just done slightly differently, whereas Angel Witch always, it seemed to me, had something that made you spin your head around and that was the thing I always looked for: a riff done differently. A riff played differently, with a different sound. I think that's what Angel Witch had. It was original because of that. A lot of bands were still playing rehashed rhythm and blues rock, whereas Kev [Heybourne, Angel Witch singer-guitarist] not so much. To this day, I don't know whether Kev listened to bands like MC5 and those out-there American bands, but there was that sort of influence there, where they took a regular riff and did something different with it. Kev certainly was able to do that.

The good thing is that Plumstead, for a few months at least, was the center of rock. I can't say it was us particularly—we just happened to be there. But the Green Man had a big room at the back. It was difficult for bands to get gigs, but because we had that in, that arrangement, the pub got noticed. So other bands would come in. We'd be playing once a month, but in the intervening time, other bands would be coming in. Half of the *Metal for Muthas* album bands played at the Green Man—people like Toad the Wet Sprocket and Maiden, they all got on to that circuit. The Dutch House in Eltham was another great gig. Slowly but surely a little circuit developed. We were constantly running into Maiden, Toad the Wet Sprocket and the like. It was competitive. It'd be, "Oh Christ, did you see Maiden? They had a bloody dry-ice machine! How did they get that? We've got to get one!"

THUNDERSTICK (drums, Samson): I played a handful of gigs with Iron Maiden. Everybody says, "You were in the band five minutes." I dunno what to say to that. Yes, in the great scheme of things I was in the band five minutes. But that five minutes was a few months. At that time, Dennis Wilcock was the singer, and he was doing a thing with a rapier, drawing it through his mouth and pretending to cut his mouth open. They were trying to push the band as much as they could, but there was no hardcore fan base there yet. It was just a lot of people who turned up to the pubs—the Bridge House, the Brecknock, Cart and Horses, the Ruskin, all round the East End.

DAVE LIGHTS (lighting technician, Iron Maiden): I think Thunderstick only did one gig with us, if I remember rightly. And that was at the Bridge House in Canning Town. It wasn't brilliant.

THUNDERSTICK: Who'd have thought something that happened in a little pub in the East End would haunt me for the rest of my life? I was having a rough time because I was having an affair. My wife had just found out. And so had the husband of the girl I was seeing. And they were at the gig, one, two, three of them. All in a row by the side of me.

DAVE LIGHTS: He'd been on something, as well. He'd split up with his girlfriend and he'd taken something. I don't know what.

THUNDERSTICK: Yes, I had taken some downers. And not only that, but I had taken delivery of a brand new drum kit, and it was delivered at the gig. And I had set it up for the very first time, and things weren't in their usual places, so I was kind of hitting some drums and hitting some rims. A lot of people would go along to just get a few pints down their neck. And everyone was chatting away, and apparently I stood up and shouted out at the people who were talking, something like "Be quiet for the maestro!"

DAVE LIGHTS: It was only about ten foot from the stage to the bar, and there were people talking. And I remember him stopping it and saying, "Shut up! Listen to the maestro!" We all looked at each other: "Oh my God." He was still just plain old Barry in those days.

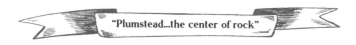

The Bridge House in Canning Town, East London, was an early home to U2, Depeche Mode, and IRON MAIDEN. "Mum, it's music, it's bands, it's not what it used to be," Maiden guitarist Dennis Stratton reassured his parents.

DENNIS STRATTON: The Bridge House was right on the Barking Road, before they built the overpass and the new station and roundabout at Canning Town. It was right on the main road and it was a huge Tudor-style pub, many floors, and it was right on the corner. It went down the hill, round the corner, so it had two massive bars. The stage was upstairs on the top bar—later they moved it down to the bottom bar. Terry Murphy had that pub, and his brother-in-law Joe Lucy—they married the two sisters—had the Ruskin in East Ham. The music in the East End in those days, everywhere had music. All the way to Leytonstone, all the way to Poplar, all the way to Aldgate. Everywhere you went.

The Bridge House years ago used to be an old haunt for prostitutes and seamen who'd come out of the docks. My mum and dad knew all about that, and when I was fourteen, fifteen, they said, "Where you been?" "I been to the Bridge House." She used to think it was like it was in the old days. "What's it like up there now?" "Mum, it's music, it's bands, it's not what it used to be." It was a massive pub. Brilliant building.

CLAIRE SCHOFIELD (fan): The Ruskin Arms was quite an intimidating pub. There was a big room at the back with blacked-out windows, and a spit-and-sawdust atmosphere. It was frequented by the Essex Hells Angels, who used to sit in the front of the pub. They were quite intimidating, but they were really nice chaps actually. Their president at the time, John, was nice. I used to chat to him. So for a young girl of sixteen it was quite an intimidating atmosphere.

There were huge numbers of bikes parked out the front, parked around the corner. A lot of biker presence. Sometimes they'd watch the bands, too. They had their corner at the front of the pub, which was known as the Hells Angels corner,and people left them to it. Sometimes there were a few fights, but Joe was a very strict manager and he wouldn't have any of it. If anything like that happened, people were thrown out immediately. He had to be a good manager with the sort of characters that came. But I used to find that although bikers looked intimidating, they were the nicest guys in the world and had the most respect for us girls and looked out for us all the time. I was with a couple of friends, and boyfriends as well. We used to go to watch the live bands.

PHIL COLLEN: Our band Dumb Blondes heard Kiss were doing all this theatrical stuff—blowing things up—so we went to this theatrical store and bought all this gunpowder. We stole a couple of dustbins and set this thing up in the Ruskin Arms to use at the end of our set and this thing went off before we even went on stage. Bang! There were bits of shrapnel flying about. It was really dangerous.

KEVIN RIDDLES: Maiden were the first of our ilk to have their own lights—the rest of us would just make do with a couple of painted fluorescent tubes on the floor, that sort of thing. But Maiden were the first to have proper lights. We bounced off each other, but it was competitive in a good way.

DAVE LIGHTS: It was a bit hit and miss, a lot of the stuff, in the early days. I wasn't an electrician and I was blowing up more stuff than was actually working. The very first light boxes I did were actually window boxes that people would put flowers in. I emptied all the dirt out and painted them up, and stuck four or five bulbs in it, different colored bulbs. The wiring came back to a little box with household switches

that I switched on and off. And then I got into pyros. That was another hit-and-miss thing, whether they went off or didn't go off. A lot of the time they didn't go off, and some of the time when they did go off it was disastrous. The wiring was just two wires, and then I'd put a bit of fuse wire across it with the powder on top, and basically just pop it into the mains. Sometimes the actual plug would explode. If that happened, Loopy [Steve Newhouse, Iron Maiden roadie] would toss on a match to make it go up.

We couldn't wait for firework night to come round, because I used to just go and buy however much I could afford. I'd get loads of fireworks and scrape them open and pour them into a tub. Sometimes you got a big flash, sometimes you got bloody sparks here, there and everywhere. It was quite dangerous. I did blow up Steve [Harris, Iron Maiden bassist] a couple of times. Once, when he was wearing PVC trousers, a pyro went off and burned them into the hairs on his legs. They should have known not to stand over the pyros. When we were doing the Kiss tour, a bit later on, Clive [Burr, drummer] wanted me to design these sticks that exploded on top. So I made this thing up with two drumsticks, and after his solo he picked them up and put them above his head and pressed a little button to a battery. But this spark flashed back and he set fire to himself. So after that it was, "No, we ain't gonna do that."

THUNDERSTICK: Samson's roadie was a pyromaniac. There were numerous occasions where we nearly blew the place apart. We did Chislehurst Caves and the first thing the promoter said to us was, "Please don't use any pyros." We go onstage, hit the first chord. Bang! A huge pyro explodes and thick maroon smoke goes up to the ceiling. The bar is almost opposite the stage. And the smoke slowly started descending over everybody. They were taking a step to the left, then another step to the left. It was if they were being chased through the catacombs by all this smoke. There was a place in Covent Garden that used to sell stage effects ignited by an electrical charge. But our roadie, being who he was, would just empty all the gunpowder in a line across the stage, and you'd get this sheet of flame that would burn across the stage. We'd be blind for about half the first song because we couldn't see a thing. And on my cymbals there would be all these tiny little weld marks, where all the gunpowder had come down on my cymbals.

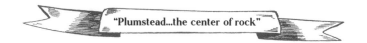
We did a place called Crackers in Wardour Street and I remember coming onstage and this guy, as we played the first chord and the gunpowder went off, his glasses go that way, he went the other way. We played Notre Dame Hall in Leicester Square, which had all this ornate wood slatting each side of the stage, and our roadie went and gaffer-taped these great big sparking things called gerbs, like roman candles. When we set them off it would create an arc over the top of the stage. You should have seen the burn marks. We burned all this lovely, ornate woodwork. Huge great scorch marks up it. We played a place with blue flashing police lights mounted in the ceiling. We walked in to do the sound check and the road crew had removed all these lights from the ceiling, taken them all down, and planted them on the backline, and used them during the gig. That was it. They went in the van and they came with us. Then we started getting into CO_2 fire extinguishers. We used dry ice, and if you fired a fire extinguisher into the dry ice, it kept it all on the floor, as opposed to coming up and the whole band disappearing into the smog. So the road crew used to nick fire extinguishers everywhere we played. There was a place in Acton we used to have to go to get them refilled.

JESS COX (vocals, Tygers of Pan Tang): There was a local guy called Davy Darko, and he had a shop in Shields Road in Byker, just outside of Newcastle. He made PA systems and things, and he also made bombs. I remember them getting us some pyro—powder in a dish and hooked up electrically and set up by hand, by our roadie Paddy. He used to set all these things off, and they fizzled and sparked up. You wouldn't be allowed to do it now. We were basically told to stay off the stage until they went off, that's how dangerous they were.

Then we moved on to buying little kits that hooked together, and had little dispensers of the various types of explosions you could get. We did experiment a bit in the early days with dodgy wiring, because Paddy was into wiring things up. He did our light show as well, which was a plank of wood with domestic switches and its own wiring that went to two wooden boxes, with tinfoil put in three separate compartments with domestic bulbs in, painted different colors. It was on-off, on-off, on-off, or all together, that was it. There was no coordination. There was one either side of the stage and that was our light show in the early days. He would do the mad pyros as well. Him and his mate Bri. Bri and Paddy, they did it all.

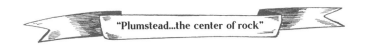

One night they had some pyros at the back of the stage and some at the front, and they said to us, "Right, we'll set the front ones off first, and at the end of the show we'll set the back ones off." Okay. So it was stay away from the front at the start, and then at the very end keep away from the back. Robb [Weir, guitar] got it wrong, and he went right to the front of the stage, and he got blown up, literally, on the first chord. Robb used to come and stand right in front of me when I was singing. Literally stand in front of me, legs astride in the middle of the stage, in front of the singer. It used to drive me nuts. So Robb had come to the front of the stage, forgetting these pyros were going to go off. This explosion took the side of his hair off.

After that, I was thinking, "Where is he?" because he wasn't coming round bugging me and standing in front of me. That night, the whole set he stood at the back. And then at the end the other bombs went off where he was standing with his white pants, and they took the backside out of his pants. We went offstage and Robb was absolutely furious. There he was with half a head of hair and the arse blown out of his white pants, so you could see his red underpants underneath with black all over them.

KEVIN RIDDLES: We didn't build pyros. We bought them. There was a lighting company called Le Maitre, and they brought out a supposedly idiot-proof pyro system, which was a plug-in box with a little cartridge. They had different strengths and designs—there'd be maroon, there'd be a confetti. We had a guy who used to look after our lighting and effects, but basically it was painting fluorescent lighting tubes. As far as pyros were concerned, we bought one of these systems because of the Music Machine, because of Maiden. Maiden turned up to one gig and they had, basically, indoor fireworks, which was what was around at the time, plus a few indoor confetti cannons. We said, "We'll do something similar," so we bought one of these systems. That was great.

There were four of these boxes across the front of the stage, and yes, I had my own mildly disastrous adventure. I used to wear these huge flared trousers, and of course the inevitable happened. I put my leg over a pyro when I shouldn't have done, and I've never had hair grow on the inside of that leg since. My trousers didn't go up in flames, fortunately, but there was the smell of burning hair and flesh. I could

DENIM AND LEATHER 75

never wear those trousers again, put it that way. But we didn't set fire to backcloths or sets or staging. We certainly set off quite a few fire and smoke alarms. We had our fair share of evacuated premises, and not necessarily due to the quality of the music. We had some fun with them.

DAVE LIGHTS: I nearly burned down the Music Machine. Basically, that was the first time we used proper theatrical pyro, from a place called Theatre Projects. But again, setting it off…It only takes 12 volts—I know this now, after—but what I'd done is wire up all this stuff, flares and smoke, and God knows what else, all on to one plug. Poor Loopy. I said to him, "Just plug it in." And bang, off it went. We blew out all the PA. Everything stopped. All the lights went out. And there was this massive display of fireworks for about two or three minutes. It didn't cause panic. Doug Sampson was the drummer and he just carried on doing the drum solo while the rest of Iron Maiden stood there waiting for it to come back on again. It seemed like forever, but it was probably only a few minutes. We turned a bit more professional after that and were able to get someone in to do it properly.

DOUG SAMPSON (drums, Iron Maiden): He'd overdone it a little bit. It was very frightening. All I could see was a curtain of flame. Everybody got out of the bloody way, but I felt quite frightened. I was quite worried. It did die down very fast. It was a bit like when Keith Moon blew up the stage. I had visions of that: "My God, I hope he ain't put any underneath the drums." It was just a wall of flame. And there wasn't enough to space to jump down from the kit.

THUNDERSTICK: There were exceptions like Keith Moon where people knew the drummer's name, but most of the time drummers were faceless and nameless, and that triggered something. I thought: "I'll create a faceless drummer." And I thought, "You can't be called Barry Graham Purkis when you look like that." So the two came hand in hand. Samson's manager at the time said, "Do you want to copyright Thunderstick?" And I went, "No, copyright that? Why?" Put Thunderstick into Google nowadays and you will come up with a huge array from vibrators to golf clubs. Little did I know.

The mask I wore was one hundred percent playing on the notion of drummers being anonymous. Our roadie was a biker with a club from the Gorbals. He had a great big chopper. These were not guys to mess around with. And I was talking to him about it. He said, "We use these balaclavas to keep our faces warm underneath the helmet. How about something like that?" I said, "That would be a great idea." So we put a bridge piece over the nose, I cut a hole for the mouth, and that was it— Thunderstick was born. And then the mask got described as a "rapist's mask." That was awful. It was because of *Sounds*. I think it was around the time I did the front cover of *Sounds*. They had all these awards and I was Cambridge Rapist Lookalike of the Year. Oh my God. Because not only that, but we used to have all these problems with Women's Lib groups.

For me, Thunderstick was always a knockabout character. Iron Maiden had their Eddie—or they hadn't got him yet—but somebody wrote to me and said, "I never used to fear Eddie, because Eddie wasn't real, whereas Thunderstick was." Then we moved on to putting me in a cage. Thunderstick played inside a cage, and at a given point in the set I would break out of the cage, the door would fly open, the strobes would go on, and I would hare down to the front of the stage to the audience, and they would visibly recoil. Oh my God! And it was a knockabout image. That was the main reason I got a female vocalist when I started my band Thunderstick. Not only because I wanted to sonically, but I thought if I got any kind of problems the way Samson did, I could say, "Go and talk to her."

DAVE LIGHTS: Eddie was called Eddie the 'Ead because of a joke. There was this couple who had a child, but it was only an 'ead. And the doctor said to them, "Look if you come back when he's sixteen, we'll probably be able to fix him up with a body." So Eddie the 'Ead, who's on the mantelpiece at home, his sixteenth birthday came along. And his parents came up to him and said, "Eddie, it's a really special day today. It's your sixteenth birthday." And then Eddie said, "Not another fucking hat." So it became Eddie the 'Ead. I had made a backdrop and squared it with loads of light bulbs all the way round it, and Eddie went on that: it was just a mould of a face. The original Eddie was just a normal face mask blackened up to be more like a skull. It was like one of those white faces people wear for Halloween. Then I made up paper-mache ones that were okay, but they didn't work because of all the blood. I used a fish-tank pump—what you use to blow air bubbles into the water. Basically, that went into one of those 3-in-One oil tins

Singer Paul Di'Anno of IRON MAIDEN and friend, backstage at Reading Festival UK, August 23, 1980.
GEORGE BODNAR ARCHIVE | ICONICPIX

with a little nozzle on it. I filled that with blood, or whatever it was. And then a tube led from there into the mouth with a little T-piece that would split round to either side and in that song "Iron Maiden," the lights around the backdrop would go on, and the power would start the fish-tank pump up, which would then pump air into the tin and that would pump the solution out of it into the mouth. And it was just a normal household switch at the mixing desk.

Doug Sampson got fed up of getting covered in blood, and so did Clive Burr. We used to use different combinations of stuff in the little oil tin. Sometimes when I put the stuff in it was a little bit too thick and it didn't come out as good as I wanted it to, so I'd thin it out with paint. I used food dye, I used emulsion paint, all sorts of different combinations. But when I used food dye, it dyed Clive's hair and it took ages to wash out.

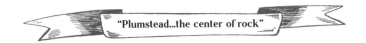
DOUG SAMPSON: I loved it. It was part of the show! I used to put my stool right under it, if I could, if I wasn't too near the wall. I didn't mind it at all. I've still got the kit and it's still covered in blood, in the food dye. I used to have long blond hair and it'd go all over me. Once I tilted my head back so it would go all over my face. I loved it. It was part of the show.

PAUL DI'ANNO: My first gig with Maiden might have been the Ruskin Arms. I was shitting myself. You'll never get two more nervous people going on stage than me and Steve Harris. Blimey. Steve used to use the khazi every five minutes, and I was like that as well. But after a couple of songs you're in it. I can't remember how well it went. But I do remember another one where I got arrested, up at the Swan in Hammersmith. That was a bit unlucky. My job at the time was doing oil drums; you got all the dents out, sprayed them up and got them ready to go back to BP. And they had those metal caps on, so you had a knife to get the cap off. I just tucked it in my bag. I took a shower at work that day, and then went up to Hammersmith with a knife in my bag. Not so smart. The cops decided to come and do a drugs raid, and I had a knife, and they carted me off the prison. Rod Smallwood had just started managing us—he had come to the gig to check us out, and it was, "You know your singer's just been carted off to jail?" I got out, in the end, and it was weird. Steve had to go up and sing. Gawd, that's not a good thing. But it still worked out alright. It's all part of life's rich tapestry. The police, being the police, weren't listening to my excuse. I ain't got a lot of love for them people.

DOUG SAMPSON: Our first gig [with Paul] was at the Bridge House, in January 1979. That was the first one, and it was thick snow, so it wasn't jammed to the rafters, but there was a good hardcore audience in there that was Maiden fans. But after that week, Terry, the guvnor, decided we were too heavy for his pub. But he had a brother-in-law who ran the Ruskin Arms, and he sent us down there. And Joe Lucy took us on down at the Ruskin. The first week we played there it was a good crowd. On the second week it was more. On the third week it was getting packed. And on the fourth week it was solid. Kids were coming in there who were just coming to see us. They weren't drinking, so Joe

used to walk round and turf them out because they weren't buying drinks. I don't suppose they were even old enough. It was brilliant, the way it was going.

DAVE LIGHTS: The band changed immensely when Paul joined. It became a proper rock band, I would say. Dennis Wilcock was good, but he was theatrical. He wasn't rock. But Paul had that dirty, grungy voice, and he loved wearing all the leather. Once, deliberately, to wind up Steve—there was a lot of windups going on—when Adam and the Ants were out, Paul plaited his hair with little bits of material. When we supported Judas Priest, Paul went down the route of wearing all those studs, but it was a good look for him. It was a good look.

CLAIRE SCHOFIELD: Every Friday or Saturday was rock night at the Ruskin Arms. You'd have a troop of people all walking down from East Ham station, all in our leathers and jeans, and you'd know they were all on their way to the Ruskin Arms. If you didn't know where it was, just follow the crowd. It was literally like that. It was really, really busy in there because there was nowhere else to go. There were always live bands—I wish I could remember some of the names of them—often local bands. But not as big as Angel Witch or Maiden, who were the big name in the East End. They were local heroes—people talked about them a lot. It was incredible, their rise to fame and how quickly it happened.

I was always with a group of girls I would go out with. There were some biker women who were pretty scary, who you would obviously not really mix with. I never used to get involved with them. Proper biker women. They'd arrive on these huge, great big trikes, with dark glasses and helmets, and they were pretty scary-looking. But people really enjoyed themselves. You'd have a glass of wine while you got ready to go out. Meet the girls in Barking, and we'd get the tube down to East Ham together and walk to the pub. It was quite a long walk from the station to the pub—it was right at the other end of the high street. And then when the pub turned out we'd all get the last bus home. My parents hated it. They didn't understand it. They were worried about me more than anything. They didn't realize I was okay and I was alright. They were not happy.

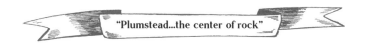

TIM CALDER (fan): I put on an Iron Maiden show! My friend Charlie's dad owned a biker's bar called Le Metro, which was well past its sell-by date. It was exactly like the Cavern—it was one of these underground sewers, in a finance area in Liverpool where there were a lot of banks, so during the day that was the clientele. Of an evening it would be a sub-biker sort of place. And they used to put on bands. We used to go down because we would get in for nothing. Charlie phoned and said, "My dad said someone's done a runner with all the money. And there's still a group who want to play. They're from London, and they're still coming up, and they're going to have the door money and my dad's going to take the bar money." This was about a week before. We made posters, and the one thing I can remember we wrote on the bottom was: "Members welcome, anybody welcome. Please bring a friend." It was almost a plea. That went up in one record shop. And on the Saturday—it was a Saturday night—we went down in the afternoon and Iron Maiden had turned up. They were happy to play pool in the back, and we played a few games of pool with them. That night, there were hardly any people there, and I got asked by the manager, "Can you please introduce them as 'The boys from the East End of London…Iron Maiden!'" There was just our mates there. The DJ booth was behind the stage, which was no higher than a beer crate. We stood there, and my abiding memory was thinking it was getting a bit sweaty. We looked at our friends, and they were laughing at us. We looked at each other: we hadn't realized we were standing underneath the prototype of Eddie, the skull. And it was pouring blood out while we were standing underneath. We ended up resembling two male versions of Carrie, drenched in blood. And we wondered why the band were going for it hell for leather, oblivious to us behind them and our mates in front of them laughing at us.

STEVE DAWSON: In Son of a Bitch [which became Saxon] we really liked the Sensational Alex Harvey Band. Also we'd done a support tour with the Heavy Metal Kids. We did about five shows with them, and they heavily influenced us—Gary Holton's stage antics.

We borrowed quite a few of their tricks of the trade. The soundman would start to fake feedback, so Biff'd give him a hard time on the microphone. And it would persist, so the soundman would come up on to the stage. Biff would have a big plastic chain and would start

whipping him with that. Then we'd all start kicking him. I used to wear Doc Martens boots that I'd painted silver, and lay into him. Biff would also, towards the end of the show, nail me to the stage through the front of these Doc Martens boots. We used to do a song called "Street Fighting Gang," which became a Saxon song, and he had a knife in a sheath. But some nights it wouldn't be a knife, it would be a cucumber, but it was a false cucumber, and when he pulled it out, it was a vibrator. So he'd put it on the microphone vibrating.

We'd do anything stupid to make a show, rather than just be guys playing music and looking at their feet. We did a show, not just a performance, shall we say. And they liked it. We had all sorts of different props that didn't really cost anything. We made them ourselves. We always had a decent light show, pinched, usually. We went to a venue with lights, we'd take a few of them. I'd been mentioning to my dad we were wanting some smoke machines onstage. And he said, "Why don't you try these?" They looked like fireworks, but they were smoke for fumigating greenhouses. We thought it would be alright, we'll light them onstage. And we got the effect, smoke on the stage, but we didn't realize they were toxic.

So we played this gig in Castleford, West Yorkshire, a small pub. We came to the end of the night, everything's going mad, there's feedback going on, so we let this fumigation cartridge off. Everybody ran out of the room, gassed, including the band. We couldn't breathe. We didn't get invited back. But there weren't no big repercussions like there would be today. It was just a learning curve. Better not do that again.

I used to breathe fire as well. We played a gig at the UMIST Students' Union bar in Manchester. I did my normal fire-breathing routine at the end, but it was a low roof and I must have got too much paraffin in my mouth. There wasn't really any substitute for paraffin. I must have taken an extra big gulp of paraffin and blew this flame, and it hit the roof and rolled down it like a big fireball and it set all the fire alarms off. Within a couple of minutes, fire brigade were there, trying to put the fire out. We would have done anything to make it a show. We were notorious among the other bands.

BIFF BYFORD: Dawson used to blow fire. That was one of his tricks. I used to mess around, really—audience singbacks, and jumping offstage and running through the audience. I used to have a set of

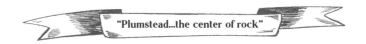
throwing knives and I used to throw them into the side of the PA. By the time we got a deal, in '79, we could do some of the big clubs and get between five hundred and nine hundred people on a weekend. We used to take the door money, and we could make £900, which was a lot of money in 1977, 1978. We weren't doing that every night. But we bought a single-decker bus and kitted it out with bunks and a kitchen, because we were all a bit handy. It was good. Bunks and curtains and a small kitchen sink—like a camper van, but in a single-decker bus. Before that we'd had a van, a tripe van that we had to paint matt black.

STEVE DAWSON: It were a Bedford Hawson van. It had been used by a tripe company called Spates. And on the side, it said, "Spates—purveyors of tripe and fine meats for all." It were a disgusting beige color. But the salesman said, "You can have that for two hundred quid." So we had it. It didn't have any heating. We had two roadies—well, I call them roadies, but they were mates who would come with us—and they were that embarrassed by it, they came one day with a tin of matt black paint and painted it. All of it. Just to cover the tripe.

BIFF BYFORD: And that's how we went round England, doing as many clubs as we could. I'd say we had a following of maybe twelve to fifteen thousand. We had a good circuit. We used to play the same places once every month. So we had about ten, fifteen places we would play regularly. And then we started getting a couple of better gigs, like the Middlesbrough Rock Garden. Our bread and butter was the northeast and south Wales.

STEVE ZODIAC: We crossed paths with Son of a Bitch quite a few times. There used to be a boarding house in Spennymoor, and when you played Newcastle or in Scotland, or even Carlisle, when you went back down to West Yorkshire, you'd often stay there, and we'd bump into them there sometimes.

Later on we played some shows with Saxon. If we weren't playing on a Friday or Saturday night and they were playing locally, we'd go out. I saw them in one of the working men's clubs. They were pretty much pure covers in them days, but they were very good. What they were doing in terms of technique, we were just dreaming of. They were about four or five years older than us, and when you're a teenager

someone who's twenty-three or -four or -five seems like an old bloke. So they were at another level.

Another guy who influenced me were Alan Barton, who were the original singer and guitar player of Black Lace. Alan were playing in a band called Love or Confusion, who were another covers band, mainly doing Sweet stuff. He were five years older than me and he were a proper guitar player, and I were still learning. He'd often sit with me, and we'd support them a lot as well. He went on to make "Agadoo." A really sweet guy. He was someone who proved you could be a professional musician and play what you loved and keep doing it and never give in. He had that attitude. He were constantly working and enjoying it and he gave me that inspiration to follow in that ethos of not caring if people think it's shit because there are other people who enjoy it. He gave me a lot of belief.

KEVIN RIDDLES: Getting hold of dry ice was a major pain in the butt. We did a classic at the Ruskin Arms. Nobody knew, not even Joe Lucy, the landlord of thirty years, that under the stage there was an extractor fan. If a particular switch was flicked, the extractor fan would come on. So we went and got ourselves a dry-ice machine, bought the blocks of dry ice, set it up, turned it on, and out came this dry ice, which immediately disappeared under the stage and was blown into the car park outside, which happened to be a police car pound. All the gig money went on buying this block of dry ice—that's how important it was. And we got no benefit from it whatever because it disappeared under the stage. Half the Maiden guys were there, and Loopy fell about laughing because he knew exactly what was going on. We didn't have a clue. We just wondered where all the dry ice had gone.

STEVE ZODIAC: I remember seeing David Bowie for the first time, and it were the first time I'd ever seen a stroboscope. Even though we had discos, strobes were rare in them days. He had this single flash thing going, and it set the mood before he even came on. When he came out he were doing his mime, then Ronson came on from the other side doing "Suffragette City." And it were the most awesome opening. All the bands I'd seen before, Sabbath and Rory Gallagher and Quo, they just had the drums on the floor and a wash on the stage, and they just walked out. There were no real stage set. But Bowie were bringing this amazing choreography, and he had this strobe and it really affected me. And I thought. "We've got to get one of them!" So we made one out of an old fan, and a piece of plywood with a hole in it. I got in my head that if we spun this fan and shone some kind of car headlight through it, we might get a similar effect. So me and my mate Ronnie got a piece of plywood attached to the front of this fan in a box with a hole in it, and this light behind it. And we were going, "Shit, it works! This is amazing!" We were looking at this thing we'd build out of plywood. And Ron says, "Right, let's give it a lick of matt black. It'll work like a peach." We were playing a small club that night, and we put this thing at the front of the stage. And we came out, with this flash, just like Bowie, and I thought, "Mick Ronson, here I come!" Fucking fan went on, and we're playing away, and house lights go up. "Can you stop playing? Can you stop playing?" All the audience were covered in black spots. All these old biddies sat there, just covered in matt black paint. We got paid off for doing that. "That's it, get your gear." It were just like *Phoenix Nights*. You're passionate about trying to give a good show and you end up getting buggered.

ROBB WEIR: We were quite an unusual act for the working men's clubs because we played our own material, rather than songs of the day, and that in itself was interesting, because if you went to see a covers band, the girls would appear down the front with their handbags, and start to bounce around to "All Right Now." When we launched into a seven-minute version of "Slave to Freedom," with the various guitar solos and harmonics and time changes, it was a little bit more intense and a little bit more for them to listen to. But we only got paid off once, at Wallsend Social Club, and then there was an uproar when we didn't come back on for the second set. Apparently it was all to do with the fact that we were too loud in the concert room for the bingo in the room adjacent to us. As we all know, bingo is sacrosanct on a Friday night at a working men's social club.

ABADDON (drums, Venom): If you've ever been in a northern working men's club when somebody interrupts the bingo, you'll know what real shit is. Even the Tygers would tell you the same. They would have to do two sets because they did the bingo in the middle. People would turn up for the last song of the first set, just to come in and do the bingo, then they'd leave.

ROBIN GEORGE (producer and engineer, Witchfinder General):
In the working men's clubs, they used to tend to use our PA rather
than their little tiny speakers when it was time to do the bingo, so we'd
just sit behind the amps and twiddle the knobs. Feedback! Feedback!
Feedback! We did enjoy it. It was a lesson in life.

ANDRO COULTON (bass, Witchfynde): Playing those working
men's clubs, they asked you to do three half-hour spots, or two three-
quarter-hour spots. The managers didn't like that, because they liked
to have two lots of bingo in. So you got to know your length of time,
and you got to be precise in how you played it. That's why we were
able to go into the studio, knock that whole first album out in two
long weekends. Because we knew the stuff backwards. We played and
played and played and played. So it was instinctive to play it.

JOHN GALLAGHER: I've just been out and drove past the patch of
that ground where Westerhope Comrades Club used to be. We got
paid off halfway through, which was a badge of honor. My mum and
dad used to go out to clubs on a weekend, and they would say, "You
couldn't believe what happened tonight!" "What happened?" "John
Miles"—who had a big hit with "Music," and it was just before that—
"he got paid off at the Westerhope Comrades!" If they thought you
were too annoying or too loud, they'd just give you half your money
and let you do the one set and send you on your way.

ROBB WEIR: I think the lowest attendance of an early Tygers show
was actually one man and his Jack Russell. It was probably our second
or third show ever, so we barely knew what we were, what we did. I
think we were being paid, I don't know, twenty quid or something to
play upstairs. So we duly set up and started to play, and you hope the
door's going to open and, you know, thousands of people, or hundreds,
or tens, or one person's going to come in, and he came, with his dog,
bought a pint, got an ashtray off the bar and tipped the dumpers out
into another ashtray, poured some of his pint into the ashtray and put
it on the floor for his dog, bought a packet of crisps, shared those with
his dog, didn't really pay us much attention while we were playing our
little hearts out, duly left, and as he left, as he opened the door for his
dog to go in front of him, the dog cocked its leg on the door and they

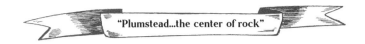
both left. And that was it, we all kind of looked at each other and then when the song finished, I think I remember we had a bit of a laugh about it, a bit of a discussion about it, and went into the next song. What else can you do?

JOHN GALLAGHER: The Hells Angels had a party out in Eckington, which is south of Newcastle. It was out in a field. We ended up playing with a generator out in a field under rapidly diminishing weather. So we played, and we played. We played "Born To Be Wild," and finished it, and they said, "Play it again." Alright. The customer is always right. We play it again. And it starts raining. "Play it again." I don't know about this, but we start playing again, and it really starts raining.

My brother goes arms akimbo, shaking and falls on the floor. Oh my God—I run over and kick the guitar away from him, and I'm trying to wake him up. And they're shouting, "Come on, play!" "Jesus, he's just had a fricking electric shock, you idiots!" And they moaned, but we picked him up and took him to the van. And when we were in there, he started giggling and said, "Let's get the fuck out of here, right now." He faked an electric shock so he wouldn't be getting real electric shocks, basically.

PHIL ASTON (guitar, the Handsome Beasts): That happened to us. Again, at that time, bikers knew what they liked and they expected you to do a certain thing. They'd booked you and paid good money, and they expected certain songs to be in the set list, and "Born To Be Wild" was one of them. Even if you didn't want to do it. From a personal perspective, they were my least favorite gigs.

JOHN GALLAGHER: The other thing would be that a lot of the clubs were south of Newcastle, and there's a huge rivalry between Newcastle and Sunderland. So once you get a few miles out of Newcastle they're all Sunderland fans, so the compère would take great pleasure in announcing: "Next up, the boys from Newcastle!" And everyone would boo. As you were playing, they would come up with requests they had written on beer coasters, and put them on the front of the stage. Quite often the request was: "Fuck off."

When you got to London, the Marquee was always a built-in crowd of people who wanted to have a good time. It was small, hot and sweaty,

tiny dressing room, and when you finished your set, all your gear had to go into the hall along the wall, which was, "Oh God," because you had to stand there all night watching it. It's a shame it's gone, like so many.

NIGEL HUTCHINGS (manager, Marquee): You went through the double front doors on Wardour Street. Box office on the left. Then there was a cloakroom a little bit further up. The Bananarama girls used to work there. Well, Siobhan worked behind the bar. Then you walked up a corridor into a bar area, where you could bump into everyone. It was like a youth club for grown-ups in there, and anybody in the music industry, if they were in town, you could bet your bottom dollar they'd be down at the Marquee at some point.

Through another set of double doors into the main auditorium area. Everything was pitch black. We changed the floor—it was a carpet up until '76, and it became a rubberized floor, which stopped the stickiness but it could be slippery. The stage was probably about nine hundred millimeters off the ground, if I remember correctly. It was pretty low, so if you were down the front you were in physical contact with whoever was on the stage. That all added to the atmosphere of the place. Out the back, you'd go through an archway and on the left were some gaming machines, which nine times out of ten Lemmy would be on. There was another bar there. Then out the back past the gents into Richmond Mews. Everything was black. The whole focus was going to be the stage.

JON DEVERILL (vocals, Persian Risk and Tygers of Pan Tang): The dressing room at the Marquee was like this tiny box—no space at all. All over the walls graffiti—artists had signed their names, drawn little cartoons. It was just extraordinary. And when you think of the people that have played that club, it was a dream come true.

DANTE BONUTTO (writer, Record Mirror and Kerrang!): You would meet in the Ship on Wardour Street, about one hundred yards north of the Marquee. Then you'd go to the Marquee, and then across to the St Moritz afterwards. That was the golden triangle of your evening: Ship, Marquee, St Moritz.

So gigs were mostly at the Marquee, and that was an amazing venue. It was a doorway on Wardour Street. As you walked through a narrow corridor, there was an outer bar on your left, where you'd have your

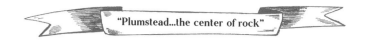
first drink. Then some swing doors into the venue, with another bar at the back. It was maybe a three-hundred-capacity venue, with a low ceiling. I remember being in there when it was really busy and it was really difficult to move. Very hot and sweaty. I remember being so uncomfortable, but having such a good time. It was really packed in there sometimes—an amazing place to play. A lot of bands would underplay there—I remember going to see ZZ Top there. People would really scale down to play gigs at the Marquee. It was always a good night. It had the vibe. In the outer bar, there would be people hanging out because you could hear the music but still talk.

It was always hard to get in to the St Moritz because the guy who ran it didn't seem very nice, but you blagged your way in. And in there it was like a nightclub. It wasn't easy to find places to drink late at night, and this was right opposite the Marquee. Lemmy would often be in the St Moritz. There were many aftershows and album launch parties in the St Moritz. It was another place to meet like-minded people. It was a boozy scene, but not knowingly. It was more that you were at a rock gig, so you'd go and have a drink. It naturally gravitated in that direction. I never sensed drinking was the main part of it. Music was way more important to your evening.

NIGEL HUTCHINGS: Generally, we'd book the headline acts through contacts we knew—a journalist would say, "You ought to listen to this band," or a record company may say, "We've got this band coming from America. We're prepared to back them by buying two hundred tickets." The thing about the Marquee was its location. It was right in the hub of everything, so it was easy for business people and punters to get to. It could be a chance thing. Iron Maiden got booked the first time because someone in the band was a carpet fitter, and was fitting carpets in the offices at the back of the Marquee.

Bands were always paid a percentage of the door. The door limit of the Marquee was four hundred, not always completely kept to— in 1976 we put on AC/DC, and they had about one thousand four hundred people in. You can imagine how that was. It was irresponsible, obviously. We did reduce it a lot, but even so we were still letting too many people in. The bands then got paid more, the atmosphere was electric. The punters loved it. When they squeezed in there it created a cooker atmosphere. People would come out at the end of the night

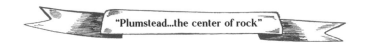

knackered and exhausted, but exhilarated, and for the bands who were up there on the stage surrounded by the lights and electrics, it popped for them as well. Sweat would be running down the walls.

We usually paid bands fifty percent of the door, and the support acts would get about £12 per person and ten people on the guest list. The main act was allowed twenty-five. Anything above that they had to pay for. Support acts quite often didn't get a sound check and they had to pay the main band for the use of their lighting engineer and sound engineer and PA. They never ended up with any money. You didn't play the Marquee to make money. It was a springboard to hopefully greater things.

JODY TURNER (vocals and guitar, Rock Goddess): My dad, as our manager, got a call: there'd been someone who'd pulled out and did we want to play? I'd been hassling him: "Dad, I want to do the Marquee." He paced all night: were we ready? And then he said, "Fuck it." We'd got a bit of press so we were getting popular. But nothing could have prepared us for that night. It was so packed. Absolutely rammed. The whole place was screaming "Goddess! Goddess!" It was so exciting but so terrifying. And when we walked on the place erupted. My dad said we performed differently: we stepped up. We rose to the occasion and it's still the best night of my life. It was pivotal. And from there things kicked off. I was crawling on the ceiling afterwards: I love that feeling after a good gig. It was such a high. It was so buzzy.

KIM MCAULIFFE (vocals and guitar, Girlschool): What a brilliant venue that was. That was a brilliant gig. It was a great size. The bloody carpet was the stickiest carpet I have ever experienced. But it was a great stage. You could see the band so well. You had the bar off to the side. A great location, great sound. It was one of my favorite gigs to play.

TINO TROY (vocals and guitar, Praying Mantis): I was going to the Marquee four nights a week, something like that—obviously I didn't pay to get in. Start at the Ship, then the Marquee, then the Moritz. It was totally nuts. And the Funny Farm in Chalk Farm.

There would always be people from bands—you'd meet up with the same crowd all the time. We bumped into Maiden quite a lot, Samson—I used to socialize with Paul quite a bit, see him round at our drummer's place, 'cause he was in east London, in Leytonstone.

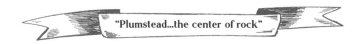
We used to hang around together quite a lot, drinking, puffing. We did some naughty stuff as well—we wrecked a whole hotel once, by a water fight that went stupidly crazy. Buckets, fire extinguishers, everything. I think it was in Huddersfield.

STEVE ZODIAC: We must have played the Marquee a dozen times and we did well there, it were a good venue for us in that period. I used to see Lemmy in the Ship a lot, and we'd chat about music. At the time Irene [Steve's wife, known at the time as Motorcycle Irene] were working for Motörhead's management—she were quite a big part of the Motörhead story in the early days. She was the classic lineup's PR. That's how we met. We fell in love at Deeside Leisure Center. I were on stage, and she were at side of stage. We were supporting Motörhead. I saw this woman there and thought, "She's alright." It were love at first sight. Love at first lust. They all said it would never last, and forty years later here we are.

4

"It was like the CBGB of British metal."

At a pub in the northwest London suburbs, DJ Neal Kay established The Soundhouse, a home for those who wanted to celebrate metal. In the process, he became NWOBHM's P. T. Barnum.

PHIL ASTON (guitar, the Handsome Beasts): The Soundhouse was the home of the New Wave of British Heavy Metal.

GEOFF BARTON (writing in Sounds, August 19, 1978): Although the sounds are heavy, the atmosphere most definitely isn't. It's pleasant and congenial with no undercurrent of aggression, no threat of violence. Bikers mix freely with AC/DC fans, "freaks" rub shoulders with "heads"…All factions join together for the sole purpose of enjoying ear-shattering sounds. For at the 'Wagon, there's no "if" about it. The kids are united…The decor resembles Dodge City, American B-movie western style, but with alternating flashing lights/darkness your eyes never really adjust to notice that much detail. A bar runs along almost the whole length of one side, so there's never any problem buying a drink. Adjacent is the sound stage, jam-packed with equipment (Gauss/Altec speakers powered by a JBS amplifier) that's capable of two thousand watts' worth of cranium-crunching power.

MALCOLM DOME (writer, Record Mirror and Kerrang!): The first time I went to the Bandwagon Heavy Metal Soundhouse was in 1977. It was full of people who loved music and had a great time. There

The Bandwagon was an unprepossessing pub in Kingsbury in outer London before Neal Kay put it on the map.
COURTESY OF NEAL KAY

was a fantastic atmosphere. Everyone would headbang like crazy and play air guitar to the songs. It was a mecca. It became a place to go on a Sunday night, or in midweek—more weekend than midweek. It was such an exciting place because everyone was there for the same reason—to have a great time listening to metal and rock that you didn't hear on the radio, apart from Tommy Vance's show. So much fun, and so many characters there. There were a lot of people who'd come regularly. Obviously people would come and go, but you'd get to know the people who went pretty much every week.

NEAL KAY (DJ, promoter, impresario): I was working in a club called Gulliver's, down behind the Hilton Hotel off Park Lane, and one night changed my life. There was a rock area downstairs, and that's where I was supposed to be working. But one night the DJ upstairs was sick and I had to fill in for him in the hated dance and soul room.

A couple of nights later this sheikh turned up in the upstairs room, and I was still there. He kept demanding I play Barry White all night long. At about four o'clock in the morning, I'd had enough. I thought this was the biggest load of bollocks I'd ever heard. They were trying to

keep him there to sell him Moët et Chandon at grossly inflated prices. In the end I went crazy and played some John Mayall, "Walking on Sunset." That did it. The sheikh went mad and sent the manager over, and in the end I walked out and told him to fuck himself.

That put me out of work, so I went trucking. The only civvy-street job I really had. Delivering furniture around London. Then my trucking buddy said, "I know you, and I know a place you are going to love. Only happens once a week, so this Wednesday we'll finish early and I'll take you to heaven," with a big, mischievous smile on his face. Alright, what the fuck. And that was the day I walked into the Bandwagon in 1975. He took me down to Kingsbury, to the Prince of Wales pub, to the Bandwagon. I walked in the door and there was this fucking great ginormous sound system, which put any club I'd ever worked in to shame. Clubland back then didn't understand anything about sound. They knew nothing. It was a really bad scene.

The Bandwagon was like the set from a cowboy western. There was a veranda running all the way down one side, so you could sit out there like the old cowboys might have done in the old days. It was alongside the dance floor, just raised a little. That was right the way down one side. Right the way down the other side was a bar. A fucking big, long bar. At the back it was like a Mexican saloon. There were swing doors going through. There was a small stage and either side of it were more swing doors leading to separate seated areas. The carpet was made of chewing gum, with a few bits of tuft in between. It never got light enough to see if there were cigarette burns.

The guys on stage were struggling a little. I was a hard-bitten DJ—if you lose the dance floor you get sacked. I was enjoying the sounds, then to my astonishment one of the guys on stage said, "We need a rock DJ here. If there's anyone who would like to try out, come up now." I took them up on it and got the job.

MALCOLM DOME: You'd go down there and Neal would be playing new stuff and the classics. He pushed Montrose quite hard, and when Riot happened he pushed them big time. So you would hear a lot of new bands, and the older stuff you wanted to hear. It was a great mix. And Neal was very good. He did a lot and was really, really committed to pushing new bands when they had talent.

IAN KELLY (fan): I started going when I was sixteen, not long after it began. I spent most of my youth in Wembley, and Kingsbury was just up the road. It was a short bus ride to my house. My best friend at the time had four aunties working behind the bar there, so we paid to get in and then that was it. So the Bandwagon was a very big attraction to me. I went there because it was a local venue.

The first few times I went there it was just ordinary club nights. One of the things that appealed to me was that the music was very varied, and they played a fair few middle-of-the-road rock numbers that we quite enjoyed. And then one of my friends told me a rock night had started. I think it was in the middle of the week, and maybe there were a hundred people there, but we loved it. From then on we started going regularly. They moved it to two nights. It was great being with a bunch of guys. You didn't have to get dressed up for a night out, just jeans and trainers and T-shirts. What the place could have done with was more females. It was really a long-haired teenage male venue. But they came along eventually.

MALCOLM DOME: It was ninety percent male. It was not a surprise at all. Ted Nugent once said that he came over to the UK, and ninety percent of the people at his gigs were men and the other ten percent looked like men. It was only much later women started being encouraged to go. They weren't discouraged. It just wasn't seen as something they were into.

KEVIN RIDDLES (bass, Angel Witch): I was told about the Soundhouse, and it was far enough off the beaten track, up the Harrow Road, almost all the way to Hendon. It was one of those things that became bigger in your head, the more you heard about it. It was just a pub. If you went round the front of the place, it was like a Toby Carvery type of pub. But it had a big back room. Initially it was one day a week, but Neal did the same as we'd done: he worked hard at it, put his own money into it, made it attractive to our sort of people. He didn't even have bands in the early days, it was just him spinning a few discs, and he gradually built it up, and it was a name that started to get spoken about.

MALCOLM DOME: He concentrated on the music. But he did silly things. He would play "Hocus Pocus" by Focus and at the end of the

"You didn't have to get dressed up for a night out." COURTESY OF NEAL KAY

yodel everyone would shout "Fuck off!" He played "Heigh-Ho," from *Snow White and the Seven Dwarfs*. So it had silly moments in there that Neal encouraged because it was part of the atmosphere. But also he would tell people what he was playing, especially if it was something new. But he was never someone to talk over records, oddly enough.

NEAL KAY: It took me a long time to get Geoff Barton down—I didn't have anybody working with me, no one. I had to do everything. I used to phone him. I used an upstairs room in the Prince of Wales as an office. I knew that if I was to make something special here, I needed the help of the media, the press of the day, whatever the hell I could do. I needed the press, and the only paper I wanted to talk to was *Sounds*, 'cause *Sounds* had Geoff Barton. All the others were covering punk and a whole load of shit, but Geoff was a true-hearted supporter of rock. So I kept on badgering him.

The press were notoriously lacking in mobility back then. They had their London office, and if they had to walk across the road to see a band it was too much. They never went anywhere. So what do I do to get attention? The answer was Ted Nugent. The record companies were stuck as well, and there was no help from the radio to promote rock. They were not interested. So Ted Nugent came to the Bandwagon in 1978 for a public appearance. CBS brought a whole load

of people with them, because they were going to make it a publicity thing. It was the worst night of the week they offered him to me—a Tuesday night. I thought, "Oh fuck, no one's going to turn up." When I announced on the Sunday night it was going to happen, I got jeers and laughter, and no one believed me. About three hundred and fifty, four hundred people did turn up. And Barton couldn't believe the audacity of a little pub in Kingsbury to do it.

I went on to have Judas Priest come, I had members of Rainbow come, I had Sammy Hagar come, I had members of Whitesnake come. "Don't tell me you can't send me David Coverdale! Ted Nugent was here last week!" And every time I did it I coordinated the press and made bloody sure it was completely covered. And in this way, everyone in the world began to find out and know my name was credible: when I said it was happening, it was. At the same time, all the record companies suddenly knew of me and they wanted me to play their latest white labels, get reaction from the kids. Then Geoff offered me the second part of what was really important: "We will print a weekly chart based on your punters' requests." Which we made, and I played the chart out on a Thursday night at the Wagon. When I did the chart, Geoff and *Sounds* always used to put the label it was on. And when it was a demo, it said so. And that told the rest of the world I was playing demos, so people started sending me more and more and more.

TINO TROY (vocals and guitar, Praying Mantis): Neal was larger than life. Especially in those days with his long hair and that big Catweazle look. He was someone to look up to, until he got off his podium, and you realize how short he was. But very animated and a very lovely guy. I've got a lot of time for Neal. If it wasn't for that man we wouldn't have got where we are today, as well as the other bands— Maiden, Samson, Tygers, all of them. He was very important and very influential. I would say he was one of the main ingredients in kicking it off, with Geoff Barton and *Sounds* magazine.

NEAL KAY: After the explosion [following the *Sounds* article] tapes started arriving from all over the bloody place. And that forced me into another situation. Not only did I have to run the Wagon, get all these things organized and sorted, but now I found myself barreling through loads and loads and loads of demo tapes and heart-rending letters:

"Dear Neal, you're the last hope we have. No one wants to listen to us, but we saw the article in *Sounds* and hope you'll listen to our tape." I had so many of those. I felt a duty, a calling, maybe. A duty to represent and stand for all of them. Someone has to stand up and front it. Someone has to win, otherwise we lose the war. And I decided that I'd go to war.

PAUL DI'ANNO (vocals, Iron Maiden): We went up to Spaceward Studios in Cambridge [on December 30 and 31, 1978], and none of us really knew what we was doing up there. We got the tracks recorded—knocked them all out in one session of four or five hours, paid the geezer, and that's it. It was the middle of the bleeding night, and we were stuck with nowhere to go. So we found a pub and had a couple of drinks and met these nurses. I chatted one up, and we ended up staying with them at the nurses' residence. It's a bit of a blur, because all we was waiting for was when it came out, and it was all pressed and we all got copies—we only done a couple of thousand, and it sold out instantly. It's as rare as rocking-horse shit now, that is. I haven't got a copy at all. It's all a bit of a blur—I remember going to Cambridge, I remember the nurse. I don't remember how many takes I needed.

DOUG SAMPSON (drums, Iron Maiden): We all bombed down there in the van. It was thick snow. If I remember rightly, we started recording it the day we drove down there, and the second day I'm sure we were mixing it. It seemed to be very fast—playing the songs once or twice then recording them. The bit about the nurse is true. We stayed round at her digs. All of us crashed on the floor round her digs. She didn't seem to mind.

PAUL DI'ANNO: Plan number one was drop some copies off at the labels. Number two was to see if we could get some work—we'd send it off to different parts of the country, see if we could get gigs. It was all down to that in the end. There must have been something more behind it, because I'm sure Steve [Harris, Iron Maiden bassist] is a bit more canny than that. Steve and me took a copy to Neal Kay at the Soundhouse.

NEAL KAY: They came up to see me, bunged that in my hand and said, "Give that a listen, mate, and if you like it, give us a call." And of

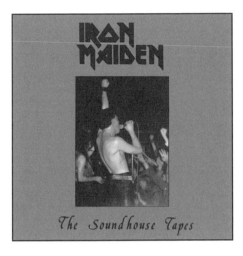

IRON MAIDEN's limited self-produced and self-released debut single, The Soundhouse Tapes, *the record that wrote Neal Kay's club into heavy metal history.*

course the rest is history. The first Maiden demo was totally brilliant: time changes, key changes, melodies, abilities. Everything was just right. Both Praying Mantis and Iron Maiden were winners. Most of the others were never going to get out of the UK. Iron Maiden hit me straight away. I took the tape; I was very rude to Steve when he gave it to me. I said, "Well, you and about five million others, mate. When I'm ready I'll call you." Took it home, put it on, that night I was jumping around the room like a blithering idiot. Couldn't stop. I phoned Steve at three in the morning. I did know one thing: I was listening to a world-beating band. No question. Songs, performance, ability, writing, singing. They had the lot. They were only playing over east London, so I didn't go to see them, but I didn't need to—I booked them for the Wagon. I never went to see any of these bands, I listened to them on tape. I was too busy as it was: I booked on spec from their tapes.

DOUG SAMPSON: Then he proceeded to play the tape down the Bandwagon. Before you knew it *The Soundhouse Tapes* was in the top three of his request chart in *Sounds* every week, which I found quite bizarre, being up there above bloody Van Halen and Priest and Zeppelin. It was week in, week out. I asked Neal Kay once—'cause he loved the band—"Did you rig this chart?" And he says, "No, I didn't have to."

KEVIN RIDDLES: It didn't take him long to realize that he'd tapped into a little well of original bands, so he'd put on a really dodgy tape of,

say, Toad the Wet Sprocket or Mantis that someone had given him from a live gig, and he would play it, no matter how bad the quality was. And then he'd gauge the reaction of people. I know he contacted bands saying, "I liked what I heard on this tape. Why don't you come and do a gig for me?"

He didn't do that with Angel Witch—we had to pester him. I had to haunt him. I suppose it would be called trolling nowadays. But fortunately he not only liked the tape we'd sent him, he had the sense to ask people—he asked people at one of the club nights. And we played the first Saturday night, when he expanded to two nights. And we packed the place. I think it had a fire limit of a hundred and ten people, and it would regularly have three hundred. You had to breathe via a raffle ticket: "Hold on, I've got a blue one, it's my turn!" It was packed to the rafters every time we played it, and it was the same with almost every band that played there. He had a knack of picking bands that suited his audience.

DOUG SAMPSON: Steve went up there to see the reaction from the people there when Neal played *The Soundhouse Tapes*. He said. "No one knew who we were and we just stood on the side. And there was all these people, and when they played one of our songs they all started headbanging." No one knew who they were—there weren't many photos of us about at that time. And Steve said. "I can't believe what's going on here. They're all going fucking loopy. We've got a gig there." When we played there, Geoff Barton came down to check us out, and I was led to understand he was a bit intimidated by it, because it was full of bikers and hardcore metal fans, and he just stood at the bar. It was a bloody good place to play.

PAUL DI'ANNO: We played up the Soundhouse a few times as well, and it was brilliant. I remember when me and Steve went up there with our girlfriends, and somebody spiked our bloody drinks. Me and Steve wasn't feeling very well at all.

THUNDERSTICK (drums, Samson): It was a haven for heavy rock to begin with. We did a few good gigs there. I don't think they knew how to take Thunderstick. It really caught them unawares, and Neal Kay started heavily pushing Iron Maiden. The first few times we played there were good. But there came a time when Samson were alienated from the crowd that would gather there.

NEAL KAY: I said to Steve at the end of that first night, "I want you back: I want you to do more dates." The most we ever gave them was £40, and that wasn't from me, it was from Malcolm Tate, the pub manager, who used to pay for the bands. It was practically nothing to get in during the week—maybe 50, 60, 70 pence, and maybe a quid on the weekend. We only ran till eleven, and to stay open to midnight we had to start serving chicken in a basket.

In the suburbs back then you couldn't get a license, and most pubs didn't want long-haired louts, which was another reason why the Bandwagon won so heavily. We would just put one band on per night—we didn't have the capacity or the room in the place. The bands would go on no later than nine-thirty, usually nine. They'd play till ten-thirty, and then I'd finish off the last half-hour while they were loading out. I introduced them, but it wasn't my show when the band was on.

PAUL DI'ANNO: It was like the CBGB of British metal. It was an important place. Bands would say, "We've got a gig up the Soundhouse, now we're gonna get noticed. People are going to see us properly, not playing to one man and his dog." It was very important.

PHIL ASTON: Of all the places you wanted to play in London—later on you might have wanted to play the Fulham Greyhound or the Marquee—everyone in Birmingham wanted to play the Soundhouse, because they had seen so many reviews of Iron Maiden.

I can remember distinctly after playing there, walking into the Costermonger in Birmingham, and knowing people knew we had played the Soundhouse. It felt like you had passed an exam to go down there, and the fact we'd gone down so well. The Handsome Beasts played there on November 22, 1980, and it was absolutely rammed. We didn't know if anyone would know who we were. We were only booked because "Breaker" was appearing in *Sounds*' Heavy Metal charts. We'd been appearing near the top of that, and Neal Kay rang us up and said, "Could you play?" It was packed, and we didn't know whether it was packed just because it was packed every week. But we went onstage and everyone went bananas. So it was a great gig. From there we could headline Walsall Town Hall.

NEAL KAY: It's no good trying to get a band on when they haven't got original material. And in my mind I formulated this equation: a band is never going to earn any money playing pubs. The band's future has

Kay's specially installed sound system gave him the ability to play records at gig volume.
PHOTO COURTESY OF NEAL KAY

to be on a big stage. It has to be capable of earning money and touring and writing and recording on a big scale. Otherwise the industry isn't going to want them.

So when I started listening to demos I was thinking about them onstage at the Odeon or bigger. Can I see them there? Is this material capable of working there? That is why turned most of them down—because they didn't have what it took. I would listen to everything, waiting for that twitch that said, "Oh yes." The third part of the equation was: this band are absolutely fucking useless in terms of worldwide success, but they will pull punters because of attitude and their style of music. One band like that was Angel Witch. Not a chance. They were no-hopers then. Never gonna go anywhere. But I booked 'em for the Bandwagon.

IAN KELLY: He loved to interact with his audience. At first he was purely up on the stage, but then he started coming down to the floor. I often heard there were big names in the place. I remember seeing this big scrum one time and I was told it was Ted Nugent. I couldn't tell you for sure. Rob Halford turned up one night, and I remember Neal going, "Rob Halford's here!" and he was going on about it.

Rob Halford wasn't there to see Neal Kay and he couldn't give a damn about the music Neal was playing. He was trying to date a friend

of mine, a guy called Sid from Hayes, who was very well known in the rock world—he used to go to every gig going, he was at the Bandwagon regularly, he was a very approachable, good-looking guy. I don't know what his real name was, but everybody knew him as Sid from Hayes. We'd spoken to Halford at a club in Hammersmith a few days beforehand, and Halford was very interested in Sid. To get rid of him Sid had said, "We'll carry on this conversation at the Bandwagon." And we couldn't believe it. Halford walked in the door. He had the leather cap on, the whole McCoy. Sid ran round to the public bar and Halford followed him.

NEAL KAY: In Judas Priest's "Living After Midnight" video you can see the cardboard-guitar boys from the Wagon. Rob Loonhouse was the first.

TINO TROY: As soon as I saw Rob Loonhouse playing air guitar to our songs, I thought, "Yeah, we've made it." It was great. It was the first time we had an audience involved that wasn't friends of friends, and we loved it.

NEAL KAY: He walked in the Soundhouse one night with a Flying V made out of hardboard—with a whammy bar. They all laughed like mad at him, but he started it all. He was the original. After he did it, loads more followed. That's what led me to do the Headbanging Band of the Year contest. We had cardboard drums, cardboard keyboards. We had road crew to unplug the cardboard instruments. That's entertainment, make 'em laugh! That's what we did.

ROSS HALFIN (photographer, Sounds and Kerrang!): For a joke, Barton got Rob Halford and some others to judge the best headbanger at the Bandwagon. So we go to Wembley one night and they're judging stupid people playing cut-out cardboard guitars. The kids were really into it, truthfully.

GEOFF BARTON (writing in Sounds, January 5, 1980): The quartet of bands taking part in the event…were made up from the cream of the heavy metal fan crop, each containing a guitar player (imaginary) of stunning expertise, a rock solid bassist (not really), a drummer (almost) of blistering power and a singer (only miming) of astonishing vocal range. One group even had a keyboard player (sort of) of such staggering ability he made Jon Lord look like Russ

Conway…I tell you, I felt privileged and, yes, even a tad humble to have been asked to sit alongside the likes of Cozy Powell, Rob Halford, Lemmy, Phil Taylor, Eddie Clarke and Steve Harris and Dave Murray of Iron Maiden and offer my expert advice…Third group Wellie and the Galoshers were the ones for me…There were five members, but with only a pair of drumsticks and a single guitar sawn into the shape of a gumboot, they were forced to, uh, improvise. And they did so, admirably, with flabby "lead singer" Jeff Goodwin doing some unbelievable athletic scissor kicks and high jumps, and one of the guitarists lying on the floor and pedalling his feet in time-honored Angus Young fashion. They chose to mime to a Priest track ("Tyrant") which had Halford holding his head in his hands…but nonetheless contained a priceless moment. During the line "Bow to your knees and repent if you please," Goodwin suddenly swung round threateningly and the rest of the band cowered and sank to the floor in mock supplication. Brilliant.

ROB HALFORD (vocals, Judas Priest): God, where did you get that from? That should have gone in my book. It's great. What Neal Kay put together was a big deal. It was extremely original. It was a great idea. It was the antithesis of disco. There were disco bars and disco clubs and disco pubs, and Neal's gone, "Why can't we have that type of experience but it's metal and hard rock?"

NEAL KAY: I started shipping the Maiden demo around record companies; A&M laughed me out of the door, said I didn't know what I was talking about. I took it to CBS, who said: "This is a joke, this ain't gonna fly." I got booted around and booted around and in the end I went to EMI. Ashley Goodall there was plotting a compilation of the new bands called *Metal for Muthas*. The real purpose of it for EMI was to woo Maiden, of course it was. They were clearly the standout band on the album. Although Toad the Wet Sprocket's blues number was great. The E.F. Band, Ethel the Frog, they were all peripheral. I knew that.

ASHLEY GOODALL (A&R at EMI for Iron Maiden): We started to pitch quite seriously for Maiden and offer options for contracts. This was when the *Metal for Muthas* album was coming together, so the plan

was to use *Metal for Muthas* as a platform to take Maiden further, giving them two tracks because they were the hot ones.

NEAL KAY: From the demo tapes that had arrived I chose the best, and if they were the best think what the worst were like. I cobbled these bands together, but it was EMI who wanted the album—it wasn't me that suggested it. I think I was up at EMI with Ashley one afternoon and we talked about all this. I said, "I've got absolutely hundreds of demos." And he said, "Why don't you put some together and let me hear it and maybe we can put a compilation album out?"

See, it's always an opportunity to move them on. I'm not a musician. It's not going to benefit me. I'm not going to go on tour. I'm not going to work millions out of all this. It was a genuine heartfelt thing to help rock 'n' roll. That's what my whole aim was always gonna be. And I thought it would be a great opportunity: finally the dam has burst. Finally, the dam has burst. Fuck everything we're going through. And not until I hear my sort of music in bloody lifts all over the country am I going to stop.

ASHLEY GOODALL: I ultimately selected them. He would have proposed some. I can't remember. We all knew about Angel Witch and Praying Mantis. There were some weird ones, Ethel the Frog and Toad the Wet Sprocket. There might have been some fillers. But Ethel the Frog sounded quite good at the time.

TERRY HOPKINSON (bass, Ethel the Frog): By the time *Metal for Muthas* was released [in February 1980], we'd split up. I'd gone. It would be interesting to speculate what might have happened had I not left, whether a recording deal might have been forthcoming from EMI, through Ashley Goodall. I would be surprised, but I don't know. We did have an album on EMI, but we'd split up.

The stuff on the album, our own album, was entirely drawn from a series of demo tapes we'd made over the previous five years at our own expense, all of which had been sent to record companies, and all of which had absolutely no response. Then in 1979 there was one of these Battle of the Bands contests. I seem to remember us reaching the national final of this contest, which Ashley Goodall was attending. It was through this contest that we came to Ashley Goodall's attention.

He became quite interested, but it was all going on at exactly the time we were falling apart.

KEVIN RIDDLES: I can safely say that when we were asked to do it, we jumped on it, primarily because the deal included an option EMI could take up to take us further. So we said, "Doesn't really matter if this works." We had one of the ubiquitous band meetings, and we said, "Hey, what's the downside?" We ain't going to say no.

Ashley Goodall, who worked in A&R for EMI at Manchester Square, was fine and he was pleasant and he knew absolutely nothing about the movement. Nothing at all. Which probably explains why there was that mishmash of bands. The guy who put it together wasn't that up on it. He was jumping on the bandwagon, and I've got no problem with that at all. But the reasons for us doing it weren't so much to do with being on that album; it was the possible follow-up that we were interested in. But it was odd. I don't remember listening to anything other than our track, Maiden, Samson. And I only listened to Toad the Wet Sprocket because it was such a silly bloody name. But other than that, I'm sitting here now and I can't remember anybody else who was on it.

Don't get me started on Sledgehammer. Two or three years later, we were booked with April Wine, the Canadian band who came over and did a few little taster gigs. Sledgehammer were opening and actually got booed off at Hammersmith. Sadly, I was on the toilet at the time, backstage in the green room, having a crap, when the door was kicked in by our sound engineer, saying, "Kev, you're onstage in one minute's time because Sledgehammer have been booed off."

THIS WRITER: Mike Cooke from Sledgehammer was our supply teacher at school in Slough for a few months in 1980. We knew he was Mike Cooke because he was called Mr. Michael Cooke, he wore a Sledgehammer button badge, and he looked exactly like Mike Cooke out of Sledgehammer, who were the only notable band in Slough and got in the local paper a lot. We used to say, "Sir, you're Mike Cooke out of Sledgehammer, aren't you, sir?" He always denied it, despite the evidence.

MALCOLM DOME: They had one great song, "Sledgehammer." That was it for me. I thought they were quite good, but *Sounds* raved about

"I was promised decent artwork..."
METAL FOR MUTHAS LP jacket and
subsequent tour ad for the London
Lyceum stop, February 10, 1980.

them. Why? I never got the obsession with Sledgehammer. I always
thought they were also-rans, never destined to be more than they
were. One good song. *Metal for Muthas* crystallized and focused the fact
there was a movement. You had two Iron Maiden tracks—I think it's
the only time Iron Maiden have had tracks on a compilation album.
They've always turned them down. Praying Mantis were there. Angel
Witch were there. Nutz were there. It was nice to see Nutz getting
acknowledged. E.F. Band, Toad the Wet Sprocket, Ethel the Frog.
Some of those choices were, to say the least, puzzling.

The cover was cheap and rubbish. Awful. As a compilation I don't
think it particularly worked because it could have been a better
collection of bands and songs. However, it did make people realize the
New Wave of British Heavy Metal had come alive, because here was a
compilation of those bands. So it did that. But as an album, it doesn't
hang together.

NEAL KAY: I was promised decent artwork, the whole bit, and they
shit on me. It was horrible, cheap, nasty, not what I wanted at all. I
was promised I could bring them all down from wherever they were
and rerecord them. Yeah, that didn't happen. Hearing it was a massive
disappointment. I felt profoundly let down by a cheap and nasty cover
and by the quality of the recordings. Maiden recorded theirs separately.
And Praying Mantis already had good stuff. Christ, it was really good.
But the others? Oh fucking Christ. The others were disastrous. I may

have phoned up and said, "Listen, why the fuck didn't you let me go into the studio and rerecord all these and make it so much better?" "Well, it's the budget. It's the budget." You fuckers.

MALCOLM DOME: Neal may blame EMI, but he was the one who chose the bands. They could have done so much better had they restricted it to NWOBHM. Toad the Wet Sprocket might have been a great blues band, but they weren't NWOBHM. And why have you thrown Nutz in, out of the blue? There should have been sleeve notes explaining why the tracks were there. The E.F. Band were basically a Swedish band, even if they did have an English drummer. What were they doing there? Two tracks from Iron Maiden made sense, because they were right in the vanguard and spearheading the movement. And were on EMI, who wanted to push them.

There was some good stuff, but it could have been so much better. It could have been so much better put together, so much better designed, presented and explained. I gave the album four stars in *Record Mirror* and I have to say I overrated it. But I did it almost because I wanted people to realize this was an exciting movement, and this represented the excitement, rather than because this is a good compilation in terms of the music. I really should have given it two and a half. But I gave it a rave review because I thought, we've got to get behind this. It's really driving this movement.

KEVIN RIDDLES: The *Metal for Muthas* album came out [it reached number sixteen in the UK albums chart], and the track by Angel Witch was on that, and Maiden had two tracks. We knew at that point that Maiden were going to go on, they were being given that extra step up. It actually reminded me that the first time I ever heard Zeppelin was on *The Age of Atlantic* album, and exactly the same thing happened with that album in 1970 as happened with *Metal for Muthas*—Zeppelin had two tracks on it, everybody else had one. So there was that slight similarity between those two compilation albums, and it was obvious even to us at the time that Maiden were going to go on with EMI. Out of nine bands on that album, only us and Maiden went on, because they had an option to bring out a single afterwards, and it was only us and Maiden that EMI actually brought out a single with.

ASHLEY GOODALL: *Metal for Muthas* came out in February 1980. What was interesting was that it didn't cost a lot of money, but it went out and suddenly all the sales guys started saying, "We're getting really good interest in this." We had good support from *Sounds* and one or two other rock mags. A buzz developed, and Tommy Vance started talking about it [on Radio 1], and it became a thing. It was a good name, it was a concept for rock music as it emerged. Because we got most of the best ones on there, apart from Leppard, who already had a deal, it was seen as a kind of street-level successor to punk and became its own entity.

The concept of aggregating it, plus the fact you had a couple of emergent bands gave a lot for the press to get their teeth into at a time when punk was waning. So it caught people's imagination. It just took off. I couldn't believe it: my first record release went top twenty. EMI couldn't believe it: "Bloody hell, what's this about?" As soon as you get surprising volumes, everyone gets very excited, so they give you more of a push, and everyone gets serious about it.

NEAL KAY: My sleeve notes on the back only caused me more grief.

MALCOLM DOME: The sleeve notes should have explained why these bands were there, where they came from. All they did was give Neal a platform for a diatribe. He used them as a pulpit for slagging punk off, and saying how great the Bandwagon was. The sleeve notes were terrible. EMI should have said no and said: "Explain why you chose these bands and where they come from. Give some background." But he didn't do that. Geoff Barton gave it a massive kicking, and it deserved it.

GEOFF BARTON (reviewing Metal for Muthas in Sounds, February 9, 1980): Straight to the point: for something that's supposed to act as standard-bearer for the New Wave of British Heavy Metal, this *Metal For Muthas* disc is a joke. And not a very funny one either. From its shabby sword and sorcery oriented cover to its clumsily written (not to say immensely bigoted) sleeve notes, the album smacks to me of being a low-budget cash in on the UK's much-vaunted metallic revival and, far from giving it a boost, cannot do it anything other than considerable harm. Apart from the two Iron Maiden tracks, *Metal For Muthas* is a bummer of the first order, a disgrace to all

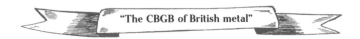

concerned with its compilation and will only delight sceptics of the NWOBHM, people who will doubtless chortle happily to themselves and use the LP as evidence for their case against the movement. And pretty damning evidence it is too.

NEAL KAY: Geoff had always been the time-honored journalist and sleeve note writer for the rock industry. And I had somehow been invited to do it and I took his thunder, and he didn't like that at all. Therefore, in retaliation, he slagged off my overlong sleeve notes, because my viewpoint was different to a journalist's viewpoint. My ways of saying things are different.

I had no interest in [Barton's argument that punk and NWOBHM should cross-fertilize]. The ethics that I have about music govern my way of music life. They are very old-fashioned. I believe in excellence of performance. I believe in professionalism, I believe in utter ability, And I believe that rock deserved the finest, the best, and punk represented an effort to wreck it completely.

MALCOLM DOME: There is a schism, definitely. I belong in the camp that believes there was a relationship between metal and punk. Metal has always taken from different areas—from soul, from classical, from the blues. And so when people say it has to be pure—pure from what? Rock and metal have never been pure. They have always come from something else. So for people to just ignore the punk influence…no, no, no.

Neal had this thing about bands deserving to be on the stage, how they are following the greats—it was one of his great monologues. And his thing about punk was: these people did not deserve to be on the same stage as Rush or Deep Purple or Led Zeppelin—they hadn't got the right. What are you talking about? These people had every right to get up and entertain, and they did. And some great music came of punk, and some great bands came out of punk. Neal, for God's sake, can you get off this bandwagon, as it were, and stop going on about how much punk destroyed music? It did not destroy music. I think it gave impetus to a lot of other young bands. And let's face it: he's championing Iron Maiden, and Paul Di'Anno was very much a punk-style front man. How do you explain that one, Neal?

BRIAN SLAGEL (fan, founder of Metal Blade Records): I was so influenced by what was going on over in the UK, and I loved the compilations they did, *Metal for Muthas* being one. I thought that if I could get all the [Los Angeles metal] bands to give me a song, I could probably scrape up enough money to press some records and put it out. I was not going to start a record label; I really did the *Metal Massacre* record because nobody could hear these bands [including Ratt and Metallica], and the only way they would get heard would be if someone made a record and got a distributor. That was a thousand percent influenced by what had happened in England. If they did it over there, maybe I could try to do it over here.

NEAL KAY: Just about everything about the Praying Mantis demo was special. Up north they didn't have any money, so when they went into recording studios, they went anywhere they could find, and the songs were often drossy. But Praying Mantis had proper songs and proper production. Did they ever. They were superb. I don't know how else to describe them. Superb in every way, and they went to a decent studio.

Praying Mantis were not a hard rock band. They were melodic, they would have suited the American market. Their vocals were good, their harmonies were good, their songs were instantly saleable. Everything about them was good. I couldn't fault them. I went crazy for it, couldn't believe how fucking good it was. It was non-stop brilliant. I started playing it as a demo tape at the Wagon. It went in the charts—the people put it straight there.

TINO TROY: A friend of mine from school told me there was this new rock pub going. Every time we used to go into town, we'd go to a disco—we used to go to Global Village, before it became a gay place. It's called Heaven now. They used to play these token four songs of rock, and then go back to the disco. So it was hard to find places, other than going to see a live band, where you could actually go and dig down and play some air guitar. We went down there, I think it was a Friday night, and it was good fun. That's how I first heard about it. And when I went there: wow! That's when I heard him talking about tapes from other bands and I gave him our demo. The tape took us maybe six hours to do and I think it cost us seventy quid.

NEAL KAY: Peter Mensch and Cliff Burnstein [AC/DC and Def Leppard's managers] turned up one night on my doorstep in Colindale. I had no idea who they were. They'd been following me. They knocked on the door at eleven one night and said: "It's too late with Maiden. What else have you got?" I reached for a bottle of Jack Daniel's. I didn't know if they were joking or not.

So I went through my collection of demo tapes and I saw the light: Praying Mantis is that band! I pulled out their cassette and they absolutely loved it. They asked me to arrange a meeting with Tino and Chris Troy at the Bandwagon. And it took place onstage while I was trying to play records. Absolutely true. Peter was trying to persuade Tino and Chris to get a front man and keyboard player to complete their sound. They needed a singer. Their backing vocals were really good, but what Mantis needed was a front man and a keyboard player. Tino and Chris turned them down. Mensch was upset about that. The next day he called and said: "Can't you make them understand? If we take them to America they will become very wealthy. You must tell them that." I phoned Tino, sat down with both of them and said, "The door is opening before you. You could be bigger than Iron Maiden because your music is radio-worthy in the States, and they are two of the biggest names in rock right now. You can't say no!" But I'm afraid they did say no. Years later the boys would admit they made a mistake.

MALCOLM DOME: That's not quite the way it happened. But he's right: they needed a vocalist and a keyboard player to bring out the AOR quality they had. They completely rejected it and several years later, when it was too late, they did it. But Mensch was right.

Neal tends to exaggerate his role. I am sure Mensch and Burnstein didn't turn up on his doorstep. There was a chat between Mantis and Mensch and Burnstein, but not at Neal's place. But Neal tends to have a worldview where everything went through him and revolved around him. But Mantis are a prime example of a band who, if they had done what they should have done, probably would have made an impact in America, but they refused to do it. They were fine with Tino and Chris Troy singing, both of whom were decent but not great. So they missed the boat in that respect.

NEAL KAY: Having recently spoken with my ex-wife, she also confirms that Peter Mensch and Cliff Burnstein did turn up on my doorstep unannounced one night. As to Malcolm's comment—given he didn't attend, I am unsure how he can be so certain that some of these events did not occur in the manner I have stated. He may believe it was exaggerating, but this all happened over forty years ago and many memories, not just supposedly mine, get clouded.

TINO TROY: Peter Mensch, just after we did the Rainbow in Finsbury Park, said to me: "You guys are great, but you need a singer. Get yourself a singer and I'll sign you." Of course, I thought, "I wonder..." But we left it too long and then when we decided to get a vocalist so we could have an identity, instead of three different voices singing the songs all the time, it was all too late.

I look back at meeting Peter Mensch now and think, "You fucking twat." I was very egotistical at the time. We were getting such great reviews, here, there and everywhere, that we thought we'd stick with what we had. We thought we were good enough, and obviously that was a very wrong move.

THUNDERSTICK: Neal, bless him. What can you say about Neal? He looked on himself as some kind of heavy metal messiah. Do you remember when Michael Jackson did the Brit Awards and Jarvis Cocker got up and started wiggling his arse? That's Neal Kay for you, and I would like to take Jarvis Cocker's place. He seemed to think he was more important than the music, but at the end of the day he was playing records. I think he thought he was on an equal standing with the musicians. I could never get my head round it.

PAUL DI'ANNO: I've heard Neal's rants. You come up on the stage, write the songs, do the rehearsals, go out on the tours, and then come and tell me you know better than I do.

DOUG SAMPSON: I always credited him with a lot of help from those early days. That was quite valuable, that business with the chart. But if he hadn't done it, Maiden still would have got through. They would have made it somehow. The band was just so out there that, with or without his help, they would have done it. It might have taken a different route or a bit longer. I don't know.

TINO TROY: Neal was a lightning rod for the movement. He's a pivotal figure. But he does love the sound of his own voice.

MALCOLM DOME: In those days Neal had no sense of humor. Now he laughs a bit about what he did in the past. But in those days, no humor. It was like he was a bible basher: "I'm a crusader, I'm the Messiah, I'm here to save music!" Neal thought that because he was one of the first to recognize Maiden, every band he championed should be seen in the same way—this is the man who got behind Iron Maiden, we should really support this band! Nah. He supported a lot of rubbish as well. Still, Neal was very important.

5

"Tommy Vance was a god."

From 1978 on, heavy metal filled the airwaves
on the BBC Radio 1 *Friday Rock Show*,
and via TV on *Top of the Pops*.

**TOMMY VANCE (DJ, Radio 1 Friday Rock Show *at 10 P.M.,
November 17, 1978—April 2, 1993):*** On medium wave and FM
stereo, this is national Radio 1. Well, hello there. This is TV on the radio,
Thomas Vance, the music vendor. Welcome to the *Friday Rock Show*.

TONY WILSON (producer, Radio 1 Friday Rock Show*):*
For about six months [in 1972/73] I produced Alan Freeman doing the
teatime weekday strand on Radio 1. He was exactly like me, a great
opera and classical music fan, but also loved a lot of the new rock music
that was happening. In spite of his huge *Pick of the Pops* career, he was
very much more of a rock fan than he was a pop fan.

In the daytime afternoon shows, we started feeding in the odd bit of
rock music, and that's where Fluff started his idea of throwing in little
five-second stabs of rock and some classical. That's where that thing
started. We started hinting at rock music in the daytime afternoon shows.
In the end Derek Chinnery, the controller of Radio 1 at the time, got a
bit fed up of it. And he said, "If you want to play that rock music, you can
have three hours on Saturday afternoon instead to do what you want." So
that's what we did.

JOE ELLIOTT (vocals, Def Leppard): People seem to forget there
was a Saturday afternoon rock show with Alan Freeman. If Sheffield
United were away, I would listen to the show, and if they were at home

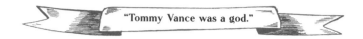

I wouldn't. So every couple of weeks I would listen. I remember being down at Weston Park boating lake with my little transistor radio, and he opened the show with "Shouting and Pointing" by Mott, so that would have been 1976. And bolting out of the boating lake as fast as I could to borrow some money from my mum to go and buy the record.

TONY WILSON: It was all rock. There was a lot of prog—Fluff was a big prog fan himself, a little bit more so than me. It was everything from Sabbath, Zeppelin, Argent, ELP, Rush and all that. Priest. Everything heavy metal and rock. But Chinnery thought Fluff was too old for the station. Chinnery called a halt to it. And it was presented as Fluff's choice to move on and do something else, but that's not how it happened.

The show ended in July '78 and I had the summer off. I came back and went to see Chinnery and said, "Right, we need a new rock show." He said, "Alright." I'd been thinking about it a bit, talking to a few people, and eventually decided Tommy would be the man. He was doing a rock show on Saturday evenings on Capital at the time, and we did a pilot, and I took it to Derek and said, "This is what I want to do." He rolled his eyes to the heavens and said, "Well, if you must have one of these old has-beens back, on your own head be it."

As far as Chinnery was concerned, Tommy was someone who had had a go at the station and had not succeeded, in the sense that Tommy and Peel and Pete Drummond were all competing for the same slot, which Peel won. Tommy subsequently let on that, with his show on Capital on Saturday evenings, what he used to do was listen to what we did on Saturday afternoons with Fluff, then go and get the records out to do something similar.

STEVE DAWSON (bass, Saxon): One of our biggest champions from the early days, before we were even signed up, was Alan Freeman, Fluff. I've got a letter from him—I sent him a demo. He said he liked it very much, and that he'd play it to people and help us all he could. And he helped us all the way through. Tommy Vance became like a friend. What happens is, if you're alright with them in the early days, they give you favors later on.

Tommy Vance did a couple of voiceovers for us. I can remember when we did Donington, we mentioned to Tommy Vance we'd done

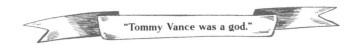
the *Friday Rock Show* prior to Donington. And we were talking about tripe. We said, "Have you ever had any tripe, Tommy?" He'd never had none. So we took him some to Donington. It were great.

PETE HINTON (A&R and in-house producer, Carrere Records): Fluff was a huge supporter of Saxon, and we courted that favor off him. I was always phoning up and sending messages. I even got a cab to drop a copy of the album at his flat. We took him to lunch. What a lovely man. Tommy Vance was a huge, huge supporter of the band.

Tony Wilson was a huge fan. Capital Radio were huge, too—the first session we did was for Capital. They did that live in the studio, before we recorded "747" and the lyrics weren't finished yet. Radio promotion was really important. The best thing I ever got for them was recording that "rock with Tommy Vance" jingle. That was great. It went on for years and years.

PAUL FLOWER (fan): In a weird way, you'd listen to the *Friday Rock Show* and—it sounds sacrilegious to say this—you'd not trust Tommy Vance as much as you would trust Geoff Barton. I don't know why that was. I didn't know what Geoff Barton looked like. I didn't know how old he was. He could have been an old geezer. But Tommy seemed a bit traditional sometimes, and although you could hear the bands there, it seemed more exciting to read about them—Geoff was more enthusiastic about the bands. He was sort of our John Peel, if you like.

MALCOLM DOME (writer, Record Mirror and Kerrang!): Peel loved his music and never really differentiated between genres: "I like it, so I'll play it." He had loved a lot of prog, before punk and new wave, and then he picked up on a lot of exciting, young, dynamic, sharp NWOBHM bands. I think he liked the rawness of some of those bands and would play them. I think he liked the aggression and the rawness and the extremity, and the fact they were pushing boundaries. And Andy Peebles did a lot as well—it's amazing, isn't it? But it showed how wide NWOBHM could be—it wasn't just Maiden and Saxon.

KIM MCAULIFFE (vocals and guitar, Girlschool): We were gigging and gigging, and there was a local youth club called the Rock, and we used to rehearse and play there. We made friends with the guy there, Phil, who had his own little record label called City Records. Friends of

ours, the UK Subs—we even shared a flat at one point, my dad used to call it "the commune"—had just recorded a single with City Records, and then Phil asked us if we wanted to do one, and of course that was it. Every band's dream. So of course we said yes, and that's where "Take It All Away" came from. "Oh yeah, we're going to be in the studio!"

Of course, we spent four hours in some dingy studio in a cellar in Soho recording "Take It All Away." As we came blinking into the sunlight, there was John Peel standing at the top of the steps. We told him who we were, and next thing you know he's playing the single on his show. The first time he played it, he said something like: "I'm not normally into this sort of music but I want to play this anyway." That was a bit of a leg-up. It sold about seven thousand, which was a lot.

ENID WILLIAMS (bass and vocals, Girlschool): John Peel's support was crucial. This was very early on. When we were doing those two gigs a week as Painted Lady, that's still one hundred gigs in a year. And we were at school still. Playing the clubs in France and Ireland got us tight. It got us together as a band. But it was grueling, and it wasn't gonna take us in the right direction to get a record deal. So having this single was so important and John Peel only needed to play it once for Motörhead's manager to hear it. If we hadn't been played on John Peel, we may have still got to the same place, but it would have taken a lot longer. Tommy Vance—great, thank you. But it would have been much, much later without Peel's help.

JOE ELLIOTT: I thrust [a copy of Def Leppard's debut EP] into the hand of John Peel. He nearly shat himself when he saw me jump up onstage at Sheffield University with a copy of it. "Play this!" "I can't. I don't know what it is. Write your phone number on it." And I did. It was a Saturday night. Then five-fifteen on Monday, I'd just got home from work and my mum answered the phone. She said, "There's a guy on the phone for you, he says his name is John Peel." Holy shit! He said, "You're the guy that gave me the record on Saturday. I'm going to play it tonight." So I rang everybody in the band.

He ended up playing the record every night for five nights. So there were three songs, two of them got played twice. People listened to that show. He was playing a lot of independent music, singles bands

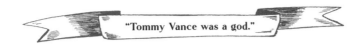

had sent in. Musically we were oil and water compared to everyone else, but the fact it was independent meant Peel was okay with it. It was a big starting point for us, because once Peel was on board, all the magazines started taking a bit more notice, then all the record companies started taking notice. That was when we started getting people coming to see us, after hearing us on national radio every night.

STEVE ZODIAC (vocals and guitar, Vardis): I have to say, I think we owe John Peel a hell of a lot. We'd done a gig at Stalybridge, and we were coming back in the van. It were late, and in his dulcet tones he went, "This is a new band called Vardis, 'If I Were King.'" And he put this fucking thing on. And we were in the van, all looking at each other. Is this happening? And then he said something about it being a great track. He probably thought we were punks. He said he was going to make it his regular play for the next five weeks. And I think that's what really kicked the momentum. He gave us a real push forward playing that. Every band needs somebody to champion them at some point. Having said that, it doesn't guarantee a damn thing, does it? I mean, you can only hope. Peel used to play a lot of hard rock, even though he got associated with the new wave and the punk thing, which I loved anyway.

TONY WILSON: In my thinking, the *Friday Rock Show* was carrying on what we'd started on the Saturday with Fluff. So there was a precedent there. A radio show is quite a straightforward thing to organize. You have in mind the style it's going to be, which is largely determined by the music and the style of the presenter, and how you want to make the thing sound. So we created a lot of jingles and music beds for Tommy to talk over, and an appropriate signature tune to set the scene. It's very much up to the DJ to fly with it and make it all work.

I was still producing Peel sessions—my life at the BBC started as a sound engineer, and I continued to work with sessions and live recordings as a producer throughout my time there. Through the seventies and early eighties I was one of the main Peel show session producers, so a lot of the early sessions broadcast on the *Friday Rock Show* were Peel sessions because I knew of them. I've a feeling we might have had some requirement to use a certain amount of session material, because of the limited amount of needle time available for

use. So it might have been for that reason, though very often they were things we wanted to play anyway. It surprises me that we played an Elvis Costello session, though that's partly because I never liked Elvis Costello, but that was personal.

But then we started to record our own sessions in autumn 1979. The first one was Def Leppard, and I remember it clearly, before Mutt Lange got to grips with them. It certainly consolidated the style of the program. And also, of course, it very much put the focus on NWOBHM, because most of the bands we did those sessions with in the first year or so were part of the NWOBHM wave.

JOE ELLIOTT: But talk about marginalized…shove it out at ten o'clock when everybody that likes that kind of music isn't at home. If you're eighteen, you've just discovered pubs: nine fifty-five, "I'm gonna leave." "Why?" "I've got five minutes to get home for Tommy Vance." Not happening. So you're talking about people who don't go out, loners, that generation's version of people who spend all day on Xbox. You're looking at people who were so into music that they'd kill their social life to stay in and listen to Tommy Vance. I'd be one of them.

Early 1980s BBC Radio One program guide showcasing prominent on-air talents TOMMY VANCE and JOHN PEEL. Both hosts' embrace of the NWOBHM on their popular shows elevated bands laboring in regional pubs to a serious national profile.

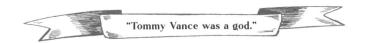

Me and my mates would sit around in one of our bedrooms and it was like a little club. It was like a POW camp, the guys who'd dig tunnels and make fake passports. That's what we were doing, in a metaphorical way, trying to make an escape route out of the mundane life we were living. We were destined to work in a factory for fifty years. How could we get out of that? Our way was listening to music, going: "I want to do that." And if the kind of music you like isn't on daytime radio, you do have to marginalize yourself. It was very, very important. And the small minority that did that, some of them became huge. I can see myself and Steve Harris and a few other people as part of that club.

KEVIN RIDDLES (bass, Angel Witch): Tommy Vance was a god at the time. Literally, you were on your hands and knees waiting for the radio to warm up—I had an old valve radio that took a couple of minutes to warm up. But the *Friday Rock Show*—if you were gigging, you got somebody to tape it for you, and if you weren't you were glued to it.

We got the initial contact with Tony Wilson via Paul Samson, and that consisted of: "This is his phone number, and this is the pub he normally drinks in, just round the corner from the BBC studios in Maida Vale. So if he doesn't answer the phone, just go and see him in the pub." And I'm fairly sure that's what we did. We got introduced to Tommy, who heard a couple of tapes, and loved what he heard. We went into the studio—you recorded on a Wednesday, it was mixed on a Thursday and broadcast on the Friday. Fantastic thing.

DAVE HILL (vocals, Demon): We did the Maida Vale session, and it was played. People the next day in town were saying, "I were listening to Tommy Vance last night and he played you!" It was exciting. On that Friday night, if you weren't gigging, you'd put it on.

ROBB WEIR (guitar, Tygers of Pan Tang): Radio's probably exactly the same today as it was back then; the presenters didn't pick any of the tracks they played, the producers generated the playlist, and the presenters were just the voice, which indeed Tommy was. He never chose any of the tracks—he was just told what was coming up and used his voice to do it. And could you have anyone better than Tommy Vance and the depth of his voice? He had the most incredible voice for late-night hard rock.

We went down to Maida Vale and we recorded four songs, one of which was "Wild Cat," I think, and Tony did a cracking job recording the stuff, because I thought to myself, "This is better than the bloody album." He really did do us proud; we were very, very pleased with it. And when it came out on the radio, it sounded great.

TONY WILSON: We'd get together on a Friday to put the show together. Most of the day we'd hang out and get the show together and usually go back to Tommy's for a meal, then come back to the studio to do the show at ten. But as with all these DJs, Tommy in particular had a very busy life with all his broadcasting and voiceover work. So we didn't meet up much during the rest of the week. He would have come in for an hour or two some other time. But it was very much left to me to organize most things. We would certainly discuss bands for sessions. I wouldn't go ahead and book something without talking to Tommy about it.

STEVE HAMMONDS (fan, music catalog consultant): Tommy Vance was famously a man with no records in his house. He didn't really know anything about music, but he was really good at what he did. The *Friday Rock Show* was so important and the sessions were phenomenal. There's bootleg albums out of Holland collating all the NWOBHM sessions. Everyone would tune in—you know all the stories about how people used to tape entire John Peel shows, and I used to do that with the *Friday Rock Show*. You'd strip the sessions out, because you could trade them. Every week there would be an old band and a NWOBHM band. The Diamond Head session was absolutely brilliant, the one with "Borrowed Time." I must have played it till the tape wore out.

DANTE BONUTTO (writer, Record Mirror and Kerrang!): A session was definitely a badge of achievement. They always sounded really good. It was important because you were on that show, and you were almost able to play live—you had that extra power and that extra edge that fans really loved. It was an honest statement, and being ingrained in the context of that show gave you enormous status and everyone really aspired to that.

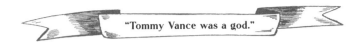

MALCOLM DOME: It wasn't just, "We're playing the demo or the single by this band." It was, "We got them into the Maida Vale studio and got them to do a session." And that did make a lot of difference to these bands, having a proper studio and a proper producer. It was a huge deal.

MONTALO (guitar, Witchfynde): We certainly did a session for Tommy Vance. I think it was after the *Give 'Em Hell* recordings. We'd done the Def Leppard tour and then we were sent out on a tour of our own. And between that time we did the Tommy Vance session, because they played it on a night we were playing in Burton upon Trent, at the 76 Club. At the time the *Friday Rock Show* was playing our songs, we were playing on stage, and twice we lost the power on the PA, and Tommy Vance lost the power of the song in the studio. It is very coincidental, isn't it? It was typical of the sort of things we encountered.

DANTE BONUTTO: I used to replace Tommy Vance when he was on holiday, and I used to be terrified doing it because I knew how important it was to rock fans. It defined record purchases. It defined your week. I guess being Friday night, the week was over, so it was a big night. He became that voice. When I hosted his show, I told Phonogram I was going to be guesting for Tommy Vance, could they give me a world exclusive on the new Metallica record? And they said yes. They gave me an acetate. That's how important the show was to the industry as well. We even ran a chart of his show in *Kerrang!* And he was very respected. You can't overestimate *Kerrang!* and *Friday Rock Show*. Having a *Kerrang!* cover and a *Friday Rock Show* session were two things that everyone wanted ticked off as a metal band.

STEVE DAWSON: Those shows had enormous power. If you could get on *Friday Rock Show*, all rock fans in England were immediately alerted to you. And if they liked what they heard, you were on to a winner. If for some reason the presenter liked you, you were on quite a bit. I know Radio 1 had a playlist, but I'm not sure if Tommy Vance chose his own songs. You only got in the position to record a session if you were doing alright. Those guys would know somebody wanted to listen to it. They wouldn't put an obscure band on unless they were a personal favorite. Tommy were great, show were great, everything were great.

PHIL ASTON (guitar, the Handsome Beasts): You release a single, it's in the local shops, it's in Virgin Records, your mum could go and buy it. And you think, "We're on our way." And then Tommy Vance's engineer is saying, "Can you do a session, because we think people want to hear the Handsome Beasts?" So we went down to London and did that. The session was done really late, so we were all very tired. It was broadcast twice, and we made sure everyone was listening. And as it went out, the phones started to ring with people wanting to book us for more gigs across the country.

We didn't meet Tommy Vance. But obviously we heard him talk about it when he played the tracks. And of course, his show was something that you all made sure you were in to hear, because it was that important to bands, because he was so supportive of young bands. Now you can get on the media because of YouTube and the internet, but in those days, to be on Radio 1 on a Friday night was massive.

KEVIN RIDDLES: Until NWOBHM bands started getting on to bigger tours, which took us around the country, you didn't get to places like Preston, like Cardiff, like St Austell, Exeter, Hastings. You didn't get to them because nobody was putting on gigs there. So the *Friday Rock Show* was the only chance you got to hear anything of the bands you'd been reading about. In a lot of ways, that's what radio did. John Peel was the same for the more alternative stuff. The only way you got to hear that stuff before you were able to see them was on the radio.

John Peel and Tommy Vance were cut from the same cloth, as far as that's concerned—they were both desperate to hear new music and bring it out to people. And it worked. It absolutely worked. If you got a *Friday Rock Show* slot, then you were getting there.

TINO TROY (vocals and guitar, Praying Mantis): It was such a strange sensation, at home, hearing us. You'd tune in, wait for it, and then you'd hear, "We're going to play some Praying Mantis," and you'd go "Wow!"

TONY WILSON: NWOBHM must have shaped the direction of the show. I wasn't an avid *Kerrang!* reader. There were times in my career that I existed in a bit of a bubble without being as conscious of what was going on in the wider world as I should have been, or could have been. I'm not sure in reality we did jump on to the NWOBHM happening as quickly as we might have done.

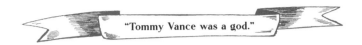
The NWOBHM phenomenon provided vast quantities of material for us on the *Friday Rock Show*, although we looked wider than that. We were also looking at what was going on in the States to some extent, although that was a slightly quieter time in America.

KEVIN RIDDLES: It was the only way NWOBHM was going to be recognized as a genre. The print media could talk about it, but nobody had the opportunity—unless you could see the bands—to make up their own minds about it. The only way to do it was via the radio. None of us had deals at the time. Maiden I think did. There was the odd compilation album, but one track isn't going to tell you much about the bands. It's a teaser. So the *Friday Rock Show*—you know one of the bands you've heard about is going to be on, because it's in *Radio Times* or whatever, or there's been a plug, so you know that's coming up, and you know you're going to get three or four songs. And that will give you a good idea of whether you like it or not.

TONY WILSON: We got sackfuls of demos. Far too many to listen to. I listened to as many as was feasible, but it wouldn't have been half of what came in, I don't suppose. It was a pretty thankless task wading through demos. You just hope to find the one in a hundred that actually says something. We began to do sessions with more unsigned bands, and later on we went on to start a demo competition, where we let the audience choose which ones they liked. Demos by the thousand, as well as label releases in vast quantities. We'd support bands because they were great and exciting in that moment, rather than because we were looking at them as likely to have a long career.

I'm always very suspicious of being presented with a band's campaign. It means: there's money behind them, they're going to be massive. And I'd think, "Fuck off, they're crap." I'm always very suspicious of anything that's overpackaged.

PHIL ALEXANDER (fan, Kerrang! editor): *Top of the Pops* is absolutely instrumental to NWOBHM, whatever anyone says. There's a slight reverse snobbery from the point of view of older music journalists, who don't ever want to admit they watched *Top of the Pops* because why would you watch something that was just pop music?

But the point is, it was the only outlet really on British television for music at the time. That and *The Old Grey Whistle Test*. And *The Old Grey Whistle Test* still seemed to have stuff that was beyond comprehension

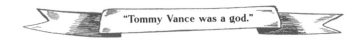

as far as I was concerned. And it was on at eleven-thirty at night. But with *Top of the Pops*, the thing was your bands were there in front of you. You could see them.

ROB HALFORD (vocals, Judas Priest): I love those *Top of the Pops* shows. Music and fashion, music and style, music and design, music and look, have always gone hand in hand, haven't they? And if you look at some of those *Top of the Pops* episodes Priest were on, we were certainly looking different. It was a veritable fashion parade on *Top of the Pops*, but we certainly almost blew up a few televisions.

PHIL ALEXANDER: The *Top of the Pops* appearances damned Priest because they blew out two hometown shows to appear on it. And I'm glad to get to see them on *Top of the Pops*, but it knackered them in Birmingham. But there is no doubt at that point there are a bunch of kids who are going back and going, "Right, okay, I'm getting into Priest."

JOHN MCCOY (bass, Gillan): The first few times, it's really exciting. It's like the pinnacle of what you're trying to achieve. That's what you grew up with. It seems impossible to describe how important that program was. If you got a *Top of the Pops* appearance, you were more or less guaranteed a chart position. [Gillan doing rock 'n' roll] cover versions was kind of a way through the yeses and noes of the BBC and everyone else involved. Doing a song that people remembered and then said, "That sounds different. Don't they look strange?" There were so many different criteria involved that you could never control.

But if you got *Top of the Pops*, that was it. And when you consider what was around at the time, there wasn't anything like Gillan. It was totally different. It was the right band at the right time. You really can't say anything bad about *Top of the Pops*.

PHIL BANFIELD (manager, Gillan): We noticed, after we appeared on *Top of the Pops*, the amount of female fans that suddenly appeared, buying tickets and coming to gigs. They weren't dressed the way the usual crowd member was dressed. And very young. And all they wanted to hear was "Trouble." They had no idea what "Smoke on the Water" was. Or "Child in Time," or anything like that. But I'm pretty sure we did convert some of them,

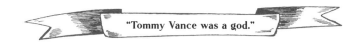

IAN GILLAN (vocals, Deep Purple and Gillan): I am not and never have been a good TV artist. I'm useless at it. I don't understand it and I don't like the compromises you have to make for it. But during those times I was surrounded by guys that did understand it, and they were great. So I got swept up and went along with it.

PHIL ALEXANDER: It felt like a triumph every time you saw one of your bands on there, whether that was Maiden, whether that was Motörhead, whether that was Saxon. That was the thing that made it yours even more. You were proud. You'd be going, "Oh, there's all this other rubbish, but my guys have made it." It legitimized your fandom and made it more of a thing. I genuinely think Maiden doing "Running Free" on *Top of the Pops* [on February 22, 1980] is a game-changing moment.

JOE ELLIOTT: The attitude Maiden had when they started out was bang on: they looked like a gang and kids love a gang. They were the first band of our time, of that kind of music, to make *Top of the Pops*.

DENNIS STRATTON (guitar, Iron Maiden): We played live. To be honest, I don't know if it was Steve's idea. There'd been other heavy rock bands on there before us, but they wanted an angle, something that had never been done before. So someone suggested playing live. Good idea. I had the perfect solution for that. At the time I was using an HH amp and Dave [Murray, guitarist] had a Marshall, but you couldn't turn it right down. So I got another HH and said to Dave, "If you turn the gain full up, turn the master right down, you'll get the sound you want but so low you can talk over it." I said, "It sounds like a transistor radio, but it will still give us the sound."

We set the gear up. We had to put toilet roll all over Clive Burr's drums so they sounded like cardboard boxes. It was still too loud. The geezer come running out of the control room with his headphones on screaming. But it wasn't loud. And then we real, when Shakin' Stevens come on, doing "This Ole House," he had a brand new pair of white trainers on, and he was over there on a podium with a monitor in front of him. So basically, he's miming, and the backing track is coming out of the speaker. As it comes out of the speaker, he's miming to it and he's dancing, and all they can hear in the control room is the single. But in the room, where we're playing, all you could hear was his trainers

squeaking. If he'd been singing live, the trainers would have been louder than his mic. That's how quiet it was. So we finally got it as low as we could before they let us do it. But that was the angle: the first heavy metal band to do it live.

PHIL ALEXANDER: I think they were the first band to play live on *Top of the Pops* since the Who. You think to yourself, "Why didn't *Top of the Pops* say, 'We're not really interested'?" I don't know why they said okay, because it wasn't like Maiden were a household name at that point. They were just one of those underground bands.

PAUL DI'ANNO (vocals, Iron Maiden): It was just a TV show. We wanted to play live, and no one had done that since the Who, apparently, and after all the ranting and raving and fighting with them over it, they finally agreed to let us do it, but it wasn't much louder than a conversation.

The way the kids were treated on that show was unbelievable. They had those great big swinging cameras, going round and round, and if you don't get out of the way and over to the next stage, you get mowed down by the bloody things. We were on one stage, Spandau Ballet were on the other side—they were shitting themselves, looking at us very suspiciously, as if we were going to rip their heads off. We played it up even more then, obviously. *[Note: Spandau Ballet did not appear on that episode of Top of the Pops. The other guests were Shakin' Stevens, Blondie, the Beat, Buggles, the Tourists, Fern Kinney, Ramones, the Whispers and Kenny Rogers.]*

DENNIS STRATTON: For me it was fulfilling an ambition. I knew it might only be once, and if the band got any bigger they would probably do a video. My ambitions started from playing the Bridge House when I was fifteen or sixteen. And they were: play the Bridge House, the Marquee, the Rainbow, the Hammersmith Odeon, go to Los Angeles, play Reading Festival. And then slowly I accomplished every one.

Me and Steve was talking the other week about our wish list, and I told him, "You know, there's one more wish on my bucket list, and you know what that is, don't you?" And he said, "Yeah, I know what that is." And that's to walk on with them once more and play one song, "Phantom" or something, before they call it a day. That's my last ambition.

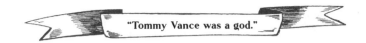

BIFF BYFORD (vocals, Saxon): We didn't physically do it for "Wheels of Steel." We did it in a studio with no audience, at the side of the main studio.

STEVE DAWSON: You were put on probation—you might go on or you might not, depending.

BIFF BYFORD: There used to be a mid-chart position and if you got in there, nearly in the top thirty, they recorded a *Top of the Pops* song for you, before the show. So a lot of bands went and did it, and a lot didn't get used because the single didn't go up. But ours did, so they played it. We didn't get the green room or anything. We didn't get to meet other bands. It was all a bit workmanlike. But if you were going to be big, you had to be on *Top of the Pops*.

STEVE DAWSON: We went and everybody were really self-conscious, not because of cameras, but because we were miming. And we didn't know what to do. Pete [Gill, drums] were alright, 'cause he'd done it before with Gary Glitter. So he knew the craic. Which helped us a bit. Your music, you playing an instrument, and performing visually go together. One thing makes you do another thing, 'cause your emotions are flowing. When you're just miming and you know you're miming, it fucks with your mind—you don't know what to do. You feel really self-conscious, even though you've done that a thousand times before, you just feel odd. And I think you can see it on our faces. If you watch that performance, it's not natural. But it was a great experience going to the BBC and going in the BBC bar that they had then and rubbing shoulders with the newsreaders and all them mob, Val Doonican and everyone, all in the same place. And you can just talk to them if you wanted to. That were a massive experience.

It was a big deal for everybody who worked with us, fans as well. Because to have a rock band on *Top of the Pops* was a rare thing. I did it with no shirt underneath my leather jacket. One, I always thought if you're in a rock band, you've got to look a bit hard and dangerous. And also, it came from playing live. You can't really wear a leather jacket for very long live, so I'd wear a leather jacket with nothing underneath it and then take it off, so I'd be bare-chested. That's why I did it on *Top of the Pops*. It weren't an intentional decision to have that image. But I were lucky enough to have had a hairy chest, so that helped. If I'd had

a smooth chest, it might have looked a bit different. But I didn't realize at the time Bon Scott [of AC/DC] had been doing it for a while. I just thought that if you're in a rock band you've got to wear black and look mean. You can't be Dave Lee Roth unless you're in Van Halen.

It's hard being a balding man in a metal band, though. A source of great personal anguish. I started losing my hair at an early age. You're always the butt of jokes, because you're surrounded by people with masses of hair. And you have to live with it. You've got to get your comments in first. You had to think about things—I didn't want to wear a hat. It weren't too bad when Paul [Quinn, guitar] joined, 'cause he were a baldy and all. So I found solace in him and being mutually fed up. Then I started wearing a headband, which meant I could comb my hair forward and hold it in place. I did buy a wig at one point, but I only wore it for two days. It were fucking ridiculous. It's what it is. It didn't affect me getting any birds—they fucking loved it. It was a problem for managers, though. They'd say: "Have you thought about wearing a hat, because when spotlight goes on your head it looks a bit weird?" At that point I should have fucking smacked him in the nose instead of worrying about it. Personal stuff like that you can only understand if it's happening to you. It's like someone saying you're cross-eyed, or you've got a big, fat belly. People who say these things to you don't realize how much it's hurting you. You can be the big, tough bass player in a heavy metal band, but you're still sensitive. All these people who slagged you off 'cause you're bald—they're fucking bald now.

ROB HALFORD: I was the first metalhead to go, eventually, with the shorn look, which seemed to be very odd to a lot of people, because everyone else in the band had long hair, and the metal scene was predominantly long-haired, denim and leather, bikers and metal maniacs. Particularly to men, because of this whole alpha male "you must have hair to be a man" thing, which is ridiculous. For some people, men particularly, hair loss can be a traumatic experience. I wasn't keen on it, but I knew it would happen eventually because my dad was that way and it runs in the family. So I knew it was forthcoming, but I just accepted it. I wasn't going to go the way of some of my friends in the business and put a wig on, but you do what's right for you and makes you feel comfortable.

Motörhead and
Toronto's Anvil deafen
Hammersmith Odeon,
June 4, 1983.

JOE ELLIOTT: We did *Top of the Pops* in 1980, but it got cut out because we did it the same day as the launch of the first Space Shuttle, which they covered live. So *Top of the Pops* was about fifteen minutes long that week. Guess who got cut off?

KIM MCAULIFFE: Vic [Maile, Girlschool and Motörhead producer] was always into the old rock 'n' roll stuff, and so was Lemmy. Vic came up with the idea of the EP with Motörhead. He said, "I've got this song by Johnny Kidd and the Pirates." It was one of his favorite songs. He put it to Motörhead, to us and to [both bands' label] Bronze, and another one of these things happened. They said, "We can release it on Valentine's Day and call it *St Valentines Day Massacre*. You do one of theirs, they'll do one of yours." It's one of those things that just clicked.

They were brilliant times. One of the most exciting times was when we all went to this massive warehouse in the East End, and picked out our costumes for the photo session. Motörhead were like kids in a toy shop, they really were. They were so excited, these grizzly blokes, "Oh look at that!" And then they got given machine guns. It was so funny. We were just laughing away. We all got dressed up and we were doing the shoot around the old docks. It was freezing. Absolutely freezing. We finished the photo session and we were gasping for a drink. We all trooped into the nearest pub—a tiny little pub—all dressed up like the cover. They couldn't believe what they were seeing. Traffic was going past beeping and waving and screaming at us, seven of us dressed up like gangsters. That was so much fun.

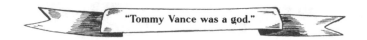
And then we got up to *Top of the Pops*! We were on bloody *Top of the Pops*! It was a dream come true, because Thursday nights that was the most exciting thing happening when we were growing up. It was the same for Motörhead as well. Any band. Their dream was to be on *Top of the Pops*. That was the pinnacle, really. You'd made it once you were on *Top of the Pops*. I'll never forget us being in the minibus on the way to the studio, and Lemmy in the makeup chair having his hair quiffed back. But once we were in the studio it was so weird. It was tiny, and the audience were literally herded around. It was funny. It was an experience, that was for sure.

We went off to Germany and did something there as well, and another couple of countries. Gerry Bron [Bronze Records founder] had his own little plane company, so we'd go whizzing around in these little bloody planes everywhere. And I guess that was all going on the bill as well. But at the time it was fun. We'd get in these little six-seaters and off we'd whizz. Off to Germany to do an interview. Then whizz back somewhere else. We didn't think about the cost. We were just enjoying it.

DENISE DUFORT (drums, Girlschool): We weren't desperate to go on *Top of the Pops*, but when it happened we were so excited because we all grew up watching it. We all sat there in front of the TV as kids, waiting for *Top of the Pops* to come on. I never thought in a billion years I would end up on *Top of the Pops*. So when it actually happened we were so excited and nervous, and it was amazing, it really was.

We were on there with Motörhead first, and then later with "Hit and Run," our own song. It was incredible. And I'm so glad it wasn't Jimmy Savile presenting. It still gets shown, and we get royalties from that.

ENID WILLIAMS: If you'd asked me what my three ambitions were at the age of fourteen, it would have been to play *Top of the Pops*, to play Hammersmith Odeon, and have a gold album. I achieved those three things. Hammersmith Odeon was what you aspired to, *Top of the Pops* was like you'd made it, and a gold album was a symbol that people liked what you'd done. Maybe *Top of the Pops* didn't matter for the heavier, heavier bands, or for people that bought loads of albums, but we didn't have money to buy loads of albums. But *Top of the Pops*—that was everything.

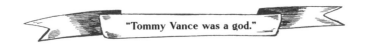

KIM MCAULIFFE: Even when we were on *Top of the Pops*, we got fifty quid a week. Everything else, God knows where it all went. We weren't thinking about that.

STEVE DAWSON: I wanted to be on that show. It was an ambition for all of us because, like you used to listen to the chart show on a Sunday, and listen to your favorite song getting up the charts, it was the same with *Top of the Pops*—you wanted to see your favorite band get on *Top of the Pops*. And when the Beatles, Stones, Swinging Blue Jeans and all them were on, it were great. But then when Nana Mouskouri were on, and some other twat you didn't like, you didn't like it. So it would be the same for our fans. There'd be KC and the Sunshine Band and then Saxon. They're all watching. The more you do it, the more farcical it becomes, because you know it's just a joke really. I think we did it seven times. We got caught up in that union strike, when we were due to be on with "747," which would have made the single go up so many places. They guaranteed you it would go up three or four places. We'd reached number thirteen with "747," which meant it probably would have gone in the top ten. But in true Saxon fashion we got scuppered. Events meant that Maiden are massive and Saxon aren't.

"Fuck me, they're young."

As 1980 approached, the major labels launched an A&R arms race to conquer heavy metal. The first bands swooped up and signed were Saxon, Iron Maiden, and Def Leppard.

PETE HINTON (A&R and in-house producer, Carrere Records):
I left university and after a while I got a position as a graduate marketing trainee at EMI. After not very long they transferred me to the A&R department. This was on the basis that I was one of the few people at EMI who actually went out and saw gigs. Every year, *Melody Maker* ran a talent competition with EMI Records. You had the final at the Roundhouse, and there were eight regional dates. The idea was that the winner got a recording session. Because I was the new boy, they said, "You're doing that." So I had to go all over the country, which to me was brilliant. I'm just out of university, and they've said, "Here's two hundred quid, there's a big hotel, keep all your receipts for your meals, bedrooms for who you want, off you go."

I was up in Leeds, where I went to university, and a guy came up to me and said, "My friends are in a band." And he gave me a tape. "Have a listen to that." That was Son of a Bitch [later Saxon]. It was one of those tapes that you hear, and you think, "Oh, these are worth going to see." They were great live. Really good. I went up to Bradford Talk of the Town, where they were playing. I was ensconced in a hotel, waiting for a cab to pick me up, and I put five pence in a fruit machine, and it wouldn't stop winning. So I went to the gig with forty quid in coins in my pocket. As I went in the cab, I thought, "This is a special day."

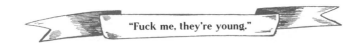

At the gig, I reckon there were twenty-six people there. The noise they made on stage was just fantastic. Biff was obviously a master of being a front man, Quinny [Paul Quinn] had a revolving guitar. Biff had this knife that he kept throwing into the stage to make a point, and it was just one of those magic nights where I thought, "God, these guys are really good." This was 1977.

BIFF BYFORD (vocals, Saxon): Pete Hinton and his boss, a guy called Freddie Cannon, worked for EMI, and we sent EMI quite a few demos. Pete Hinton came to see us in Bradford. He said the band were great, and he worked for EMI and he'd be in touch. We didn't hear anything for a while.

PETE HINTON: Me and my boss Freddie Cannon offered EMI Son of a Bitch. And they said, "No, not really." I don't know why, a reason was never given. EMI had had their fingers burned with rock; they'd had success with Tom Robinson, but that wasn't in that vein of rock, if you see what I mean. I suspect, because of that, these big record companies had the power to wait to see if a genre was developing and then they'd move in with their money.

STEVE DAWSON (bass, Saxon): At the same time, Claude Carrère had got in touch with Freddie Cannon and asked him to set up a branch of Carrere Records in England. I think mainly because he'd got wind of this new thing that were starting with rock music. And he set up Carrere Records UK with Pete Hinton as his A&R man.

MUSIC WEEK *REPORT* (June 2, 1979): When Claude Carrère appointed Freddie Cannon to set up his UK operations, it was assumed that the label would be aiming to repeat its disco reputation which is so good in France…"Not so," explains managing director Cannon. "We got away from disco as everyone else was jumping on that bandwagon. We want to sign English acts and make them long-term projects to be broken worldwide. We are open to a variety of artists and we believe the product that comes out of England can also be very successful in the US." Cannon is aiming now for 10 acts, five of which have already been signed. One of their newest signings, with tracks already in the can, is the reformed Mud, which now includes a belting young lady called Margo. Also on the label is Sheila and a new rock band Saxon. Peter Hinton is A&R manager.

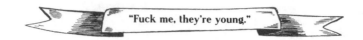

PETE HINTON: I was Freddie's assistant at EMI. So he took me with him. The original idea of Carrere was to be an outlet for all the European disco stuff, but we wanted to kick off the UK label with Saxon, absolutely we did. I get the impression heavy rock wasn't really fashionable then—we signed them in 1978. Iron Maiden still didn't have a deal. If someone said Saxon were the first NWOBHM band to be signed, that would be correct.

I particularly liked things like "Frozen Rainbow," where you could develop an idea, and you could really get the emotion, really showing off the songwriting side of it. But the beauty was they could write the other kind of music too—"Big Teaser" was literally a cross between rock and pop, power pop as they called it in those days. You could see that had chart potential. One of the strengths was that they were a northern band, and they talked about their lives, and their lives were motorbikes and cars and girls. I think it was with that real-life aspect that it all came together.

BIFF BYFORD: I don't know how this happened but we got signed by Queen's management, Trident. I don't know if maybe Pete or Freddie had been in touch with them. But they got in touch with us and said they had a deal for us with this Carrere Records. So that's how we got involved with Carrere and Trident—they brokered the deal and got us signed.

STEVE DAWSON: I were at home at my mum's. That's where the band phone was, my mum's house. And the phone rang. It was Dave Thomas [of Trident]. "Can you get to London tomorrow?" "Well, we can, but we've got no money." "We'll send you some money to come on the train." We all got on the train at Doncaster and went to London. They met us in London, and they gave us £80 each, saying, "We want you to smarten yourselves up a bit."

BIFF BYFORD: They told us to get our hair cut and go and buy some nice clothes. So that's when me and Dawson went and bought new leather jackets, when we went to London before we flew out to Paris to sign. They gave us £300 or something to smarten ourselves up a bit. So that's what we did. I bought the one with the white collar. He bought a black one.

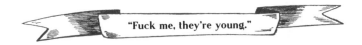
STEVE DAWSON: We were serious about our music, but we weren't really bothered about our image—whatever sufficed, we wore. But they gave us £80 each. And Pete [Gill, drums], being a bit more worldly-wise, said, "Right, we need to get up Kensington market." We went up Ken market, and in them days there were hundreds of stalls inside in an old store, but they were all individual stores. Pete had been there before. He says, "Right, we're going up to Buck's Boots first." They made handmade boots. So we all bought pairs. I think Graham and me bought a pair of snakeskin boots each. Biff bought a pair of white high-heeled boots. Pete Gill bought some white boots. Paul Quinn got some high-heeled black boots. The fella said, "Come back tomorrow, they'll be done."

Then we went and bought skin-tight black jeans. And we all wanted a motorbike jacket each, but we didn't want them all to look the same. So I bought a normal black one, Biff bought a black one with white lapels, Graham bought one with tiger-skin lapels, Paul bought one with blue lapels. Pete spent the most money of the lot. He bought one of them Marlon Brando ones, proper American job. We got shoes, jeans, a T-shirt and a leather jacket for £80 apiece. We put 'em on as soon as we bought them. We were staying in this hotel at Piccadilly Circus, and then flying to France the next day. Nobody had ever flown before. We went to Heathrow, got on the airplane and went to Paris, went to Claude Carrère's office.

BIFF BYFORD: We signed the deal and Claude left, whisked away somewhere on his yacht. Pete [Hinton] leaned back on the table and it cracked right down the middle. It was a huge glass table. A work of art by some glass artist. It collapsed. We didn't hang around for long. They didn't sack him though. But he never went back there, in all the years he worked for Carrere.

PETE HINTON: Claude had left the room and I literally just leaned against this bloody desk. I didn't sit on it. I just leaned against it and it broke. I was fucking horrified. I didn't realize that because Claude Carrère was a multimillionaire he had the best of everything. Me and you, we'd have a bit of glass that cost thirty quid. His cost thousands. But he forgave me. The band still laugh about that. Gits.

DENIM AND LEATHER 137

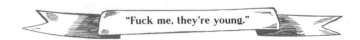

STEVE DAWSON: [Trident] gave Pete Hinton some money and said, "Come back in eight hours, take 'em round Paris, a bit of sightseeing." When we come back, we went in, a piece of paper was shoveled under us nose—"That's your recording contract, sign it." Which we did. Got back on the airplane, went back to England, and we had a record deal. Just like that. No understanding of the consequences. Nobody cared. We've signed up now, we've done it.

BIFF BYFORD: We changed the name to Saxon, I think, because the record company didn't like Son of a Bitch. They didn't think Americans would go for it. And they didn't think it translated into French very well. I wasn't really that keen on the name by that time, anyway. They actually came up with Anglo Saxon, which we didn't like. But Saxon was pretty cool. A friend of ours at art school came up with the artwork and basically painted me as a warrior for the cover. And they did the logo as well, which was great.

STEVE DAWSON: It were great recording the first album, because we thought we'd made it, in a strange way. Not that we were ego tripping or anything, but there were an inner glow among everybody. You've got to think there'd been seven constant years of non-stop struggle, with only one thing in mind, and that's to sign a recording contract. When you've actually done it, you're in a strange situation where you don't realize that's only the beginning of it. No thought that it'll not sell. No thought that there might be no more money. You're in a false situation of endless money and endless success. You're not thinking that it could end. So we were having a great time. We were all staying in a B&B, full of old people. We weren't used to hotels, so it didn't matter.

BIFF BYFORD: It was a cheap place where actors stayed, so they were pretty good with people coming in late at night, and then staying in bed—you could have breakfast any time you wanted. It was a theatrical bed and breakfast. We had the attic room, which was like a dormitory, and we all slept in the same room. So it was just like a transit van, really.

STEVE DAWSON: And there were various antics went off there. There was an evening meal, if you were there. One night we were all in there, and Pete Gill says, "If everybody chucks in a couple of quid, I'll eat the entire cheese board." So, we thought, that's easy revenue,

SAXON (from left: Biff Byford, Steve Dawson, Pete Gill, Graham Oliver, Paul Quinn) laying siege to Cardiff Castle, Wales, May 28, 1980. GEORGE BODNAR ARCHIVE | ICONICPIX

that—he'll make himself ill. So we all threw some money in, the cheese board come round, and he took everything off the cheese board, and it were quite big. And he ate it. Everything. In London, there used to be a place called Chicks and Chocs, which were a forerunner to KFC, a chicken place, but they also served gateaux. We went in there one night and Pete Gill said, "If you chuck some money in, I'll eat a full industrial gateau," which he did. But then he proceeded to be sick afterwards.

It was not so much chucking TVs out of the window, because we never did that. We never had enough money to pay for that. You chuck a telly through the window, you get a bill for five hundred quid. I think our Yorkshire heritage stopped us doing that.

JOE ELLIOTT (vocals, Def Leppard): We didn't just want to play working men's clubs, playing covers and earning a few bob. The idea was to go through everything that everyone else did: sleeping on people's floors, going up and down the M1 in a transit van, playing to no people and a dog in New Brighton, which we did once. And working our way up until an A&R man spotted us and we got a record

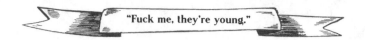
deal. Everyone from the Beatles to Elton John had done that, but you weren't going to get it going for you unless you had songs you'd written yourself.

So we made an EP at Fairview Studios in Hull. Mick Ronson used to work in there, 'cause he's from Hull. Wow, Ronno's done demos in this place, an eight-track studio the size of your average kitchen. It cost £148.50. We budgeted for a £150, but I think we took three cassettes less than they expected. We had £1.50 left over, with which we bought fish and chips to share between us in the back of the car, while listening to the cassette driving over the Humber Bridge to go back to Sheffield, going, "We just made a record!"

I had to borrow money off a woman at a factory where I was working. Twenty-five percent interest she wanted, so she lent us £450 but wanted £600, so we knew it was an exercise in promotion, not making money, because we were never going to make any money. By the time you add in the cost of the sleeve we did, and the fact we were selling them for a pound, we were probably going to make about £60 if we sold a thousand of them. And we were going to give at least a hundred away, because we posted them off to as many record companies' addresses as we could find on the back of other people's albums.

RICK SAVAGE (bass, Def Leppard): From the EP we got the airplay. From the airplay we got record companies interested. It was going quickly. Then from all that we started to get in the national music press.

JOE ELLIOTT: There were two Leppards at the time. There was lying Def Leppard, who would turn up at a working men's club promising the MC we would play "Tie a Yellow Ribbon." We'd announce: "This is a song by a band called the Nolans," and we would play "Answer to the Master." The working men's clubs would pay you £350; to play the Wapentake would cost us £45—they'd pay you a fiver and it cost you £45 to rent a van. You'd have your mates helping you load in and load out. So we had to play the working men's clubs to fund playing where the rockers went.

DAVID BATES (A&R at Phonogram for Def Leppard): My parents had decided in their infinite wisdom—or madness—to move from just outside London to Sheffield in the late sixties. I ended up there, which

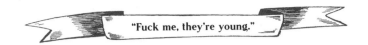

wasn't great, because if you were from the south you were immediately hated and picked on. Having been expelled from school in London, this was supposed to be a brand new start. I ended up going to two schools and getting expelled from both of them. Nobody else would take me, so I had to get work and eventually I became a DJ.

I was DJing in Sheffield and I became quite well known. I had a relationship with the local press and the local radio, and there was a guy called Keith Strong who was the main music journalist at the *Star*. I used to work with a guy called George who was a DJ as well. He ran the Buccaneer, where I worked, and the Wapentake. The Wapentake was the rock gig in Sheffield. It was where Joe and the other lads used to sneak in underage. And then I left Sheffield and went back to London and eventually ended up getting a job. I became a scout for Phonogram, and all these people from Sheffield were telling me about this young band. That's how I came across them. I was getting the word from people I knew in the city itself.

JOE ELLIOTT: We had A&R men falling over themselves to see us. We played the Retford Porterhouse one night and eleven of them were in the audience, including Dave Dee, as in Dozy, Beaky, Mick & Tich.

DAVID BATES: Def Leppard at the Porterhouse. That was the gig their management invited everybody to. That was July 26, 1979. It was not the greatest of gigs, one had to say. It was bizarre because it had this enormous pillar in the middle of the stage. And I do mean enormous. I don't mean six inches across. This thing was about eighteen inches across. Right in the middle of the bloody stage. A round pillar holding up the entire building. Stupid thing to have right in the middle of the stage. And there were probably, I would guess, ten to fourteen people from record companies. There were probably about ten other people in the audience. And the venue held about three hundred. This vast, cavernous gig, with about twenty-odd people in it. But they came on and it could have been Madison Square Garden as far as they were concerned. And they were playing to that.

The shocking thing for me immediately was: "Fuck me, they're young." They were really young. I had seen young bands in punk and new wave, but these guys…they were young. I was floored by that, and by their confidence. To do a gig in front of a bunch of record company

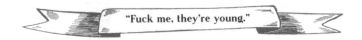

people and very few fans, that's very hard. It's very, very, very hard. To do it in front of a bunch of sozzled old A&R people, who are all thirty to forty years old. who've come up reluctantly from London, that's got to be one of the worst audiences to play in front of. But they did it like it was Madison Square Garden, sold out, and the whole place was with them. It was fantastic.

JOE ELLIOTT: We played the Middlesbrough Rock Garden the night after, and of the eleven, I think six dropped out and five came again, Dave Dee not being one of them, because he sat next to me at the bar after the Retford gig and said, "Don't move much for a front man, do you?" And I laid into him and said, "Shut up, you fat cunt."

DAVID BATES: This was my smart bit of thinking. Having seen everybody at the Porterhouse, I thought: "That's it. They'll all go back to the hotel, get pissed up and then go home the next day." But I went to Middlesbrough to see them play the next night at the Rock Garden.

Middlesbrough itself was a town that was in decline, I think that's fairly safe to say. It was a city that people had passed by. It must have been tough living there. And the one place they had was the Rock Garden. I remember going down there and thinking, "This is a weird crowd, man." There were a lot of people. It was sold out. But when you saw fifty punks going in, fifty skinheads going in, then a whole lot of rock fans going in, you thought: "That's a strange chemistry that's going on there."

And about halfway through the gig, the biggest punch-up started. As in a classic cowboy saloon fight, with glasses flying around everywhere. I was stood near the sound guy, so I could duck and hide behind the equipment. But it was a full-on, over-the-top punch-up. The amazing thing is, they ploughed on. Like in the film *Roadhouse*, where the house band has wire mesh in front of them, and the bottles go flying and smash on the wire and the band carries on playing. It was pretty much like that. They dealt with it, it was remarkable. I went back to see them and they were all fine. The weird thing is, a year later I went to the same place to see the Teardrop Explodes play. And exactly the same crowd. And exactly the same thing happened again. I went to the Rock Garden three times in my life, and every time there was the biggest punch-up. And after that I thought, "I'm never going again."

DEF LEPPARD in leather (from left: Steve Clark, Rick Savage, Joe Elliott, Pete Willis, Rick Allen) backstage at City Hall, Sheffield, Jul 20, 1981. ADRIAN BOOT | URBANIMAGE/ICONICPIX

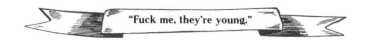

JOE ELLIOTT: A copy of the EP ended up in Chicago, and none of us know how. But it ended up on the desk of the A&R department of the Chicago branch of Mercury Records [part of the Phonogram group] which happened to be run by Cliff Burnstein. Cliff Burnstein's best mate was Peter Mensch. He was now working for Leber–Krebs, who managed Aerosmith, AC/DC, Ted Nugent, New York Dolls. Very credible management company. And Cliff Burnstein had heard this EP and played it to Peter. He basically, as the head honcho of the Chicago branch, managed to get in touch with the London office and say, "There's a band called Def Leppard. Under no circumstances let them sign for any other label."

DAVID BATES: I'd told the London office about them. But I was only a scout at this point; I wasn't allowed to make offers. I said how much I wanted this band. I think the powers that be thought, "Yeah, it looks pretty good. Here's the press, they're young." Either they said or I said I should look after them. That was it. We made them an offer, which was pretty much what they wanted. And we went up to Sheffield to sign them.

JOE ELLIOTT: When the bidding wars did get going—in fairness to [original managers] Pete Martin and Frank Stuart-Brown, they initiated it and were in charge of it along with whatever lawyer we had at the time. It got to a point where whoever bid £100,000 on it, Universal would come in with £100,000 and ten pence. We signed to Phonogram and we were ecstatic about it: Thin Lizzy were on Phonogram! Some great bands. We felt this was what we wanted.

We used all our homemade, cottage-industry punk ethos for a while, but having seen the Clash "sell out" by signing to CBS, we weren't that kind of band. I wanted to be on the same label as the big stars. We didn't want to be on Jet Records or Carrere or any of these crappy little labels. We wanted to be on a real label. So we were ecstatic, and it was a six-album deal, so we felt an enormous amount of security.

RICK SAVAGE: I'm led to believe there were a lot of companies interested. You never really know because people can say a lot of things to get you onside. When it came to the crunch, it was put to us that Phonogram had come up with the best deal. It was a five-album deal, and the advance was far bigger than anyone else. At the time we just

Cronos, Mantas, and Abaddon of VENOM sparing neither the meek nor the mild in 1983 at London's Royal Docks.
FIN COSTELLO | REDFERNS

Rob Halford and K. K. Downing of JUDAS PRIEST tempering Britain for what was soon to come, City Hall, Newcastle upon Tyne, 1978. RIK WALTON | ARENAPAL

From top: *IRON MAIDEN (L-R: Dennis Stratton, Paul Di'Anno, and Steve Harris), Hammersmith Odeon, London, March 14, 1980*. PETE STILL | REDFERNS; *IRON MAIDEN's three 1980 "yellow" singles—"Sanctuary," "Running Free," and "Women in Uniform"—had Dennis Stratton on guitar. Far from the fantasy fare of later years, the sleeves by artist Derek Riggs depict topical horror scenes under the street lamps of London's back alleys.*

Clockwise from top left: *Joe Elliott of DEF LEPPARD takes America for Sheffield, August 1981.* AL MUNSON;
the luminous Kevin Heybourne of ANGEL WITCH, Reading Rock Festival, August 24, 1980. PG BRUNELLI | ICONICPIX;
Rob Halford of JUDAS PRIEST bringing denim and leather together, Pier 84, New York, July 31, 1981. FRANK WHITE;
Guitarists Robb Weir and John Sykes of TYGERS OF PAN TANG. COURTESY OF TOM NOBLE

From top: *DIAMOND HEAD*, Lightning to the Nations *tour, Rock on Tyne Festival, Gateshead, August 30, 1981.* COURTESY OF BRIAN TATLER; *IRON MAIDEN in broad daylight, May 1980: (L–R) Dennis Stratton, Paul Di'Anno, Steve Harris, Dave Murray, and Clive Burr (latter two flashing* Metal for Muthas *tour shirts).* GEORGE BODNAR ARCHIVE | ICONICPIX

The resounding look and sounds of KERRANG! plastered British newsstands with the new HM heroes starting June 1981.

As promised, TANK are only mentioned in passing in these pages—aside from this smouldering evidence of the band (L–R: Peter Brabbs, Algy Ward, and Mark Brabbs) in its natural habitat in 1982.

Clockwise from top left: *Guitarist Robb Weir and vocalist Jon Deverill of TYGERS OF PAN TANG, Reading Festival, August 28, 1982.* GEORGE CHIN | ICONICPIX; *Jody Turner of ROCK GODDESS in London, 1984.* RAY PALMER ARCHIVE | ICONICPIX; *Bruce "Bruce" Dickinson, Chris Aylmer, Thunderstick, and Paul Samson of SAMSON.* FIN COSTELLO | REDFERNS

From top: Phil Collen and Joe Elliott of *DEF LEPPARD at Hammersmith Odeon, London, December 5, 1983.* PETE STILL | REDFERN
RAVEN going crash bang wallop by the sea in April 1985. RAY PALMER ARCHIVE | ICONICPIX

From top: *Conrad "Cronos" Lant and Jeff "Mantas" Dunn of VENOM.* PETE CRONIN | REDFERNS; *NWOBHM fashion attack by Killers-era IRON MAIDEN guitar duo Adrian Smith and Dave Murray, the Palladium, New York, July 24, 1981.* FRANK WHITE

Above: *Mark Gallagher, Rob "Wacko" Hunter, and John Gallagher of RAVEN,
Newcastle, 1981.* RIK WALTON | ARENAPAL
Facing page: *A grown-up Girlschool makes a mockery of nasty habits.*

During their first visit to America, IRON MAIDEN and Eddie attempt to hail a taxi at Gramercy Park and Lexington Ave., New York City, July 1981.

GEORGE BODNAR ARCHIVE | ICONICPIX

From top: *Paul Di'Anno and blood-red IRON MAIDEN haunt New York City, the Palladium, July 1981.* AL MUNSON;
*Total destruction by pyro (carried from England in checked baggage) at VENOM's first U.S. show
(with support act Metallica), The Paramount Theater, Staten Island, April 22, 1983.* DANNY FALCON

From top: *DIAMOND HEAD* on stage "lived up to everything I had hoped in terms of the music, in terms of the songs and the spirit," according to Metallica's Lars Ulrich. COURTESY OF BRIAN TATLER ; Hell-o America! *DEF LEPPARD* toured the US hard in 1980 and 1981, but MTV's embrace of "Bringin' on the Heartbrea vastly changed the scope and shape of the band's U.S. profile. Joe Elliott greets the Stateside welcoming committee in Rochester, New York, September 1, 1983. MICHAEL OCHS ARCHIVES

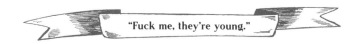

thought, "Wow, they've given us this money to make good records!" We didn't realize an advance is just a loan that you're gonna pay back. And also they were the company that showed the most interest, and it felt like they really, really believed in us. Most young kids are just happy to get a deal. It was an incredible feeling—we can now give up our day jobs because we're professional musicians! Even if we might be starving, we are professional musicians. That was so cool, to be able to concentrate on that, every single day, for as long as we wanted.

JOE ELLIOTT: We had four gigs supporting Sammy Hagar, and this is where it gets interesting. Peter [Martin] and Frank said to us: "We've got you the AC/DC tour." And we were, "Fucking hell!" They were promoting *Highway to Hell*, and they were going to do four nights at Hammersmith and two in Glasgow. This was going to be amazing.

Turned out they didn't get us the gig at all. What happened was: Burnstein had said to Mensch, who was looking after AC/DC, "Take them out and see what they're like live on a regular basis." He'd seen us a couple of times in little clubs—Wolverhampton Lafayette, where my trousers split and it was a bit of a disaster—but they could see past the cock-ups that there was something there.

CLIFF BURNSTEIN (comanager, Def Leppard): I said to them, "Hey, it wasn't a great show, but you're doing fine. Unconsciously, you're doing everything right for America." I don't think they believed me.

RICK SAVAGE: Cliff then joined Leber–Krebs with Peter Mensch.

JOE ELLIOTT: Cliff just wanted to cement that thing, and Peter [Mensch] watched us night after night. So he really had to bend AC/DC's ear to have us out—they wanted Maggie Bell to open for them—but he talked them into it and they were really great to us. Bon Scott was an absolute diamond—I still owe him a tenner. But that tour wasn't Peter [Martin] and Frank. It was Cliff and Peter [Mensch] pulling strings from behind the scenes that none of us knew.

RICK SAVAGE: AC/DC's UK tour in 1979 was the first thing that gave us another leg-up, but it also gave Mensch and Burnstein a leg-in. They were muscling their way in and elbowing Frank Stuart-Brown and Pete Martin out of the way.

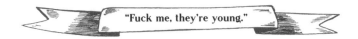
PETER MENSCH (comanager, Def Leppard): I was getting friendly with the group during the AC/DC tour. Then Rick came up and asked me to do him a favor. He wanted me to hang out in the dressing room and make believe I was interested in them, to make their managers work harder.

JOE ELLIOTT: During the AC/DC tour it became painfully obvious to us that they were out of their depth. I'll never forget this one time they were talking about making it more of a show. Now we were a band who used to dress up and leap about a bit, like UFO. We were like five Pete Ways. Well, four Pete Ways and a drummer. Pete Willis [guitar] said, "What, stop the show and bring out a table and do some card tricks?" And Frank Stuart-Brown went, "Yes, exactly, something like that!" And that's when we went, "Okay, we're done. You've got to be kidding."

RICK SAVAGE: With all due respect it really didn't take much thinking about. We were young, impressionable people and they were a management team that looked world class, even at that age. To be managing the Scorpions and AC/DC, to be part of that sort of stable—well, sorry to the current management, but we've got our career to think of here and we genuinely believe these people will take us higher than you can. So it was one of those things. It cost us to get out of the contract but we would have done anything to do it.

JOE ELLIOTT: We said, "Will you manage us?" Mensch said, "If you want us to manage you, and you're serious about it, it's going to cost you a lot of money." And we said, "How so?" "We're going to have buy you out of your contract." Long story short, that's when we made the decision—halfway through the AC/DC tour. It wouldn't have gone into litigation and all that nonsense until after the tour. Steve [Clark, guitar] was very reluctant. "I really like Pete and Frank." Yeah, because they're your fucking drinking buddies. But Mensch and Burnstein had all these big dreams, and we thought, "They manage all these massive bands and they want to take us on and nurture us? That's just too good to turn down."

We ended up giving up all royalties on our first albums, just to get out of that contract. We were completely skint by the time we went in to the studio to record *Pyromania.* We were in it up to our necks with the label. Thank God back in those days record companies had money to burn and invest in a band.

NEAL KAY (DJ, promoter, impresario): The phone rings one day, and it was Peter Mensch on the phone. He said, "Look, we want you to help us with this Def Leppard thing." I said, "What do you want, Peter?" He said, "Look, we want them to sign with us so we can take them to America and make them big. You'd want that, wouldn't you? We've got a problem: the band and their parents need convincing to leave Frank Stuart-Brown's management and come to us." And I said, "Hang on, whoa, whoa, what is all this?" He said, "Look, we can do more for them than Frank can. He's only a small operator, we're worldwide. And it would really be in the band's interest to sign with us and you must realize that." It's that moment: do I become a cunt? Do I sign up for cuntsville? They put me on the horns of a dilemma. They offered me money as well, which I believe I took, shamefully. I don't know how much it was. I can't remember.

So the day came and I went down there and the Leppards were there and their parents were there. And Mensch was there, and Burnstein was. This was at Phonogram London. And I remember going into a room with the band and their parents and explaining to their northern mentality from Sheffield why it would be best for them to join these two who would almost assuredly get them where they wanted to go and give them the career of their life if they do as they are told. "It's a golden opportunity. That door is right in front of you. Once you walk through it you will never ever look back." And I hated myself, but how can I deny the world that band? I felt that way.

JOE ELLIOTT: That's absolute bollocks. It never happened. The guy's been smoking his granny's underwear.

NEAL KAY: The meeting did happen. Maybe the band was not in that room with the parents and me at the time. However, I did get paid for that meeting to encourage the parents to leave Frank and sign with Peter and Cliff. These days, I am sorry that this slightly grubby little thing has come to light, but it is worth mentioning that it is not a figment of my imagination. It is the truth. It happened. It should be noted that my involvement in the meeting to help persuade the parents to sign to Peter and Cliff was perhaps meant to be off the record, which may account for the general lack of knowledge around this event. It is not my intention to upset Joe Elliott or the other members of the band

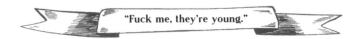

with this history. I have always had a healthy respect for the guys and their music. There is no gain for me to have fabricated any of this.

DAVID BATES: Cliff and Pete moved in on management, and those guys were from A&R backgrounds. Guess what they wanted to do? They wanted to A&R it, which is pretty much what happened. Here's the thing: the band wanted to make it in America. And if you were a rock band, that was your number-one destiny, your number-one desire. You can either be someone that's just been made an A&R man and is on his first record. Or you can go with two hotshots who are doing it in America and know what's going on. It's clear and obvious. It was hurtful to me at the time, but clear and obvious why. And I didn't have any animosity towards the band, or Cliff and Pete. It was done for the right reasons, and you can't argue. It worked.

RICK SAVAGE: They made a huge difference with their knowledge, their ear for what sounds good. Our previous management were preoccupied with getting us gigs, liaising with the record company—standard stuff. All of a sudden Burnstein and Mensch came along and they almost became part of the band, in the sense that they were just so interested in the songs we were writing, wanting to hear them and give opinions on them, on which parts of the songs could be better.

  They were objective. But they were objective in such a positive way; it was amazing. We felt we were in the big leagues, with the big boys. You couldn't put a value on it because, through Peter Mensch, along came [producer] Mutt Lange. He heard our music and said, "Yes, I can hear it. I can see what you're saying. I want to produce these guys." Which was another step up the ladder.

JOE ELLIOTT: Eventually Mensch and Burnstein worked to leave Leber–Krebs. They were very fair about it. They said to us, "We're leaving to set up our own management company. You can stay with Leber–Krebs or you can come with us." I think we met Leber or Krebs once, when we opened for AC/DC on my twenty-first birthday at the Palladium in New York. One of 'em stuck his head in the dressing room and said, "Nice to meet you, boys," and left. So we had no emotional connection to Leber–Krebs at all, but Peter and Cliff were there twenty-four hours a day, seven days a week, so it made no sense not to go with them.

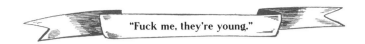

ASHLEY GOODALL (A&R at EMI for Iron Maiden): I joined EMI late in 1978, I think September. I was on a graduate trainee scheme, and you had to go round the departments and do a month in each one, and after that, if they liked you, you got a gig. My heart was in A&R and I really pushed the boat out on that. After six months, they said, "Can you come and join us as a junior A&R guy?" That was around Easter '79. I was delighted. I'd loved my month in A&R, going out to see bands, going through the tapes.

EMI when I arrived had just had Paul McCartney & Wings's "Mull of Kintyre" at number one and had had a denouement with the Sex Pistols, so we had a job on our hands to change perceptions from it being the "Mull of Kintyre" label to trying to get with the kids where the new bands were coming from. Toxic is too strong a word, but we were not on the menu for up-and-coming bands. The most exciting we got was Tom Robinson. We were not in a good place.

What then happened was I started to get out there and find out what was going on. Punk was sort of past its best, to be honest. But in my travels I noticed that there were big crowds at the Music Machine in particular for heavy metal. I used to go down there and hang out quite a bit. There were quite a lot of bands getting bigger crowds than the punks were. The punks were at the Marquee and it was waning a bit. But the heavy rock bands were getting much bigger crowds, much more determined crowds. That was interesting. I chatted to Neal Kay who used to do gig nights at the Music Machine, and we got quite friendly.

Maiden emerged as the interesting one. I think the first time I saw them was at the Swan in Hammersmith, and there was a football crowdish group of people wearing the same T-shirts, slavish followers, all really into the band. That was impressive. Then I think they did a gig at the Music Machine and I thought, "This is it. These guys are hot. They've got a big following, it's growing fast. This looks like a band that is on the move, that I like, that the public like." They had a clear plan.

NEAL KAY: I put Iron Maiden on frequently at my Music Machine shows, and at the Bandwagon, where they pulled huge crowds.

KEVIN RIDDLES (bass, Angel Witch): On one of those Music Machine nights, where nobody wanted to do the headline slot, the bill was White Spirit, a great little band from up north, Angel Witch, and

ANGEL WITCH (from left: Kevin Riddles, Dave Hogg, Kevin Heybourne) perform at the Music Machine, Camden, London, March 23, 1980 . GEORGE BODNAR ARCHIVE | ICONICPIX

Maiden. We got into the habit of drawing names out of the hat to see who would get the headline slot. This particular night Ashley Goodall had turned up, so everyone thought, "Blimey, something's going on." We didn't quite know what.

Somehow, Maiden got the middle slot, which worked out absolutely perfectly for them, because they turned up with the biggest pyro show any of us had ever seen. A brand-new Eddie skull motif out the back filled up with pyros and God knows what else. They put on the best show they'd ever put on, and we discovered later the reason they had done that was that they knew EMI were turning up that night to decide between Maiden and Angel Witch as to which one they gave the deal to. Our management didn't know anything about that, but Maiden did. I'm not saying they did anything underhanded, but if we'd known what they did, we'd have done exactly the same thing. But their management was better than ours. Their management made it their business to know exactly what EMI were thinking and they took advantage of that knowledge. I don't begrudge them one iota, I just wish we'd had that information, because then it would have been a fair fight. That's the difference between good management and management.

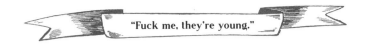

ASHLEY GOODALL: I met the [Iron Maiden] manager, Rod Smallwood, who I think originally had bad vibes from EMI in the early seventies when he was managing Cockney Rebel. I think he might have had a problem with EMI. So EMI were not top of his menu. I was into it. I watched them develop. And because I'd seen all these bands like Angel Witch or Praying Mantis, I thought, "There actually there seems to be a movement going on." And I thought, "Hang on, I've got a studio at EMI in Manchester Square, I've got a number of bands here, why don't we pull together a heavy metal album?" And I shared this with Neal Kay, and he said, "That's great, why don't we do this?" He suggested trying some bands.

I went to my bosses—this was pretty much the first thing I did at EMI—and I said, "I think there's an opportunity here, can you clear it and can we do it?" They said, "Yeah, fine." I brought the bands in. Some of them recorded in the studio in Manchester Square, some of them had tracks already. Maiden lent us "Sanctuary." That seemed to work rather well. As that was happening, Maiden were rising quite fast. It was clear they were becoming a bit of an act. And so my job was to get the company interested in the band.

You couldn't just go and sign a band without the marketing department and everyone wanting to decide if they could work with them. I had to wind up EMI. I had to get my boss on board. I had to get the marketing guys down. The next stage was to see if all the other guys were prepared to support a band like Maiden. And actually the results came back pretty well. And as Maiden got hotter, all the signs were good. They were getting better gigs, they were doing their own single. They had a cohesive view of what they were doing. Their manager was on the case. And they were determined about where they were going. And the press were picking up on them very fast. So all the signs were there to say this was a good thing.

We then got to the stage where we were looking at Maiden quite seriously as an act. I got the marketing department on board, I got the company on board. And we started to bid for them. I can't remember, but all the record companies were interested. But because it was heavy rock it wouldn't have been everyone's cup of tea, but the guys who got rock would have tipped up for it. There was a lot of negotiation—we had to commit to two albums firm, which was a big deal in those days. Good royalties. We had to commit to a lot of tour support, which these

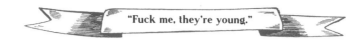

days sounds odd, but was probably more expensive than the advances. The plan was to put them on the Judas Priest tour, to buy into that. So the whole Maiden plan became quite clear, and *Metal for Muthas* became part of that implementation plan, even though it had preceded Maiden. It became very helpful that Maiden had two tracks on it.

NEAL KAY: Rod Smallwood invited down someone from EMI A&R to the Bandwagon. He said, "You have to see them in their home." It was arranged that Brian Shepherd [EMI's head of A&R] would come and see the band. Come the night it was full. They had one hell of a following. But they had such a following Shep could only get in at the very back—and in front of him were some fans with a big banner. Sheppy said, "I couldn't see anything, but I heard it, and the people love 'em, so I'll sign them." The night the cheque came through we went out to a restaurant in Swiss Cottage: Rod had the cheque and it was for £40,000.

PAUL DI'ANNO (vocals, Iron Maiden): Oh gosh, it was amazing. We'd finally made it. But then EMI spent their time trying to keep us away from their other acts. Cliff Richard was EMI. He probably would have shit himself if he'd met us. Pink Floyd were on the label, Queen were on the label. I was a huge fan, and I hoped I'd get to meet them, but I never did. I used to go up to EMI offices and raid them every month, get the swag bag out and come home with all sorts of albums.

MUSIC WEEK *report (December 15, 1979):* EMI has signed the group Iron Maiden to a long-term worldwide recording deal. The band is currently touring the UK. A single is planned for January with an album to follow in March, and the group are featured on Radio 1's *Friday Rock Show* on December 14.

ASHLEY GOODALL: The fact they had a loyal crowd was a sign of the fact they had got it together. But actually what lay behind it was that they were good musicians. They could play. There were great guitar licks, and Dave Murray and Steve Harris could play. That's number one. Number two, they had an attitude onstage that wasn't old-fart heavy rock. It wasn't slow, pompous stuff. It was fast, it was adrenaline-driven. It had taken something of the punk ethos and transferred it to heavy metal. So the effect of punk was an adrenaline kick into the

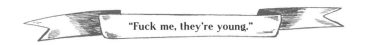
older genre of heavy rock, if you like. That was the transference that happened there.

You had this new form, and a younger group of artists coming through, who were faster, younger, streetier, and fresher than some of the old guys. I always looked to see whether people can write their own material—fundamental. And they could. They had a sense of cohesion to their music that didn't obviously copy other people, even though they looked to other bands like Judas Priest and Wishbone Ash a bit. They had a sound of their own, and the writing was their own, and an attitude. The core is always: do they have good material? Can they play? Are they doing something different? What's the attitude? Have they got followers? Have they got a clear plan? Have they got a good manager? All those things came together, which gives you confidence.

It was quite clear that Steve was the driving force behind it. But also Di'Anno was an interesting character. Steve was slightly more recessive. Is controlling too strong a word? There was a sense he was the ultimate decision maker, but he wasn't always the guy that did the most speaking.

DENNIS STRATTON (guitar, Iron Maiden): It didn't matter who managed them, Rod Smallwood or whoever, they would still be where they are now. It was Steve's determination, positive thinking, iron fist. He didn't suffer idiots. He would speak his mind and sometimes get angry with Paul, because he'd act like a dick. You could tell it was Steve's vision. He could be a little bit of a dictator.

ASHLEY GOODALL: The drummer [Doug Sampson] I didn't know and he got changed quite quickly.

DOUG SAMPSON (drums, Iron Maiden): It was health issues. I had a virus and I couldn't shake it off. I was feeling rough all the time and I said to Steve, "I don't think I'm going to be able to carry on with this." He said, "Give it till Christmas." But it came to a head, and we came to an amicable agreement that I needed to go.

ASHLEY GOODALL: Rod and Steve understood upgrading. Bands aren't static. If there is a weak point and your objective is to be successful and deliver then you have to upgrade. And that's exactly what Maiden have done. They were unbelievable. That tells you there

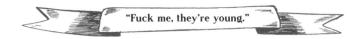
was a rising tide of musicianship. I remember in the first sessions the drummer was a bit loose. He wasn't quite solid. Di'Anno I thought was alright, but I think they had some personal tensions there. That sense of "We're going to make the best band we can" has prevailed, because they've delivered all these years. Maiden had a brand image, at least they had a logo, that was very distinctive. And that gives a strong sense of identity. Steve had been a draftsman, and he had a good eye for what cut through.

THUNDERSTICK (drums, Samson): They all looked exactly the same. Automatons. "Oh, we're heavy metallers!" Bad News Tour, really. We always used to call it "Putting the cunt kit on."

DENNIS STRATTON: The cunt kit. I had to get a black leather jacket. My hair was long anyway so it didn't matter. I've always been a jeans and T-shirt man anyway. I had to get a leather jacket, but they were all wearing the biker's jacket. The black one with the zip and the lapel. We went to a motorbike shop over in Leytonstone, round the corner from where Steve's uncle lived. I saw this other black leather jacket with padded sleeves and a round neck, and I fancied doing something different because that was me. So that was what I did.

Regarding the stage uniform, they all wanted you to wear black. That's why I had a black pair of leather jeans, and we always wore the white high tops. But Rod got the hump because I went and bought a red pair. And that got to be a bit of a trademark. I used to have a black pair as well, but he only got the hump when I wore the red trousers. I always used to wear a white kimono, because it was a bit different.

We were in Lido di Jesolo in Italy in 1980 [on a break during a European tour with Kiss], and it was when Kiss did three shows in England. We got the message through that Kiss didn't want us supporting them in England, so we had to wait in Italy. It was lovely. We had about eight days on the beach. Rod gave us orders before he flew back to London that everyone had to wear a leather jacket. It was nearly ninety degrees. So me and Dave Murray went out and bought white linen shirts and shorts and we walked around with flip-flops on. You can't wear leather in that heat—you'll die. I saw Paul walking around sweating with his leather jacket on, and I thought: "I ain't doing that."

PAUL DI'ANNO: Rod never told me to grow my hair. He knew what I would have said. I weren't no yes-man. I don't think everyone should look the same. I like a bit of individuality. As long as it all fits in and you're doing your job. I didn't look like a traditional metal singer, because I wasn't one, let's be honest. But it seemed to work. I was just trying to be me, and I always have done. What I'm comfortable with, some people may not like it, but fuck it, they ain't wearing it, are they? Bollocks to 'em.

ASHLEY GOODALL: What we added at EMI was the graphics and the Eddie character. I remember going through album covers and artists. We were looking at Frank Frazetta stuff, but actually we got to Derek Riggs, who effectively created the Eddie character, and that has been a constant in the visual part of their brand, almost to the exclusion of what the band looks like. And they were always very keen on merchandising. That was another switched-on part of what they were like as a band.

With Eddie, Derek Riggs came up with a cover with the Eddie character on it, and it seemed right—a punky horror show. We were in Wessex Studio doing the first album, and I remember it on the pool table. We were given some options for covers and artists, and Eddie was the one. That's what prevailed. Once the album was out and the character was established, he became a thing. It evolved because it was working. But Eddie only came once they were pretty much established.

PAUL DI'ANNO: That was amazing. When we got pictures of artwork for the first album, that was brilliant. We opened these portfolios up and got on to Derek Riggs. There was a few other artists they had in stock at EMI. But all of a sudden that face just jumped out. "Cor blimey, that's a bit weird, you know?" We all agreed it looked great. It had longish hair, but slightly punked-up, looking really weird. We loved it. We were looking at it, thinking that when the album came out, and people were looking through the racks, that was going to jump out at you, wasn't it? We thought it was great. We loved it.

ASHLEY GOODALL: Rod was very much in control, but through Steve. And Rod had clear views about what he wanted and what kind of band they were going to be: they were going to be a beer band, not a drug band—I don't think he wanted them being a bunch of dossy

Monumental and continental IRON MAIDEN (from left: Dave Murray, Adrian Smith, Eddie, Paul Di'Anno, Steve Harris, Clive Burr) Paris, March 1981. GEORGE BODNAR ARCHIVE | ICONICPIX

hippies. He felt they had to be quite streety—blokes who drank beer, not hippies shooting up. He was good. He was a very effective manager.

Ultimately he also knew that at EMI, even though he might have had a twitch with them back in the day, he was dealing with different people. And he knew EMI had international muscle to deliver. I was always taught as an A&R guy that EMI was international. You're not going to make money out of the UK, so go international. Knowing heavy rock could go internationally, they suited EMI very well. Germany, northern Europe. America to an extent, the Far East and Japan. EMI are very strong in those markets, and I think Rod knew that.

When it came down to the fight for the band, EMI's muscle worked out, the fact we spent a lot of time with them at a human level—I'd spent time getting to know the band, believing in them, putting a bit of time into the studio. Rod was talking to my boss Brian Shepherd on a deal level, so that was all working well. He could see EMI were revved up, and when you've got a big machine like that ready to go, why wouldn't you want to use it?

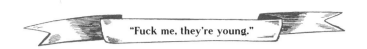

Once the first album came out, I'd only been out of university a little while, and I thought: "This is what happens, you have hit records." I looked at the other bands. I looked at Samson, who I didn't think had the songs and weren't that great. I looked at Angel Witch, who did get signed, but they weren't sexy enough. I like bands to be a bit sexy: I like the charisma with the music, and I'm not sure the others had that.

Half the trick of A&R is saying no. In any development you tend to get a couple of leaders, whether it's Duran Duran and Spandau Ballet in the new romantics, the Clash and the Sex Pistols in punk. You get a couple of lead bands in a wave and the rest you take a view on. We had Maiden and we were quite happy with that.

STEVE DAWSON: Rod Smallwood once said to me, "Your management are takers." Whereas he was investing in Maiden's future. If your commission is on the gross, which our management was, it's irrelevant if there's any money left at the end. So, you go on tour that grosses a quarter of a million pounds. But it costs you £245,000 to do it. Five tour buses, twenty trailers, fifty crew. And you're losing money. Our management still got twenty-five percent commission on a quarter of a million. Whereas Iron Maiden, they looked at it in the long run.

As far as Peter Mensch goes, he'd already done it with other bands, so he saw the potential in Def Leppard as a young pop-rock band who could get a massive audience in America. And they were willing to invest a lot of money in them, making those albums that made them big. You thought they'd never recoup, but they did.

It's better to have a small piece of a big pie than a lot of a small pie. And that's what Iron Maiden and Def Leppard's management did. And ours didn't. Because they just thought: "They've got five years so we'll milk it." And that's exactly what happened. It was our fault for being naive. You can be bitter about it, but there's no point really. I could think, I wish Saxon were playing the O2 like Maiden and Leppard, but that's just how it goes. But our managers didn't see further than a few years down the line. Otherwise they'd still be managing the band now.

"Dear Mr. Barton, grovel grovel grovel"

Sounds and its star writer Geoff Barton became the kingmakers of the NWOBHM, and tried cutting Def Leppard down to size. They had the power to anoint new bands, and carried that power across in June 1981 to launch the future bible of metal, *Kerrang!*

PHIL SUTCLIFFE (writer, Sounds): It always seemed that *Melody Maker* was the staid, mainstream one, and *NME*—which of course we called "The Enemy"—was out in front. Heading into autumn 1976 there was a key change. There was a cover that featured Justin Hayward and John Lodge of the Moody Blues, and Alan Lewis, who obviously had put them on the cover, cried out when he saw the final cover: "We've got a couple of hairdressers on the cover!" That was a key moment of realization: Jesus, this is what rock 'n' roll has come to now.

So he was wide open to punk, and the people who brought it to him initially were Jonh Ingham and Vivien Goldman. The paper carried on running old stuff, but a lot of was edged aside by punk bands. For three years before the NWOBHM was declared, those two things existed side by side.

ROSS HALFIN (photographer, Sounds and Kerrang!): The *NME* was so socialist, and up the workers and John Peel, that anyone who liked rock music—like Steve Harris or Joe Elliott—was laughed at and shoved to the side. It was either pub rock with all the old bores or the nods who liked so-called punk.

JOE ELLIOTT (vocals, Def Leppard): I used to buy *Sounds* and *Disc* and *Record Mirror.* I didn't buy *NME* because it was the enemy.

KIM MCAULIFFE (vocals and guitar, Girlschool): *Sounds* was more rock. *NME* was more punk. And *Melody Maker* was more serious. *Sounds* was more fun. And we got on the front cover of *Sounds.* We did the interview in our local pub, the Leather Bottle, and he said that was appropriate because we wore leather and we'd got a lot of bottle. It was quite important to get in *Sounds*, because that's how people got to know you, and then *Kerrang!*

PHIL SUTCLIFFE: I think Alan was a fairly cool observer of the scene, and thought: "We have this readership base of heavy metal followers, we've got a lot of punk followers. We need to be alert to what is happening." And I think they were spotting something that was happening, rather than inventing it. And that was with writers tugging at his sleeve, going, "This is happening! This is happening!" Geoff Barton was saying, "This is new," having been himself a totally loyal heavy metal and prog rock writer for the four or five years I had known him.

ROSS HALFIN: Alan Lewis was a great, great editor. He was the one that let everybody have their parts—like Geoff had the rock stuff, which I liked doing as well. And the reason was that instead of going to Bradford, I was able to go to Hawaii or Texas. Alan would listen to Barton and do things like put Rob Halford on the cover when I shot him at home, in front of his council house in his stage gear. I was surprised it went on the cover. It was just a thing Geoff and I went to do in miserable Walsall, where Rob lived, on a rainy day. And Alan Lewis put it on the cover. Alan was very visual.

PHIL SUTCLIFFE: It's not that everybody else was barred from writing about heavy metal at all by Geoff, and I did. But he was the expert. So anything in that area, I'm sure Alan would turn to Geoff and say, "What do you think of this lot?" and take his view into consideration. But when Geoff started to enthuse about this, he paid more attention for sure—"This bunch of bands you've been telling me about, they're a movement." And if you can genuinely see something—a very good editor will be looking, and Alan was a very good editor—it's a matter of

saying, "Are we going to look silly?" And Alan decided no. And that we would give it a name—the New Wave of British Heavy Metal—which is a crucial moment. It really is. Christening the baby.

MUSIC WEEK *report (February 9, 1980):* Average weekly sales (UK and Eire) for the six months July–December 1979 were: *NME* 190,605, *Sounds* 132,459, *Record Mirror* 125,984 and *Melody Maker* 121,407... Alan Lewis, who has seen the circulation of *Sounds* double since he took over as editor four years ago, said: "It's a victory for rock against seriousness. Music can be art, but mostly it's entertainment. We are not ashamed to give readers what they want, rather than telling them what to like. We were the first with punk, which did us a lot of good, the first with two-tone. And we were the only paper to keep faith with heavy metal, which the other papers have suddenly rediscovered. The kids create the trends and all we have to do is stay on the case."

MALCOLM DOME (writer, Record Mirror *and* Kerrang!*):** *Record Mirror* took rock and metal seriously enough to cover it, but they only dabbled in it. They did a little bit on the NWOBHM and bits on Maiden and Samson and so forth, but they didn't really take it as seriously as *Sounds*. But *Record Mirror* was much more of a pop-dance publication, whereas *Sounds* were very much involved. They gave Geoff Barton a lot of leeway to write about rock and metal. He wrote about American bands like Kiss, Angel, Styx, Rush. So at a time when *NME* and *Melody Maker* just didn't get it at all, *Sounds* did give Geoff the opportunity to cover those sort of bands. So they were giving it much more exposure than *Record Mirror*. He was the only person championing those bands in the UK media. The only way you really knew what was going on was to read what Geoff was writing.

PHIL ALEXANDER (fan, Kerrang! *editor):* Anything Geoff Barton writes, I am into. So when he writes about Wire's *Pink Flag* album I go out and buy *Pink Flag* because Geoff Barton wrote about it. The truth of the matter is, I can still remember the photo caption, which includes the words "bleak, mesmerizing." And of course that is an astonishing record, but it tells you about the power of the personality within that journalistic generation—whether it's Geoff or Pete Makowski or Jon Savage. Even Garry Bushell writing about street punk. There's this raft of people you can identify with because their personalities are writ

SAMSON drummer Mel Gaynor and vocalist Bruce Dickinson, Reading Rock '81 festival, August 29, 1981; Dickinson's last Samson performance before joining Iron Maiden.

JUSTIN THOMAS | ICONICPIX

large in the pieces they write. They are part of the story, inside the story, along for the ride, rather than the distance that comes from the *NME* and *Melody Maker* and people like that.

And as a result of that, that's what makes *Sounds* successful. That is really crucial. That is a real thing. These aren't fanzines, but they're written from the point of view of a music fan, and I think that's a massively crucial part of what happens from '77 onwards.

LARS ULRICH (fan, drums, Metallica): The first thing you would do every week in *Sounds* was to go to Geoff Barton's playlist, and you'd read about things like Silverwing's "Rock and Roll Are Four Letter Words." "My God! Silverwing have got to be greatest band in the world if they're on Geoff Barton's playlist!" But it's four dudes out of Macclesfield, and they all have day jobs at the local chip shop or the local bicycle dealer, or whatever.

None of this is meant disrespectfully, but it became a thing of making rock stars out of anybody who had a local band. I still put on that Silverwing song "Rock and Roll Are Four Letter Words" four or five

times a year, and to me it still sounds as great as it did the first time I heard it. But I think in context it was easy to get swept up in what the press created, in order for this whole thing to shift issues every week.

BRIAN SLAGEL (fan, founder of Metal Blade Records): Oh my God, Geoff Barton was so important. Before the internet we were barely able to speak to anybody over in the UK. So every week we got *Sounds* and it was gold to us. Whatever he wrote about, we would try to get that stuff. And when I was lucky enough to get a job at a record store and bring everything in, it was still *Sounds* I went to, because he was the voice of what was going on over there. Anything he got into, we had to find it.

PAUL SUTER (writer, Sounds and Kerrang!): When I was reading *Sounds* before I was writing for it, I developed an understanding of what the writers liked. So you'd read a review by Geoff Barton and see he liked bands for two reasons. Either they were gloriously great or ridiculously absurd. You'd read a Geoff Barton review and go: "This means they are gloriously great, so I might like it." Or, "This means they're ridiculously absurd and it's probably really crap so I'm going to ignore it."

MALCOLM DOME: Knowing Geoff, he could sometimes champion bands without knowing why he was championing them. He would like the fact they were daft. There was a quirkiness about what he liked and didn't like. He would overstate things, but in a comic-book type of way. Take Kiss. He loved writing in glowing, ridiculous, over-the-top presentations. Because he thought he was the only voice over here that was being heard on their behalf, so he had to make a big deal of it. And I think the same was true of NWOBHM and some of the acts he championed.

ROSS HALFIN: It took me a long time to realize this, but Geoff would only do things where he could see the joke. I thought Geoff really liked music, but he didn't. The reason he liked Kiss was because he thought it was funny that they wore makeup. And then he liked Rush because they dressed up in women's kimonos and sang about science fiction. He loved Ted Nugent because Nugent was ridiculous. If Geoff Barton can't see the joke, there is no band. There was a band called

Silverwing—some rich kid from Cheshire, and his mum paid for it. We went to his mum's house and I'd never been to the outskirts of Manchester before. I didn't realize there was all this wealth, like in Surrey—all these mansions. His mum was loaded and they couldn't play. They just let off a silly flash pot and Geoff wrote that they were the greatest thing. But he was taking the piss, and no one realized. It was all about what he could laugh at and take the piss out of.

MALCOLM DOME: That's harsh. Geoff had a really odd sense of humor, and I'm convinced he loved Kiss because they were ridiculous comic-strip heroes rather than because he genuinely thought they were the greatest band in the word. It's harsh to say he didn't like music, because he did. But sometimes his love of music was colored by a love of and appreciation for the larger-than-life images these bands had.

JENNIE HALSALL (publicist, Samson, Rainbow, and Monsters of Rock): He was just a kid. He was a baby. And he had a baby face. He was a really nice guy, a real sweetie. And so was Malcolm. They were both eager little beavers. It's that eager innocence that pushes everything in your sight out of your way, because you're climbing the ladder to get where you want to be. But Geoff and Malcolm were the people who would do you a favor. *Melody Maker* wouldn't. *NME* definitely wouldn't.

PAUL BIRCH (founder, Heavy Metal Records): When I first met Malcolm and picked him up, he was wearing a skullcap, and he was quite a modest figure. He came up with his girlfriend. And I thought,"Not what I was expecting from a heavy metal writer." He looked like he'd just left the synagogue. A nicer man you would never meet, and obviously he knew his subject inside out. He was quite a powerful force to be reckoned with. If Malcolm didn't like something, he would let his opinions be known. They went straight to the point— reviews could literally make a band or break a band.

PHIL SUTCLIFFE: He was kind of "the boy Barton" in the office. I think he was younger than any of the rest of us, and looked it. He looked like a young lad, quite innocent.

ASHLEY GOODALL (A&R at EMI for Iron Maiden): *Sounds* was really important. People ignored heavy rock. But *Sounds* was talking to

that audience that was not being served by other media. They got it. Geoff Barton was very helpful. If you got the front page of *Sounds*, that was very important, and getting gig write-ups. So yes, really important. That was part of the menu of things you looked for: Tommy Vance, *Sounds*, good live shows. That helps create the buzz. Malcolm Dome was very useful—a great Maiden devotee. He went on to *Kerrang!* and flew the flag high. The most unlikely of people. A little Jewish guy with a cap on, rather nerdy, sweet, quite intellectual, always turning up to Maiden gigs. It was an interesting blend, but he was always incisive and intelligent, and one of the flag bearers.

TONY WILSON (producer, Radio 1 Friday Rock Show):
I've always put the power of the printed press higher than ours. Considerably so, in fact. Essentially in those days it would be *Kerrang!* Their ability to flash the whole image and style and excitement graphically in front of the reader with interviews and record reviews— very brash and excitingly presented—I always felt that would have much more impact than what we were doing.

Though it's true a magazine doesn't convey the music to you. That's certainly the other side of the story. With Saxon, it was a great tribute to us, the "Listen to the radio on a Friday night" line in the song "Denim and Leather." That was something that kind of told the story a bit.

SIMON PORTER (publicist, Venom, Girlschool, and Motörhead):
Absolutely. Press really was more important. You can go back to Zeppelin and Purple: radio and TV wouldn't touch those sort of things. It was all press. Or *The Old Grey Whistle Test*. A front cover of any of the music papers was absolutely huge. And of course all the record shops used to sell the rock papers, so you'd have people browsing. Someone would be on the front cover of *Sounds* with their album in the racks next to it and there was that association.

DANTE BONUTTO (writer, Record Mirror and Kerrang!):
I bought all the other magazines. I tried them all, but that voice in *Kerrang!* and *Sounds* of Geoff Barton, and Dave Lewis and Robbi Millar and Pete Makowski—this great team they had was very important and gave it a very credible and informed voice. I think it was by far the most important thing. They put Samson on the cover of *Sounds*— Thunderstick—without them having done that much. So they were

"In those days, if you were a rock fan, you were buying Sounds.*" Heavy rockers, Thunderstick, and Angel Witch take the covers of Britain's NWOBHM-iest music paper.*

really championing this new thing. I guess having scored heavily with punk, they were taking chances with bands, and they were in a place to champion a new movement. I guess in those days, if you were a rock fan, you were buying *Sounds*, because there wasn't *Kerrang!* yet. *Kerrang!* stole its thunder on the rock side, but there was a moment where *Sounds* was absolutely the one.

And Geoff—I became a writer because of Geoff Barton, and I'm probably here today because of Geoff Barton—was revered and massively respected. And I would have thought he sold a lot of records as well. A good review in *Sounds* would have sold a lot of records. A front cover certainly would have sold a lot of records and would have put a group on the map. The Geoff Barton interview was big, so him going to interview Def Leppard in Sheffield would have put that band on the map, without any question at all.

ROSS HALFIN: Barton got a letter from a guy called Joe Elliott, saying he had these demos. Because Geoff liked championing the underdog, he convinced *Sounds* to let us go to Sheffield to do a feature on this group called Def Leppard, which Geoff loved because it was like Deaf Leotard. We go up there, to a working men's club, and we get paralytic. I'd never been to a working men's club. It was stupidly cheap, so we were all drinking shorts. We were used to being in London and paying a fortune. Barton was so drunk I took a photo of him with his head in the little PA bin. We ended up at Joe's mum's after, and I had a piss in

the sink. We were appalling. Joe is a perennial northerner—like "Ee up, lad"—and we saw them in this working men's club that was just empty. Some old blokes with flat caps watching them. Geoff came back and he was so excited about this idea of them being the underdog that he wrote this massive piece on them.

JOE ELLIOTT: I wrote Barton a letter. "Dear Mr. Barton, grovel grovel grovel. Will you please come up the M1 [motorway] and see our band grovel grovel grovel?" He wrote back, saying, "Dear Joe, thanks for your letter. As much as I am enthused that a band like yourself is doing what you can to keep the flag flying for rock music, at this juncture in time I am not able to take a trip up the M1, but I wish your band much success." That was our Decca Records turning the Beatles down moment.

We put out the EP, and I sent it to Geoff with another letter, going something like "Remember me? I understand you can't come up to see us, but here's some music to listen to." He writes back and says, "I want to come up and do a piece." We hastily arranged a gig and it just happened to be at Crookes Working Men's Club, which made it very iconic because of the juxtaposition of this brand new rock band and the working men's club. Ross was a year older than me and Geoff was a bit older. And drinks were subsidized, so you could get a shot of whisky for 25 pence and a pint for ten pence. And they got bollocksed. And they were down the front headbanging. It turned out to be a really great article, and that was the beginning of a love–hate relationship with Geoff. The hate would come about six months later. But then the love would come back as well.

GEOFF BARTON (writing in Sounds, June 16, 1979): Def Leppard burst onstage at about ten p.m. and your immediate impression is how good they look: from left to right guitarist Pete Willis, diminutive but cool in white shirt and grey stain strides; tall, lanky Joe Elliott, garbed in a full silk shirt and narrow, figure-hugging "leather" pants; drummer Rick Allen, bare-chested and already slick with sweat atop his riser; and bass player Rick Savage and guitarist Steve Clark, resplendent in leather/leopard-skin combination outfits, both possessors of fine heads of tightly curled blond hair. Eminently presentable, not a single pair of time warp Angel Witch-style loon pants in evidence, thank God. And the music? High-powered heavy rock played to a degree of tightness usually only achieved after a half-dozen gruelling American tours. Neat duelling guitars and a titanic rhythm section...the EP, good as it is, doesn't even hint at Def Leppard's live dynamism...Joe Elliott hasn't got a great voice, but he has got presence and, really, that's half the battle.

RICK SAVAGE (bass, Def Leppard): It was huge, the support *Sounds* gave us—and Geoff Barton in particular—at that time, and that coinciding with the launch of the EP. And what do you know? In the *Sounds* readers' poll "Getcha Rocks Off" was the single of the year. Forget "Another Brick in the Wall," that came second. This is pretty stupid really, but that's the impact the newspaper had.

ANDRO COULTON (bass, Witchfynde): You know we had that track "The Devil's Gallop," beginning "This one's for you, Geoff"? We badgered Geoff Barton because he wrote about the New Wave of British Heavy Metal. He'd come up and see Leppard at some crummy place, but wouldn't come and see us. So we started ringing up and asking for Dick Barton. And of course all the guys at *Sounds* took that over, and I don't think Geoff liked that.

We had spare time in the studio, so we got the guy who owned the studio to play piano—he'd got an old upright piano, and he knew the *Dick Barton: Special Agent* theme. We got a sound effect of a scratchy record, and then we were, "How many stars are you going to give it?" The "two stars" was from Alan Campion of Rondelet Records. Anyway, Geoff reviewed the album and he did give us two stars. He was not a happy chappy.

ROSS HALFIN: He was so powerful. He was. Because at the time everyone took him seriously. He was a champion of UFO. He broke Iron Maiden, I don't care what anyone says. He broke Def Leppard. He really did. He started *Kerrang!* And he would stand up for you. I didn't realize till later he was taking the piss.

STEVE DAWSON (bass, Saxon): I'd walk to local newsstands, and all the local kids would be shouting, "You're in *Sounds* this week!" They were glad for you to be in it.

SIMON PORTER: Geoff was really important. If he didn't like something, then it was the nature of the business that there weren't many alternatives to go to, so it was important to get Geoff on board. In those days, if you got a front cover of *Sounds* for a rock act, it was as good as being on the way to having a hit album or sold-out tour.

KEVIN RIDDLES (bass, Angel Witch): He was the kingmaker. I'm sure he had that vision for himself, and it was a mantle he embraced. He made Leppard, simple as that. Without Geoff Barton, Def Leppard would probably still have done something, but they probably wouldn't have done it when they did, and as big as they did. Without any shadow of a doubt, from that point of view he gave them their leg-up. I think probably the same with Maiden. With Angel Witch he never liked it. It was as simple as that.

We were never going to be a Geoff Barton band. There were bands around at the time that we looked on as Geoff Barton bands. We were never going to be, in his eyes, that sort of West Coast pretty-boy type of band. We were never going to appeal to young ladies. My good lady wife just said, "Oh, I dunno." Angel Witch was not the sort of music you were going to put on the tape player in your convertible muscle car while you drive Route 66. That was never going to happen with Angel Witch. We weren't that type of band.

I always thought we were a fans' band. And Geoff always wanted to be part of a slightly different version to what Angel Witch was. It wasn't that he wanted the limelight—there were probably only six people who knew what he looked like—but he wanted that Geoff Barton byline to mean something, and the more people that saw it, the more that byline meant. So he wanted that association with the more American, AOR type of music, and the more photogenic bands were the ones he was interested in, so Leppard were perfectly made for him. Absolutely tailor-made for Geoff, and vice versa. They were exactly the band he was looking for.

DAVID BATES (A&R at Phonogram for Def Leppard): Geoff Barton turned on them pretty viciously.

GEOFF BARTON (writing in Sounds, March 1, 1980, cover-lined: "Has the Leppard Changed its Spots?"): In a mere eight months the Def ones have rocketed to prominence from obscurity

and at the moment I feel like I'm standing on an observation platform watching their tail flares flicker as they shoot further and further up into the sky, waiting for them to be swallowed up by the stratosphere and disappear completely.

JOE ELLIOTT: When he first came to see us at Crookes Working Men's Club, I picked him up at the train station in my works van, took him to my mum and dad's house. My mum made him cheese and ham sandwiches, a cup of tea. Go to the gig, drinking subsidized alcohol. Having the time of his life. Cut to January 1980, we've got a record deal, an album in the can, and he gets picked up at the train station by someone from the record company, not me. He didn't like that. And maybe he was suspicious of our performance that night, which was a little subdued because we'd found out Bon Scott had died the night before. One reason or another, he thought we'd gone corporate. But it was more there was so much to do that I didn't have the time to fetch him. And neither should I have fetched him. That's not the way it would have worked if he'd gone to see UFO. But because I did it a year earlier, that set a precedent in his mind.

What was unfair—and this isn't a go at Maiden—is when he had a go at us for going to America. Iron Maiden went to America four months before us, but he didn't say a thing about that. And we went to America having done forty-five gigs in forty-seven days, January through March, in the UK, in every nook and cranny around the UK. Then we put the album out. Then we did twelve city halls. There was nowhere left to play in England by the end of April. Of course we were going to go to America next.

MALCOLM DOME: I think Joe's being naive and unfair. And I think he's doing a disservice to Geoff. By that time Geoff had been writing about music for several years. He was used to major labels' treatment. Geoff was not naive. I honestly think Geoff didn't so much turn against them as expect more from their first album than was there. He also seemed to think they were trying to sell out to America, and I do wonder if part of that was that they got American management. I think that's got a lot to do with it. I think in his mind, he had championed them so much and suddenly felt they were on a major label, they've got all these other people around them, you've become too big now, I want

to put you down. Which is very unfair. But I think Joe's being naive if he thinks Geoff's feelings were hurt because Joe didn't pick him up. I don't think Geoff would ever have expected that.

But *Sounds* turned against Leppard because Geoff did. And I think Geoff set the benchmark for that because he'd been a real champion. I'm sure there would have been a lot of talk about them going to America. The irony being that Maiden went to America before Leppard. But Maiden were the working-class heroes, and Leppard were seen as wannabes who wanted to sell out to America, putting spandex on and selling millions of records and hanging out in limos. That was very unfair. So there was that ridiculous nonsense that was going on at the time. And I think *Sounds* turned against them simply because Geoff no longer wanted to support them.

JOE ELLIOTT: I was pissed off. Completely pissed off. And what started to leak out in the early days was that "Hello America" was deemed to be this sell-out song. Now, once that gets said, you can't put it back in the bottle. We'd been playing that song for two years, and nobody blinked an eye. We played it the night him and Ross came to Crookes Working Men's Club and they were headbanging to it. They didn't come up to me afterwards going, "What the hell was all that about?"

As I've explained a million times since, when you work in Osborne's in the basement with no natural light in an office the size of a tiny bathroom and you start writing lyrics for this band you've just got together, it's not unusual for an eighteen-year-old, naive kid to start saying, "Get me out of here." And you start dreaming about what's above ground. I was not dreaming about the streets back up to my mum and dad's house, or the cold, breezy parks I used to play football in. I started thinking about *Charlie's Angels*, or the articles Barton himself had written about Kiss playing Detroit Cobo Hall. And by the way, they didn't pick him up at the airport when he flew out to review that gig. So my reaction was: "This is bollocks. This is totally unfair."

It affected our popularity in the UK. Absolutely it did. I've got proof of the fact it did. The album came out and did really well, so it didn't affect us right there and then. It wasn't like the day after the article came out, we disappeared from the face of the planet. But what happened was, after Reading '80, it sort of started to peter out.

Reading was August. After we did America, we came back to the UK to do Reading. And then we went over to Europe with the Scorpions, and then we came back and we started to get ready to do the second album. But it kept getting put off and put off and put off. And we got bored. So we said, "Let's do some shows." We booked six locally. When we played Burton upon Trent in January or February there was a queue round the block of about five hundred that couldn't get in. And when we went back there nine months later, two hundred people turned up. Chesterfield Aquarius Club, there was barely anyone in. It was a disaster. But it was so under the radar we got away with it.

As people, as well, we were suffering. It was all balanced out by the fact we'd made great inroads in America and slightly in Europe, so if there was a bit of backlash in the UK, we'd have [management team Peter and Cliff] Mensch and Burnstein going, "Don't worry about it. It'll sort itself out." So we were being talked off any dangerous ledges by experienced managers, and our own young bravado of "Fuck them, if that's what they think about us." But it wasn't the fans; they were very loyal to everything they heard from the mouth of the god that was Geoff Barton.

ROSS HALFIN: Barton took them to task over that first album, and they didn't like it. I don't care what Joe says, Leppard got full of themselves quickly, which Iron Maiden never did. Geoff made a conscious decision to take them down a peg or two. Absolutely he did.

RICK SAVAGE: I got the impression that from a journalistic point of view it was time to try and bring the band down a peg or two, and he was able to do it. *Sounds* in particular had really championed the band in the previous year or fourteen months, and I think it was just their turn to go, "Let's bring them back down to earth a little bit."

It started, I believe, with this impression that we sort of turned our back on the UK and went to try and further our career in America. During that period—the first nine months of 1980—we still played more gigs in the UK than we did in America, but it's perceived as if we turned our backs on England and went to seek riches across the ocean. It was far beyond our intelligence to think on such a business level. We'd literally run out of gigs to play in the UK. Anywhere between St Austell Pavilion and Exeter Roots nightclub all the way through

to Aberdeen University, we'd played every one and all of them in between from the previous November, December, January, all the way through up until early summer. We had nowhere else to play, we'd nowhere else to go. The album was out, we'd done well. We started on the nightclub circuit and ended up doing the city halls, and that was it.

What do you do? We couldn't go and make a new album. We were getting offers from America, initially to go over and support Pat Travers, but also with a view to supporting the Scorpions and Judas Priest. It was a no-brainer. "Fantastic—yeah, let's go." And it just got perceived in a slightly negative way. And I think our next gig back in the UK would have been the Reading Festival. So any steam that needed to be let off from whoever, it was a perfect opportunity to do that.

JON DEVERILL (vocals, Persian Risk and Tygers of Pan Tang):
The first thing Joe Elliott said at the Reading Festival in 1980 was something like, "Hi! We've just got back from America." The audience booed. The whole thing was that Leppard had sold out to America and saw us as a second-class market. It was all about America. Who cares about the UK, because you don't sell any records there, anyway? I remember the way they looked. It looked like they were trying to be Duran Duran, not heavy rock. There was a real kind of American feel to them. It was all a bit false. I don't want to slag off Def Leppard, but I'm sure they don't give a flying fuck what I think. They had one of the worst receptions I've ever seen of any band. The only other one I've seen like that was Jayne County, who got canned off and couldn't finish her performance, which was terrible. But Def Leppard were so badly received that day. There was a lot of stuff thrown on the stage that day. It took them a long time to recover from that.

RICK SAVAGE: It certainly wasn't as bad as was made out. That's the first thing. That gig was actually quite good. I've got to be honest, it was pretty good, and we went down pretty well. It's just that it was our first experience of a major festival and, in that day and age, people threw things at every band. It was part of the festival-goer's mentality; it wasn't necessarily an indication of dislike or anything like that. It just happened. I think nowadays crowds are a lot more understanding and a lot more forgiving and a lot more into lots of different styles of similar music. It's not as partisan, you know?

Debris and litter: The August 1980 Reading festival became an endurance test for bands besieged by missiles. Those present remember Def Leppard bearing the brunt of them. READING POST/MIRRORPIX/GETTY IMAGES

I think in those days, if you were a Motörhead fan there's a possibility you would hate Def Leppard, or if you were a Whitesnake fan, you would hate Iron Maiden. It could be all kinds of different reasons. And obviously at a festival, it's a prime place to show your allegiance to one type of band and your anti-allegiance to the others that might be on the bill. So that went on all the time. Yeah, we got things thrown at us. I do believe so did Whitesnake, who actually went on after us.

JOE ELLIOTT: It gets tiresome. People think I'm being overly defensive. But I'm not. I'm telling you how it was. We got shit thrown at us, but everybody got shit thrown at them. People were throwing shit and they didn't even know who was on stage, they were that pissed. Girl got it way worse than us, and they hadn't been to America. They got it because they were dressed up like Japan or the Bay City Rollers. They were "poofs" because they weren't Judas Priest. Whitesnake got shit thrown at them, UFO got shit thrown at them. Everybody that played that thing got shit thrown at them.

MALCOLM DOME: Joe claims they went down really well. But I was at Reading. I was in the audience that day. I know how they went down. Not as dreadfully as has been claimed, but they didn't go down that well. They were following Slade, who absolutely stormed it, and they had a hard time. It didn't help that Joe came on and said "Now for some proper music." Which he meant as a joke, because he's a massive Slade fan, but it backfired because no one got the joke. And at that time Leppard were on a down with British audiences because they'd got the bad press in *Sounds*, and people were not turning against them, but less convinced by them: "Oh yeah, look at these smart-alec know-it-alls, cocky arrogant sods."

PETER MENSCH (comanager, Def Leppard): When the first tomato and beer can hit the stage, I knew this was it. Def Leppard were happening in America and they were coming back to England where four months before they were doing eighty-five percent in theaters. But to come back following Slade, combined with the fact that people thought we had sold out, that was it. We were gone.

MALCOLM DOME: I don't think it's healthy Geoff had so much power. I don't think music journalists should ever have that power of life and death over bands and Geoff, to a certain extent, did. If Geoff wrote about a band did people sit up and take notice? Yeah. But to be fair it never gave Geoff an ego. It didn't. But I don't think it was healthy. To be fair to Geoff, with Leppard he accepted and admitted he got it wrong.

PHIL SUTCLIFFE: Geoff was already an established journo. But he became a lightning rod for NWOBHM. Heavy metal, I suppose, had been a part of the orthodox music industry—the way in was to get your tape to an A&R man. Not that journalists were irrelevant, and we did get tapes sent to us all the time, and punk encouraged that direct contact. But with the New Wave of British Heavy Metal they started thinking in a punk way about the industry while not making music that was anything remotely like punk. And part of that would be to find your journalist—and Geoff was the man to go to, and he had the openness to step outside what he was being strenuously fed by the big labels and be a bit punky in attitude.

That was a distinct change, with journos becoming more directly involved and getting closer to what was happening. Of course, the editor had seen that happening with punk, and had also shown his bosses that it worked as opposed to it closed the paper down, which it might have done. And so they pulled that off in a more minor way.

The other evidence of this, and Geoff's oomph, was *Kerrang!* You could actually start a whole new publication off this genre. It was brought to life by the New Wave of British Heavy Metal. I believe Geoff coined the word "kerrang" and it lasted because it's such a perfect word for the heavy metal guitar sound. So those things were about enthusiasm and journalistic flair. There was a lot of brilliance involved in that. He was narrow—one of the music journalists most narrowly devoted to a particular genre that I have ever encountered.

PAUL SUTER: He struck me as almost shy. He was very quiet, almost introverted. But then so was I, so I didn't count that as a negative. It just meant it was hard to relate to him. At *Kerrang!* I got to know him a bit more, but he was the same guy—he'd have his desk at one end of the room, and he'd sit there quietly doing whatever he was doing. The only time he ever came out of his shell, really, was when he was firing me in October 1985.

STEVE HAMMONDS (fan, music catalog consultant): Then *Kerrang!* came along and changed it for everybody. *Kerrang!* was the first magazine to really get a grip on it.

ROBB WEIR (guitar, Tygers of Pan Tang): *Kerrang!* made a huge difference. We had kind, sensible, considered reviews in *Kerrang!* And when it came out, the readership was massive—they couldn't print enough copies. It wasn't a newspaper, and it wasn't a color magazine. It was something in between.

PHIL ALEXANDER: *Kerrang!* comes out of *Sounds*, the champion of NWOBHM, and it is launched purely because every time *Sounds* did a cover with a metal band, they saw their sales go through the roof. And with Geoff Barton, it was not him going. "I want to launch a magazine called *Kerrang!*" It was actually Alan Lewis who said to him, "This is all really working. Why don't you draw up a magazine that could work?" That this would be a magazine in full color as well was really, really fascinating.

That first issue comes out, and it's the first magazine devoted specifically to hard rock anywhere in the world, and it completely

changed the landscape on a global basis. I can tell you there is clear proof of this from the simple fact that I bought a copy from my local newsstand, and what happened on the back of that is that it just set me off on a path. And the same is true of Lars Ulrich. At the *Kerrang!* awards two years ago, I said that both Lars and I bought a copy of that first issue and, without it, neither of us would be here. And the Danish voice comes out from the audience: "I bought two copies! Because I thought one of them would be collectible!"

LARS ULRICH: It was billed as a *Sounds* heavy metal special, and the word *Kerrang!*—which Geoff Barton had dreamed up—was supposedly like a guitar sound or something. It made us very happy and very enthusiastic. Obviously at that time—the fall of '81—heavy metal and the New Wave of British Heavy Metal was becoming a pretty far and wide movement, certainly in England. It was incredible to be able to sit there and look through a glossy magazine and see color pictures of all your favorites. That was pretty crazy.

One little detail that you don't think much about is that all those weeklies, all four of them, were black and white. And so *Kerrang!* was the first time you saw any of these pictures in color. I guess it was more about pictures than text, but it was a great part of the fact that this was becoming a movement that was reaching more and more people.

MALCOLM DOME: NWOBHM's momentum and dynamic gave Spotlight, which published *Sounds*, the interest in doing a one-off. The original *Kerrang!* was a supplement in *Sounds* at the end of 1979: Thunderstick from Samson was on the cover, and most of the bands in there were NWOBHM bands.

JENNIE HALSALL: It was a great cover. There's always a hook that helps sell copies. Every heavy metal fan bought *Sounds* because they knew they'd always get what they wanted in there. I didn't think that up—*Sounds* did.

THUNDERSTICK (drums, Samson): At that time the rest of the band thought Thunderstick was going to be the person to open the golden gates. It was all for the good of the band, so they were behind it. I thought it was odd. It was odd to walk past the magazines and newspapers on the shelves and go, "My God, that's me." Very strange.

My wife at the time used to work in London. She was getting the train home and there were all these copies of *Sounds* hanging up in the racks. She went, "Oh my God!"

MALCOLM DOME: And it was NWOBHM that then drove them to think in 1981: "Let's do a color magazine." Angus Young was on the cover, so there were established bands as well, but there was a lot of NWOBHM content in there. That's what really drove the whole idea and revitalized the rock and metal environment to the point that people were getting excited about it again. I'm sure NWOBHM was behind it.

Hardly anyone was on *Kerrang!* staff in those early days. It was treated as a bloody joke. Spotlight, the publisher, owned *Record Mirror, Sounds, Music Week*—*Kerrang!* was part of that. We were on the first floor above Covent Garden tube station, and in those very early days Dante was on staff. Alan Lewis from *Sounds* and Alf Martin from *Record Mirror* oversaw things, but they weren't full-time at *Kerrang!* There was a designer, [Steve] "Krusher" [Joule]. I don't even think there was a secretary. There was no one. The very first proper editor was Geoff, and that wasn't till 1984. Geoff had been made editor of *Sounds*, and they didn't feel he was right for that job but didn't want to lose him, so they made him editor of *Kerrang!* That was the reality of it.

ROSS HALFIN: Geoff came up with the idea—and it got shot down— of doing an annual, like *Beano* or *The Dandy*. And he wanted to call it *Kerrang!* But the reaction was: "We're not doing an album at Christmas called *Kerrang!*" The idea was laughable. How it worked was, the only way color was used was if someone bought a color ad—that's why you would very occasionally get a color cover of *Sounds*. Somebody started buying color ads, and because of that they had to produce a one-shot, a one-off magazine. So Geoff said, "Let's do *Kerrang!*" Just to humor him, Alan Lewis agreed to this one-off magazine.

Everything for *Sounds* was done in black and white, but I had just done AC/DC. I normally shot black and white, but Geoff said, "Did you shoot any color?" I said, "I shot eight frames." You didn't want to waste film, so you'd save it in another camera and use it for another gig. And I had eight frames of Angus Young and they weren't very good. But Geoff went, "Great!" And that's how *Kerrang!* got its first cover.

We put together this magazine. And everyone laughed at it, but it sold out. Absolutely sold out. Everyone was like, "Wow, what's this?" We did four magazines, then there was a big strike and it got taken off Geoff by the editor of *Record Mirror*, who did the next few issues that didn't sell before it came back to Geoff. It was monthly, but it ended up being biweekly.

BIFF BYFORD (vocals, Saxon): Metal got so big that *Sounds* couldn't handle it any more. They had to launch *Kerrang!* It was so big it created a new magazine.

DANTE BONUTTO: People would often just turn up in the office to hang out and give you something. Lars Ulrich from Metallica was always in the office hanging out, so people saw it as the place to be, to make connections. But we were doing it very much as fans, as professional fans. The great thing about *Kerrang!* at that time is that our publishers pretty much let us get on with it, and do what we wanted. There were no shackles on what you could do or say, which meant you could really put forward your point of view and take this thing on and champion whatever you wanted.

And no one ever knew what the magazine sold. I don't think we ever sat down and discussed circulation because it seemed irrelevant. People were going to buy that magazine, so long as you were true and didn't take the piss. It did have great integrity. Because you did what you genuinely thought was good. It wasn't about pulling an ad into the magazine, which happily did come. It wasn't about the circulation figures. We never checked those out that much. We got great feedback from the fans and that was the main thing. And we felt that was something important.

PAUL SUTER: It certainly gave metal new reach because it was the first publication solely devoted to championing hard rock and heavy metal. There hadn't been that before. The supporters of hard rock and heavy metal had always been fairly clannish. And now they had got a publication, which was leading the charge. Everything coalesced around it. That became a prime moving force, even internationally. Its power had a lot to do with the fact that heavy metal and hard rock couldn't get on the radio, except for Tommy Vance and sometimes John Peel. So the press was what sold records and what broke bands in

Britain, and it became particularly important to the whole scene. If you didn't have the support of the flagship publication, then you were kind of fucked.

A *Kerrang!* review became more important than a *Sounds* review, and that happened fairly quickly. I guess over the first ten, twenty issues of *Kerrang!* it was gradually building, and it reached the point that the publishers and the editors real, "Wow, this is actually happening, this is a thing." And that's when the full-time commitment came, and they got their own office, and they started taking on more writers, such as myself. It wasn't a side thing from *Sounds* any more, it was a thing all of its own and it was rapidly becoming influential, and part of that was reflected in the fact that the record companies saw *Kerrang!* was becoming influential, therefore they were putting advertising money into it, therefore *Kerrang!* could afford to expand and become a full-time thing because they got the ad revenue. It became a virtuous circle.

PAUL BIRCH: Pages were not cheap. So we were paying a lot of money in advertising. But they were everything. But when *Kerrang!* became more frequent, it became very hard to keep up with the output they needed. The label in the end was probably releasing thirty albums a year.

MALCOLM DOME: We kept on looking for new, exciting, young bands who maybe wouldn't have got the time of day otherwise. We did cover a lot of those bands, so I think we did give it extra legs. You can argue maybe we gave it too many extra legs. I don't think so. I think we just saw a lot of young talent that was coming through as NWOBHM started running out of steam. We had pages devoted to new bands. I think we did look to promote talented bands who were coming up at the end of NWOBHM, and sometimes not so talented bands, which was inevitable.

PHIL ASTON (guitar, the Handsome Beasts): *Kerrang!* appeared and it was very easy to send off a little message and get yourself into the news section of *Kerrang!* And if you got your name in, you'd go to the pub and you'd have it under your arm to say, "Look! We've been featured! We've got this gig."

TOM GABRIEL WARRIOR (fan, founder of Hellhammer, Celtic Frost, and Triptykon): I managed to save enough money and talked my mother into helping me go to London in 1981. I hardly ate. I spent all my money on New Wave of British Heavy Metal singles, and that was really a breakthrough. I went to HMV on Oxford Street, where they had a rack with New Wave of British Heavy Metal singles, and we were blown away. I basically bought every single on that rack. Then everybody gathered at my house and everybody taped what I had bought.

I actually discovered the first issue of *Kerrang!* when I was there. I came back with vinyl, T-shirts, the first issue of *Kerrang!*, which opened an entire universe, and every seven-inch single that we could get a hold of. But walking past a newsstand and seeing a dedicated heavy metal magazine, that was the ultimate. Because in that magazine, of course, were all the ads, so we were able then to get some more material by mail order and we found out about bands we had never heard of. *Kerrang!* really opened an entire universe. I got a subscription for *Kerrang!* so I had all the early issues, and every issue opened yet another universe.

CRONOS (bass and vocals, Venom): One of the reasons I had a war with *Kerrang!* was that they started pitting bands against each other. It seemed ridiculous. You had one week of them being on your side, and the next week it was someone else. It got really petty and that's why we ended up at war with the press, so when we had interviews to do we would just lie and go off on tangents and talk about whatever we wanted. One guy was desperately trying to talk about the connections between the bands that came into Neat and I just wanted to talk about all the different star systems.

PAUL SUTER: At *Kerrang!* Malcolm and I were the ones who provided most of the information for the news pages, because we'd gotten a lot of contacts in America. I was working days at Heathrow Airport, and I used to come into the office on a Friday night after I had finished work. They closed the offices down at nine, and there would be Malcolm, Dante, myself, and a couple of others would drop in. Malcolm and I would be on the phone talking to our friends in Los Angeles and New York, and finding out what was going in so we could run news pieces.

And the phone bill got rather high. Bear in mind I'm there on Fridays, and the rest of them are there all week. But I got told I couldn't use the phones any more because I was running up the phone bill. Okay, fine, I'll just have to make my calls from home.

And then RCA were paying for me to go to Los Angeles to do Jefferson Starship, Autograph, Mr. Mister, and I was due to leave on the Monday. Went into the office on Friday: "Where's Malcolm?" "Oh, he just went to Los Angeles." Fuck, if he covers the bands I'm being sent out to cover, I'm in deep shit. So I said, "Look guys, I'm not allowed to use the phone. Someone dial the number for me, we've got to ask him what he's doing there." And they said, "Don't be ridiculous. Dial it yourself." So I did, and I said, "What are you doing? I'm supposed to be coming out for a trip, are you gonna cover these bands?"

Then on Monday, Barton called me at work, screaming his head off: "You used the phone! You're fired!" I'd been weaseled on. I blame petty jealousy. And I believe that it was what started the fragmentation in the metal press. *Metal Hammer* was there already, but *Kerrang!* was a real force at that time, and a lot of the people on the paper saw that happen and thought it was really wrong. So it split the team apart and people drifted off and started *Raw*, and it screwed the whole situation. *Kerrang!* had been a real force and it fell apart after that.

STEVE HAMMONDS: I had to gird myself to talk to Geoff. He was really important. He was very knowledgeable, but he went off to edit a car magazine. He doesn't speak to anyone any more. He doesn't speak to Malcolm, and Malcolm's been his friend for thirty years. Very strange.

8

"I was once punched in the face by nothing at an insane asylum."

Venom, Witchfinder General, Witchfynde, and Demon
led NWOBHM's embrace of the occult,
one of metal's eternal themes. For many bands,
the devil was just a gimmick, but not for all.

CRONOS (bass and vocals, Venom): I've always been interested in the occult. I've got green eyes, I'm left-handed. It's the Black Sabbath thing: it works so well. You've got horror movies, and you've got horror music. It's always been my thing. I never wanted to be an Elton John, singing love songs. He does it so well, but I don't think I could do that. Same as I don't think Elton could sing "In League with Satan."

RITCHIE BLACKMORE (guitar, Rainbow): Having done some research into the paranormal, I've found that most apparitions and ghosts really don't happen in old castles and houses: they can happen anywhere. They can happen in a brand-new house, depending on the ground and the kind of energy that the people themselves bring into the house. Even watching TV and the ghost shows, they complain of demons and things and I noticed they always have religious pictures and crucifixes up, even before they start the investigation and get to the bottom of why it's haunted.

I'm always taken by the fact that the people involved are often religious. I don't know if that taunts the ghost, or sets off an energy that excites them. I was watching a show last night, and they were

investigating this house and sure enough there were crucifixes and religious pictures all over the place. It's strange they hadn't figured that one out and thought it might have been causing ghostly activity. If it's a poltergeist it usually comes from kids anyway. I find it a fascinating subject, because we're all going to end up going somewhere and it would be nice to know if it was a nice place.

MONTALO (guitar, Witchfynde): People always have to put you into particular pigeonholes. We accepted that. But the occult has many different disciplines, and it's not possible to define them under one name. None of us were interested in anything terribly negative.

MALCOLM DOME (writer, Record Mirror and Kerrang!): Ah, Montalo, the Satanic milkman!

JOE ELLIOTT (vocals, Def Leppard): Witchfynde supported us! I wouldn't remember any of Witchfynde's names, except didn't one of them have a weird name? Mandrax? Montalo! He used to play guitar through a Pignose amp and it sounded horrendous. I'm sure they thought it was great, but it was just this big, fuzzy noise that sounded like a washing machine.

MONTALO: When we first got together the four members of the band each had different interests within the broad spectrum of the occult. I was more interested in natural magic, which tends towards the Wicca elements, and as part of that the high priestess that I knew at the time in Sheffield gave me the name Montalo. It doesn't have a meaning. It's just a name.

MANTAS (guitar, Venom): I've been questioned so many times about the Satanic, the Devil, blah blah blah. Go back way into, I don't know, the 1920s, go to the Delta, and you've got some guy sitting on a porch with an acoustic guitar and a slide singing about the Devil. The Devil's always been in music, we were just the ones who pushed it to the forefront.

KEVIN RIDDLES (bass, Angel Witch): This six-hour East German entertainment extravaganza was broadcast across all of Germany, and an hour and a half of it was the East German border guards' band playing East German classics. And they just happened to sling us on in the middle. The producers were terrified, not so much by the material, more by the visual clues that we were of the occult persuasion: I used to wear a huge cross, which my mum had given me, about three inches tall. A big old chunk of steel. You can see me wearing it in the rehearsal. When we did the live transmission I had to take it off and cover up my hairy chest. Kev [Heybourne, Angel Witch singer-guitarist] was told to take off his bracelets and his Egyptian ankh. Like most people, they didn't have a clue what an angel witch was, and neither did we. The main thing was the visuals.

DAVE HILL (vocals, Demon): I wouldn't say I was particularly into the occult, but I always liked the Hammer stuff. I remember growing up and watching all the Christopher Lee stuff and I thought they were great.

ABADDON (drums, Venom): The occult was almost in the mainstream—it was accepted at the movie theater. You think about the seventies, you've got *The Exorcist* coming out, and *The Omen*, and the Hammer House of Horror was in your face all the time. And again, a couple of years earlier if something like that had come on the TV, your dad would have said, "Get to bed." But now I was at an age where I could sit up and watch it with my dad. And so it all happened at the same time. The excitement around *The Exorcist* being released was incredible; it was palpable, you know?

If Hollywood could be at the front of it, then everyone else was going to follow, and it's when it gets a bit darker and turning into murders and things and music is in the background where somebody committed murder, that's when people jump on it and say it came from heavy metal. Well, hang on, we probably got it from being inspired by Hollywood. It's about where you are at the time and the youth that carry the fire. We wrote a lot about history—we wrote about Countess Báthory and stuff like that. So we would look into stuff. And then you'd see Peter Cushing in a Countess Báthory movie and think, "Hang on, they're based on real events." You'd get into it and start being inspired.

FENRIZ (fan, guitar and vocals, Darkthrone): One had the occult influence from the sixties, when the cauldron was already bubbling with Coven, Black Widow, and Black Sabbath. In fact, I think it was a red thread throughout fuzz guitar's existence. Combine that with a lot

of the folk rock that didn't exactly feel Christian but pagan as hell. Yes, I get an anti-Christian vibe from Steeleye Span. There, I've said it! Top it off with some Vincent Price movies.

BRIAN SLAGEL (fan, founder of Metal Blade Records): Metal and horror movies go hand in hand. We grew up watching that kind of stuff, and I think that imagery just goes perfectly. If you were a horror-movie fan, then singing about all that stuff is perfect. We loved horror movies, and we loved metal, here are all these bands singing about the same thing. And it's rebellious, it's against the grain of the norm, and a lot of us into the music had those against-the-mainstream vibes. So lyrics like that pushed the boundaries. And look, I grew up as a big fan of Alice Cooper and Kiss and both those bands—especially Alice Cooper—pushed the envelope very far in terms of that sort of imagery. So it's natural bands that came after would pick up on it.

MALCOLM DOME: Why is metal obsessed with the occult? Now there's an interesting question. I think it's the dark side, and the rebellious nature of metal. Black Sabbath started it by picking the name Black Sabbath and talking about occult things, and other bands picked up on that darkness, which works really well with the music. As Rob Halford once said, you can't really be from Birmingham, play heavy metal and sing about flowers. Somehow it works with the music. You get very few true Satanic worshippers in metal—it's all about image. But it just works with the music. The extremity of horror works with the extremity of metal. It combines so well.

I think it also played a part in the macho presentation of metal. It didn't have any shock value—it was like Dennis Wheatley or Hammer horror. So there was no shock inside the metal community, but outside, people were: "How can you talk about Satan like that?" It was just fun. "You're messing with things you don't understand"? Come on. There was a *Newsnight* interview with Venom, and Paxman asked: "Are you Satanists?" "Of course we are!" In their Geordie [Newcastle] accents. They were not at all. Not one bit.

ABADDON: It was a hangover from the Judas Priest thing. Judas Priest were in court over the suicide case [in 1990, they were sued in Nevada by the families of two fans who shot themselves, the families claiming the boys had been compelled by backwards messaging on records. The

case was dismissed]. They couldn't speak about it to the press because it was an open case. We were the next best down the line. And the first thing Jeremy Paxman said was, "Are you a Satanist?" And I said, "Yeah." They had this guy, a priest I think he was, from Birmingham. He had a lot of equipment to play records backwards. Paxman said, "You can't deny this. You can clearly hear what you're saying!"

And I said, "Yeah, but that's on a song called 'In League with Satan' and it's off an album called *Welcome to Hell*. It's written there in English on the front cover. You don't have to spend thousands of pounds of other people's money in order to say that. If you don't want your kids to hear it, it's written there in English on the front cover, there's a pentagram, it's got lyrics on the back—'We spit at the virgin you worship!' It's right there. We're not hiding anything. If we play stuff backwards it's as an effect. It's not to preach to anybody. We're a Satanic band singing Satanic lyrics and playing as heavy and as fast as we possibly can."

MANTAS: Do you know one of the most embarrassing things? One of the most embarrassing things for me was when I see fucking Abaddon on the Jeremy Paxman show on fucking BBC news. "So, Mr. Abaddon are you a Satanist?" "Yes." He's no more a fucking Satanist than my cat! Fuck off ! None of us were, don't give me that bullshit.

PHIL ALEXANDER (fan, Kerrang! editor): It felt really dangerous. It felt completely at odds with everything else that was out there. And it sounds so absurd to say that now. When you listen to them now, what do you hear? You hear fairly normal stuff, in a lot of ways—it doesn't feel completely groundbreaking or insane or anything like that. But when you heard "In League with Satan" in 1981, even the title was just like, "Is this real?" Obviously, there had been bands with Satanic connotations and what have you. It's hard not to talk about Sabbath in relation to that. But Venom's rawness and lyrical stance was so extreme. It felt completely different to everything else. It also felt as though it was ours. That's the biggest thing.

TOM GABRIEL WARRIOR (fan, founder of Hellhammer, Celtic Frost, and Triptykon): I can only speak for ourselves, but for us [the occult element of NWOBHM] was massive. We already felt with Black Sabbath that these topics suited that kind of music very well,

the heavier edge of music. We were not Satanists—we were very much against organized religion in any shape or form. Nonetheless, the lyrical topic matched not only our personal interests but it really fit the music like a glove. Of course, many of these bands just used it as an image, but bands like Witchfynde were immeasurably important to us and have influenced me for the rest of my life.

MONTALO: People get curious about how things are and why things happen. They are just mystified by it, and it has a particular allure to certain people. It's a matter of trying to control the energies inside yourself, and if you go too much down the left-side energy you're going to get caught up in all this negativity and possessions. You've got to learn to control these energies so you stay in the center, so you don't go to the negative and demonic, or to the right, and the apparitions type of thing. I still practice [Wicca].

ANDRO COULTON (bass, Witchfynde): The name is an unconventional spelling. It was done that way before I was even in the band. I think they just wanted to be different and not just be like the film *Witchfinder General*, which is where it came from originally, the Hammer horror film. They wanted to make it more Olde English with the "y" and the "e" at the end. The "e" isn't pronounced at all, so it's just Witchfind. It did cause some problems, but the fans who'd been with us since the mid-'70s knew.

And it's actually in the song "Into the Ages of the Ages." They then thought that was called "Witchfynde." But it wasn't. "Into the Ages of the Ages" is the Wiccan equivalent of Amen. It's in three sections, and in the center one, after the spoken-word part, we had incense burners onstage with a tube clanging out in time. It was more like a ritual than anything else. It was probably more occult back in the day than it was by the time we ended up in the New Wave of British Heavy Metal.

MONTALO: Originally, we had a sort of a stage show. We had props—candelabras and incense burners and things like that. And we used to have different people come on stage, models and people like that, a bit bizarrely. And then we went through a stage of having dancers as well. It was only really when we went on the Def Leppard tour that we had to slim it all down and get back to doing rock. The people who came on stage used to act out parts of the songs. Sounds a bit bizarre now, with

The mysterious moods of WITCHFYNDE: Give 'Em Hell *(1980) and* Lords of Sin *(1984).*

the health and safety, but they used to present the vocalist with swords or regalia, and things like that. I guess we got a reputation for being a theatrical band—that was all part of it in the initial stages. It was more theatrical. Even the simple thing of having candles on stage is a no-no these days because of health and safety.

TOM GABRIEL WARRIOR: It was the mystery, with Witchfynde. You have to realize we are talking about the time before Wikipedia and YouTube, and you would only know about these bands from what was on the back of a seven-inch single or the back of an album, which usually was very little. You would read lyrics and interpret all kinds of things, and fill the gaps with your own fantasy. But that was the appeal: to not know every detail, and to think these bands are mysterious. They come from somewhere in the British Isles and you knew what it looked like over there. You knew the graveyards, and everything in your mind matched it. There again, Black Sabbath had done it, but they all did it in a more modern and advanced way. They took it one step further and it was like a magnet to us.

ANDRO COULTON: For years, we only played in Derbyshire. At Cromford, near Matlock, there was the Black Rocks Club. That was a small club open on a Friday night. Rock only, one band on, and a disco. Then you'd got the Monsal Head Hotel, which back then was a bit of a dump. They had regular rock nights there. We played in Buxton, we played in the mining areas of east Derbyshire, it was amazing—we used to do one pub where the landlord said, "If they like you they'll clap, if they don't like you they'll throw bottles." We used to fill that one. We'd go back and we were immediately asked to go back again. We were filling the place. That shut because the landlord was jailed for setting fire to a barn to get insurance money. He was also a volunteer firefighter.

We moved down to the Brimington Tavern, just outside Chesterfield, which became our home gig. The last time we played there, after the Def Leppard tour in early 1980, we were four times over the fire limit. We had a massive fan base in the Nottingham and Derby area. We played a lot of gigs in Nottinghamshire. And then we extended it out. The *Melody Maker* gig guide always gave the phone number of the gig, and we used to phone them up. So we played in south Wales, in Ellesmere Port, Canterbury. But we never played in London. Everywhere else.

We had a big, massive fan base in Thetford. First time we played the Music Machine in '79, we were first on. Iron Maiden second, and Saxon top of the bill. We came out and there was a big rush to the front of the stage, and it was all these kids from Thetford. It felt like a home gig. So we did have quite a big following.

DAVE HILL: The music room at the Brimington Tavern was about as big as a small front room. Imagine a drum riser with the drums on it. We had a piece cut out of the front of this drum riser, and before we came out the lights went down. Drummer gets on the riser. But then the roadies push out to the front of the drum riser this grave, from underneath it, and I'm in this grave and I'm covered over by newspaper and leaves. The lights would come up, the drummer behind. I would put my hand against the newspaper to give the impression someone is going to rise. And they'd burst out. It wasn't a con, just a grave on a little trolley.

At the Brimington Tavern, there was a fireplace, and to get underneath the drum riser, it was so tight that I actually had to get into the fireplace. It was rammed—which probably meant twenty people. And when I managed to get out of the grave, the crowd were behind me, they were in front of me, they were at the side of me. I was in the middle of this crowd, with these horns and this latex suit on. It was absolutely hilarious. It didn't resemble a gig; there was nothing resembling a stage.

KEVIN RIDDLES: Angel Witch got our Baphomet logo as soon as I joined [in 1976]. I'm trying to think exactly where that came from. I know it came from the same idea as the debut album painting. We'd seen it in a book, and it was one of the things stored away for the future, in the dark recesses of the memory palace, to surface later. But the Baphomet thing was very early on. It was days after I joined that we started talking about how we needed a logo. We needed to get something out there, and Kev came up with the idea of Baphomet because there was film out at the time where it was a main part of the film. It lent itself to what we were looking for. It was as synonymous to us as Eddie was to Maiden. When we saw the design, with Angel Witch over the top of the Baphomet, it just worked.

We didn't have a professional-looking backdrop until the Music Machine days. I'd worked at the Playhouse theater in Harlow and made some friends there. One of them was a set designer and a scenery painter, and we got him to do a full-size scenery cloth when we knew we were doing the Music Machine, because it was the biggest gig we'd ever done. It would have been the only place to hang something like that. Prior to that, I don't remember us having a backdrop. Until it was the full monty.

PHIL COPE (guitar, Witchfinder General): We had a Witchfinder General banner behind the stage. The banner belonged to Black Sabbath. It was about twenty-five-foot long and two-foot deep, and it was plastic. And we stole it—acquired it—from the Birmingham Odeon in 1978 when Sabbath were gigging there that night. As you walked into the foyer, it was up high, from one side of the room to the other, and it said Black Sabbath on it. We all looked it and said, "Oh, that's cracking." Sabbath did a great gig and as we were coming out, Zeeb [Parkes, Witchfinder General singer] got hold of one end and I got the other, and down it come and off we went. Witchfinder General got painted on the other side and we used that at every gig we did, that banner. Thanks to Black Sabbath!

A few years ago, when Tony Iommi got throat cancer, I was thinking of putting it on eBay to raise money for his cause, but next thing I know he was okay. I suppose it's worth some money today, but sorry Sabbath.

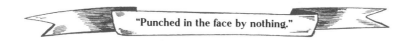

PAUL BIRCH (founder, Heavy Metal Records): Their demo tape popped through the post, and Ian Bridgewater from Langford's record shop in Wellington spotted it and said, "Paul, this is it, this band is extraordinary." It wasn't that they were terrible, but that the demos were terrible, but the songs were there underneath.

PHIL COPE: We decided we needed a record. We had to pay Paul £1000 for him to release the record, which back in 1981 was a damn lot of money, an awful lot of money. I think we had to sell half our PA to raise the money, but we felt it was the thing to do.

PAUL BIRCH: I don't believe that's correct. The way production works is that record companies specify and pay the cost of production, but they recover the cost of production from royalties. They only had a £2000 PA? The group never performed. Did he mention that? Money was recouped from Witchfinder General but they did not pay up front.

PHIL COPE: We recorded the "Burning a Sinner" single in somebody's garage in Aldridge in a matter of hours. Heavy Metal Records were pressing five records at the same time, and they set up the mastering to suit this one group. We had already put a lot of bass on our record, because that was our sound. And of course they just churned out the other four records. When it came to our record, the bass was that high it just distorted. The record came out awful, really, but in a way a lot of people tell me that was the start of doom metal, believe it or not, because it was that distorted.

PHIL ASTON (guitar, the Handsome Beasts): The first single, when it was cut, the grooves only went across about a quarter of an inch because they'd used some sort of device to master it without paying for a human to do it. Because the singer Zeeb had said he wanted to sound like Sabbath, they'd taken all the treble out. And they just left it thinking it would be alright because maybe the Sabbath fans would find it cool. There's a *Spinal Tap* element to all of this. If that film had come out any earlier, people would have thought they were a rival band. Like Venom, you'd never have guessed Witchfinder General would be so influential.

MALCOLM DOME: Heavy Metal Records was looking for shock value, and Witchfinder General's album cover for *Death Penalty* was an example of that. [The cover featured the glamour model Joanne Latham, apparently being killed in a ritual sacrifice in a churchyard, while topless.]

PAUL BIRCH: Joanne Latham, the month we launched that album, she was the centerfold in *Penthouse*. We were deliberately courting controversy. I had no idea that the whole thing would give rise that it eventually did to: "Topless woman in Satanic ritual!" We knew we had to create outrage, because outrage caught the attention of the Sunday papers. And it was the Sunday papers where they sold twenty million papers, in those days. We needed the outrage.

PHIL COPE: I think the first album cover worked very well because it was really early in the morning—it was about half five when we got over there. To be honest I was still half cut from the night before, because I'd been down the Royal Exchange in Stourbridge and I'd drunk a bit, so I was still out of it. I think it did look good, whereas the *Friends of Hell* cover, by the time they'd got everybody down there at Enville, a good way away from where Paul lived in Wolverhampton, the sun had started to rise. It was already half seven, a quarter to eight, and it looked like a comedy of errors.

PAUL BIRCH: I don't suppose I did them any favors with the record sleeves. Sorry about that.

MALCOLM DOME: Paul paid more money, I think, for Joanne Latham to be on the cover than to produce it. I think they were given a day and half to record the album. And how much money was spent on Joanne Latham for the album cover? A lot more than Witchfinder General were allowed to spend in the studio. And then he was shocked and horrified that people didn't think the album sounded very good. Well, sorry, but it's your fault.

PAUL BIRCH: No, the cover wasn't the most expensive thing. We spent a significant amount of money in the studio. How much did we spend? You're asking me to go back forty years, and from memory I would have said the two Witchfinder General albums cost between £10,000 and £20,000 each to completed production.

WITCHFINDER GENERAL: The stark reality, and the scandalous fantasy.

PHIL COPE: Paul Birch paid for the studio time, so *Death Penalty* was done in two days. We had Pete Hinton who had produced Saxon. He came down. Lovely chap. Really got on well with him. He was a good pool player as well. But Saxon and Witchfinder sounded completely different, and the bass got left behind.

PETE HINTON (A&R and in-house producer, Carrere Records): I was trying to remember whether it was two or three days with Witchfinder General. I suspect it was two days. It was the day the Pope came. I drove up from London to Wolverhampton, and the Pope was helicoptered into Wembley Stadium and I got stuck on the North Circular. Then, fuck me, he got helicoptered into Coventry City's football ground, just by the M6 motorway. So I was desperately late for the session. Held up by the Pope. And it was just a weekend. It was a very strange weekend because of that.

PAUL BIRCH: I was thinking: "I just have to push the boat out here, just in order to be able to get any kind of traction." Otherwise I've got no start in getting the record sold, unless people are talking about it. But if they're talking about it, even for the wrong reasons…

I remember the *Sunday People* took it up, the competitor to *News of the World*. They took it on almost single-handedly: this album had to be banned. Course, the more people of parent age said, "You shouldn't be listening to this," they created a market for it. But as long as people in the press were talking about it, because we knew we were never going

to get any of this stuff played. And really, what I knew as a promotion man was: you had to get music played on the radio, and if you couldn't, what could you do? Getting people to talk about it was the main thing.

PHIL COPE: We was on our local news, and to be honest I thought we were going to end up with a hit. I don't think my parents were pleased about it. And looking back on it now, I don't think it was the right thing to do, but when you're only twenty-one you go along with anything. But no, that kind of publicity isn't very nice publicity, so they weren't very pleased.

PETE HINTON: I got paid nothing. Nothing at all. I had become quite pally with Paul Birch. I really liked him and what he was doing, and I thought I would help him out. So I didn't get anything for that. He promised me points on the album. I read, after it had been released, that it had sold sixty thousand copies in the first week. I remember this so clearly. I phoned him up and said, "Sixty thousand copies? That's really good." He said, "Yeah, it's brilliant." I said, "I'm looking forward to my cheque then." He said, "I don't think so, Pete. They were all picture discs, and picture discs are exempt from the contract."

He might have given me a hundred quid for petrol, but that was it. If he gave me a hundred quid for petrol and we used two reels of tapes, that album cost three hundred quid, plus £50 a day for the studio. So four hundred quid.

PAUL BIRCH: What year was this? Did Pete say when he was last in contact with us? And has Pete got a copy of the agreement? All of that would be helpful. Otherwise, it's a bit like me saying to you, "Back in 1986 you never paid your gas bill in the September quarter of that year. How do you account for that?"

ROBIN GEORGE (producer and engineer, Witchfinder General): Did I get paid [for engineering Witchfinder General's *Death Penalty*]? No comment. I would have got per diems. But there were no royalties. Don't be daft. But that was Paul's style. I produced a Wrathchild album for him that was really special, I have to say, and he put it out, it charted, and he never did a second run. It sold out, and he never did the second run. That was his style. Get in the money. Go and do something else. I was promised points on Witchfinder, but Paul was such a sly bull. I didn't even bother trying to collect them. It was pointless. I'd have liked to see royalties off Witchfinder.

PAUL BIRCH: Pete and Robin were paid for their work. Pete was working for Carrere Records at the time, and was paid an advance. Robin would have been paid through the studio, because he was an engineer. We only paid producers. Engineers are the responsibility of the recording studio. So if he wasn't paid, it was for that reason. Can I just say, these people are not wallflowers, Robin George and Pete Hinton. But they have never complained to us.

ROBIN GEORGE: Did the band get any?

PHIL COPE: I haven't made a penny from either of the first two albums. Never made a penny. Not to this day. I've had an IOU—this is going back to 2004 or 2005—from Paul Birch for sales in the UK and abroad. But I've never had a penny come through. But what you never had, you never miss. I'm sixty-one now and I'm talking about Witchfinder back in the early eighties. It could have been a nice little pension if he'd paid me a little bit of royalties, but I think Paul's let a few groups down over the years. We're not the only ones.

ROBIN GEORGE: That's exactly what I thought he'd say, unfortunately.

PAUL BIRCH: Zeeb Parkes was paid on behalf of the group, and then Phil said he was shocked because Zeeb had never told him that he had been paid on behalf of the group. Phil Cope has been in touch with us recently saying, "You owe me royalties." We do owe you royalties, but you hadn't been in touch with us for 20 years. I'm not a psychic. Contact us and let us know. We sent Phil Cope an onboarding form for him to give us his bank account details in order to pay him. He refused to give us the details. What am I meant to do?

The fact is that Phil has been absent for 20 years, and then comes out of the woodwork and says "You owe me 20 years' worth of royalties." We're very happy to pay them. It is not unreasonable for us to ask for royalty onboarding forms after an artist has not been in contact for such a long time. I have spoken to you more about Witchfinder General than I have to Phil Cope or Zeeb Parkes in 30 years. They just have not spoken to me. Not picked up the phone. And the very first thing

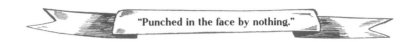
we hear from them is from Phil, it's hostile, and it gives no address or phone number or contact details, only a Sky email address.

We went to the Musicians' Union and the PRS and to PPL [the UK royalty collection bodies for songwriters and recording artists] and to the record industry, to the BPI, asking if anyone had got any details for Witchfinder General, and no one had. We identified each musician in the group and asked the union if any of them were members. We did the same with PRS to find out how we could contact them. What more can we do than that? I'd encourage Phil to sit down with us and talk about all his concerns.

PHIL COPE: We had a third album all wrote, but we felt at the time Paul Birch was failing to come up with the royalties for a lot of bands, including ourselves, so we decided to try and get out of the contract. We were advised to see a solicitor in Baker Street, London. We took the contracts down to him. He read through them. He ripped them up in front of us, threw them in the bin and said, "You are no longer under contract to Heavy Metal Records."

So we had an album all ready to record, but no other record company came in for us. We'd spent all the band's funds on the solicitor to get out of the contract, and the album never got recorded. And we all decided to carry on with our jobs and that was the end of the group.

Paul didn't seem too bothered. He'd signed quite a few bands by then, and a lot bigger bands than Witchfinder, so I don't think he was bothered. I was gutted. I remember going on a building site and seeing the cement mixer going in the corner and thinking, "God, I could just jump under a car." All my dreams had been dashed.

I had chances to join loads of bands or go back into club bands, but I didn't want it. That was it. Everything I wanted to do was with Witchfinder, and when it come to an end, that was it. My guitar went under the bed and it stopped there for years. In fact, it rusted away. When I got it out twenty years later, the pickups had all gone rusty. My old 1964 Gibson SG was all battered and worn.

BEN WARD (fan, vocals, Orange Goblin): Around that time there was a plethora of New Wave of British Heavy Metal bands that were all doing great music, but Witchfinder General always stuck out to me. When we first started Orange Goblin, we came from that doom metal

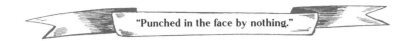

scene, and Witchfinder General had more of a kind of doom metal sound. It was based on the Black Sabbath template. The guitar tone was similar to Sabbath. Zeeb's vocals were very similar to Ozzy. The imagery around the band had a darker, more evil feel. In the early days of Orange Goblin we were really heavily influenced by Witchfinder General, because they encapsulated both the doom metal that we loved and the New Wave of British Heavy Metal. It was a combination of the two. They're a bit of an enigma, really.

MALCOLM DOME: It was very much the birth of doom. It's unfortunate it ended up on Heavy Metal Records. Had it been on a different label, not necessarily a major, but a different label, I think it would have sounded better for a start, and probably got more promotion for what it should have got promotion for—the band and the music, not the cover.

BRIAN SLAGEL: They had a little bit more of the blues; doom clearly came from this time period. You ask a band like Candlemass, who were one of the originators of doom, they would immediately tell you that NWOBHM bands like Witchfinder General were a huge influence.

TOM GABRIEL WARRIOR: I was such a huge Black Sabbath fan in the 1970s, and Witchfinder General were right down my alley. That's one of the albums that changed our lives. Also the *Soviet Invasion* twelve-inch was monstrous in its influence. The second album is also good, but the first album is a milestone, a doom metal milestone. They were unusual for singing about psychedelics, too, and that also connects to Witchfynde, whose music had a strong psychedelic touch to it. *Death Penalty* is perfect as it is. That ludicrous cover was perfect for us at the time, and the production, you can hear it's Heavy Metal Records but that's perfect as well.

PHIL COPE: You'd got Motörhead coming along, Saxon were a very good band, Iron Maiden was just coming on to the scene and it was speeding up the rock sound, whereas Witchfinder tried to keep the music slow and heavy. But to be honest it didn't really work because the majority of the people was moving with the times and they liked that fast music, and we got left behind. That was the only problem.

MALCOLM DOME: Were they looked upon as being hugely influential at the time? Not at all. But suddenly you had people like Lee Dorrian out of Cathedral going, "Oh my God, Witchfinder General! That album's amazing! Those albums really changed my life!" But at the time, they didn't get any respect. Pagan Altar the same—another band who when they were coming up in 1980, everyone looked at and laughed at. And then years later, people said: "Look at what they were doing! It's so far ahead of its time. It's brilliant."

PHIL ALEXANDER: The thing about those Witchfinder General albums comes back to building on what was already there. Lee Dorrian and I have talked about this previously quite a few times, but there weren't very many NWOBHM bands who basically go, "We really like Sabbath, and we're going to be more like Sabbath." But Witchfinder General clearly do, and they make their garage version of Sabbath.

PHIL COPE: I'll put my hand up and admit to copying Tony Iommi. It wasn't original. Because it was Sabbath with a few riffs altered.

PHIL ALEXANDER: It's raw-sounding. These are underground records, made by people in fairly basic circumstances. The Venom records are exactly the same. Despite Venom's insane pronouncements about wanting to be the biggest band in the world, they're not making records like that. That's not how it is. If you wanted to be that, you would have been Def Leppard, of course.

ABADDON: We had our Satanic image very quickly. I was bringing all this stuff to rehearsals early on. I wasn't going to be wearing stuff I would wear on the street: I wanted to look different. I wanted to be different, I wanted to have an Abaddon personality. I didn't want to have a Tony Bray personality within the band.

   With the whole Satanic thing I was reading a lot. Conrad was always influenced that way. The Satanic imagery with upside-down crosses and pentagrams just became…dead obvious what our first album cover and single cover were going to be. There was never any question that it was going to have a pentagram on the front. It was my artwork. The only thing was that the logo that I did was one of the first logos that you couldn't read properly. Dave Wood at Neat said, "Can you have another look at your logo? You can't read it." And I was, "Yeah, but that's the thing. People are going to walk into a record store, pick up this thing

VENOM in 1980
(clockwise from top left:
Anthony "Abaddon" Bray,
Clive "Jesus Christ" Archer,
Conrad "Cronos" Lant, Jeff
"Mantas" Dunn) haunting the
very depths of Wallsend.
A certain part of the band's
appeal lay in working out
whether they were really
as evil as they claimed.
RIK WALTON | ARENAPAL

with a gold pentagram on the front, look at the logo, go, 'What the fuck does that say?'"

I've never been in advertising, but I guess the first rule of advertising is: get it into people's hands. Get your product picked up, get it looked at. Then people have to choose to put it down again if they've picked it up, and it's in their consciousness, in their psyche. "Did you see that band?" "Yeah, I picked it up, what a pile of shite." "Oh, have you heard it?" "Well, I haven't actually listened to it, I just picked it up." "Well, I picked it up and took it home and Mam and Dad made us put it in the bin." I've heard so many stories about people who were scared of the album. They put it back and they had to go out the next week and buy it and thought, "Shit, I've been thinking about that all week."

MANTAS: I've read so many times how this member changed the course of the band, that member changed the course of the band, he designed this, he did that, blah blah blah. The pentagram, I mean I've heard so many times Abaddon say, "That's my fucking design." No, it's fucking not. It's the Sigil of Baphomet, it's been around for hundreds of fucking years. You did not design it, you monkey, you copied it off the front of *The Satanic Bible* and made a couple of adjustments.

Now it's as shocking as walking around with a crucifix around your neck, it's nothing, it's absolutely nothing. Back then it was something because nobody had stuff in anybody's face. You had Sabbath, you had Black Widow, I suppose there was plenty of bands dabbling in it before us, nobody really pushing it to the forefront.

CRONOS: Some people took it really badly. And when we came to do the third album, *At War with Satan*, where one song took up a whole side of the album, there was a local guy who was known for his beautiful handwriting, so I asked him if he would write out all the lyrics for the inner sleeve and we would pay him a large sum of money. He read it and he refused to do it because of the content of the lyrics.

HMV also banned the album, wouldn't have it in the shops. It reminds me of when my mum told me about how they wouldn't show Elvis on the TV except from the waist up. And you look today and what bands are doing now with beautiful Satanic imagery, like Behemoth. Could you imagine if a band like that had come out in the eighties? The police would have arrested them.

MANTAS: It didn't surprise me that people took it seriously. If my memory serves me correctly, the week after our first interview with *Sounds*, the letters page was doubled. Because there was so many fucking complaints about us—and a lot of people going, "Yeah, fucking great band." It was shock. Why did Alice Cooper do what he did? Shock value. Why did Kiss do what they did? Shock value.

It's like every kid wants to rebel against their parents, and I've spoken to so many—and I'm talking probably hundreds or even over the years thousands, because it's been a long fucking time—fans who say that their parents took their Venom albums and threw them in the trash, or wouldn't even allow them in the house, because they're blasphemous. I suppose, yeah, looking at it people would go it is fucking blasphemous. But nowadays, what can you do that'll shock anyone? Nothing. You turn on the news channel, that'll shock you more than any band or film or anything like that.

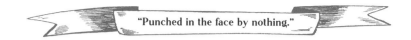

CRONOS: We'd heard of other bands who'd try to come up with slogans and stuff, like Angel Witch. It was too softcore—Britney Spears could've sung that, it's not even slightly scary.

MONTALO: I'm quite insular as a person, and we in Witchfynde were quite insular as a band. We wouldn't have gone out of our way to see any of these other bands. We did used to maintain a tight-knit relationship within the band. It was only if we were on the same bill as them that we got to see them.

ANDRO COULTON: Montalo was heavily into the occult. He was a member of a Wiccan coven. He had books, and he knew how to do spells and anything. I was interested in books before I was in Witchfynde. I went with Montalo to an occult shop in Northampton, but I never really practiced it, but I was interested in the study of it and reading what it was all about.

Gra [Scoresby, drums] was never really into it, and Steve [Bridges, vocals] definitely not—now he's a lay preacher in the Church of England and won't have anything to do with Witchfynde. I said to him, "If you look at most of the lyrics, you can take them as being occult, or you can take them another way." "Give 'Em Hell," there's nothing occult in the lyrics to that—it's about getting sacked and getting arrested. The only slightly occult bit is the first verse, "There never were three wise men," being the fact that they were magi, which means they were occult adepts. That's the only bit that is slightly occult in it. It got less and less as we went through the years. You've got "Tetelestai," which means "celebration," which we used to play last and people loved because it's really uplifting. But that's the limit of it. There was one member who was extremely into it. I was involved to a certain degree.

MONTALO: I just always felt connected to nature. It is still the case. It's just a way of life, really. Every one of us has got the energy within them to connect to the wider natural energy, and it's just a question of being able to harness that and control it better.

My parents were certainly supportive of the music, but there were times they got worried about certain involvements, but that's just how it was. It did cause some tensions, but when anybody gets into a routine

that's different to their own people naturally have concerns. But I came out of it fairly unscathed and it continues to this day. There was never anything particularly hairy.

ANDRO COULTON: On Halloween we used to go to Stanton Moor where there are standing stones. All sorts of weirdos up there. But I wasn't into black magic as such. We didn't do it for black magic, so much as just magic—occultism as a pagan religion. The goat's head is Celtic—it's occult in the sense that everything that isn't Christian is occult. But it's not the evil side of it.

It was a bit menacing up on Stanton Moor. There were practicing occultists and Satanists around at the time. Quite a few dodgy people. So we decided to bin it. It felt quite malevolent. We've always said, "Don't piss about with things like Ouija boards." You need to know what you're doing before you do anything with the occult because you can really leave yourself exposed. So we would try and talk people out of doing things unless you get an education before you start messing about with things. And you never do anything on your own, ever.

Montalo told me he knows of a guy who'd made all the circles, like in *The Devil Rides Out* [Dennis Wheatley's 1934 novel, adapted into a film in 1968], out comes a demon and he couldn't be touched because he was in the circle, and he burned the house down around him. So, you've got to be very careful what you do with all this. There are things out there you can't see. I was once punched in the face by nothing at an insane asylum.

TOM GABRIEL WARRIOR: I was in the Midlands in October 1983, visiting some friends. We walked through some town and my friend said, "Just down the road lives Montalo of Witchfynde." Just to know that was magical: this mysterious guy who plays this completely unheard-of music lives down the road. It was a really naive, innocent time, but not in a negative manner. It left a lot of room for your own interpretation and creativity because you always had to fill the gaps.

DAVE HILL: Mal [Spooner, Demon guitarist] was a far more avid reader than I was, but we read up on Aleister Crowley, and how in Paris in the twenties he supposedly summoned up the Devil. We did read about it. But what we did with *Night of the Demon* is probably from growing up reading Dennis Wheatley and watching *The Devil Rides Out*.

It was definitely the Hammer thing for me that started us to do that first album. Once the album was out, I must admit we were explaining!

There was an artist who did the *Night of the Demon* cover, and I thought it was pretty astounding when I saw it: wow! We'd sent down some of the tracks—it ended up coming out on Carrere with Pete Hinton at the helm—and we hadn't got a cover. And Pete sent it round to the artist. The first time I saw the cover was in the record-shop window in Hope Street in Hanley, and there in the window he'd got various album covers, and I saw six of what turned out to be *Night of the Demon*. And I stood there like a kid on Christmas morning with my mouth open, thinking, "What the hell?" It reminded me of the film *Carrie*. As soon as I saw it, a shiver went down my back. And I thought, "What have we done here?"

The demonic side, which we became known for, happened for me the moment I looked in that window and saw what someone else had thought of the material and how he'd put it into a cover.

PETE HINTON: The first Demon album came to us, and Freddie Cannon [head of Carrere UK] really, really liked it. The one thing I didn't particularly like about it was the mix, so I said, "Can I remix it?" I remixed the first album to give it much more of a rock feel. And also I directed the cover. The artist was Robin Behling, and he was from an agency. I used to brief him on what we wanted for the covers. I just said it had to be demonic. And he came up with that [hands reaching out of the earth to rip intestines from a cross gravestone]. I said, "How did you come up with that?" And he said, "I'd like to tell you I took loads of mescaline." It's quite *Carrie*, isn't it?

DAVE HILL: The press we got from *Night of the Demon* was very, very good, but it went very much down the occult side. We were doing things anyway, but when you start reading what the press is saying, you think, "I can't just walk out here in denim and leather, we're going to have to come in on the back of the album."

I always quite liked taking things on and trying to do something with the stage show. We were playing in little places, backstreet pubs. We had a drum riser with two crosses on, and I had to crawl round the back and then come out from underneath. But initially we didn't have a latex suit. I was made up, by myself, so for an hour—while the band were having a drink, and after we'd sound-checked—I'd be getting

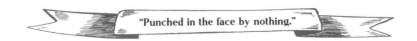

ready. I'd then crawl through the drum riser, and in front of the drum riser we'd have this grave. And I'd go and collect leaves from any park. I remember doing it when we played the Marquee, and it had been raining, so we had to dry the leaves out in the afternoon. We'd take them to the venue, and I'd go through the back of the drum riser, under the drummer, and there was a grave there that I came out of. We put some newspaper just above me, and then put the leaves on it. The light would be shining on it and I'd burst out. All this didn't happen on a Kiss budget. It was put together on a wing and a prayer.

When the album started doing well, we thought, "We must get something better together." So we got the latex suit that looked like it was covered in intestines, which I could pull on, instead of spending an hour doing makeup. And by then we had a roadie who could go and get the leaves and dry them out. I'd come out, and the horns would pierce through the newspaper, the leaves would fly up in the air. It was trial and error. I sang the first two numbers with the demon head on and the original one was so heavy, like an old diver's suit, and I'm singing two, three numbers with that on. I would take it off and my face would be painted. I'd have a skullcap on to do "Sign of a Madman," and rave around the stage like some kind of madman.

And in keeping with the first album, "Father of Time" was featured on the album, so my wife got me a white gown, and I got a mask. And then we added things as we went along. When I look back and see the old films it is quite funny. I think we must have been mad. There was no big money behind us or anything. And we did get some weird followers. But at the end of the day most people understand it was rock 'n' roll. Say you'd had ten gigs in a row, when I put on the suit again and got into the grave, and I'd think, "God, it's smelling a bit in here." Once we had a day off I'd get them cleaned up. But when you're lying in there, you'd realize, "This doesn't smell too good." Plus all the leaves we'd collected and dried. I was quite often glad just to get out of the grave, even though I had to wear a head for the first two numbers and try to sing through it.

DAVE DICKSON (writing in Kerrang!, July 29–August 11 1982): What strikes you first about this band are the visual theatrics, and, to be perfectly honest, they're risibly inept. Vocalist Dave Hill begins his act topped with a tinfoil goat's head mask, then replaces that

DEMON faced the twin perils of not being taken seriously, and being taken too seriously.

with a skullcap and a blood-spattered face before donning a "Father Time" mask for the song of the same name, which quite frankly looks plain ridiculous. I cannot conceive of the possibility that Demon take themselves at all seriously but I find their dabbling in the occult, their glorifying of the Black Arts and their usage of the symbols of the cross and blood more than a little disturbing. I suspect that if they really knew what they were making play at they would immediately reconsider their whole stance…Taken in its proper context of comic-book entertainment this is quite fun. I just wonder how many of the teenage fans the band attracted to the Marquee on a Monday night saw it that way.

DAVE HILL: I think he was taking it a bit seriously, but I don't think it did us any harm. But yeah, we used to get a lot of that. You worry when they're not talking about you. It all added to what we were doing.

PETE HINTON: I took Malcolm Dome up to see them in Leek. Malcolm was deeply unimpressed. But both Demon and Witchfinder General have this local innocence about them: "You may do things differently in London, but this is what we do." They had that non-London lack of sophistication and both bands were the same. Dudley and Leek.

DAVE HILL: Demon was on our *The Unexpected Guest* tour, and we were coming close to the end of fourteen dates. One of the last dates was in Leek, where I lived, an open-air gig on Leek football ground. So the local paper had put plenty in, and a couple of days before the gig they asked if I would meet someone at what used to be a graveyard in Leek. They said we'd do a photo shoot at midnight. So me and Mal turned up, and they were taking photos, me in the latex suit, and the police got wind of it. Next thing we heard sirens, and I was chased through these woodlands. I eventually came out of the woods, and it turned out I knew the police officer. He says, "Is that you, Dave?" We got cautioned. Next thing we knew we were all over the papers for blaspheming.

Then a chap rang from one of the Sundays wanting to come and take more photos in the graveyard. Looking back, it was a wonderful promotion tool, but we didn't know anything about it. Over the years it's like the story of Robin Hood: it's been added to. I've heard we were arrested, put in jail. It's become like folklore. Pity we didn't know before, because we could have played on it and promoted ourselves even more.

MANTAS: Do you know what? In 2018—April 30—I had a massive heart attack and I died in the back of an ambulance. I was clinically dead for five minutes. And what got me back was not God, was not the fucking Devil, was not a deity, it was the trained, skilled fucking doctor and nurse and paramedics who attended the scene. There was no conversations with God, no devils, fuck all. It's bollocks. The whole fucking lot of it. The more I read about this and the more I hear about it it's like, "Oh, fuck off."

TOM GABRIEL WARRIOR: We were really disappointed when in one of the early *Kerrang!* magazines Venom gave an interview and said it was all an act. And the interview was very comical. It wasn't really a serious interview. To say it cruelly, they were in a very childish mood, I think. For us, it shattered a world because we had taken it seriously.

They were really extreme. We thought they were really like this. And that was part of the appeal: the extremity of the first Venom album. It was very disappointing to see that it was just an image. Of course, many of these bands just used it as an image, but bands like Witchfynde were immeasurably important to us and have influenced me for the rest of my life.

9

"Are you better off being a superstar with £150 million in the bank, or just living a normal life?"

One of the greatest NWOBHM bands never
became stars, but Diamond Head—four school friends
from Stourbridge in the West Midlands—left a legacy
that dwarfed that of many more successful acts.

LARS ULRICH (fan, drums, Metallica): When Diamond Head
finally showed up on my radar in October of 1980, that went
somewhere deeper and connected at a deeper level. They really were
for me the ultimate of those bands.

Obviously, what we did in the early days of Metallica, there was
nobody closer to us influence-wise and inspiration-wise than Diamond
Head in the first six months or year when we started. We've never
shied away from shouting from the rooftops about everybody who's
ever turned us on. We started as a NWOBHM cover band. We started as
a Diamond Head cover band. The first show we did, we played four of
their songs. We have never been shy about talking about that.

MALCOLM DOME (writer, Record Mirror and Kerrang!):
Diamond Head was like being swamped by an orchestra. It was
something truly spectacular. They had world-class songwriting and
they had long songs that sounded quick. And they had the ability to do
short songs or long songs and make them all work within a Diamond

Head framework. And what they were doing was dramatic. There was a drama about it that really captivated you and didn't let you go. And every time I saw them I thought they were incredible. I thought they were going to be the band to come out of NWOBHM. And of course it didn't happen. I will always maintain Diamond Head were the band who should have come through from NWOBHM.

KEITH KAHN-HARRIS (fan, sociologist, and writer): That one Diamond Head song, "Am I Evil?," you can hear it resonating up to this day. It's because of the riffs. They just wrote brilliant riffs.

They seemed to be influential with the elite—at Wembley Arena in 1990, there was the thrash concert, the Clash of the Titans. And Dave Mustaine of Megadeth brought Sean Harris of Diamond Head onstage to do "It's Electric." And he was greeted with tepid applause. That seems to be a sign of how they were an elite metal obsession, forgotten in the grassroots for reasons I don't fully understand, when a lot of worse bands did much better than them.

Hardly anyone heard the first Diamond Head album at the time, but everyone who did formed a band, which is what they say about the Velvet Underground, and the Sex Pistols gig at the Lesser Free Trade Hall. Which is cold comfort if you are the band itself, of course.

BRIAN TATLER (guitar, Diamond Head): The band met at school. We were all in the same year. Col [Colin Kimberley] was born in '59, everyone else was born in 1960. Col went to a different school, but I'd known him since I was eight and we stayed friends—and we're still friends now, which is amazing. I've known him more than fifty years. I had to talk him into playing bass. He didn't play bass. I said, "If you buy a bass, I will teach you." He thought that was a fair deal. So he bought a £30 Kay bass, which is probably the worst bass in the world, but it did for then.

Sean was at school as well. He used to come round my house occasionally 'cause we had a tree up the garden, and he used to be able to jump out of the tree, whereas I was scared. It was too high for me. He was a good footballer, Sean, in the school team. Somebody heard him sing, on a school bus trip, and when I was looking for a singer, just before we left school in 1976—I was asking round 'cause I could play guitar a bit by then—we auditioned a few chaps. They'd say they could sing, then they'd come round and they ain't got a clue.

Sean came round, and he could sing. That's it. He's the man. It was as simple as that. We did a little blues jam and he made up a lyric and that was it. Done deal. Sean's the singer.

SEAN HARRIS (vocals, Diamond Head): They invited me down because Brian had heard of my infamous bus-trip singing, and we all went round his house to jam some blues riffs on guitar. That was it. A week later, in class, I was formally invited to form a band with Brian, even signing a contract with Brian and Dunc [Duncan Scott, drummer].

We began as a trio with no name, no songs, no direction, other than if I remember rightly, Brian showed me a black and white picture of Dunc and Bri dressed up like extras from a sixties *Doctor Who* episode, in front of a giant cardboard mock-up of a Moog synthesiser, complete with kung-fu dagger and a witch's hat. And that was it. We were off. We had no idea what kind of music we were going to be playing. We shared a liking for Lizzy and Purple, and stuff like that. But we didn't have a clue what we were going to do: learn it as you go along, make it up.

BRIAN TATLER: We had a biscuit-tin drum kit, homemade. A big black plastic winemaking tub for the bass drum, a biscuit tin for the snare with a chain on top. It had biscuits in it. We took the biscuits out and it went "CLANG!" and we thought, "That's no good." We put the biscuits back because it was like a dampener. It sounded okay with the biscuits in. And a couple of sweet tubs, and a deflagrating spoon we'd nicked from chemistry, which was a little thing that went on top of jars. That looked a little bit like a cymbal. So we had that for a cymbal.

That lasted for a bit, until we did our first gig in February 1977. As we got towards that gig, we had to pressure Duncan to get a kit. We couldn't go on stage with that; it would have been embarrassing. So I thought: "We'll paint a drum kit on to a big piece of wood and put him behind it." We didn't do that, either. So he borrowed money off his mum—I think it was thirty-nine quid—and there was a second-hand drum kit in the paper, a John Grey Autocrat kit. He bought that and off we went. We now had a group.

SEAN HARRIS: It was a bit of a mess that night, to be honest. We weren't very well organized. But it was fantastic to be doing something different to everyone else.

BRIAN TATLER: Apparently there were 181 people there, and it was 30 pence to get in. So we made some money. It was at our old school, High Park School in Stourbridge, where we'd all been apart from Colin, and they let us have the hall because we were old boys. We loved it. It was ever so exciting to actually get on stage and play to your mates.

We did all our own songs apart from one cover—by a band called the Tuff Darts, "All for the Love of Rock 'n' Roll." We learned that and did that. At other gigs we did "Paranoid" once or twice. We never did covers regularly. We'd do 'em for a bit then chuck 'em out.

We didn't do many gigs in the early days. The Mere Hall was in front of no one. We said we wanted to play the Mere and they said, "Well, come down on a Tuesday and we'll have a listen." We set up and started playing, and this bloke went into the back room after a bit and didn't come back out again. We were playing to no one. Instead of stopping us and saying, "No," he just disappeared and we never saw him again.

SEAN HARRIS: The reason we took the time [before playing live regularly] is just that it was all new and we were all learning to play, and we were developing our style over those two or three years. Brian and Dunc and Colin were still going to work. I preferred living on the dole and writing songs into the tape recorder, using my mouth to make distorted riffs. We were always writing. We never considered covers because we couldn't play well enough.

Sometimes I'd have the whole song sung into a tape recorder to take to Brian. "Helpless," "The Prince"—most of them came about like that. "It's Electric" came about by the archetypal way of Brian and me in his bedroom on a lovely summer afternoon—he'd think of the verse riff and I'd think of the chorus riff and that would be it. But "Am I Evil?" must have taken eighteen months to two years just to get all the bits together.

Ninety-five percent of the early songs we discarded because they weren't good enough. It was only later on that I started to develop my own style, when I'd got a bit more confidence and we'd done a few things, and I felt good about what we were doing.

BRIAN TATLER: The lack of gigs forced us to write. Every week we'd get together, maybe twice a week, and all we'd do is write songs. We'd put them straight on to cassette, and we'd listen, and we'd go, "That

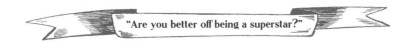
bit's not very good, we'll change that bit. That riff's good, put that riff there," and we'd learn the art of songwriting and arrangement by trial and error. We made these little cassette albums and we kept doing that.

Eventually we'd have a gig and try the songs out, and we realized slow songs don't work live. If a song didn't work live we'd scrap it after one go because we seemed to be able to write quite quickly. I think we were a really creative band, and we seemed to be able to write a lot of stuff. There was a satisfaction in the writing, and I think we just got better and better and better quite quickly.

We played a couple of biker pub gigs and they'd all be headbanging. We knew then what our goal was. We had a style and a sound, and we were trying to emulate the classic seventies band, but move it forward a bit with the speed and some of the energy from punk rock. Priest had already opened the door with songs like "Exciter" and "The Sinner." We went down that route, trying to write fast songs to excite a crowd who had never heard any of our material before. That can be hard—it's different when you've got an album out and they know the material. But if they've never seen you before…We'd just go mad to try to excite them, and people reacted. We'd end up playing two encores. The early gigs, once we could actually get them together, were very encouraging.

SEAN HARRIS: Dunc was very soft. I don't remember having an argument with him or Colin, ever. Or even Brian in the early days. I was a bit of a bully, I suppose: "Get this done, get that done, play this like that, play that like this." And in the early days they didn't mind it. Later on it became a bit of a pain, I suppose.

BRIAN TATLER: Sean and I became the main writers and Colin and Dunc…it was a bit like chiefs and Indians. There were two chiefs, which was me and Sean, and two Indians, Colin and Duncan. They weren't as outspoken as Sean and I. And they weren't as inquisitive, questioning everything: "Why is the PA like that? Why have we only got a thirty-minute set?" Me and Sean would question everything. I don't know why we were like that.

SEAN HARRIS: I enjoyed being the front man; it suited my character, I think. I've got a big gob. I like bossing people about. I think I know better than everybody else. And I had a better perm than Brian. I liked being the center of attention.

Being in the band in the early days, it set us apart—we were totally apart from the normal day-to-day stuff, and you think it gives you the opportunity to be apart from normal society and be an artist. I liked the idea of that. You felt quite free, free to express yourself. Free to wear spandex in the middle of the afternoon, when you're nineteen. That's fantastic. You could wear one of those tied shirts that Robert Plant used to wear. Youth's a wonderful thing. You've got so much power and everything's ahead of you.

BRIAN TATLER: I didn't know what else to do, really. I didn't want to be a mechanic. It's a kind of dream, but you hold it in because you don't want people to laugh at you and scorn you. Realistically, I was thinking all along, "At least give it everything, because you never know, and if you don't, you'll regret it." I didn't want to wake up one day aged thirty wishing I had done this or that. I just thought, "Give it everything you've got while you're young, while you've got that kind of energy and enthusiasm, tap into it and go. And if it don't work out, it don't work out, but at least you've tried."

MALCOLM DOME: Sean's mum and her boyfriend at the time, Reg Fellows, comanaged the band. Very nice people, who did their best for the band and were very well-meaning.

SEAN HARRIS: My mum [Linda] was Reg's girlfriend at the time. They heard what we were doing, and I think she just advised him to take a look at us. He was a businessman who was into other stuff, and there was a certain point where we needed financial help, or at least we thought we needed financial and business help.

PETE WINKELMAN (friend of Diamond Head, owner of Milton Keynes Dons F.C.): Reg used to take seven sugars in his tea. He's not with us any more, but when I look back at the fact that he had seven sugars in his tea and did that probably thirty times a day, along with seventy cigarettes, it's not a surprise he's not with us any more.

He was a local businessman. He owned a packaging company that made cardboard boxes. He had the Jag, and some money, and a love for Sean's mother. That's what made him support the band.

SEAN HARRIS: I don't think any of us were that business-minded in them days. We weren't thinking about it like we would now, having a

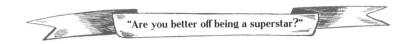

business plan. We didn't do any of that at school. We were lucky if we got O-levels [basic high school diplomas]. If somebody was interested, was prepared to come to the gigs and had an opinion, and was prepared to put his money where his mouth was, that's all you needed.

BRIAN TATLER: Linda must have got Reg to come and watch us at a gig. I think I remember him coming—he had a cigar. I think she said, "My son's in a band, come and see him. They're really good." He must have liked us. He was probably interested in Linda. Even though he'd been married and got three grown-up sons, I think there was a romantic thing going on where he was interested in Linda, who was divorced from her husband, who used to sing light opera.

Reg began to put money into the band. We sent a tape to *Sounds* in 1979 and Geoff Barton put it in his playlist. A really rough demo. We'd done a five-track demo in Kidderminster that we paid £25 to do, and we sent that to Geoff Barton and he put it in his playlist.

SEAN HARRIS: After he heard our demo, Geoff Barton wrote the amazing thing that there were more riffs in one of our songs than Sabbath had in their first four albums. That blew it out of proportion. It made us think the magical spandex was working. People were starting to get it. We were starting to get into a groove, too—we had a good set, good numbers. It was probably better that we hadn't been playing for those three years because it took us that time to really craft ourselves into a working unit. It's like momentum in football—we had a bit of momentum by then. We thought we were at least as good as the rest.

BRIAN TATLER: Peter Mensch of Leber–Krebs was looking for talent at the time. Def Leppard did the *Highway to Hell* tour with AC/DC, then two of the dates—Newcastle and Southampton—were postponed into January 1980. Leppard by this point had disappeared to start work on their album, and so I think Peter Mensch would have gone to maybe Geoff Barton or Malcolm Dome or Paul Suter and asked who was hot. And they would have said, "Diamond Head." So he gave the two dates—there must have been fifty bands he could have had—to us.

You drive all the way to Newcastle, you play to three thousand people who've never seen you before and don't know any of your material and have all come to see AC/DC and you go down really, really well. That was a bit of a light bulb moment. That was our thirty-third gig, and the

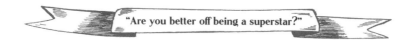

fact that they loved Diamond Head was, "Bloody hell, we can do this."
We definitely felt the world was our oyster.

SEAN HARRIS: Ah man, that was a dream come true. I'd been to see
AC/DC about thirteen times. And Dunc had even made a little cut-
glass goblet for them. We did Newcastle first, and it was sensational
because the crew were just so good to us. Rather than take the piss
out of us, they took pity on us—tuned the drums up for Dunc. They
made us so comfortable that when we got on to play, it went too quick.
Newcastle Mayfair, no colors in the lighting gels because the gels
hadn't come, and that was absolutely sensational.

We met them afterwards; they invited us back and passed around a
Coke can with some hashish in it, which I thought was very convivial
of them. They were very nice. And very short. All of them. Bon Scott
was drinking all the time, and popping this and popping that, but he
was ever so nice. We were a bit overawed. I was always overawed in
the company of my heroes; you never know what to say. They were the
biggest crowds we'd ever played to—real crowds. We couldn't imagine
anything bigger than that. Those two gigs were the first times where we
sensed, "Maybe this is our time." Two gigs with AC/DC and we could
stand on our own. The people hadn't come to see us, but we still went
down well.

We were probably a bit unconventional with our spandex, but that
was one of the turning points where you start thinking about yourself
a little bit differently. You're going to be more objective, looking at
what you're doing and how you're coming across, because now you're
actually competing with your heroes. It was nerve-wracking, but they
went so fast. You're so fired up and so nervous and so anxious, that you
don't notice the first twenty-five minutes, and it's only a forty-minute
set. Our songs were so fast anyway, but at least we didn't do a Little
Richard and do it as fast as we possibly could just to get offstage.

BRIAN TATLER: Peter Mensch duly came to the dressing room and
had a chat. And at the time, I didn't think anything of that. It was
interesting to talk to someone with an American accent—he may have
been the first American I'd ever met. He was interesting. And then in
hindsight, I think the manager of the main band doesn't normally go to
the support band's dressing room for a little chat.

I could see what he was doing. He had come to check us out and have a word and see if we fitted his criteria: "Are these guys ambitious enough? Are they going in the right direction? Do they want it?" He didn't get to manage the band. That could have been because Reg and Linda would repel all boarders: "We don't want anyone else taking our babies off us!" It could have been Sean going, "I don't want him managing Diamond Head, Linda's the best manager." I'm speculating there, but it's based on logic. We were great at those shows—we were a great band and Sean was a great singer. We had the songs, we had the singer, and that's what you need. And we looked good.

SEAN HARRIS: He's a manager. He's in the music business. But I didn't know anything. There were rumors, but there are always rumors in the business, ain't there, about stuff like that? People do come and see you and check you out and see if you're available. But he never spoke to me. Whether he spoke to Reg, or to anyone else, I do not know. I know Bud Prager was interested at some point, Foreigner's manager. I think Reg had been speaking to him. I wouldn't be surprised if Mensch was interested—we were quite hot at the time.

MALCOLM DOME: What summed Reg and Linda up as having no clue was that Diamond Head played with Silverwing in Portsmouth in early '81, and I'd got a lift back to London with Reg and Linda. And at one point, Reg said to me, "There's interest in America from this guy called Bud Prager, who wants to manage Diamond Head in America. Do you know him?" "I know of him, absolutely, he manages Foreigner." And Reg said, "Who?" And then *Foreigner 4* came out, biggest album in the world, they were huge. And he had never heard of Foreigner. Linda hadn't heard of them. How could you not have heard of Foreigner? Come on. They had no clue who Foreigner were. At that point, I give up. They meant well for the band. They did their best. It just wasn't anywhere near good enough.

BRIAN TATLER: We went to a studio in Worcester to record the first single, "Shoot Out the Lights." We did it in maybe a day, A and B side. Then Reg got the idea to do an album ourselves, and we could own the album rather than worry about a record deal. So he got this idea in his head that we would record the album ourselves, then take it to record labels and we'd license it to the label.

DENIM AND LEATHER   215

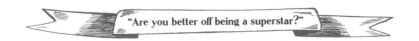

I didn't know what that meant. It was a handshake deal between the studio owner and Reg, that he would have half the publishing, and we'd get to have a week in the studio. And we thought, "Right, we ain't actually got to pay for it!" Whoops. We signed a fifteen-year publishing contract like idiots. So we went in the studio for one week and recorded seven songs. Mixed them. Stopped in a little cottage up the road. Just worked and put the album down.

SEAN HARRIS: When we did the album, we liked all of it, but the stand-out tracks were "The Prince," "Am I Evil?," "Sucking My Love," "Helpless"—they just stood out as a benchmark of the way we wanted to be slightly grandiose with big arrangements and changing tempos, quite out there as far as trying to be progressive, but at the same time bludgeoning you to death, and being quite tight and concise at the same time as having all this sort of stuff going on.

LARS ULRICH: What exactly they did on *Lightning to the Nations* and over those first couple of years was exactly the recipe for what I was looking for. They still came out of the Deep Purple/Black Sabbath/Led Zeppelin lineage, but they had a different kind of energy. Some of their songs were quite fast—"Helpless" and "The Prince" were fast songs, but they were not punky-fast in the way that Motörhead was or Judas Priest were on "Exciter."

"Helpless," if you're going to get into the specifics of it, was an F-sharp, which is a really heavy key, and it had this riff that kept repeating over and over. There was a simplicity to it but it was really, really just about the riffs. First and foremost about the riffs. Their songs were arranged a little more adventurously. So the songs would be these journeys. They had a singer who could really sing, and a guitar player who could really play guitar. And solo. And the rhythm section were very supportive in the right way. And they had just enough of a "We're the natural successors to Led Zeppelin" attitude.

MALCOLM DOME: *The White Album* [*Lightning to the Nations* is also known as *The White Album* because it came in a plain card sleeve] happened and it was great. It was absolutely superb. And I saw them do a show at a disco in Swindon. The place was packed and they went down so well they had to come back and do five encores. They had planned one. They kept getting called back, and in the end they had to say they could only play the songs they'd already played. "We haven't got any others!" At that point, I thought: "They're gonna be huge. Nothing's gonna stop this band. They're amazing."

Sadly things did stop them. *The White Album* is certainly one of the best albums to come out of NWOBHM. And it should have been the springboard to enormous success. They had an epic quality about them. It enveloped you. It was like you were in the middle of something truly momentous and theatrical. And their music was heavy, powerful, but it also had subtle touches. "In the Heat of the Night," even in demo form, is a song I still listen to and think, "This is so incredible." It showcased Sean's vocal range, Brian's ability on guitar to go in a swoop from something in your face to something much more laid-back and even sinister. They had it all. In Sean and Brian they had the new Robert Plant and Jimmy Page.

BRIAN TATLER: I used to think we were as good, if not better than, all the other bands. I used to think Sean was the best singer of the whole lot. Bruce Dickinson's great, but I thought Sean was better. I used to think, "That's a bit of luck, innit, that we've got the best singer in the whole fucking movement?" No matter what band I caught sight of, I thought, "Sean's better." I thought I was good—I was a big fan of Michael Schenker by this point, who was *the* rock guitarist, and so I wanted to be a bit like Schenker.

PETE WINKELMAN: I remember going to Warrington—was it the Red Lion?—a hundred miles from Wolverhampton. They played their set to about three hundred and fifty people in this pub, and they wouldn't let them off the stage. They literally wouldn't let them off the stage. They played their entire set twice and the place still wanted more.

I remember thinking, "If this can happen in Warrington, it can happen all over the world." Those kinds of little instincts you get. I was witnessing something very special, and it was to my great disappointment that I wasn't able to be a better influence on them, because I didn't have the experience at the time to push them in the direction of getting serious support behind them, because they would definitely have benefitted from that.

Dazzling DIAMOND HEAD (from left: Duncan Scott, Sean Harris, Colin Kimberley, Brian Tatler). COURTESY OF BRIAN TATLER

MALCOLM DOME: Sean had great charisma. Great personality. Great singer. Bonkers. But had that special something that made him stand out. He had the ability to front the band without overshadowing Brian. He and Brian were a tremendous team, a force to be reckoned with up front, and behind them you had a decent rhythm section. There was something about them no one else had, not Leppard, not Maiden, not Saxon. They had it all. NWOBHM was set up for them to happen and somehow they didn't.

BRIAN TATLER: The Holst intro to "Am I Evil?" was an afterthought. The main riff came first. I came up with that in my bedroom, taped it, and I played it to Sean and Colin, and whoever came round for our band practice. We used to do two a week—one in my bedroom and one somewhere else, someone's garage, Colin's dad's factory—and we knew it was good, so we worked on it. We built it. I figured out I could go up to B, then back to E would be the chorus. That same riff gets played for two and a half minutes—we never moved off that riff. But what helps is the drums move upside down and go back straight. And the snare goes on to a one instead of a two. We put that song together bit by bit. Adding the fast bit.

And at some point I thought we could put "Mars" at the beginning: we could do a big intro, and join it to the song with a guitar part. I wouldn't do that now. I wouldn't say, "Here's a bit where I'm just going to go widdly widdly widdly for a bit." I wouldn't have the confidence. But people love that bit. So what do I know? People like confidence, don't they, but you don't realize at the time that will work.

It became seven minutes and forty seconds long and it's hard to put myself in the mindset of what I was thinking when we were writing that song. It took a long time. It took over a year before we recorded it properly. We'd definitely played it live. And we added bits. I'd forever be trying to work out the solo, Sean would forever be trying to work out the lyrics. Sometimes I wouldn't know what the lyrics were until we got into the studio and he'd record the lead vocal and you'd finally think, "That's the lyric." It would be in flux up till then. He'd be constantly changing it. And I'd be constantly trying to invent the perfect solo.

In the studio, we changed the solo. And we wrote the bit where it goes from A to F to A sharp to F sharp and back to B. We didn't come up with that till we were in the studio and I wasn't happy with the solo bit. Then it was final. That was the finished arrangement. But we'd been messing with it for months and months before.

PHIL ASTON (guitar, the Handsome Beasts): There was a lot of jealousy of Diamond Head. The first album, there was a story that the money was put up by their parents. I mean, why not, if your parents could do that? And then there was the fact that they hadn't paid their dues in the way a lot of bands had. There was a kind of feeling that you had to do fifty gigs in Birmingham before you could even approach London to do a support gig. It was like some kind of apprenticeship.

Whereas Diamond Head just went straight to London. And people thought, "Oi, that's not fair! They've broken the rules!" But that was the right thing to do, and they had the song "Am I Evil?," with that riff, and that captured the imagination—it was mysterious. But as individuals themselves at the time, their egos were turned up to eleven, and I think that's what you needed to be noticed, really.

BRIAN TATLER: The album was sold via mail order and we sold it at gigs. There were one thousand pressed, and they sold out pretty quickly. Then we did another thousand, and they sold as well. And Reg and Linda didn't pay for the advert in *Sounds*.

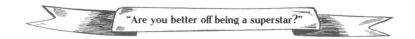
SEAN HARRIS: I am not aware of any such thing.

BRIAN TATLER: We had to go to a solicitor's office where Spotlight publications tried to sue them for the money. We got roped into being directors—I don't know what that meant, aside from take legal responsibility but get none of the money. We had to attend the meeting at the solicitors'. I vaguely remember it but I didn't have a clue what was going on. Stiffing *Sounds* for the price of five ads? What were they thinking?

SEAN HARRIS: We were surprised the majors weren't coming in for us. That might be because we were from the sticks, Stourbridge, and most of the majors are based in London. They want you to have management that they like, and an agent that they like.

BRIAN TATLER: I would imagine Reg and Linda were being a bit unrealistic in their demands, and labels would probably say no. I can remember conversations where labels would say they'd sign us for two singles, and if they didn't do well, that would be it. Maybe we had unrealistic expectations about what kind of deal we could get— Zeppelin signed to Atlantic for £200,000, and that was never going to happen. I don't have much business sense even now, so I didn't really get involved in negotiations. I hoped the management knew what they were doing. I trusted them to do it, and I would concentrate on writing songs and doing gigs. I didn't know what else to do. We definitely thought we should be on a major: that was the only goal.

  The one-thousand-copy pressing was partly about money, partly about just getting it out there. I suppose Reg thought, "If we can't get a deal we'll do it ourselves." But I don't know if that was a wise thing to do. I would imagine he turned up at the A&R guy's office with this album, and they'd be, "What's this? A band from Birmingham? A heavy metal band?" It don't work like that. If you're an A&R man you want to sign the band, and maybe pick the tracks, do a single, build the vibe. You don't just give them a copy of the finished product and say, "Here, put that out." Who does that? They'd want to pick the producer, the studio, the budget, the artwork, everything. They'd want all those boxes in place, not: "Here's the album, you do the rest."

  It didn't really dawn on me about the management situation. It took me a long time to realize that if the managers are amateurs no one will touch you with a bargepole. I didn't know that at the time.

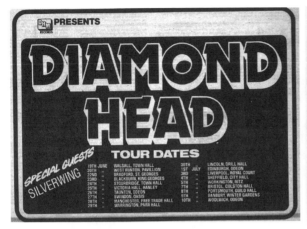

DIAMOND HEAD 1981 tour poster. Seventeen-year-old Lars Ulrich of Metallica flew from Los Angeles to attend the final date; Diamond Head was a true cottage industry, selling directly to fans via self-financed ads in the music press.

MALCOLM DOME: I think it's one of those things that could really have worked for them. There was rarity value. Everyone wanted to get a copy because it wasn't available. "How can we hear this?" So it could have actually brought huge momentum for them. But it was wrong, I suppose, because it was the best thing they ever did.

LARS ULRICH: There was an address on the back of one of those records: "Write to Diamond Head at Bagley Street, Stourbridge, West Midlands." And I did. And to my absolute astonishment I got a letter back from Linda Harris, who turned out to be Sean Harris's mother. And so the lead singer's mom was running the fan club, and I was like, "Wow. That's very cool."

BRIAN TATLER: We did the big tour of the UK in 1981 that Reg funded. It was a tour of Odeon-sized venues, but instead of using a proper promoter, he did it all himself, and we did posters ourselves. You know them big A0 [3' x 4'] posters? He printed one design for each venue. In Birmingham we had to post them ourselves. We had to go round in the middle of the night with a bucketful of fucking wallpaper paste and stick them on. We'd get letters from councils saying, "You have to take it down or we'll sue you."

We'd be doing places like Hanley Victoria Halls, which held about two thousand eight hundred people, and there'd be two hundred in.

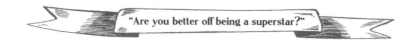

And he'd hired a PA, lighting rig, tour bus, so we spent about thirty grand on all this periphery. He must have just thought, "If you book a big gig, they'll all come flooding in." But you have to have sold thousands of records to do that, and we were just a cult band.

The jump to these venues was just ridiculous. It seemed exciting to have a tour bus and all that, but I just thought after a bit, "This is a bit shit: you're playing great big venues to nobody." There's no fun in that. And at the end of it all we owed Reg a load of money. It was his own fault, and he shouldn't have been putting his money into it.

SEAN HARRIS: I don't think we sold out anywhere, and we were playing Birmingham Odeon and places like that. I was a little bit disappointed that we weren't sold out, but we were probably overreaching a little bit. We still had eighteen hundred people at Hammersmith and fifteen hundred in Edinburgh. Manchester Apollo was almost sold out. I thought it was fantastic. That's when we thought we'd arrived. As a performing band, that was our high point. Brian would always remark about promotions, so he might be right. But I don't remember the venues being half empty, but I'm always the guy who sees the glass half full anyway.

LARS ULRICH: In the summer of 1981, after school finished, I threw it all to the wind and jumped on an airplane to London. I had worked as a newspaper delivery boy to save up for a ticket. There was a Diamond Head tour that summer, and I timed it so I could show up at the last show. I ended up at Heathrow the same day Diamond Head were playing at the Woolwich Odeon in July of 1981. I found a bed and breakfast, left my bag there, and made a pilgrimage to the Woolwich Odeon.

Somehow I got word to Linda Harris through someone in Diamond Head's crew that Lars from Newport Beach, California, is here, and is there a way to get a message to somebody in the band? Linda Harris came and found me and ended up inviting me backstage, and that night I ended up hanging out with them all night. I went back to my hotel, and the next day I took the train up to Birmingham and ended up staying with them in Stourbridge for the next four weeks or so.

SEAN HARRIS: God, he was a scrawny little chap, with a funny, strange accent.

LARS ULRICH: The show lived up to everything I had hoped in terms of the music, in terms of the songs and the spirit. It's a little fuzzy sometimes to remember exactly what the emotion was because you don't go super deep when you're eighteen. But I'm pretty sure I was probably a little surprised: it was a little smaller than I had expected; it was probably a little more DIY than I expected. I don't want to use disrespectful words, but it was a little smaller and more homegrown than I had expected.

If you read *Creem* magazine, or an issue of *Circus*, you would read about people that were touring and playing big venues and had record deals and were fully fledged, functioning rock 'n' roll outfits. But this was just four dudes who lived on almost the same street, went to the same school, and the mom and the stepdad were managing the band and running the fan club, and they scraped a few thousand pounds together and made their own record and printed them out on a white label and sent them out themselves. That part of it maybe didn't quite come across when you were reading *Sounds* every week. With the distance you build it up to this grandiose thing.

But I'm not knocking it, because it made me realize I could do it myself. I could go back to America and do this myself. I didn't know what a major label was. I didn't know about A&R guys. That was a whole different thing. That was the grown-ups. This was a different thing.

BRIAN TATLER: That was the positive of that tour. He was a fan. He'd got into us because we had "It's Electric" on an MCA compilation called *Brute Force*. He loved that track and decided that when the mail order thing appeared in *Sounds* he was going to buy the album. So he sent for his album from LA. We thought: "Ooh, we've got a fan in LA!" We were amazed at that. "Blimey, someone in America's bought it!" I don't think anyone had flown from America to see us before, so we were very impressed.

He came backstage, and we knew his name because of him writing to us. We met him, this seventeen-year-old kid, with a funny Danish-slash-American accent. And he was so full of energy and enthusiasm for not only Diamond Head but all things NWOBHM. I said, "Where are you staying?" He said, "Dunno, just come from the airport." So I said, "Come with us if you like, jump in the car." We were driving back home, because this was the last gig of the tour, when the Woolwich riots were on. A lot of people hadn't gone, and a lot of mums and dads said, "You ain't going to Woolwich when there's a riot on." But Lars had thought: "This is what I want to do."

LARS ULRICH: I ended up staying with them in Stourbridge for four weeks or so. First, I landed at Sean's on Bagley Street. His mom and his mom's partner, Reg Fellows, he was kind of the manager and she was the den mother. Sean's house was ground zero for the band, and there was a lot of activity there. Sean had a sister, she had a boyfriend; Sean had a girlfriend. There were people in and out. It was a pretty communal experience. And then the other guys would come over and hang out. They played some shows, and I drove with them to the shows. I became sort of the fifth wheel and hung out with them.

BRIAN TATLER: Everything was based in Sean's house in Bagley Street, Lye, where his mum lived. Apparently, that house had been bought by Reg for Linda and the family, and that became Diamond Head HQ. Sean had a lot of control now, so if Sean didn't like something it wouldn't be done.

LARS ULRICH: Then I stayed with Brian for a couple of weeks at his place, which I think was in Wollaston. That was a different affair. It was just Brian's mum and dad and Brian. It was very quiet. We would listen to records and stay up and watch Deep Purple videos.

BRIAN TATLER: I was still living with my parents, so he slept on the floor in a sleeping bag, my brother's old sleeping bag. He stayed for a week. We would go to the pub, have a couple of pints, and he went to Pinnacle, the distributor, and came back with about fifty albums and singles. I thought, "He's got loads of money, this chap."

All these NWOBHM records, we went through 'em, putting them on the record player. We would listen to them—"That's shit, that's good, I like that riff." Sean used to say Lars would get up in the night and raid the fridge. Eat all the food. "Where's all the bread gone?"

SEAN HARRIS: We had our bed on the floor, me and Vick [Harris's girlfriend, and later his wife], and he used to sleep at the bottom of the bed. I had this old record player, a portable one, and Lars used to lie at the bottom of the bed listening to "It's Electric." All night.

MALCOLM DOME: They had one guy, called Charlie Eyre, who was an A&R guy at A&M who was so in love with them and wanted to sign them to A&M. And when A&M refused he quit the company and joined MCA. And he first thing he said to MCA was, "I'm only coming to you if I can sign Diamond Head." So he left one company and went to another only to sign Diamond Head [in 1982].

Unfortunately it was the wrong choice, because he was so in love with them he couldn't see the big picture. I remember talking to Charlie when he was at A&M, and him saying, "The biggest problem Diamond Head have got is their managers—whoever signs them is going to have to insist they change manager." Well, Charlie signed them. Did he insist? I don't think he did.

Had they had Peter Mensch or Rod Smallwood, or a different type of manager, I think the story would have been very, very different. But Charlie signed them to MCA and either they didn't listen to him or they didn't want to listen to him, because Reg and Linda stayed involved and that was a huge error.

BRIAN TATLER: When we signed to MCA, it became apparent that they didn't like the management situation.

PETE WINKELMAN: Reg and Linda cared very much about them, but the trouble with being a parent is that you are overprotective, you only want the best. And if you only want the best, you don't trust other people are going to want to do their best. The music business is full of horrors and at the time they were genuinely trying to do their best.

BRIAN TATLER: It was a five-album deal. I think Charlie thought we were going to be like Queen or something, that we were going to be massive. He really believed in us. He had stayed in touch, and because he totally believed in us and thought we were brilliant, we all thought, "Okay, he's going to bat for our cause. He believes in us. Let's go with him." I didn't know the A&R men from the other companies—they hadn't made themselves known. But he'd been to see us five or six times, and he was just waiting for the green light. I don't think the advance was much—it might have been five grand.

JON DEVERILL (vocals, Persian Risk and Tygers of Pan Tang): When Charlie Eyre arrived at MCA it got worse for Tygers. Charlie Eyre's band was Diamond Head. He signed them to MCA. As far as we

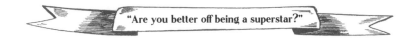

were concerned, he just didn't want to know. When all's said and done, he was doing what he thought was right, and I don't want to badmouth Charlie. He's not the first A&R man to favor one band over another.

SEAN HARRIS: MCA seemed very nice, but I'm not sure they really got it, in hindsight. But at the time they was as excited by us as we were by them.

DANTE BONUTTO (writer, Record Mirror and Kerrang!): They were one of the last bands to get a deal. All the NWOBHM bands were getting deals, and MCA eventually signed them. I remember going to the MCA offices and interviewing them when they'd just signed the deal, and it was almost like they were the last ones through the door, when they should almost have been the first ones through the door.

If you look at those early *Sounds* features, they were being hailed as the new Led Zeppelin. And I can see where that was coming from, but what a thing to have to carry with you as a young band. I don't know why it took them so long to get a deal, but they certainly weren't signed straight away. But if you compare their management to Rod Smallwood with Iron Maiden, and how important he was in making a positive difference, it just goes to show your paths can go down the right or wrong direction.

SEAN HARRIS: Reg made a bad mistake in the deal. Instead of going for big advances he went for points. So then we were all beholden to them for the budget. We couldn't do things of our own accord, which we'd always done. Wrongly or rightly, hit or miss, although we'd always been on a small budget, we'd always been able to do pretty much what we wanted to do. We didn't know anything about producers or engineers or any of that rubbish. We just used whoever was about at the time. So they picked the producer for the *Borrowed Time* album, Mike Hedges, and I don't know if that was the greatest choice in the world, but we weren't making those choices.

MIKE HEDGES (producer, Diamond Head): At the time I was super, super, super busy. I'd been doing the Cure, Siouxsie and the Banshees, the Associates, mixing the Thomas Dolby record. I was literally flat-out. I was flavor of the month at the time, quite honestly, because I was having a lot of hits. Charlie asked me to do it.

I was a very odd choice; it did seem like an odd fit to me. Charlie's reasoning was to find a different sound, instead of doing the same old same old. And quite honestly, in that genre at the time, everything sounded pretty much the same. Charlie's reasoning was: "Let's try and be a bit more adventurous, sound-wise." So there was a lot more digital reverb, and it wasn't just room ambience.

I know, at the time, a lot of the heavy metal fraternity were saying, "You can't do that." But you know what? Listen to Metallica records from two or three years later and it's not a million miles away, to be quite honest. The Americans picked up the heavy snare and digital reverb and developed it and have done it ever since. It was slightly ahead of its time, I think.

It got a lot of flak for not sounding like every other heavy metal record, but it did fairly well. Possibly not quite as well as it could have done. I always felt they could have had another single. A lot of people said it should have been Chris Tsangarides doing it, and if he had done it, it would have sounded amazing because he's a genius producer, but it would have sounded like all the other bands.

We were doing very long hours and everyone was getting very tired, but Sean and Brian particularly, my God they were good. Seriously good. Sean was banging out those amazing vocals one after the other. What a genius.

SEAN HARRIS: I can sort of understand a little bit why some people were a bit disappointed, because the material had been around for a year or two so they didn't consider it new. But making a record for worldwide release for a record company was new for us. We did the best we could with what we were given. I don't know what else the record company could have done. For its time, *Borrowed Time* is okay. It's probably not the tour de force it could have been. Why that is, I don't know. The production's not great, I don't think.

BRIAN TATLER: Part of me feels it wasn't as good as *Lighting to the Nations*, whereas the first album was hit after hit. *Borrowed Time* didn't have a lot of power. I think the two rerecordings of old songs were good, but the production—it was okay. I don't like to pour cold water on it because it's one of my babies. A lot of people, it was the first record they could get hold of because they could just go to the shop.

They didn't have to send off mail order. So it was the first album to a lot of people. And we were doing well by that point—we went back and did another Odeon-sized tour, and we were getting a lot of people. It was all going really, really well. We did Reading Festival, which was fantastic.

SEAN HARRIS: We were doing the best we could, but the horse had bolted. I don't even know why we went back into the studio to make a new album [*Canterbury*] when we'd just done one. They're paying for it so they must be insisting on us doing it, I think. Because I can't think of any other reason we'd be doing it. We'd only written three or four songs. The other ones had taken three and a half years to write—three and a half years to write one hundred and fifty songs of which about fifteen were any good. Now we've got three or four songs and we're meant to make an album? For the life of me, I have no idea why we didn't just go on the road. I don't understand. That was the beginning of the end, that was. We weren't ready for that.

I don't think we consciously changed direction. I suppose we'd been doing the other songs a while and our heroes were Queen and Led Zeppelin, mine in particular. We were blissfully unaware that we were cornerstones of a new movement in heavy metal. If somebody had told us what we were doing, then maybe things might have been slightly different. But we were just doing what we always did: trying stuff out.

Unfortunately now we were in a situation where we were going to have to do twelve new songs in six months, and it took us a while to put the material together and arrange it. We weren't able to do things quickly, and we didn't know we'd invented a formula. I was definitely a little ambitious on the *Canterbury* album. I wanted to be like Queen and Simon and Garfunkel and U2 and all them sort of things rolled into one. It wasn't a conscious decision. I think it was psychologically, physically and mentally the wrong thing to do, at the time.

BRIAN TATLER: There had been more than three years between *Lightning to the Nations* and *Canterbury*. And I think we had started to become more about the vocals than the riffs. We'd walked away from heavy metal a little bit. Instead of thinking heavy metal was everything, we were starting to listen to all sorts of other things. But it didn't quite work. What we should have done is been like Judas Priest: just be a

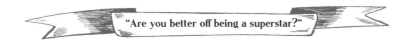

heavy metal band. Sean was starting to slag off a lot of other bands in the press.

SEAN HARRIS: I have been accused of that by some, but not by others, I will say, however, that there is a certain arrogance that comes with the territory of being the screaming front man. I actually believe that I'm quite humble and down to earth most of the time.

BRIAN TATLER: I was sort of trying to keep Sean happy: "Let's write an acoustic song, whatever. Whatever will work. We've got to write songs and keep going, and I'll try anything." I'm fairly open-minded, I haven't got blinkers on.

I don't think we appreciated what we'd got and I don't think we appreciated what we lost. And I don't think we appreciated songs like "Am I Evil?" for what they were—forty years on and it still sounds good. So you obviously had something, but we were prepared to throw that away because it wasn't successful back then. We hadn't turned into Led Zeppelin. We were still struggling to pay bills. So we were constantly looking for a successful formula.

And Sean was very much wanting to become some kind of pop star. He was a big Bolan fan in his youth and it became all about the vocal and Sean becoming a star, rather than knuckling down.

SEAN HARRIS: I came close to feeling a trifle "detached" whilst appearing to have a nervous breakdown during the making of *Canterbury* and Linda had to come to London to peel me off the studio walls so that I could finish the record, as no one else could get through to me. For the next few years I was a little "vacant," maybe, but I was physically and emotionally exhausted.

MALCOLM DOME: Had they signed to a label that was more formidable, more determined, more committed, had they had the right people around them at the time, I think they could have done something. The right producer, the right A&R, the right management. Yeah, they could have done.

It wasn't over by '81, but when *Borrowed Time* came out, it was: "Well…It's alright." But it wasn't quite the way it should have been. And it could not live up to the hype or get anywhere close. It wasn't well produced. Somehow they lost the excitement they had on *The*

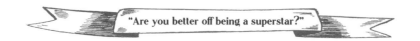

White Album, something that made you feel you were in the middle of a theater, and it became a good album, but no more than a good album. At that point, it had gone. And I think they knew it had gone.

So *Canterbury* felt like it was, "Well, we'd better try something different." And *Canterbury* was a better record, I think, than *Borrowed Time*. But they confused the audience. The cover looked like a seventies prog record. It was the wrong sleeve as well. I like it a lot, but why are you doing an album like this? You're actually confusing your audience. It finished off any opportunity they might have had to make any sort of headway.

BRIAN TATLER: And then the first twenty thousand copies were mispressed. But we should have been able to overcome that. Just move on and do some more. It was one thing after another, and we felt a little bit beaten down. And when it came out, Geoff Barton didn't review it. Paul Suter didn't. It was someone called Winston Smith at *Sounds* who reviewed it. Obviously, the big boys had said they didn't want to do it. "I ain't going there. I don't want to slag them off, so you do it."

SEAN HARRIS: We weren't in a good place. I ended up pretty much having a nervous breakdown at the end of that record, because of the work, and I'm sure everyone was stressed by it. Colin had been threatening to leave for a while. Ever since we'd gone to MCA, he didn't like the politics of the record company—and he was right— messing in everything. Everything had changed all of a sudden. We were like puppets on a string being rattled around. Six months in London, fetched and carried, to put this thing together, not knowing why we were doing it, other than we were under contract to do it. All the normal circumstances had been completely changed. We weren't strong enough to deal with it.

BRIAN TATLER: After about a year, MCA had started making overtures to get rid of Reg and Linda. I think they'd gone to the US to meet the head of MCA America, and the word back was: "They don't know what they're talking about, they're idiots." So they wanted them out. Sean was just so loyal to his mum that eventually MCA pulled the plug and walked away. They said, in the boardroom, "Either you change your management or we will drop you." Sean wasn't interested. He said to me, "My mum is the best manager in the world." I didn't know what to say to that.

SEAN HARRIS: I vaguely remember a meeting with MCA after finishing *Canterbury* and they wanted us to remove our management. I was in my "vacant" period at the time and so I just shrugged my shoulders and said nothing. There was only Brian and me now and Brian had an opportunity then to say what he believed should happen and he said and did absolutely nothing. Was that decision then made by me alone?

Under the guidance of our management team we made an album that would influence the world of metal music in a profound way forevermore. We achieved our goal of a worldwide record deal with a major label. We achieved worldwide renown, and for a few years we were an ace band getting better all the time, playing concert halls with an ever-growing fan base.

Now if you had asked whether we could only go so far with our set-up you may have an argument to make—remember we were all amateurs until we got the deal. The truth is we all believed that the record company, with its knowledge and contacts, would help take us some way towards where we needed to go, but that failed to materialize because the record company had no vision for the band.

BRIAN TATLER: I couldn't separate Sean from his mum. And instead of changing management we let them drop us. Stupid, innit? We got dropped on January 1, 1984, when they didn't pick up the option to make a third album. It's not entirely Sean's fault. It's partly my fault. What could I do? I couldn't tear them apart. It was impossible.

SEAN HARRIS: It's unfair, the way my mum and Reg have been blamed for what happened. They weren't perfect and they made mistakes. And, yes, you can definitely argue, and it would be perfectly valid, that a Peter Mensch would have made things better, but not necessarily. It's easy to say that with hindsight, but what is success and what is failure? Are you better off being a superstar with £150 million in the bank, or just living a normal life, and having a family, and not having been divorced five times? I haven't been divorced. I've got the same missus I had then. I've got two wonderful children. I might not have a great big mansion in Hollywood Hills. I haven't done what I should have done—I should have made a lot more albums. But that's what happens when you get disillusioned by the music business and everyone in it. Even your best friends lie about you.

I'm not bitter. I still love music. But, yes, I've always been a little bit upset. It's justified on the one hand, but unfair that they've become the scapegoats. We have to take as much responsibility—me and Brian and Duncan and Colin—as anybody else. It's easy to point the finger at a scapegoat. I find it difficult to talk about it because I think my mum has been unfairly criticized, when she was just trying to do her best, like the rest of us. Both me and her have been rightly criticized—I've been criticized for not wanting to let go of stuff, for holding on to stuff, and wanting stuff to be a particular way. Fair enough. I am a bit like that. That's why I haven't put anything out for about twenty years probably.

Criticism is fair when it's warranted, but if we all take a bit of the blame, that might be a bit more reasonable. All of us could have said no. Brian and I stayed together through thick and thin more or less for thirty years, on and off, so there must have been something good in it.

BRIAN TATLER: What happened later was incredible. Metallica covering Diamond Head has been my main source of income for thirty years. They've done four songs: "It's Electric," "The Prince," "Am I Evil?" and "Helpless."

When they did *Garage Inc.* in 1998, I went over to the studio where they were recording in Sausalito. They recorded "It's Electric" and played it back to me. I said, "How many copies do you think it will sell?" They said, "Five million, something like that. So the beers are on you."

Bear in mind the most copies we ever sold of a record was probably twenty-five thousand or something. Suddenly we've got four songs on an album that's going to do at least five million. The biggest metal band in the world name-checking you in every magazine in the world: you couldn't buy that.

SEAN HARRIS: Metallica's success is sort of a vindication of what we did. In the sense that we were right about what we were doing. We were right enough to influence the most important metal band of the last forty years. That has been a vindication. And the fact I get royalties means I can still survive as a semi-professional musician. That would be the reason we're not bitter.

LARS ULRICH: There wouldn't be Metallica if it wasn't for Diamond Head.

10

"I don't think I spoke to him after that."

The rising NWOBHM fueled several bands formed from the ashes of Deep Purple: Ritchie Blackmore's Rainbow ditched swords and sorcery for hits with Graham Bonnet as singer; David Coverdale's Whitesnake began a journey to stardom; Gillan became *Top of the Pops* regulars.

DANTE BONUTTO (writer, Record Mirror and Kerrang!): Ritchie Blackmore and Ian Gillan were always part of our world. They were never seen as being, "Oh, this is an older generation." They were very revered. NWOBHM was not trying to burst that bubble. They were not having a pop at any of the old musicians. They had massive respect for them. Because the NWOBHM guys were really good musicians, they were part of the same tradition, but they had a young energy and spirit.

MALCOLM DOME (writer, Record Mirror and Kerrang!): Blackmore, Coverdale and Gillan were three very strong characters who were already very successful. But I think they all took notice of what was going on in the scene and knew, "Okay, we have to change where we're going with this, because it's going to sound old-fashioned."

Rainbow was Blackmore and whoever he brought in. Whitesnake was Coverdale and whoever he brought in. They had some fabulous lineups, of course they did. But the groups were very much those three individuals. Gillan were probably more of a band, even though it was called Gillan. With the exception of Bernie Tormé leaving and Janick Gers coming in, they kept the same lineup throughout, whereas with Rainbow it was: "What mood is Blackmore going to be in this morning?" "You're out." And Coverdale was desperate to break America and wanted good-looking young musicians, so, "You lot are out and I'm getting this lot in." Coverdale is ridiculous, but he knows he's ridiculous and he's a total charmer.

RITCHIE BLACKMORE (guitar, Rainbow): There have probably been four hundred and five people in Rainbow. I've been told it's because I don't pay anybody, and I don't see why that should make a difference. You know, if you're into music, you should do it for nothing. In fact, that's the way the music business is going, isn't it? I thought artists were expected to play for nothing.

JENNIE HALSALL (publicist, Samson, Rainbow, and Monsters of Rock): I started doing Rainbow's press in the late seventies. Ritchie Blackmore was horrible. Ritchie thought he was some kind of mystical being and he really only liked girls with massive tits that looked a bit fairylike. Because I was really good at my job, I worked out that the less I saw of him and the less he saw of me, the better it would be.

I was up at a gig in Liverpool, and I drove up there with the manager, Bruce Payne. I spent most of the evening, if he was coming down a corridor, walking the other way.

RITCHIE BLACKMORE: My reputation keeps the people that I don't like away from me, and the people I'm friendly with, they know that I'm not that way. I'm definitely not a guy that comes in the dressing roomsaying, "Hey, everybody, what a wonderful life." I'm usually brooding about something which I think is wrong. I think part of it is I care so much about getting the music right, and things just have to be right, and if I think someone's slacking that's working with us, I get very upset about that.

I just can't go on stage and say, "Another day, another dollar," which I've heard a few people say. I can't go along with that at all. It's got to be as good as you can do. And to my own detriment, sometimes if I'm not playing well on stage, I'll purposely play even worse; I'll tear it apart, because I'm so disgusted with what I'm playing that I'll go the wrong route: instead of trying to make it better, I'll go the other way and really make myself sound bad. Which is a kind of a strange outlook, I suppose.

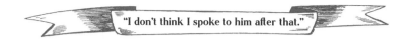
JENNIE HALSALL: It's probably right that he used his reputation to keep people away. If you're being Ritchie Blackmore, and if you are not the persona you are projecting, then you just put that out there and keep yourself to yourself. It worked well for both of us.

ROSS HALFIN (photographer, Sounds and Kerrang!): Blackmore was the best laugh. He has the best sense of humor. It's all about the windup. The problem is other people are at the end of the windup. I remember getting totally pissed in Denmark with Rainbow and going back to my room. And there was nothing in my room. No furniture, nothing. I had to go down to the front desk, and all these businessmen are queueing up to check out, and I had to go, "My room. It's gone." Pardon? I had to go upstairs with the manager, I'm barely able to walk, and show him the room. He looked at it, said, "So I see," and gave me another room. That's the kind of thing Blackmore would do. Blackmore was great fun.

RITCHIE BLACKMORE: A lot of the stories are exaggerated because people think, "Oh, we can jump on this one." I love hearing the stories about what I'm supposed to have done. And it's interesting how they can be so untrue. I suppose as long as people are talking about you, that's the main thing.

JENNIE HALSALL: That night in Liverpool when I was obviously definitely running away from him, he made me sit down and talk to him. But it was very odd. He used to do tricks—so-called magic—to people. I suppose he expected to impress people.

DENISE DUFORT (drums, Girlschool): Okay, he was weird, and we heard all the stuff and rumors about him, but he was so good to us, so nice to us [when Girlschool supported Rainbow on tour]. He even invited us out with him. And he showed us magic tricks. He was really nice to us. Everybody knows he can be an arsehole, but to us he was brilliant and he was a lovely guy. I'm not just saying that. It's true. We never had any problems with him.

KIM MCAULIFFE (vocals and guitar, Girlschool): Ritchie was so brilliant. He was just mesmerizing, and such a laugh. He used to have this man who would come to us and say, "Mr. Blackmore would like your presence on his side of the stage tonight." Then when we'd go

RAINBOW singer Graham Bonnet in coral red and man in black Ritchie Blackmore bringing the first Monsters of Rock festival at Castle Donington to fruition, August 6, 1980. ALAN PERRY | ICONICPIX

out for a drink afterwards in a club, it would be, "Mr. Blackmore would like you to join him at his table." He was brilliant. He was hilarious. I wouldn't have believed he was like that.

He did this trick. He put a coin in my hand, and he told me it was getting hotter and hotter and hotter, and I had to drop it because it got boiling hot. How he did that I will never know. He loved the band. I know most people didn't like him, but we obviously got him at a good time.

GRAHAM BONNET (vocals, Rainbow): Before Rainbow I was doing solo albums which were very successful overseas, but not in England and not in America. What happened was, they were playing a game one night, Cozy Powell [Rainbow drummer] and Ritchie and Roger Glover [Rainbow bassist]. What they were doing was spot the tune, basically. And one of the tunes was one I sang with my cousin Trevor Gordon as Marbles back in 1968, that Barry Gibb wrote, called "Only One Woman." Ritchie said, "Where is this guy now?" And Roger said, "I'm working with one of his friends, Micky Moody. I can get in touch with him."

So Roger Glover called me up and I went over to Switzerland to do an audition with a song I didn't really know all that well because I didn't know who Rainbow was, to be honest with you. I learned this one song, "Mistreated," and that was my audition piece. The audition was in a huge room with a balcony going around it. You could imagine the minstrels up there. It was a bit overwhelming for me because I really was a fish out of water. I went in there to the room thinking, "Oh shit, I'm going to fuck up on this, aren't I?"

So what I did was, I didn't sing on microphone. I stood in the middle of the room and sang it to myself, twice. And then they said, "We can hear you." Don Airey [Rainbow keyboard player] said, "Graham, this time try it on microphone. Give yourself a rest." So I did it another two times. And I remember the girlfriends who were staying with us all came into the room, and they were all smiling and I thought, "What's happening?" And they told me: "The job is yours. Now we can hear you even louder." When I went back to England, I said to my manager, "I don't fit with this band at all." He said, "But they've given you the job!" I said, "I know, but I don't know if I can do this—a whole album of hard rock." He said, "Come on, Graham!"—as a manager, of course, he was thinking of his own pocket.

MALCOLM DOME: The jazz rock of the Ian Gillan Band was fine, but it was really not going anywhere. Whether Ian was influenced by the fact that NWOBHM was changing the landscape and it was okay to play hard rock I don't know.

PHIL BANFIELD (manager, Gillan): Ian had come to my office, just before Christmas in 1976, with a coach and some members of the band on there, and a bar. So we had a drink and he asked me to come and see the Ian Gillan Band at Dunstable Queensway Hall. So off I went, and stood there and looked at the audience and thought, well, "Smoke on the Water" in a jazzy form didn't really work. So after a couple of drinks I went backstage to say hello, and told him the truth. Thankfully he was alright about it. The rest of the band I could feel their eyes on the back of my neck. But it was said and done.

JOHN MCCOY (bass, Gillan): At that time, I was recording the first Samson album. I'd done a lot of work at Ian's studio [Kingsway Recorders in central London], producing other bands and playing sessions there. I came across Colin Towns, the keyboard player from the Ian Gillan Band. I think we were in a session together or he'd come down to the studio and dropped in to listen to a couple of things that we were doing with Paul Samson. Colin invited me down to the Marquee to see Ian Gillan Band. I'd been a fan of Ian and we'd known each other since I was in a band called Curtis Muldoon who were signed to Purple Records; I think we did two or three support gigs to Purple, which I loved. I just absolutely loved that band.

Colin sort of intimated that things weren't well; IGB were having a hard time. I think their record deal had expired and they couldn't get a renewal. Ian couldn't get arrested, couldn't get a deal, because IGB had not been well received by the fans or the industry. When I saw them at the Marquee, it was exciting—the place was full—but it all seemed a bit strange to me. It seemed like Ian plus session men. Fantastic players playing incredible music. But the style of music went over half the audience's heads. They didn't get it. They wanted to rock, they didn't want to think. And I was one of the ones that wanted them to play Purple-type songs.

In the encores of the IGB set, they did "Smoke on the Water," and to me it was really not "Smoke on the Water." It was a strange version of it that just didn't have the bollocks. It's so hard not to be cruel, but it was cabaret bland. Everybody was playing great stuff but it wasn't heavy enough. It wasn't a great gig. At the end of the show, people started shouting, and they weren't shouting "IGB! IGB!" They were shouting "Gillan! Gillan!" The first thing that I said when Ian and Colin asked us to make a permanent band was it had to be called Gillan. It's so obvious.

IAN GILLAN (vocals, Deep Purple and Gillan): Colin was the catalyst for the change of lineup after the funky-jazz period we went through. He brought in a song called "Fighting Man" and started playing it at the Bechstein piano in my studio. And the other guys just started laughing. I said, "What's funny about that? It's great." But they all just poo-pooed it, at which point I fired myself from my own band and moved on with Colin. You've got to follow your feelings as best you can.

PHIL BANFIELD: A couple of months later I got a tape couriered over to me, and Ian had done what I has asked him to do: go back to being a rock star. I loved the tape, and he got what he wanted. That was the tape that became The Japanese Album [the first Gillan album in September 1978,

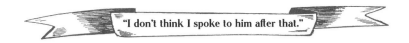

which was not released in the UK]. That's what the audience wanted, that's what his fans wanted.

JOHN MCCOY: We needed a rock hero, a guitar player. And I knew immediately who that player should be. It was my old friend Bernie Tormé. At the time, Bernie had a deal with Jet Records, with the Bernie Tormé Band. So I talked to our agent and said, "Is it possible to organize a support gig for this band?" I got the Bernie Tormé Band as the support act to Gillan at, I think, Brunel University.

I said to Bernie, "When you're doing your sound check, make sure you do something good. You know, you really perform." And he went, "Fuck off, what the hell are you talking about?" And when Bernie was doing the sound check, I got a hold of Ian and said, "Just come over here and listen to this guy." Bernie was playing on his own. And he did what Bernie does, which is what no one else could do. And Ian just looked at me and said, "Yeah, it has to be, doesn't it?" And I think that's where the band really took off.

IAN GILLAN: I saw Bernie Tormé when he was the opening act for an early incarnation of the Gillan band and it was a cold winter's day. We were going out to get fish and chips after a sound check, and I just stood in the gallery and watched Bernie standing there, but it was like watching Hendrix. He was so into what he was doing: he wasn't rehearsing or practicing. He was just into it so much that he would kneel down on the stage, because he got into the theatrical delivery. I thought he'd be perfect for our band, and that changed us and improved us. McCoy changed us and improved us. And Colin Towns did more than that. He was amazing.

JOHN MCCOY: When we sat down in Kingsway, sitting round on flight cases or whatever and had a meeting with me, Bernie, Mick [Underwood, drummer] and Colin, Ian said, "Right, well, the situation is this: everybody gets paid the same. Everybody gets an equal share." And I found that quite surprising. If Ian had turned around and said, "Look, I'm Ian Gillan and I get ten times more than you," we'd have still done it, because it was Ian Gillan and he had the best voice in the industry in that kind of genre. I was in love with what we were doing. So it seemed like a bit of a surprise for him to just say everybody gets paid exactly the same. I just thought, "What a fantastic guy he is, but he's a millionaire so he probably doesn't worry about that too much." To me, Ian was a millionaire. We went to gigs in his Rolls-Royce. The whole thing seemed perfectly legit. I didn't find out till too late that things had gone drastically wrong on the business side of things.

DAVID COVERDALE (vocals, Deep Purple and Whitesnake): I loved the orchestral aspect I had learned working with Ritchie and with Jon Lord in Deep Purple, with the classical elements they had introduced. When I say symphonic rock, I don't mean like Queen's drama—"Bohemian Rhapsody" or whatever—but taking something and exploring it, using a band as an orchestra, a rock orchestra, as it were.

Everything sounds so clichéd now, but that was what I was formulating in my mind, and it was very easy for me to pass on some of the offers that were coming my way. The biggest lesson I have learned in my life is to be patient, because I work very quickly once I make a decision. But there was no aspiration from me to compete with the level of volume that I had been working with. I wanted to be heard, as it were. I can't say Deep Purple weren't musical because, holy shit, they were unbelievable musically. I thought, "I need people to help me grow. If I can help them to spread their wings and fly, that's going to be the deal. That'll be the exchange."

If you look at the first Whitesnake, which was in essence put together as the Dave Coverdale Band, unfortunately—that was more of a promoter thing—it was to promote my solo album *Northwinds*. Because there was no support from media at that time. And according to record companies and the majority of music papers, there was no audience for a dinosaur such as me.

BERNIE MARSDEN (guitar, Whitesnake): I have to give him the credit where it's due. He was the one who didn't entertain the David Coverdale Band. He wanted a name. And we messed around for probably a month thinking of names. I think it was me who said, "Well, you called your first solo album *Whitesnake*, and you always wear white snakeskin boots. Why don't we call the band Whitesnake?" So it became David Coverdale's Whitesnake up on the posters. And by the time the *Trouble* album came out it was just Whitesnake. It was always a band.

NEIL MURRAY (bass, Whitesnake): *Trouble* had all these mixed influences, bits of fast, fusion-y kind of jazz-rock grooves, and we hadn't really quite got our direction. By late '79 into 1980 and *Ready an' Willing*, that's when I would say that solidified the band's direction, which I wouldn't say was very heavy at all really. It depends on your point of view. Certainly not compared to the new wave of metal bands.

My take on it, really, is that they were taking their influences from heavy rock bands of the late sixties and early seventies, whereas we were taking our influences from the music of the sixties, and probably from a wider range of music, with a lot more black influences, it has to be said. It may have got filtered down a lot, with the result that we sounded quite a lot like Bad Company, rather than B. B. King. But that's just the natural process of it being filtered through half a dozen thirty-year-old white men.

GRAHAM BONNET: Rainbow had started making [the 1979 album] *Down to Earth* when I joined. They'd started doing everything. I didn't write anything apart from the melodies. Roger would work with me, come to the hotel room every morning, knock on the door, and say, "I've got a lot of tape for you to listen to. I've put down a rough melody. And now you add to that." And that's how we did it. We did each song about three times each in different melodies, and Ritchie would come in the next day and choose which melody he liked the best. When that was done, Roger would think about words.

I'd never done words for something like this: I didn't know what you were supposed to talk about. Dragons? Chains? Whips? Not that there's anything wrong with songs about dragons. It was just something I couldn't relate to. I said to somebody, "It's like Jack and the Beanstalk or something, might as well sing about Jack and the giant coming to get him." I wasn't quite sure what to do, so Roger said, "I'll get on with it then." And so Roger wrote all the words, but I made up the melodies from Roger's rough ideas. I should have got recognition as a songwriter on the album. I didn't even think about that.

Once it was done and out of the way I thought, "That's it. That was a session." I wasn't expecting to do any more. But they called me up for gigs. And I thought, "Well, this is going further than the recording." Although I had joined the band, I didn't realize what was coming up.

I had never toured in my life and I wasn't expecting a tour. When I toured with my cousin in the sixties we did about four gigs, and that was it. But heavy rock bands tour all the bloody time. I didn't realize that was coming up, and suddenly these months of gigs were in front of me and I was very worried about it.

RITCHIE BLACKMORE: What happened with Graham was, when he first came into the band, we were basically a long-hair kind of band. In '79, everybody kind of wore denim outfits and had straggly hair or whatever. And I had misgivings about the way he looked, because I thought he looked a bit like a kind of a Las Vegas casino man.

DAVID COVERDALE: We had a rivalry to the point that Ritchie and I had a physical confrontation in Munich. I had just finished mixing [the 1980 album] *Ready an' Willing* and I'd flown over to Munich, and I was invited to see Rainbow. The rivalry was there in terms of success: they'd do four nights at Hammersmith, we'd do five. Just silly stuff. Silly, silly stuff. We actually had a physical altercation backstage. The promoter invited me in, and it got very, very, very nasty in the corridor. It was really uncomfortable for a lot of people and entirely unnecessary. I did not start it. And we were pulled apart and that was it.

We used to record at the Arabella House in Munich, and they had apartments above the Musicland Studios. Super studio. It was perfect. You could go down a special elevator into the basement studio from your apartments. On these apartments there were doorbells, and you could slide a piece of plastic across it to make it ring and then run off like schoolboys. But they scribbled a bunch of black magic shit on my door, and my child was there. My baby. They woke us up in the middle of the night, and my hand was really swollen from the earlier scenario. And I thought, "This is unforgivable. I'm going to stuff it down his fucking throat." And from then on that was one of my driving forces. I was always uncomfortable with that hate, but I perpetrated it just as much as the other side. That personal element really charged me. We went into a very unpleasant, unsavory rivalry, until I had the *1987* album which just blew everything out of the water.

NEIL MURRAY: They were rather silly, sniping at whatever. I think David was really dismissive of Ritchie's guitar solo on "Since You Been Gone." But myself and Bernie were still good mates with Cozy Powell and would go and see Rainbow. It wasn't quite our thing; it was a little bit too heavy metal actually. I wouldn't have gone out and bought Rainbow albums. I would have heard them, but it wasn't my cup of tea. There was rivalry in terms of ex-Purple people playing the same sort of gigs, and selling the same number of albums. There was a lot of focus on the ex-Deep Purple guys from journalists, and we had these T-shirts made up that said "Deep Purple" on them, and then in little letters. "No, I wasn't in Deep fucking Purple" for me, Micky Moody, and Bernie. We were kind of distant from it.

BERNIE MARSDEN: We built our audience gig after gig. From three hundred to five hundred to a thousand to one thousand five hundred. It was tremendous fun, and the camaraderie was great. Jon Lord is on record as saying it was the best time he ever had in a band in his life. We laughed ninety percent of the time. I remember reading stuff about the New Wave of British Heavy Metal, which we never ever associated ourselves with. Even though we did gigs with Saxon and other bands in that genre, we just saw ourselves as a rhythm and blues rock band, really.

NEIL MURRAY: To some extent, there was a reverence for anybody who had been in Deep Purple, but I don't think any of us in the band felt on the same wave as the New Wave of British Heavy Metal bands. You meet people who assume that because you're playing a similar kind of music, which comes under the same umbrella, that therefore you love the same guitarists as them or were influenced by the same bass players, and you often have to nod and leave them in ignorance.

DAVID COVERDALE: No question Whitesnake benefited from the New Wave of British Heavy Metal. Absolutely.

NEIL MURRAY: That's probably right, but it's not something I've thought about that much. To me at the time it seemed to be something perfectly acceptable for people to dance to rock music, for it to be on *Top of the Pops*, for bands like us to make fairly commercial hit songs. So in one sense, you're probably right. But in another, none of the stuff that got in the charts was sounding very similar to what the NWOBHM bands were doing.

GILLAN (clockwise from top center: John McCoy, Ian Gillan, Mick Underwood, Colin Towns, Bernie Tormé) on the Dorset coast, May 22,1980. BRIAN COOKE | REDFERNS

IAN GILLAN: I remember very well the excitement of injecting some new attitude into our music. I remember the terrible headlines of Emerson, Lake & Palmer and the pomposity of rock at that time. Punk was coming in and I used to drink with Boy George in the early evening drinking sessions around Holborn, and it was exciting. It was something fresh, going back to "Louie Louie" and the three-chord bash, heads down. It was all that youthful energy, which was fantastic. A lot of great young bands were coming up at the time who also saw it as a way of playing rock music that was rejuvenated. But Gillan wasn't responding to that. Like everything in my life I've never really thought it through. It's pure fortune. My songwriting and style has always been dependent on the people I'm working with.

PHIL BANFIELD: I was going round the labels, and I was being rejected, because at that point the New Wave of British Heavy Metal, as they called it, hadn't quite taken off. Ian came to my office. We sat down and said, "Okay, we're going to ring every label there is to see if we can get a deal." And Acrobat wasn't our best choice. They had pop acts. They had Dollar. But they showed an interest, so off we went and signed with them.

JOHN MCCOY: The *Mr Universe* album was quite a turning point. It was on an unknown label, Acrobat records. We were on tour and we arrived at a hotel in Bradford, went into the reception there, and there was a fax message at the hotel from Phil Banfield that the album had gone into the chart at number eleven. I literally fell on the floor in the reception. I just had to sit down and then I lay on the floor going, "What?" After years and years of hard work, for me personally getting to that stage was what I'd been working for: a hit album.

The *Mr Universe* album really set things on fire. So when we booked a Marquee gig and it sold out immediately, we thought we'd better do two nights. And that sold out. So we had the three-night stint at the Marquee in summer 1979. I remember we had an oxygen tank in the dressing room because it was full to capacity twice. There was such a buzz about the band. It was so hot, so airless in there. It was just, "This is what's supposed to happen, this is what a gig's supposed to be like." There was a real sense of excitement about Ian singing hard rock again. Everybody was very positive about him going back to what they called his roots. It seemed ideal. It seemed like the right band at the right time.

MALCOLM DOME: When Gillan emerged with *Mr Universe*—killer record.

PHIL BANFIELD: It was a huge deal for Acrobat. In fact it made them bankrupt because they didn't have the funds to keep the album stocked up, and they certainly didn't have the funds to pay us. They went into liquidation and we were released from the contract. Then I was getting lots of enquiries from labels, in particular RCA. They were offering lots of money, and then when I asked them what they thought of Ian's music, they had no idea what it was about. And I knew the people at Virgin very well, and I was talking to Steve Lewis [deputy managing director] at Virgin one day, and he said, "What are you up to?" I said, "I'm just sorting out a new record deal for Ian Gillan." He said, "You haven't come and seen us." I said, "You don't have any rock bands. You wouldn't be interested."

He went off and the next thing I knew, Richard Branson and Simon Draper [Virgin owner and MD] got in touch, and they wanted to meet Ian, and so Ian went, "That sounds good, because Virgin is halfway between my house and the studio at Kingway, so I can stop in." We went round to Virgin and they couldn't have treated us any better. All the staff came down and met him. They just made him feel very welcome. What they were prepared to pay wasn't as good as some of the other labels, but you could see the enthusiasm they had for Ian, so we signed.

IAN GILLAN: I suppose it was an odd group of people. The odder the better as far as I'm concerned. I love eccentricity. I love people who give character. You could find five people equally adept with their instruments, but it's the one with personality who's going to work best on stage, certainly. I remember that from being a kid, how I idolized Cliff Bennett's voice, but how disappointed I was because he just stood there immobile while the rest of the guys were rocking and throwing shapes and putting heart and soul into it. He was a very conservative character who didn't project very much and spent a lot of time with his back to the audience. I love people who are able to deliver on stage and, boy, we found a few then.

JOHN MCCOY: I got my image through the curse of alopecia, which is the medical condition which makes your hair fall out. When I first met Ian, when we were signed to Purple Records, I was a great big, hairy monster. I had long hair and a long beard. I think it was in 1977 I developed this hair loss thing and great clumps of hair would come out. It happened very, very quickly. Within about two weeks, I did not have any hair at all anywhere on my body. I was in shock and was told by medical people that nothing could be done in this case—it may or may not come back. I was offered all sorts of stupid wigs and different methods of curing it, and nothing worked. So when I discovered that the hair in my beard had started to grow, I let it grow anywhere that it would. It was almost as if it was a purposeful thing: I had no hair and a goatee beard. It was a gift that I didn't realize at the time.

But as soon as I had that image, my phone didn't stop ringing because everybody was talking about it. In those days, nobody in a band had a bald head and a beard. Also, I've always had a problem with bright light. And that's where these sunglasses came from. As I say, it was like a gift from God. All of a sudden I had this image, which had been dumped on me but worked incredibly well for me.

When I was working at Kingsway, and Ian would see me and say, "Hi," I don't think he actually connected me with the guy that he knew from Purple Records. It slowly crept up on him, the slow realization of who this lunatic was. But it kind of spurred me on, realizing the difference that image made for me. Because instead of being that fat, hairy bloke at the back of the stage playing bass, I was part of the image. And with myself standing next to Ian—in those days, he had very long hair—it was quite a surprising look, and then you get on the other side Bernie with his ridiculous performing image. I mean, he didn't look like anyone around at the time anyway. It was a very, very, very strong front-row image.

RITCHIE BLACKMORE: I was a little bit nervous about [Graham Bonnet's short hair and clothes], but he had such a great voice, we went, "Oh, it doesn't matter." His hair was extremely short—"Maybe he can just grow his hair a bit, we'll rough him up a bit around the edges." But he never took to that. I would say to him, "It's probably a good idea for you to just grow your hair a bit, look a bit scruffy, you know. We've got three months before we go on the road and it might help, for people to accept you in the audience." And he didn't seem to take that in.

And what happened, I think it was Newcastle City Hall, we even had a roadie guarding his room, because he was threatening to go to have his hair cut, and it was very petty, but it was like it became an obsession. I said, "We're going to have to have someone watching him, because he'll just go off down the road and get his hair cut, just before the show." And one of the roadies volunteered. He said, "I'll watch him, I'll make sure he doesn't leave his room." So he was like a prisoner in his room before we did the show.

And sure enough, he got out the back window, apparently, in the Holiday Inn in Newcastle, and he went and got his hair cut. So, of course, when I saw him on stage, I hadn't seen him before that, and sure enough, he'd had his hair cut really short. So he was doing it just to annoy me, and I was like, "You know what, I might just hit him."

I'm glad I didn't hit him, but it crossed my mind to hit him. Because I saw he'd gone out of his way to go against the grain; not that I should really be in a position to tell people what to do—it was just the thought, you know, the principle was, "Look, we've got to roughen ourselves up a bit for the audience," and he went the other way. So, I went, "Okay, you want to play that game, I'm going to have to hit you." But I didn't. I mean, it sounds really petty, but it's the principle, "I'm going to do my own thing and go against the grain of what anybody says." I just took that as an insult. I don't think I spoke to him after that. But that's true, that's what happened. These things, these petty things, come along on the road sometimes.

GRAHAM BONNET: There's a resemblance to the truth, but it didn't happen that way. It's a better story. It might have been Newcastle, it might have been Scotland. I can't remember. I was with my girlfriend, just hanging out in the hotel room bored shitless. We were going to go for a walk and I said, "I need a bit of a haircut anyway." So I went and got my haircut. And that's all it was. I got a haircut.

And as I said, we never saw each other until we were on stage. So they didn't see me until I walked on stage with my new haircut. Ritchie saw it and he disappeared behind his amps for the whole night. He played behind the Marshall stack. That was his protest.

The next morning, I was told by somebody: "Ritchie wants to have a meeting in his room this morning. A band meeting." I thought, "What the fuck is that?" So we went into the room, all of us, to see Ritchie. We all said, "What's up?" "It's Graham's hair." So the whole room bursts out in laughter. "You got us in here at this time in the morning to talk about Graham's fucking hair?" "But it's not long!" Ritchie wanted that rough and ragged look, and I was the opposite. I looked like a fucking game-show host.

Everybody thought it was so ridiculous, and Ritchie eventually got used to me having short hair. That's just the way he is. I think I said something like, "Ritchie, I'm in this band because of my voice, not what clothes I wear or how long my fucking hair is." I said something like that, but probably a bit gentler. Because he would go wild sometimes and it would end in a fight. So I would break it to him gently: "This is me and you are you. And I am not known for long hair and spandex. That's not my thing." It took him a while to get used to Mr. 1950s. That's what I am and what I've been since my brother came back from the barbers with a great haircut years and years ago when I was a kid, before I was old enough to get a DA. I wasn't going to change because of Ritchie. My manager said, "Calm it down! I don't want you to get chucked out of the band!" I said, "I won't be. It's just him."

DAVID COVERDALE: There was no conscious image-making in Whitesnake compared to other bands. John Sykes would later tell me that Whitesnake were not glam enough. That Tygers of Pan Tang would say: "Sounds too much like Whitesnake." And meanwhile we were writing songs that exist today. By the time of *Ready An' Willing* we had an extraordinarily secure rhythm section to build on, with Neil Murray. To me, Neil is the unsung hero. I'm always complimented on my guitar players, but I've had great drummers and great bassists. And if anything stands up from the early records, it's his amazing, melodic bass playing. He's a super musician, lovely guy. Ian Paice [former Deep Purple drummer] coming in was great.

With "Fool for Your Loving," Bernie had done an interview with B. B. King for *Sounds*—a young, white blues guy interviewing one of his heroes. And B. B. was fully aware that we'd done Bobby "Blue" Bland, because Bobby and B. B. were very close, and that one of the songs we were auditioning musicians with was a slowed-down version, which Micky Moody and I arranged, of this dance song "Ain't No Love in the Heart of the City" from Bobby Bland's *Dreamer* album. That came up in conversation, and B. B. said, "Why don't you guys write something for me?" That was when B. B. was working with the Crusaders.

If you listen to "Fool for Your Loving" without the tough guitars, you can hear B. B. But Martin Birch and I were sitting listening to it, thinking, "Actually, this is pretty good." And that was our first international hit. You can hear the collective experience of us all knowing each other, and having Ian Paice, who was determined to make a statement on his first Whitesnake record, and he certainly made a statement.

BERNIE MARSDEN: The biggest change was Ian Paice coming in. Paicey brought a kind of sharpness. And because I had worked with him for that year and a half with Paice Ashton Lord, I could formulate songs in my head knowing what Ian Paice would do with them. "Fool for Your Loving" is a classic example of that. And we had the late Martin Birch there harnessing the whole thing. Once we had that triumvirate of Paice, Lord, and Coverdale, with the three relatively new guys, that was as tight as it got. And Martin was the seventh member, without a doubt.

NEIL MURRAY: "Fool for Your Loving" was a very catchy riff. I'm biased in that I took a lot of trouble over the bass playing on it, and I wish there were ten other songs that are as well known for my bass part. So I'm biased in a way. I feel more attachment to it than I do to "Here I Go Again." But we should have had more songs as good as "Fool for Your Loving."

BERNIE MARSDEN: "Fool for Your Loving," Cozy Powell heard the backing track. He came to the studio and shook my hand and said, "You've got a hit." That was without the top line. He just thought it was so good. Gary Moore, bless him, said he'd heard it on the radio, didn't know what it was, and thought it was great. And then the solo came in, he said, "That's Bernie. This is Whitesnake." So there was an identity thing.

The overriding thing was that the BBC played it. I think it's as simple as that. The BBC put it on the playlist, so when people said, "The BBC doesn't play enough rock music," they could say, "We play Whitesnake." And they did, for two years. A lot of that is to do with Tommy Vance, but a lot of other jocks were fans, too, and were telling us, "You deserve to break through."

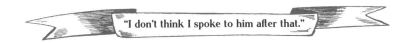
JOHN MCCOY: [That Gillan became a successful singles band] is probably down to me. I'd been working as a producer for a long time and I'd got a whole stack of songs suitable for singles. I suppose because we got the success with the singles, you think, "Oh yeah, continue in that vein." It was weird, going from like the normal rock, Marquee-type audience, to having kids on the front row, young girls and young boys screaming at the band, and it was a different world. But we were managing to cover all the bases at the time.

We were having fun doing the singles and I think it came as a surprise to Ian. At the end of the show, the audience quite unprompted, from nowhere, would start singing—"Whoa oh oh oh ohhhh." It reminded me of the old Gary US Bonds hit "New Orleans," and I thought, "This whole audience knows that hook. They know that little tune.' And they're actually singing it to the band to get them back on stage. And at that moment, I had a blinding flash of inspiration. I could hear the arrangement and Ian singing that song straight away and it was a pretty special moment. I mean, I didn't think twice about it. I have a mental pile of old songs that I like to rearrange into a new rock version. And that was one of them. And "New Orleans" became a big hit for Gillan.

PHIL BANFIELD: We'd gone to Friars in Aylesbury, where we were doing a show. All of Virgin Records came up. And in the afternoon, during the sound check, they did the song "Trouble" [a 1958 Elvis Presley hit], I don't know why, but they did it. Simon Draper was stood next to me, and he went, "That's a hit single." So Simon Draper, being the managing director of Virgin, told that to Ian, and the next thing we know we've recorded it. I remember getting on a phone call and ringing Ian in Blackburn, I believe it was, where they had appeared the night before. I woke him up and told him, "Well, we're doing *Top of the Pops* this week. You've just charted." He was over the moon. The band were over the moon then, as you can imagine. I also have to say a big thank you to Dave Lee Travis, who played the song every afternoon on his radio show. And the other rock 'n' roll covers ["New Orleans" as an A side, "Lucille" as a B side] were because of that: if ain't broke, don't fix it. That was the idea.

GRAHAM BONNET: Of course it was great to have a hit single. Who'd have thought I'd be recognized in the street once in a while? It was great for the ego. I thought at that point, before I joined Rainbow, I'd just be another guy making records for no apparent reason. But I never ever thought "Since You Been Gone" would be in the chart. Everybody hated it. They didn't want to do it. It was left as one of the last tracks. But it turned out pretty well and it became a hit record. As soon as that happened, the tours started coming in.

PAUL LOASBY (promoter, Monsters of Rock): The end trigger for Monsters of Rock was the 1980 Rainbow tour, for *Down to Earth*. This was in February/March. It gives you some idea of the madness here. They did two nights at Wembley and Ritchie refused to do an encore. The audience went wild, and I went up on stage to say, "That's it, the show's over, please go home." I was met by a barrage of seats—the damage was enormous [it was estimated at £10,000 and police made ten arrests while clearing the arena]. We worked overnight to make the second show happen, which it did. And he did do an encore. But I thought of all the power that was involved.

JENNIE HALSALL: Ritchie wouldn't come back out. You've never seen me run so fast. He decided he'd had enough. All I know is I had to answer the questions. I had to deal with the media that were there. I don't even remember if I had a quote. I know Cozy Powell was furious, absolutely furious. We never understood why he did that. But when the chairs started flying we all ran.

GRAHAM BONNET: I think somebody was injured badly that night. One of the audience. It was a bit strange. I think Ritchie had had a bit too much to drink and just couldn't be bothered. Which we all do once in a while. Back then everyone was boozing it up like fucking idiots. I don't know if he just was tired, but it caused a bit of a problem with the crowd that had come to see us. I had no clue about it. By the end of the show we all got in the car and went. So I didn't know until somebody told me the next day and I saw photographs and thought, "Bloody hell."

THUNDERSTICK (drums, Samson): Ritchie Blackmore didn't want to do an encore because he'd had a howler of a gig. He went backstage and jumped into his car and went back to the hotel. We'd had a good gig. We went down really well. We did an encore. The rest of Rainbow were milling around backstage going, "Where's Ritchie?" And he'd gone. And so they didn't come back. That's when everyone started ripping out the chairs and throwing them on stage and rioting.

When it was covered, in *Melody Maker* or *Sounds*, they said: "Great gig by Samson at Wembley Arena, and the support band Rainbow weren't too bad either." After that we were chucked off the tour. That was the end of that. Saxon took over from us and then they got thrown off as well. It was a prerequisite for working with Rainbow.

BIFF BYFORD (vocals, Saxon): It's difficult with Blackmore because he is a bit of a unique figure, so you take him as he comes. He can be a bit dismissive. We crossed paths with him a few times. We did a couple of big shows with him in 1980. He kicked us off the Wembley gig, I don't know why. The rumor is we went down too well, but I don't know if that's true. He was alright, but there were a few moments. Generally he just keeps himself to himself. Some of the antics—walking offstage—were a bit odd, but that's his decision, not mine.

STEVE DAWSON (bass, Saxon): We did plenty of gigs with Blackmore. We were kicked off the tour twice. Once in England, once in America. We were going down well, and they tried all different techniques to fuck us up—no water or liquid on stage, no setting guitars on fire. Blackmore went and sat in the audience at one gig. He were pulling faces at us to try and fuck us up. And that were the English tour. It just got announced we weren't going to do any more after the show at Deeside Leisure Center, I think.

And then in America we did a gig in Texas and next gig were a two-day drive away for us—they were flying. Ritchie wanted us to play football with him the next day. And when we said we couldn't possibly get there, we were off the tour. But he's an eccentric madman. Stuff like that is normal to him, I think. It broke our hearts because we were doing really well on that tour.

IAN GILLAN: Gillan was big and spreading and ripples were going out around Europe, Japan, and South America. Never made a dent in America.

PHIL BANFIELD: Gillan attempted to try and break the rest of the world. We toured Europe—that was successful. We went to Japan—that was so-so. Australia was okay. And then we went to America, which probably was the biggest mistake we made, because it cost a fortune to do. Ian was paying for it all out of his Deep Purple royalties, and we should never have gone. It's that same old story: you've broken in England so you think you can break the rest of the world straight away.

America was having so much success with their own bands—with Journey and Styx and REO Speedwagon. It was called soft rock or something. But they were all over the radio and for any British rock act to get on the radio was very, very difficult. Today I know that Iron Maiden are very successful in America, but it took them a long while. And they probably had a lot more money put behind the band than we did at the time with Gillan. Because Virgin wasn't established at the time in America, and Virgin had problems getting distribution, and there was only so much money they were going to put up for tour support. It's very, very expensive having a band on the road.

We couldn't get on shows. We played in Atlanta, for example, when across the road the Police were playing in the bigger venue. The Police came over to our show afterward and Sting had a photo with Ian Gillan. We should never have been playing in Atlanta the same night as the Police, but the American agents didn't research things. They just threw dates at you, and I'm probably just as much to blame because I didn't research it. Being an agent myself, if the Police were playing in Newcastle, I would be avoiding playing Newcastle that night. So you assumed, wrongly, that the agent in America was on the case.

JOHN MCCOY: When we first started, when we finally agreed it was going to be a permanent band, I think we were on £40 a week, which back then was enough to survive, incredibly. We all made contributions to the writing, so the publishing was a separate issue. And was kind of your bank account, your pension money—your publishing money was there. And the money that we received on a monthly basis was, I dunno, the highest it ever got was about £200 or £300 a week. But money from the record royalties and touring receipts and merchandising, we never saw anything from that at all. We weren't aware of what the income was, and there wasn't time to think about it, because you had to get on a plane to go there or go to a studio and record this. So the whole thing was built on trust, and I had no doubt whatsoever that things were absolutely fine. But unfortunately things weren't fine.

We were in Germany on tour in June 1981, and Bernie was able to see certain accounts and sales figures, and I think it blew his mind a little bit how much was being made that none of us were aware of, and that was just one territory. So over the next few days, Bernie started saying to Ian, "Where are the accounts?" And to Phil Banfield, "Where are the accounts? You've been promising accounts to the band to let us know the state of things." I don't even remember where the gig was, but Bernie was literally onstage screaming in Ian's ear, "Where's the fucking accounts?" mid-show. It really got quite out of hand, and we finished that show and Bernie wouldn't go back on until he saw the accounts: "Where's my fucking money?" The next morning, Bernie said, "I've had enough. I'm going." I said, "What do you mean, you're going? We've just been told we're on *Top of the Pops* tomorrow." And this day was the first day off in weeks, and we were all looking forward to just collapsing. "But you've got to go back for *Top of the Pops*." "I'm not doing it unless I get my accounts." And I tried to reason, but he just said, "F-f-f-f-f-fuck that. I'm going."

PHIL BANFIELD: We were in Germany and "No Laughing in Heaven"—I have no idea how Virgin did it, because it was definitely not a record that was going to get played on the radio—had become a hit. And we were asked to come back to do *Top of the Pops*. As Bernie told me later, John McCoy loaded the gun and Bernie pulled the trigger. McCoy encouraged him to go missing and said we wouldn't come back to London to do *Top of the Pops*. We had no idea McCoy had told Bernie this. So then McCoy said, "Don't worry about it. We'll go back and do it without him." And that's what we did.

At that point, Ian had said, "Well, if Bernie's doing that, he's fired." And we got Janick Gers down from Newcastle, and we sat in the hotel room that night with Ian and I think Mick Underwood going over songs, because then he was going to fly out to Germany with us the next day and become the next guitarist. Of course, then we found out what happened with Bernie, and that caused another rift between McCoy and other members, and then the arguments just carried on and on and on. [Note: Bernie Tormé died in 2000. In interviews before his death he said he left Gillan because he was unhappy about money, the final straw not being paid a fee to appear on *Top of the Pops* to perform "No Laughing in Heaven," but also said he was provoked into doing so by McCoy, who he said was the best-paid member of the band.]

JOHN MCCOY: When we got back to the UK, I spoke to Bernie and he told me he'd got this lawyer and they were investigating, and did I know that money had disappeared and not gone to the band? There were so many things you wouldn't believe. Oh dear. Some problems here. So I had to get myself a lawyer and Mick, I think, had the same lawyer. Colin was in a different position because he'd been around so long, and his songs were signed to Ian's publishing company. He had a different kind of business relationship with Ian that none of us knew about. Colin was squirming and embarrassed about it all. As far as I know, he was getting more than anyone apart from Ian. At that stage you start to examine things and think, "Hang on, this can't be right."

I can remember being at gigs where there were bagfuls of money, where the guys doing the merchandise would talk about how brilliant it was, and there were all these banknotes walking out of the door. Some of that should have been for me, shouldn't it? It sounds very naive, considering I had been in the business for quite some time. But as I said, it was all built on trust. I didn't doubt Ian for a minute that everything was fine and we would get accounted to and paid our due. But that wasn't to be. The accounts never appeared.

And on the last tour we did, Ian had started travelling separately from the band; we didn't get to see him until we were onstage. He had a bodyguard with him—what he thought was going to happen I don't know, but he had a guy standing at the side of the stage, he was that concerned. I think perhaps because of Bernie's outburst on stage, which nearly came to blows, but he had this ridiculous bodyguard with him, who was a guy called Jimmy the Con. He was a bouncer from a club in the Midlands. He was a lovely guy but not too bright, shall we say. That was weird. We were close friends in my brain. All of a sudden you can't get near the guy because he's got separate transport, separate dressing room, and you can't go in there. It went very sour.

PHIL BANFIELD: John, Colin, all of them were always in the studio hanging around. They'd be doing solo stuff, because Ian never charged them to be in the studio. Everything was just losing money. You can't run a studio just for you and your mates to go in and play there. You have to have people coming in. The bills have to be paid.

The best thing that happened to Ian was losing everything in 1982 and 1983. He lost his house, the studio, the whole lot. He couldn't have a bank account. He couldn't have anything. And he remembers it to this day. I took over all his finances, setting him up with new bank accounts, new bank managers, new this, new that, and I stopped him spending money. He is the first to admit: "I'm not a businessman, I'm a musician. I write. That's all I want to do. If you want to have all the crap of dealing with it, deal with it." So I did. That's why I'm still here.

The main reason we continued touring as much as we did was the band members were paid every week whether we worked or not. The band members didn't understand how much money was going out on a weekly basis. They all had their own personal road crew. Plus the other crew. They were all on wages every week. When you're running something like that, it was probably costing £3000 or £4000 a week, and when you'd play somewhere like the Rainbow you'd be lucky if you picked up £1000. Ticket prices weren't the same as they are today.

And the merchandising sales weren't that huge, because you had all the bootleggers on the street and they were very threatening people. You couldn't take action against them. The band thought, because they saw lots of people with a Gillan T-shirt on, that it was our merchandisers that were selling them. No. If you're out walking towards the show, and you don't know that's a bootlegger, and he's selling the T-shirts for fifty percent of what you're going to pay inside, what are you going to do? Things like that. And when you did 30,000 records to get in the charts, you're not earning the same royalty rate because Virgin are not paying for that extra record [The first 30,000 copies of Gillan's *Glory Road* album came with a free LP]. We had to pay for it. As my wife says, because she worked at Virgin, there is no such thing as free in a record company.

But they would get sick of being told there was no money. They would say, "We just earned £30,000 on a festival." To them it was just £30,000. Well, who paid to get you here? How did you fly here? You're all driving round in a limo now, because you didn't like going in a minibus. If you wanted more money, you should have said, "Let's stop spending it on this or that." But no. And you wanted better hotels. The problem is, artists complain about their managements because they took no interest. They wanted to go out and travel and have a good time and travel to the next show in as much luxury as they could and stay in the best hotels and then one day they get a bill. 'Oh, you didn't tell me it was costing that." You don't need someone to tell you how much these hotels cost; you're staying in them.

IAN GILLAN: It wasn't a designer group, and I think the oddity of it all, and the eccentricity, was part of the strength of it. It had a vibrancy, but it burned out—you can only keep that excitement going for so long, in the image sense. And of course the human chemistry was very volatile. I was probably the most volatile member, but we just hadn't quite grown up enough. We all had things to say and everyone made mistakes. I'm not going to name names. I just have fond memories really.

JOHN MCCOY: There was this thing about us not being able to continue because Ian had a problem with his throat; his nodes had gone and he needed to rest his voice. He told us partway through that tour. All kinds of weird things were going on, but I couldn't get close to talk to him about it because I still didn't believe myself that there was any problem. I just thought, "Well, Bernie has overreacted and I am sure it is going to get sorted." I think he has said in the past the band cost him too much, but at the time he wasn't saying anything at all to the band. He didn't speak to us. He just avoided us at all costs, apart from onstage.

PHIL BANFIELD: The truth about the matter is that he did have problems with his vocals, and a rest was ordered. He had to go to Germany and had his tonsils taken out, which was a scary thing for him as a singer. [Gillan himself has said accusations he did not have vocal problems were "lies."]

JOHN MCCOY: It all came to a horrible end at Wembley at the end of the final tour. It was absolute chaos at the end of the show. Everyone was asking, "Where's Phil? Where's Ian?" They left the show immediately and went. And it turned out on that night, the guys in the crew—lighting, sound, stage—were all wandering around saying, "Where's my money?" Because they expected to get paid. Everybody was confused. Coming offstage at Wembley, you think you've achieved something. But all I could achieve was to ring up and hire a van and load up my own gear out of Wembley and drive off into the night. It certainly wasn't rock-star status. It was very hurtful, in fact. I know people hear me talk about it and find it very hard to believe their hero Ian would do anything so bloody awful to his friends. But it's what happened.

PHIL BANFIELD: John McCoy is completely wrong about that. Ian was the last person to leave, alongside me. The road crew were in dressing rooms with the other members of the band partying. The road crew, on the instructions of the band, each personal roadie had to go out on to the stage and strip down the equipment that we had loaned from Marshall, and put it into separate vehicles to be taken away. No, Ian never left. I remember Mick Underwood and his family coming into Ian's dressing room while Ian's mother and everyone was there, and they were cuddling each other and crying, as you do at a farewell thing.

IAN GILLAN: After my last gig with Gillan, I went for an Indian meal afterwards with Rodney Marsh [former QPR and England footballer]. Rodney being Rodney, at some point in the evening he went, "That was great. I really loved it tonight. Great band." And then, with a twinkle in his eye, he said, "But it's not as good as Deep Purple, is it?" The next morning I woke up and called Jon Lord and we had a nice chat and the seeds were sown for a possible get-together. But it wasn't possible at the time, so I joined Black Sabbath.

JOHN MCCOY: I was very sad. Very disappointed. For all kinds of reasons. He ruined one of my favorite bands. I had always been a Sabbath fan up to that point. I couldn't even listen to it, it upset me that much. Up to that point I had been thinking, "Maybe he is ill, maybe his voice is going." But obviously not. I was devastated by that.

It had been the greatest time in my life. I had never been busier. I was absolutely snowed under with work, which was why it was such a big thing to start the Gillan band. I was doing good. I was getting loads of session work, I was getting production work, and I totally wiped that off to concentrate on Gillan. But that period from '77 to the end of '82 was a fantastic period for me. I loved the band, I loved what we did, and I guess I loved Ian at the time. But now I just feel disappointed in him and what happened.

PHIL BANFIELD: It ground me down. If the band members had said to me, "Let's sit down and talk about this because we're concerned,' that would have happened. But no. One by one they just chipped away at each other. The band probably would have broken up regardless of Ian's vocal problems. They were just fighting, bickering, having little digs at each other. I was sitting between them all trying to be the peacemaker.

DAVID COVERDALE: Initially the money was so bad that I split percentages. But I found I was doing so much fucking work that ultimately that changed. The lightest aspect of my financial worth now comes from the early days.

NEIL MURRAY: When you've been in something that's extremely successful and played huge gigs in America and had lots of adulation and lots of money coming in, you always want to get back there, really. I'm split, really, musically and personality-wise in terms of David and Whitesnake altogether, because I can see both sides of it. He did change. But he also educated himself a lot. He was sort of a man of the people, salt of the earth, very normal type of guy when I first knew him. There weren't that many airs and graces, really. But maybe it comes with the territory—he educated himself in terms of food and drink and music and art and whatever else, and probably some of the women in his life had quite an effect as well. And he could quite easily have been just your typical working-class rock singer made good. I enjoyed the fact he became more educated, and I had more in common with him later on, when we could talk about things more. Whereas it worked the opposite way with Micky Moody, who felt more and more alienated from who David was.

Now, I wouldn't disagree he's taken it too far; I think a lot of that has to do with him moving to America in '85 and having American management ever since, and American girlfriends and wives, and huge success in America. In recent years he has become much more nostalgic about the early years and given them much more credit. Certainly, he's had nice things to say about me. So that's nice to hear.

In the initial five years, the problem was that though we'd used David's Deep Purple connection in order to get management right at the start, and then used the management's connections to get a record deal and maybe leapfrog ahead of some of the other bands that were coming out at the same time, you still have this all-pervasive music business attitude: when money comes in, the person who receives it thinks, "Oh, I could buy a new house with this instead of passing it on to the band." Over the first few years he got pretty disillusioned with the amount of money the management was making, because it was also the publishing company and the record company. It was all under the same roof. So it was very difficult to keep tabs on where the money

WHITESNAKE (clockwise from top: Jon Lord, Mel Galley, and David Coverdale)
Saints and Sinners tour, Hammersmith Odeon, January 5, 1983. GEORGE CHIN | ICONICPIX

was going. Even then, it wasn't an equal situation financially. Certainly, David was able to eventually do a bit of blackmail and say he wasn't going to go on tour unless they gave him some money. But I think also, because of the Deep Purple connection, because the manager was part of Deep Purple's old management, Jon Lord and Ian Paice were getting a wage that was far higher than me, Micky, and Bernie. But I didn't know that at the time. Maybe they didn't know that. Maybe they thought we were all getting the same. But it's water under the bridge.

Certainly, by the time of [the 1982 album] *Saints & Sinners* there were all sorts of things David wasn't happy with. We'd had enough success in the band for him to feel that some people weren't really pulling their weight, and just coasting along. Musically it was starting to get a bit samey, and he was very unhappy with the management situation as well. He had to find interested parties, and there were various managers sniffing around in early '82. Basically Geffen Records in America came along and put some money in and allowed David to buy himself out of the various contracts. But that started the whole thing of him being in charge.

BERNIE MARSDEN: David got wind of another deal, and somebody said to him, "The only way you can get out of this is by breaking up the band and then you can start again." And that's what he did. At the time it was a shock, but hindsight's a wonderful thing. You can't look back and say he shouldn't have done that, because if he hadn't have done that, if we'd had another two years and another couple of number-one albums, we still probably wouldn't have made any money. He went on his own, and struggled for a year and a half, then came through good. Ironically with a song he and I had written together in the last days of the original lineup.

It would have been great if we'd had a good row and a fight. But we all just went, "Oh, see you later then." There was no future. The bigger we would have become, the less we would have got out of it. But I wouldn't change anything, apart from reading contracts more carefully.

DAVID COVERDALE: It was artistic, the reasons I thought, "Fuck. I've got to change this." I'd written the song "Crying in the Rain," and a couple of the guys felt it was like a Black Sabbath song, and I'm going, "Well, I don't hear that at all." Hendrix tied together blues, soul, cosmic, surreal poetry, image, sex, muscular music and riffs. All these things I felt we could go to, but I felt we couldn't do it with reluctant musicians. I had to find musicians who had the same vision. There are still some resentments—I've made my amends and it's up to other people whether to turn down the handshake. I did my part, so *whatevs*.

GRAHAM BONNET: We never saw Ritchie very much. He was always with his girlfriend. Wherever we went, she was with him and he didn't participate very much in rehearsals for the follow-up album. That's one of the reasons I left. Ritchie would give Roger and me an idea on a cassette machine, and he would bring it to the band. But we were never all in one room at the same time.

[After Monsters of Rock] Bruce Payne called me up and said, "Where are you, Graham?" I said, "Well, I've left the band." He said, "What if we get another singer to sing the songs you don't like?" "Nah, that wouldn't work, and I want to do something else." I didn't really want to do something else, and I made a big mistake there. I should have stayed for another year or two, but Rainbow was very much like a revolving door. I never saw a bloody penny. I never saw anything. I must have made a lot of frickin' money that I don't know about.

RITCHIE BLACKMORE: I like to be dangerous in that area [of changing lineups]; I like to take on the challenge that we can change anything and still keep going. But it doesn't help the momentum. Even some of my favorite bands, I get used to the members, and when they change, I'm kind of disappointed, but I don't play by those rules; I'm my own worst enemy sometimes. I know that it will not be good for the popularity of the band, but I still do it, because there's something in me that has to go against the grain. You know, I don't like to be a dead fish, swimming with all the other dead fish, I like to go upstream sometimes, against the flow, and it's almost like a challenge for me.

I liked Rainbow right in the beginning, with Ronnie Dio. I also liked the American era [immediately after Bonnet left] of songs like "Stone Cold" and "Street of Dreams." I think you go through these periods of being with the same people for so long that their idiosyncrasies get magnified, including my own. It's a bit like being married, it's hard to keep it all together, I suppose. And I've noticed that a lot of bands, even the people I look up to, like whatever, can only take so long before they change and go somewhere else.

"Look for the backwards shit."

Based in Newcastle, a declining industrial city in the northeast of England, Neat Records became the world's first independent specialist metal label, offering the world Tygers of Pan Tang, Venom, and Raven and many others.

ABADDON (drums, Venom): Newcastle isn't a very big place, and the towns on the outskirts—South Shields, Hebburn and Jarrow, and Wallsend on the other side of the river—had a really healthy hard rock contingent. There were people going to specifically hard rock pubs, biker pubs, this kind of thing.

At chucking-out time everyone would gravitate to Newcastle and all the pubs in Newcastle. All the lads from Hebburn and Jarrow and South Shields would all stay in our own pubs, but once we got to Newcastle we would mix with everybody from other towns, from Wallsend and Tynemouth and North Shields. And when that had finished we'd all go to the Mayfair, especially on a Friday or Saturday night. The Mayfair was open till two or three in the morning, and that was just hard rock and heavy metal. You were always mingling with new people.

IAN RAVENDALE (writer, Sounds): The social club circuit is pretty well gone now, but at that point there were thousands of social clubs where beer was ten pence a pint and you could get in free. There was a bingo you had to sit through. All these people who had started off in the late sixties wanting to be in real bands drifted on to the social club

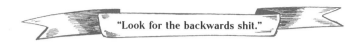
circuit because there were gigs there. There were social club agents, and they could pay. Around that time a successful social club band would be getting around five hundred quid. Now, five hundred quid in 1980, that's a large amount of money. Hard rock bands had been popular and successful in the northeast for many years, that's just the way it was. Rock and metal was what musicians wanted to play and, to a large extent, it's what audiences wanted to see.

JOHN GALLAGHER (vocals and bass, Raven): The northeast was always big for hard rock. Still is. Back then it was a religion, it really was.

TOM NOBLE (comanager, Tygers of Pan Tang): Because they played their own material, it was harder to get the Tygers gigs because what the clubs wanted was bands doing covers. So we went to an agent in Newcastle, who only operated in the northeast. He got the band gigs in these tough working men's clubs, mainly in County Durham, where on a Friday night people would come in from their hard day's work, before Thatcher shut all the mines, and they would want to go to the club.

ROBB WEIR (guitar, Tygers of Pan Tang): These were times when there were shipyards, there were Consett Steelworks; it was huge employment, and there was a big, big, healthy rock scene. It wasn't like today where everybody struggles to get people out of their lounges. When a band was playing, it was well attended. It was a more nine-to-five world back then, and a Monday-to-Friday world, so with the shipyards and stuff like that, when the whistle came on a Friday, they wanted to go out, they were looking forward all week to going out and enjoying themselves and having a good time, and what's the point of spending your hard-earned welding money and going out and not enjoying yourself? So I think it was a vastly different mindset then. I think that's where the passion came from, when people came out to see their favorite artists and their favorite bands.

ABADDON: But you also have to remember you're going into a period where the mines were closing down. A lot of industry was vanishing. The shipyards were struggling. Everybody was employed within a handful of industries and that started to thin out quite dramatically, and

there was a lot of anger among my father and my uncles and people like that. It wasn't sweetness and roses.

There was also the punk thing kicking about, and skinheads, so there was anger on the streets as a background to the music. The northeast did have a background of anger, and the noise of the industries and the noise of the anger was pretty prevalent when I was growing up.

MANTAS (guitar, Venom): It was an escape as well, that was the thing. Every concert you went to was a release, was an escape from the mundane. I can remember doing a video documentary where the cameraman was in my car, we were driving around Newcastle and saying, "We come from Newcastle, it's a rough area, there's some great people here but there's not much in the way of love and flowers in Newcastle." And that was absolutely true. It was a hard, industrial city.

JOHN GALLAGHER: I saw people who were in my class who were incredibly smart. People would get A levels, go to college, come home and they would be on the dole. What's the point? And it became more and more obvious. I ended up getting a job with the government, as a pencil pusher for the Health and Safety Executive, which was a cake job—with flextime and everything. That worked out great until 1982.

PHIL SUTCLIFFE (writer, Sounds): The Mayfair was a great venue. One of my all-time favorite places to see a band—it had standing room and sitting room. The sound was good—maybe someone had designed it acoustically in its dance hall days—but it was the place where heavy metal bands tended to be.

They had a promoter—an Italian guy, I think he was—and they had rock nights on a Friday, where you would get really significant metal bands every week. There were plastic pints trampled underfoot until they were like sand, and a balcony where you could sit at a table and peer over and have a drink. It was a good-time place—very rarely any significant trouble, because the Mayfair bouncers were renowned and you didn't fuck about. The crowd was great—they gave back to the bands. And the bands were happy to be there.

ROBB WEIR: We all used to meet on Monkseaton station, and as the train made its way through the stations up towards Newcastle it gathered probably ten, twelve of us. We started off at a pub called the

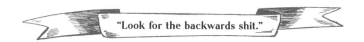

Man on the Moon. We would then go to the Farmer's Rest and have a pint there. From the Farmer's we'd go to the Percy Arms, which was a big biker bar on the Haymarket, and have a final pint there and then down to the Mayfair.

You would walk in, you would go to the box office and buy your ticket. You'd then go down about five stairs, turn to your right, and that would open out into a huge balcony area, and the balcony went right the way round the whole of the venue. The balcony was huge. And there were two bars on the balcony and a food bar as well, at the far end, where you could go and get a dog-burger with semi-fresh cheese. When it was combined with several pints of Heineken, I suppose it was alright.

JESS COX (vocals, Tygers of Pan Tang): There was a band called White Spirit, who were a huge deal around here. They were the gods of the area. There were some smaller bands, but we started to hear about other bands once we got mixed up with Impulse recording studios, because the owner there, David Wood, clocked something was going on, and Dave was never one to miss the opportunity to make a few bob. I think he put an advert out, asking rock bands to send him their demos. He got bombarded—Raven, White Spirit, Fist, all these bands—and when we went to the studio, we got given all the demo tapes to listen to. Even the studio assistant, Conrad Lant [Cronos], had a band, Venom.

JOHN GALLAGHER: There were obviously a few bands who'd been hanging around or playing in their bedrooms, and all it took was one or two to get some notoriety, enough for someone to say, "We could do that. We should be doing that right now." You had Saracen and Mythra. There's been a tradition of great music out of this area forever. We had to come along and ruin it.

CRONOS (bass and vocals, Venom): I was going out to local bars at weekends to see bands. "Oh, there's a band called Raven! There's a band called Tygers of Pan Tang!" So I'm hanging around when they're putting their gear away after a gig, and I'm saying, "Where the fuck did you come from?" And they're, "We're just local guys, been playing for a year or two." Wow!

NEAT RECORDS treats (left to right): Raven's "Don't Need Your Money" 7" (1980), Venom's "In League With Satan" 7" (1981), and Tygers of Pan Tang's "Don't Touch Me There" 7" (1979).

A lot of the information we used to get was from *NME*, *Sounds*, the music magazines. And everything was London, London, London. But here we are in Newcastle as there's a scene going on. The bands were getting up week after week and playing their arses off. It was awesome. It was all about the love of rock music.

ROBB WEIR: We played a Wednesday night residency at Mingles in Whitley Bay.

TOM NOBLE: This was probably the end of '78. Mingles was low-ceilinged, one big room in an L-shape, with a bar. It probably held a hundred and fifty, two hundred people, and it was packed with people who were there to listen to the music. Robb was also a DJ there on a Wednesday night, when his band played. So before they played, Robb did the DJing. It had a great atmosphere because there was only one reason you would ever go there, and that was to listen to music. There was never any trouble on any night I was there, or anything like that. It was right on the seafront, in the Esplanade Hotel, which has now been converted into very expensive flats.

DAVID WOOD (founder, Neat Records): I'd been running Impulse Studios since 1966. For years we did things in rock, folk and pop music. By 1979 the idea of an alternative label, Neat, came up. We recorded a couple of odd things at the beginning. Motorway was quite good. I think Andy Taylor who ended up in Duran Duran was in the band. Then we did this young girl who was a singer round the clubs in the area, Janie McKenzie. That was just an effort to make a pop song.

STEVE THOMPSON (house producer, Neat Records): It was highly speculative. There was no plan. Neat wasn't planned to be a heavy metal label.

DAVID WOOD: Conrad Lant came and worked as a tape operator.

STEVE THOMPSON: Conrad was such a nice lad. He was sixteen years old, and he was on employment training—ET, which we called Extra Tenner. They massaged the unemployment figures, so he got his dole money plus an extra tenner. He was so helpful. He was so keen. He would do anything anybody wanted. His official title was tape op, but he was the gofer. He was there when we recorded the Tygers. He would be there that night. He just used to bang on about his own band as well. He would have been there for Neat 1 and Neat 2 as well, but with the Tygers it was coming closer to a genre he was interested in.

CRONOS: The guy who ran the place was a bit of an Arthur Daley, you know? His eyes kinda went "Ker-ching!" I said I was going to all these bars in town and watching all the bands, Raven, White Spirit, Tygers of Pan Tang, blah blah. He'd say, "Which ones do you think are the best?"

We came up with this £50 demo offer and the bands could come in [and pay to be recorded]. So effectively I was the A&R. I went from the studio guy, learning how to plug things in, to studio assistant, to engineer, tape operator, blah blah, and then to the fucking A&R department.

JOHN GALLAGHER: I think there are delusions of grandma there. I don't think there was any one person at all. Conrad had nothing to do with us going in there. Conrad doesn't need to say that. He has quite a legacy just from doing Venom. You don't have to tell stories like that. He's believing his own press at this point.

STEVE THOMPSON: Conrad didn't play any part in the direction Neat took. He must have become a bit of a fantasist.

TOM NOBLE: I've read numerous articles suggesting Steve Thompson started the idea of Neat as a heavy metal label. Or Steve and Dave. Actually it was the band, the Tygers, who put them on that direction. And it was us who showed them how to market a record as well, when we used to sit there packaging them up and ringing people. That's

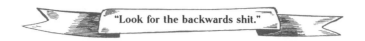

when they began to think, "Oh, we can do this." And then the major success came with Venom, which was something completely new.

ROBB WEIR: The Tygers played in Whitley Bay High School, after school, as it were, in one of the gymnasiums. Our set, our songs, our self-compositions, as well as a few covers. Went down an absolute storm, and two lads who obviously were at school, they knew that we were on and they brought their dad along, who was called Dave Wood, and of course after the show, Dave Wood came up to us and said, "I really like what I heard, very exciting. I've got a recording studio in Wallsend, would you like to come down and record some of your songs?" to which, of course, we were absolutely elated.

STEVE THOMPSON: Although they were very raw, they were very open to ideas, and by then I was really experienced in the studio. They listened to my suggestions, and I did a lot of tightening up their songs and shortening the introductions and just getting to the hook quicker. We finished it and I put it to one side. It was perhaps a few weeks later that David said, "Have you mixed that stuff with the Tygers yet?" I said, "No, David, it's really rough. Have you listened to it?" He said, "No, I'm not interested. All I care about with this band is making a splash, so we should get the product out."

I was impressed by their enthusiasm and their willingness to try anything. "Don't Touch Me There," when we tightened it up, it had something to it. I was using some fairly accomplished session men at the time, and if you compared the two, the Tygers would come up wanting, but what they had was attitude in droves. They weren't accomplished musicians, and they'd be the first to admit that. But they had huge belief in what they were doing, loads of energy, and you could sense that.

DAVID WOOD: We said, "Let's put it out and see if we can get some interest." All those singles were all pushed out to try and get interest, much the same way as the punk market worked. You'd put out a single and get somebody to write about it. The secret, I found out fairly quickly, was that you had to get some decent journalists on your side who were interested in what you were doing.

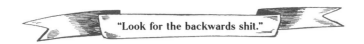

TOM NOBLE: The advantage for me was that because I'd been working at Radio Newcastle, I knew how it worked to get records played. So when the single was made, basically Grahame [Thompson, Tygers comanager and brother of Steve] and I promoted it.

Neat—this is not a derogatory remark—didn't know how to promote a record. They really didn't. But we did. So we used to go in every week during the first week after the single came out, and target people to send the single to, to try to get it played and reviewed. And Impulse let us use their secretary to send them out, let us use their space to get everything organized. So we used Neat like an office.

And the key one was, we sent one to John Peel. And two nights later we were driving home and it came on the John Peel show. That was a massive foot in, that happening.

JESS COX: David had started to see the national press and he's a businessman, and he's like, "Oh yeah, what's all this?" So he's gone in and went, "I'll put it on my record label," to Tom Noble. Next thing I knew, Tom Noble was saying to us, "We're putting it out as a record." Okay, yeah, whatever.

I just remember being at the studio and being told, "Sign this piece of paper. Just sign it—it means you'll get your record out." So we all just signed it. And it came out. We thought, great, sell that at the gigs. But obviously they put it in the paper, and the first lot went pretty much overnight. And then they just kept pressing it and selling it.

It started getting into the charts in *Sounds*, the companies came round to see us, and we got a session with Tommy Vance on Radio 1. The single came out November '79, and by March '80 MCA Records wanted to sign us.

ROBB WEIR: I wouldn't use the word "surprised" about the way "Don't Touch Me There" took off: I was elated, I was full of expectation, and it very much surpassed all our expectations. I think initially there was a thousand printed off, which we were selling at gigs, which was quite an unknown thing—there weren't many bands selling singles at gigs because most of the bands that played in those situations played covers. So when people were coming in and they saw a single there, it was very much, "Oh, wow, what's this?" and of course the thought of taking home a record—which was a seven-inch single,

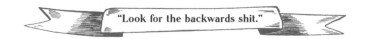

it wasn't an album, so it was quite portable, it could go in a bag or whatever—meant it sold so quickly, it was ridiculous.

I think the first thousand sold within three shows, and we had to go back to David, saying, "They've gone!" And so I think then he had another two thousand or three thousand of them pressed up, and we went again with it, and then MCA became interested.

TOM NOBLE: It wasn't a surprise actually, because I'd been living in this world of independent punk singles I was being sent to play on our radio show. And I knew if you made a record that was different to something else and you could get it to journalists and radio people, then you could make a success of it.

We thought we might do about a thousand, but then on Neat we did four or five thousand. And then, of course, MCA reissued it and did a whole bunch more. I don't think David Wood realized the impact it would have on him and the future of his studio.

DAVID WOOD: I was pleased, obviously, because we got a foot on the ladder, which meant that when they did a deal with MCA I was able to speak to MCA on behalf of Neat and say, "There's these other acts as well—Fist and White Spirit." They went along with Fist and White Spirit and did albums. I was trying to put ourselves into the marketplace through MCA. Not a lot of that happened then, not like today when people produce their own things and take them to the record company and release through the company while still being their own thing. I suppose we were in a way trying out a new angle.

Fist and White Spirit didn't really happen—which was a shame because they were terrific bands, very popular live. They signed direct deals with MCA. We had done the singles with them, so we got some sort of sales off that, and there was a carrot dangling to get them interested in the other acts that were coming along.

TOM NOBLE: People have often asked me, "Were you all friends?" Actually, not really. The bands didn't really socialize. They weren't particularly friends with each other. There was huge rivalry, particularly directed at the Tygers because they got the recording contract, they were doing the national tours. It wasn't this great, friendly bunch of people. But certainly the fact there were so many bands did create a large impetus.

FIST (L–R: John Wylie, Harry Hill, Dave Irrwin, Keith Thatchfield) out for a stroll in scenic Newcastle upon Tyne, circa 1980. RIK WALTON | ARENAPAL

STEVE THOMPSON: I began to realize there was something happening and the Tygers were part of it. Some other bands had come along—Dave had signed Fist and White Spirit, and in what seemed like a very condensed time, a whole movement seemed to have started. I wasn't surprised. I was bemused. I was just along for the ride, really. It was fine, it was exciting, but we couldn't maintain it. We were using quite a small pressing plant and pressing up a thousand at a time. Eventually we were doing three thousand at a time, and we couldn't maintain it. So eventually a deal was done with MCA and they took on the product. They were able to service the demand that we couldn't.

TOM NOBLE: One Friday night I was at Radio Newcastle, where I used to go every Friday night to look at the new releases, to prepare for the radio show, and one of the secretaries said, "There's a phone call for you. It's a guy from MCA Records." So I went and answered the phone, and this guy said, "We'd like to sign the Tygers." I said, "Who are you?" And he said, "I'm Laurie, I'm the managing director of MCA Records." I said, "MCA Records, Tom Petty's label?" And he said, "Yeah." And I said, "Wow. You want to sign them?" He said, "Yeah. We came to see them and we think they're good enough for us to sign."

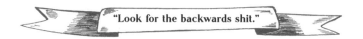
Several labels came to see the band. We had Phonogram there, who weren't interested. The guy from EMI who had signed Iron Maiden, Ashley Goodall, came to see them at Newcastle Mayfair and passed on them, which destroyed us, because he came to us and said, "Sorry guys, no." He was putting together tracks for the *Metal for Muthas* album, and said, "Would you like to go on here?" And the band—in the way bands can be quite arrogant—said, "No, if you don't want us for your label, we're not giving you a track for your sampler." The guy from Chrysalis came to see the band at Sunderland Mecca Center. He too passed on them. We were beginning to think, "This isn't going to happen." So MCA were the band's saviors, really.

MALCOLM DOME (writer, Record Mirror and Kerrang!): Neat became one of the important independent labels. It gave us Raven, Fist, Tygers of Pan Tang, Venom. It gave us a lot of really good bands. And it was really important that Neat gave these bands the opportunity to be heard before some moved on to bigger things.

Neat, on the ground, were very important. It was very much a case of grassroots. They had their studio there in the northeast, and young bands coming through the door saying they would like to do something. So it did encourage that whole scene, by getting bands in and giving them the opportunity to be heard before anyone else got hold of them, and maybe when no one else would have got hold of them.

Some of these bands would probably have put out their own self-released music. However, having a label like Neat there, that seemed to know what they were doing, was hugely important. And David Wood seemed to be really keen to encourage young talent and give them the opportunity and the springboard to show the world what they could do. They made the northeast a hotbed.

STEVE HAMMONDS (fan, music catalog consultant): Neat was very collectible. The first two singles were rubbish, but even the Motorway single goes for a lot of money now, if you can get it. There was a stamp of quality with Neat, in a funny sort of way. Neat carefully chose their tracks, certainly for the first twenty, twenty-five singles. Everything on Neat was slightly different. They didn't follow a format. Guardian [another Newcastle metal label] was good, but Neat was a really interesting label.

IAN RAVENDALE: Tom was pretty much switched on to the scene, Dave Wood—as he would admit—wasn't. It could easily have not happened for Neat. Motorway and Janie McKenzie were what Dave was into. That was what Steve Thompson was into. It was the fact that Tom was more switched on, and the fact that Geoff Barton had picked up on these Neat bands, and also—of course—Tommy Vance. He was playing the Neat stuff. So it was a combination of things. Dave was and is a businessman, so he was listening—he said to me, "I thought it was too loud the first time round. I really think it's too loud now"—and without one or two of those elements it wouldn't have happened.

TOM NOBLE: If I recall correctly it was me who said, "There's this band called Raven," 'cause I'd been to see Raven in a pub, and they were just great. And I gave them a whole bunch of other names.

JOHN GALLAGHER: We played a show at Balmbra's [in Newcastle], and Tom Noble came up and said, "Loved the set. Would you like to do a single for Neat?" And I said, "Let me think about it. Yes." I think I literally said that. He said, "Okay, let me sort out an audition." So about a week later we brought our gear in and recorded three songs live to two-track. From there, "Let's do a single." So we went in with Steve Thompson producing and Mickey Sweeney engineering and did "Don't Need Your Money" and "Wiped Out." It was very organic. Put it together, picked the live shots. Iconic song, iconic cover. And we were off to the races. I've no idea how many were pressed. That type of information was a tightly guarded nuclear secret.

IAN RAVENDALE: I became aware of them when they first auditioned for Neat. The thing with Raven, unlike with Venom, was that you could tell they really had the chops. What it sort of was, I remember thinking at the time, was the heavy metal version of the Ramones. They looked a bit like that as well. But they were nice guys. Raven were certainly pretty musically accomplished.

ABADDON: Raven were fucking great! I remember the first time I seen them—I was like, "Fucking hell, that's a fucking good band." But you know why they were a good band? They worked and worked and worked and worked. They never stopped fucking playing. It showed when you seen that band live, they were seasoned, they were ring-

DENIM AND LEATHER 275

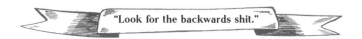

crafted fucking musicians. I think if you could swap these two bands around and put one where the other is now, I think Raven should be where Anthrax are, dead right. I'll fucking say that, I'm not afraid to say it. There's bands out there that Raven would blow away. Really fucking good band.

STEVE THOMPSON: I thought Raven were terrific. The first I heard of them, I had been out of the picture doing other stuff and the label had become heavy metal. I had not produced White Spirit or Fist. So Dave said, "There's something come along I want you to do."

We sat in the studio one night, just me and him, and he played me this rehearsal tape. They'd been in when I wasn't there and laid down three tracks, and it was really interesting stuff. It was thinking man's heavy metal. Some really clever riffs, some stops and starts. It almost had elements of jazz in a way. I don't think anybody's ever said that, but their approach—the structures and the interplay between the musicians—was amazing for three people to be doing that. So I said, "Yeah, let's do it." We picked one of the songs that would be the single from the three we had.

And Dave said, "We've now done three singles, it's maybe time for an album. Are you up for that?" I said, "Yeah, okay. Sounds interesting." He said, "The band's on at Mingles next week. Go down, check them out at the gig, and get to meet them, and then take it from there and let's do an album."

I'm stood against the wall at Mingles and I'm only six feet away from the band, on a stage about six inches high. They know I'm there to check them out. They know what's coming. Dave would have prepped them: "We're gonna do an album and will you work with Steve Thompson?" And in the middle of one number John Gallagher points his Fender Precision bass at me as if it's a gun or a lance and then he leaps from the stage and hurtles towards me with the machine heads of his bass coming towards my head, and he stops half an inch short of my throat. And he's still playing. He eyeballed me, and I didn't flinch. I couldn't. I was against the wall. I eyeballed him right back and neither one of us blinked. Then he winked and went back to the stage and I thought, "Oh, right, that's a test, and I think that I passed."

So I went back in the studio and Dave said, "What do you think?" I said, "I don't know if I'll survive the experience, but let's do it. But an

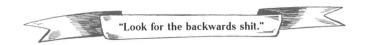

album is going to take possibly four weeks, and I'm not going to spend four weeks in a studio with those guys."

JOHN GALLAGHER: By his own admission we were doing his head in. He could only be in there two or three times a week because we were just so intense and full of it.

STEVE THOMPSON: They weren't session guys—they were doing their show in the studio. They were leaping all over the place. So we had to mic them up carefully. Rob [Hunter, drums] was in the drum booth. We put John's bass amp in the vocal booth, and then Mark [Gallagher, John's brother, guitar] and John were on the studio floor. They were just going crazy in there. The headphones were flying off. I gaffer-taped the headphones to their heads, otherwise they would have been flying blind.

JOHN GALLAGHER: Impulse Studios was the dressing rooms of an old theater. The theater had been turned into a bingo hall and it had a suspended ceiling. Above that suspended ceiling was thirty or forty feet of dead air. And in the dressing rooms upstairs they had a huge metal door. And you would open it at night and they would put a speaker and microphone and use it for reverb. The dressing rooms were stone, and they were very cold. It was very bare bones.

They had a sixteen-track Ampex machine from Trident in London, and they'd recorded *Ziggy Stardust* on it. The thing was as big as a refrigerator and had these huge modules for each track. The tape head looked as though someone had ground it down. It had been used for so long, it was so worn. But two-inch tape, sixteen tracks, big fat sound. Desk very bare bones. It had a reverb unit and the famous rolling space echo, which would be on every Neat act. They'd all have that…that… that… at the end…end…end… of the song…song…song. It's all they had. So when you wanted to be creative, you had to do things yourself, or maybe get the sound effects records out. There was no "Let's get a synth in and dial up sound seventy-five." There was none of that nonsense. It was very organic.

STEVE THOMPSON: I said with "Rock Until You Drop," it's got this stompy start, and it would be great if we heard a huge army coming over the brow of the hill. So we ran a few mics into the toilets. The

brick and concrete was very bare—only the studio had any softness to it to deaden the reverb. So we sent the guys to the toilets to march in tempo. And I thought we would get this cavernous sound in the toilets, but it was just twee and rubbish.

So I went down to the coffee machine and had a coffee. I thought of trying to get some gravel from somewhere, but it was the middle of the night. So I finished my coffee and scrunched it in my hand and it made that noise. So the room next door to that, the tape store, that's where the coffee cups were. So I went there and got a load of plastic cups and thew them on the ground and marched on them and it sounded about right. But we needed to do it three or four times to build it bigger and bigger and bigger. And each coffee cup would only last one march before it was destroyed. So I went and got the whole lot. We went through three thousand coffee cups, but we got the sound.

Now the next morning, Dave said, "What's going on? What's with all the coffee cups?" "Just wait till you hear this track, man, it's incredible." And he says, "But think of the cost!" All he cared about was the cost of the coffee cups, and all I cared about was the music. It was only coffee cups. It didn't cost the earth.

John reminded me of what happened after that. John said, "We had two stereo microphones in the toilet, and we'd done the marching, and I went in to take a dump. You took those mics and mic'ed my arse up as I took a dump." Remembering my influences, going back to the Beatles and George Martin and backwards tapes, we reversed the sound of John shitting and put that into the tracks. We put it on the album. I can't detect it, but it is there somewhere. So when you're looking for the Satanic messages, look for the backwards shit.

JOHN GALLAGHER: We put out the first independent heavy metal album. And that comes from sitting in a room with a guitar and there's nothing there and you come up with a song. And you've done something that wasn't there before. You've created something out of thin air. And that times a thousand, you've actually done a record. All the bands you've worshipped for so many years have done that, and now you've done a record, too. That was a very big deal.

DAVID WOOD: They were a terrific band in the Athletic Rock area. Fantastic. And it went into the charts, which was unbelievable.

Basketball jerseys, elbow pads, and shinguards—John and Mark Gallagher of RAVEN playing "athletic rock" to win, November 1982. FRANK WHITE

JOHN GALLAGHER: Athletic Rock was a stupid saying from Dave Wood. We just saw an advert that said, "Athletic Rock from Neat." What's that? He said, "Well, you wear those running togs, and you bought the hockey pads, and the hockey helmets—Athletic Rock." Well, it's better than being told you're like this band or that band. We'll take it. We'll work with it.

IAN RAVENDALE: Of all of the bands, Raven were the most influential. There was no one like Raven. And bands like Metallica cite Raven as being the band that showed them the way.

MALCOLM DOME: Raven were very important in terms of their influence on the whole thrash movement a few years later.

TOM GABRIEL WARRIOR (fan, founder of Hellhammer, Celtic Frost, and Triptykon): Raven's first two albums were extremely important.

TOM NOBLE: What we didn't know [when Tygers signed to MCA] was that Dave had signed a nice little side deal with them to take the single, which also guaranteed him a small percentage of the first

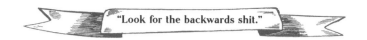
album. And MCA, for some reason, hadn't told us that. It wasn't a huge percentage, and perhaps Dave did deserve something for what he put into the band. What Robb didn't like and I didn't like is that we only found out afterwards about this.

ROBB WEIR: We were sold to MCA, effectively.

JESS COX: David Wood was a character. Dave knew how to get a good deal for himself, let's put it that way. It only came to light for me when we signed this deal with MCA, and it was disclosed that Dave Wood had to get four grand buyout and two percent of our royalties on the first album. I just hit the roof. "What the hell's this? What do you mean, Dave owns us?" I'd forgotten all about that piece of paper we signed. I said to Tom Noble, "You said I had to sign that so he could put the single out!"

Basically, I was told to shut up and get on with it. The rest of the band were telling me not to rock the boat, and I was livid. We weren't getting a lot of money anyway—I think it was thirty grand to record the album. But that was everything—that was what we had to live on. We got £6 a week after we signed to MCA. And that was to pay the rent. And if we went on tour we got some per diems, and it was something like £3 a day and a kebab. Even on the *Wheels of Steel* tour [supporting Saxon] we were getting nothing.

ROBB WEIR: When we opened up for Magnum in March of 1980, our management allowed us £1.50 a day. Just that. They said, "You have a rider in the dressing room, so you'll get fed at least once a day. You should—you should—get breakfast in the guesthouse, so your £1.50's enough to buy your lunch."

But we tried to beat the system, because we had a one-ring Calor gas stove in the back of our hired estate car, with some tins of Irish stew, and we used to buy loaves of bread and some Stork margarine, and we used to have Irish stew on toast at about four o'clock when we arrived at a venue, and invariably, Magnum would join us, because the smell was irresistible. So it wasn't just the four of us for tea; I think I was cooking tea for about ten people.

JESS COX: So to have someone given four thousand quid—which to me was a lot of money—and two points on the album, when you were

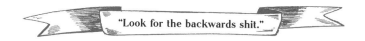

only getting twelve points anyway, I wanted to know why we were lying down and letting this happen. But I had to just forget it. That was my introduction to Dave, but that's every local band's introduction to Dave. Dave was a character.

I'm not blaming him—he was a businessman, and he saw a business opportunity. Probably what he gave us, looking back, was free recording time for the single. But he then owned the rights to the single, because he owned the recording. If we'd paid for it, we would have owned it. But he jumped in and did a canny deal. I don't blame him for it now. So we had to buy Dave out to be on MCA.

ABADDON: I was working at a factory and I was called in by the bosses. I had my union shop steward on my side. And they called me in. They had my time sheet, which was worked out into days and half-days throughout the year. And it was supposed to be clear, unless you had your holidays, and that would be black for two weeks. And if you were late it would be red. And mine was like a patchwork quilt. It was all bloody colors. And this guy came out with the best bloody line I've heard in my life. I guess I was pushing twenty, and he said, "Son, you'll have to decide if you want to piss off round the world being an international rock star, or if you want to work for us."

Seriously? You're asking me that? The shop steward was saying, "You can't do this to this lad." But I was, "Honestly? I'm just going to go. Forget it." I went and told Eric [Cook, Venom manager], because he was in the same factory, and he nearly fell off the trestle he was standing on. Then he handed in his notice as well.

To be fair, when we were nineteen we both put in for voluntary redundancy anyway—well, they're paying off all these older guys— but when we asked they told us we were taking the piss. We signed on the dole and we were getting thirty quid. But later on I got called into the dole office and the woman said, "Can I have a quick word?" So I went in and she had all the singles, all the albums, and I think the Hammersmith Odeon VHS and a couple of T-shirts. She said, "Is this you?" And I was like, "Yeah." "What the fuck are you doing signing on the dole? You look like you're some fucking mega rock star or something." I said, "I'm fucking penniless." She went, "You absolutely cannot be. Get out there and sign off." So I did.

I went to Neat Records and said, "I've given up work because of the band. I've been thrown off the fucking dole now because of the band.

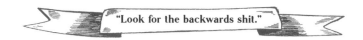

What are we going to do?" So Dave said, "I'll give youse all thirty quid a week." And that's all we ever got off Neat Records.

MANTAS: To this fucking day I have never ever seen a Neat Records royalty statement.

JOHN GALLAGHER: It probably took us about a week to start distrusting Neat. It was obvious the type of operation it was, which was why we were looking for the first opportunity to get out of there. He was paying us twenty quid a week. Whatever came in came in, and he would just pay us twenty quid a week. It was kind of like the Motown deals, except nobody was buying us Cadillacs.

DAVID WOOD: That's a disappointing thing to hear, to be honest. A major label has a massive structure and still doesn't get it all right. A small label is often hanging by a thread. It's just trying to make some sort of headway. Tony Wilson at Factory had a looser relationship with bands than we would ever have. We were trying to get things going. I would say we spent time doing that and perhaps didn't have the facility to do all the things bigger companies would do. But it wasn't for want of trying and enthusiasm to get things going.

We were self-funded, with various business loans. None of that area would have been discussed with the bands. I would say, if they mean I was tight, I would say no. If you haven't got the money, you can't do certain things. There's no other way forward, unless you want to go out and borrow it. I wasn't living the life of the lord of the manor, and I'm still not. There were no suitcases full of money, and I've got the bank statements to prove it.

TOM NOBLE: I tried to pry Raven away from Neat. I said to them, "You can do better than this, guys." But they seemed to be quite happy to stay there.

JOHN GALLAGHER: There was a period during the recording of the first album where we were courted by a guy who used to manage the Groundhogs. He looked at the deal and said, "This is rubbish. You guys could do so much better." He came up and talked to Dave Wood and had him cowering within about five minutes. And we were going to get off the deal, and then he just disappeared. Well, I guess we're

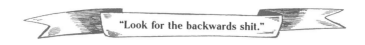

in a deal with the devil we know. At least we'll have the record out, and we'll go from there. And if there were any enquiries about [taking over] management, they would have been quashed very quickly at the source. And I'm sure that happened a few times.

MALCOLM DOME: What went on behind the scenes is between the bands and him. A lot of them felt he didn't do justice by them in terms of the deals he gave them, and that perhaps he didn't play fair with them. Whether that's true, who knows. But it's true he didn't know much about the music, but what he did know about was saying, "Okay, these bands are getting a bit of a buzz. I think we should put something out by them, so the buzz can get bigger and the label can get bigger."

In terms of "Was he a fair record company person?" I think at any record company bands hate certain people or hate the way they're treated. It's the way bands are. But bands stay because it's better the devil you know. Don't forget as well that he did do a deal with MCA in the early eighties, which gave White Spirit, Fist, and the Tygers an opportunity to put stuff out through MCA, so it wasn't all bad.

DAVID WOOD: We ended up paying for all sorts of things. We would try and do some merchandising and stuff. You had to hire a van, drivers. You had to pay for hotels. It never paid for itself. So we went the other way of trying to get some revenue from selling bits and pieces. With Fist, I remember we bought a tour bus for them, which was one of the biggest mistakes we made. It was a single-decker that had been converted into a touring caravan kind of thing. It was massive. It had a shower, a toilet, it had a kitchen and a comfortable seating area, bunks and everything. We got a guy to drive it.

They went out on tour—we paid for them to go on a UFO tour; it was many thousands of pounds—and the bus seemed to be a good idea because it would save on hotels and what have you. But after the first couple of weeks the driver got back in touch with us and said, "I'm not doing this any more. The bus is like a pigsty with this lot." He retired.

The worst thing in the world happened. We couldn't find anybody to drive the bus, and eventually found someone who'd been driving a pop van around, selling bottles of lemonade. He seemed alright. He had experience of a big vehicle. He brought it back in many pieces. He hadn't got the foggiest. So we parked the bus up securely in a lorry

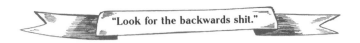

park and I put it up for sale. A year and half later someone came along saying, "I hear you've got a bus for sale." I took him to have a look, and he offered me five hundred quid for it. I snapped his hand off. It cost a fortune in upkeep.

MALCOLM DOME: And some of these bands never took full advantage of that springboard to really make an impact. I mean, Raven ended up on Atlantic, but did they really do anything? Not really. They became a Metallica support band, and then for a while they became a hair metal band, sadly. So while they can moan all they want about their treatment by Neat, they didn't take the opportunity when they were off Neat to do anything. I love Raven, though, I have to say.

JOHN GALLAGHER: Neat definitely had cachet: if it's on Neat it's got to be good. And the initial track record was good—the Tygers, the Fist single, the Raven single, Venom of course. In their own way they were all great. But somebody said Dave Wood started a snowball and then ran out of snow. Because there's a finite amount of really good bands. You can't just keep saying, "Here's another new band, and another one!" It just doesn't work that way.

IAN RAVENDALE: Think about Merseybeat: yes, you've got the Beatles, but by the time you get down to the Dennisons or whoever it is, it's the law of diminishing returns, isn't it? Which is not to say that the forty-seventh band to show up is not a great band. Who knows? But by then it doesn't matter if you're a great band—you're the forty-seventh band. Some people will have bought that record because they were buying all the Neat Records. I suppose if the records got crappier and crappier they might stop, but I'm sure Neat had its own fan club of people buying Neat Records because it was Neat Records. I'm just glad these people have been successful in their different ways.

12

"Your head grows and you start to have a bit of an ego."

Through 1980, Def Leppard, Iron Maiden, Saxon, Girlschool, Diamond Head, and Tygers of Pan Tang released landmark albums and gilded their reputations. Judas Priest's *British Steel* bound all the threads together.

MALCOLM DOME (writer, Record Mirror and Kerrang!): It was only in retrospect you think, "My God, what an amazing year 1980 was." It didn't feel like this would be a year that we would look back on as a turning point. But we all knew something was going on.

BIFF BYFORD (vocals, Saxon): Nineteen eighty was the year that was the catalyst for everybody. If you were going to make it—if you were going to be selling out venues and doing the obligatory *Top of the Pops*, if you hadn't done it by '80, you weren't going to be one of the top three or four bands later on.

JOE ELLIOTT (vocals, Def Leppard): Making *On Through the Night* was a piece of piss. It was done at Tittenhurst Park, owned by Ringo Starr. He'd bought it off John Lennon. It's the house where Lennon shot the "Imagine" video, with the white piano in the white room. That specific room had been turned into a games room. It was a live-in and we drew straws and I got Lennon's bedroom. They've hated me ever since.

We moved in for three weeks to John Lennon's mansion, and it was beyond surreal. As we moved in, who's moving out but Dr. Hook and

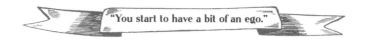

the Medicine Show. They invited us to smoke a bit of weed—and I'd never done that in my life—drink some beer, play some pool. And so I had a game of pool with Ray Sawyer, and I beat him. I got on the phone and called my mate in Sheffield, Andy, and said, "I just fucking beat 'Sylvia's Mother' at pool!" He goes, "Well, he's only got one eye, so how fucking hard was that?"

We're hanging out with Dr. Hook and the Medicine Show for two hours as their crew are getting their gear packed and our couple of guys are bringing our stuff in. We set up on the Friday night, and on the Saturday got fired up and ran through a few songs, and almost by early Sunday morning we had the backing tracks for seventy-five to eighty percent of our record. I could have sung better, but I could have sung worse. It is what it is.

RICK SAVAGE (bass, Def Leppard): The songs we'd do in the early days were basically a collection of riffs. We found that very easy—me, Pete [Willis] and particularly Steve [Clark]. It came natural to us to just come up with guitar parts that we would then try and glue together if they were of the same tempo and in the same key. After that we left it to Joe. We gave him the rough outline of the music and the chord progressions and the riffs: "Sing over this, Joe, or whatever, 'cause we ain't got a clue. Here's the music, now make a song out of it."

Even now, we still believe writing's our biggest strength. Not just from an ability point of view, but from a respect point of view, and recognizing the song is the most important thing you can do. Not a guitar solo, or doing something outrageous to make the front pages of the papers. It's the song. If you have to play this way to project the song, that's what you do, because the song is king. And we're all slaves to the perfect song, and we spend our lives trying to write it.

TOM ALLOM (producer, Def Leppard and Judas Priest): They looked like they'd been doing it for years. They were really accomplished and they looked like stars. I went up to Sheffield and did a few days' preproduction with them. It was very rough and ready. The rehearsal room was on the first floor of a building where there was a bloke downstairs making cutlery. There was a great big hole in the wooden floor and you could look down and see him working. They had to put a bit of board over the hole in case you put your foot down it. I think the only reason he could keep going with the work was that he was making quite a lot of noise as well.

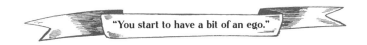

RICK SAVAGE: That's not far off the truth, in fairness. It would have been our first real rehearsal room. It was in a complex, a tiny factory, size of a kitchen, where independent people would make knives on lathes and little things like that. It was a really, really old-style complex with older machinery, and there just seemed to be one room that came available. It cost us £5 a week. It was somewhere to go, somewhere to rehearse, and also somewhere to store your gear in between gigs.

So it was perfect because it became our little den. Apart from being just our rehearsal room, it was a place we'd hang out. We'd go there, bring the girlfriends and things like that. It was brilliant. Absolutely brilliant for £5 a week. I mean, it was falling down. The whole place was falling down, but we were grateful for it.

JOE ELLIOTT: Tom Allom was a ringleader, not a producer. He was a good producer, but producers are employed by the record company, not the band—or that's the way it was then—and the word to him from the label was, "Capture the energy." So Tom documented who we were. He improved sounds here and there and we would do things again if they weren't good, but he didn't want to overdo it. We overdubbed the overdubs, but it was only to make the guitars sound bigger.

DAVID BATES (A&R at Phonogram for Def Leppard): The cover was terrible. Because I was the junior A&R man, I hadn't learned the ropes yet, but I was learning, as in, "In the future I will be saying something about shit album sleeves." That's what you call an album sleeve by numbers. Not something you would want on your living-room wall. Even a fantasy painting might have been better than the cover we had. More or less anything might have been better than the cover we had.

For the band, and for me, it was a learning point. At some point you've got to stand up and go, "Fuck that." And to do that, you have to be the person that comes up with the idea of a) the sleeve and b) the designer, and work with someone. What you don't do is hand it over to a record company's art department, because one day they're doing Nana Mouskouri and the next day they're doing Def Leppard.

JOE ELLIOTT: We saw the cover and went, "Okay. A truck going through space? With a guitar sticking out of the back of it and the moon in the background? Who the fuck came up with that? It's just awful..." I don't know why it wasn't ever challenged. It was probably five naive,

DEF LEPPARD on Spooner Road, Sheffield, July 20, 1981. ADRIAN BOOT | URBANIMAGE/ICONICPIX

shy kids going, "We're signed to a big label. Maybe this is what Elton had to deal with." We were wet under the collar. That's when we started to learn: this is how it works.

So when it came to [1981's second album] *High 'n' Dry*, we said, "We're taking charge of this," and we went with Hipgnosis because we'd grown up with their sleeves for UFO, Zeppelin, and Pink Floyd. So that album made us start wrestling back control of our own art.

MALCOLM DOME: At the time I thought *On Through the Night* was good—I would have given it three and a half stars out of five. Now, I think it's really strong. I think it really catches them at a time that should have been captured—with that energy, with that rawness, with that power. In retrospect, I think it's a better album than I did at the time. A song like "Wasted" is still one of my favorite Leppard songs. It's an anthem and it always came across really well live. And still does.

JOE ELLIOTT: The album's recorded but not out, so we do the clubs, where people are just listening to music they've never heard. And then, when the album comes out, because we'd done that, the album sold well enough to go top twenty, so that happens and the articles get a bit

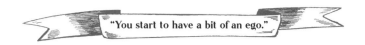

bigger, and the advertisements are in all the right magazines, and all of a sudden it's time to play the city halls. But at the same time, we had to make it a bit of a package, like those tours in the sixties. We were expected to play a full ninety minutes, but we only had an hour and ten's worth of music. So we did what happened when we went out with Nugent. We would take out Magnum and a local NWOBHM band. We had Tygers of Pan Tang in Newcastle City Hall. I don't remember who those third-on-the-bill bands were, but it was a good package. Because there was going to be three hours of music, we were okay to only have an hour ten.

I remember when we did the City Hall in Sheffield we had to play "Ride into the Sun" twice because we didn't have enough material. We played it early in the set, and there was such a clamor for another encore, we had to play something again. It's in Leppard lore that me and Sav [bassist Rick Savage] chalked on the wall of Sheffield City Hall in 1978: "Def Leppard will play here in 1980." And we did. And we sold it out.

We were that ambitious—fifteen months previous we were scribbling that on the City Hall wall because we were having to walk home, because we had to make a choice after rehearsals: either go into the Sheldon for a one-pint, four-straw, twenty-minute drink and walk home, or don't go to the Sheldon and have the bus fare to get home. We chose the former. We had a quarter of a pint each, and me and Sav took the long walk home to Bramhall Lane and Crookes and Broomhill, which would have been four miles. It wasn't warm. The shortest route home would have been walking straight down the side of the City Hall. It was one of those moments where you're walking along, kicking cans, doing whatever you do, and you see a white stone, pick it up and do what teenagers do. I was hardly Banksy, but prophetic maybe. Lo and behold, fifteen months later we'd sold the place out.

TOM ALLOM: We finished *On Through the Night* in mid- or late January, and the first week of February I was in with Judas Priest, doing *British Steel*.

ROB HALFORD (vocals, Judas Priest): *British Steel* is a unique album, in sound and production and engineering from Tom. Tom made a very special record for Priest, really directing us to cutting away all

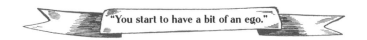

the dead flesh from the songs and just getting them really, really precise to do the job they needed to do. Tom gave us some valuable insights into putting across the minimalist point of view to maximum effect. Sometimes bands are in that creative place, where things appear to come easily. But they don't. It's out of your control as far as the creative bursts of ideas you have, whether it's Glenn Tipton [guitar] waking me up in the night to write "Living After Midnight," or the jams for "Stealer" and "Rapid Fire."

A lot of it has to do with being there in the building together. When you're writing, a lot of the stuff that happens when you're not writing has an effect on the way you write. It's that being with each other all the time, from when you wake up in the morning to when you go down the pub at night. All those elements. There has to be some harmony in all the chaos of making metal, and I think that had a great effect on us. What a great facility, too, that magnificent house that belonged to a Beatle. I'm sure all those little things played a role in how we forged the metal so efficiently.

K.K. DOWNING (guitar, Judas Priest): We didn't have much written. We set up a rehearsal room there and we put songs together while we were recording them. But that was okay. We would go to the pub and come back and plug in. We'd play before we went to the pub, we'd play when we came back. We were pretty prolific back then.

Songs like "The Rage" and "Living After Midnight," definitely they were born in the studio, and there would have been other tracks as well. With "Living After Midnight," we came back from the pub and Glenn plugged in and he got a riff going on and of course you could hear it all over the house, so eventually we got up and just joined in. I mean, there was no set hours when you would sleep anyway.

TOM ALLOM: Writing usually started with guitar riffs, and then a vocal idea—not a finished vocal, just the idea, a sketchy melody, and then get the lyrics in. There were certain times when a lyrical phrase came to mind first. But it was easy because us all being there meant it all gelled and happened at the same time really. The arrangements were pretty straightforward. There wasn't anything very elaborate about them, and they were quite hard-hitting.

I had some input in the lyrics of one or two tracks—I enjoyed working with Rob and coming up with ideas. I can't say I contributed

Rob Halford in denim and leather and Glenn Tipton of JUDAS PRIEST. FRANK WHITE

greatly to the lyrical content of the album, but one part of the producer's job is to be involved in that. We were very much on top of each other. Everyone was very much involved in all aspects of it.

K. K. DOWNING: We were so competitive, especially me and Glenn. Glenn knew that if he was lazy I'd do it all. And vice versa, you know. Eventually we decided to form a team, me, Rob and Glenn, where all the songwriting was split equally, so no one person kept pushing their ideas. So it ensured that the best ideas were selected really. For the right reasons. And that was the right thing to do, I'm sure.

TOM ALLOM: Everyone knows about the breaking glass sound effect in "Breaking the Law." That was smashing milk bottles on Ringo's terrace. And shaking the cutlery tray was famous. We wanted the sound of marching feet in "Metal Gods," but it wasn't just a cutlery tray, actually. It was also the legs of mic stands, with the rubber feet taken off—you couldn't just sample sound, you had to get it in time with the music, because we didn't have sophisticated sampling. And I thought, "What about some cutlery?" So I got all the cutlery out of the kitchen drawer. It was a mixture of those two sounds.

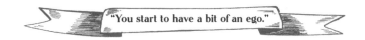

There were other sounds, too. On "Metal Gods" there was the sound of a whip, which was a guitar cord being slapped heavily on to a flight case and then heavily compressed. There was a laser beam, which was a billiard cue going through the air. It was fun doing sound effects in those days.

ROB HALFORD: We were just a little bit outside of the box for NWOBHM because of the specific timing of it. But we felt connected in the metal way, and in the British way. But we were there before that kicked off, and I think it's fair to suggest we were part of the inspiration for the way metal grew from the early seventies.

TOM ALLOM: I don't know whether we thought it was changing heavy metal, but I think we all knew by the end of the album that we had made a good album that really captured what the band was about. And we proved to be right. It was the first big success the band had had, and it clearly had an impact on the heavy metal scene, and on the rock scene. Because we were making an album at a time when heavy metal was being discussed a lot, *British Steel* was a great title for the album.

MALCOLM DOME: They absolutely created something and Priest's influence has always been underplayed. They were very important. Not just in terms of music, but the image. You look at the image around the time of *Unleashed in the East* [1979], when they suddenly went into leather and studs, which became really the metal uniform, and that came from Priest.

K.K. DOWNING: Since the beginning of time, bands that wore the same clothes on stage was a no-no, because of all the Merseybeat guys. When Hendrix came and Cream came and had photographs taken, they were all idealizing themselves as individuals with their own look. So basically, if you get three guys in a band, they all look really cool as individuals, as stars in their own right, but together, they make this kind of superstar band. They all look super cool, and they've all got their own images. So that became a trend. What it was is just staying away from anything that was remotely pop-looking.

I did a U-turn at some point. It suddenly dawned on me that if we're the same, we would look stronger as opposed to weaker. We wouldn't have to wear all the same suits like the Beatles—we'd have

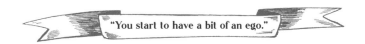

to design our own clothes, but they all came together. It's almost like *The Magnificent Seven* in a way—they've all got their own identity, but they've all got the gun belts and they've got the hats. Or it was almost like one of those military things, where everybody's got their own look, but they're all a part of the platoon, you know? So I'm thinking they look fearsome together. They're different, but they've got things in common, and I thought that that's really the way we ought to go with metal and that's what happened.

We started to design our own look that had that leather and studs and color in common. That added strength, because I would stand behind the curtain with my bandmates, ready to go on stage, and I would look across at everybody and it was a good feeling of strength that we were uniform, we had this connection. That was a turning point.

ROB HALFORD: I think there's this feeling in a band of wanting to find unity, as far as the visual side. And Ken was the first one to adopt that change in what he was wearing, and it became something we all picked up from and developed, pretty much all the same time.

K. K. DOWNING: I went to Andy's in Goldhawk Road [in west London] and had some boots made. And it kind of felt good, you know, and then I had a leather waistcoat made. I still had black satin trousers and a black shirt, but then I had a leather choker with studs, and I liked how that looked. And I've got studs around the shoulder. And eventually, when the money came in, we were able to recruit a good tailor to make everything, that was all leather and studs.

Me and Rob had to go to Mr S. Don't know where that was located, but it was called Mr S. A lot of it was for the gay guys that wanted to be fitted with something different and stuff like that. I think they made some theatrical stuff as well, you know. And so, we went down there and got measured up, me and Rob and I was kind of tactfully hoping, anticipating the rest of the guys would think that we looked pretty good. It was so rewarding when I saw so many other bands kind of doing the same thing. I really liked it.

ROB HALFORD: Once I personally attach myself to an idea that can be developed and explored, I just go for it. And so I'd go in and out of various sex shops in London, and it became part of the overall imagery of the band. There was nothing more attached to it than that, in reality.

ROB HALFORD *in full regalia:*
Hat, sunglasses, whip, studs
from head to foot, Madison
Square Garden, New York
City, October 2, 1982.
FRANK WHITE

There have been many, many references—"Because you were dressed like that, we should have known you were gay." Well, I always find that a little bit insulting. That was never my intention, personally. It was always just about looking the best way to fit in to the band and that particular moment. And it just so happens there is a subculture in the gay community that is the leather scene. But I never went, "Oh, let me utilize this in an ambiguous way." The only time it sometimes rattles my cage is the assumption of some form of intent on my part, that I had some kind of agenda. That was never true.

K.K. DOWNING: Heavy metal needed to be more than just a name, it needed to be a thing, it needed to be identified. If a band wanted to be heavy metal, you needed to add some of that look, at least in part. That's what I think.

MALCOLM DOME: And they were the first band to really call themselves heavy metal. Sabbath never did. Sabbath were always heavy rock. Priest embraced the term heavy metal, and made it okay to call yourselves heavy metal. So they were massively important.

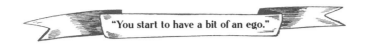

And the sound was instant: you listened to a Priest song and you could hum it, rather than it being lots of different parts, trying to be all symphonic. And they had no blues in there. I'm sure they could play the blues if they wanted, but they were metal. This was the template, not just for them but for what came later.

K. K. DOWNING: I was never a blues player. In fact, I first auditioned for Judas Priest and they were looking for a blues player but I wasn't that. I was moving beyond that and even now I'll never play the blues. It never enters my head. What we wanted musically just wasn't there. We grew up in very industrial areas. It wasn't pleasant. Blues music just didn't have that kind of attitude and aggression. It was all a bit laid-back really. And the lyrical sentiments? Yeah, fine, I get it, my baby just left me, but I was looking for a lot more than that.

ROB HALFORD: There are many definitions within Priest as regards heavy metal. You know how some bands have an exclusive sound and stick with it? With Priest we had the core of that, but as we've said many, many times, we had a sense of adventure and never restricted ourselves. We never put the blinkers on. We went into many different realms of metal.

BIFF BYFORD: With *Wheels of Steel*, we were writing songs together rather than picking songs from three or four years before we had joined together. You have to remember that quite a lot of them tracks had been played with other bands—the first album was basically the same tracks as the demo tapes we had been sending out. "Frozen Rainbow," I wrote that with Paul; "Judgement Day" is a Coast song; there must be five or six of those songs. The songs we wrote together—"Stallions of the Highway," "Backs to the Wall," are very similar to *Wheels of Steel* in style. The first album was a mixture of songwriters, but *Wheels of Steel* was very focused, and the same people writing.

STEVE DAWSON (bass, Saxon): That were the first time we'd gone somewhere specifically to write songs. We were up in this rehearsal room in the mountains of Wales. We'd just been dropped by Trident. So it were a case of, "It's now or never, and we're gonna show 'em." So there was a bit of anger in the writing that we wanted to use to prove them wrong, that they'd made a mistake.

SAXON, first show of the Denim & Leather tour, Brighton, October 7, 1981. GEORGE BODNAR ARCHIVE | ICONICPIX

When me and Paul Quinn [guitarist] drew up the music for "747 (Strangers in the Night)," we fucking knew it were gonna hit. We sat down and we'd been watching a program about an airplane that couldn't land because there were a power cut in New York. And it was nicked a bit off Frank Sinatra for "Strangers in the Night," and "747" were a good thing to sing. So we've got a 747 that can't land—what sounds good? And then Biff came up with a melody to sing those words. We had a great tune.

"Wheels of Steel" was a great groove in the style of AC/DC. "Motorcycle Man," because we were mad on motorbikes. We had the idea to have the sound of a motorbike, and we thought: "How can we match the sound of a motorbike? It's got to be an aggressive fucking noise." Not a lot of people know this, but "Wheels of Steel" came from steam locomotives. We had another song, later on, called "Princess of the Night," about the same subject. I'm a massive steam engine and classic car fan. Anything old is a major like of mine. So I thought, "A steam engine's got wheels of steel. That's heavy." So I mentioned that to Biff. And he didn't see it. But what he saw was a car. Which hasn't got wheels of steel. Not really. They've got steel wheels and rubber tires. But you can't sing "Wheels of Rubber."

And we were all mad on American cars in the early days. We had a band car rather than a minibus, and we bought American cars 'cause they were big. They had a bench seat in the front, which meant you could get three in the front, three in the back. More room. So we had a Chevy Chevelle, which is a really sought-after car now. We got it cheap because someone had run into the back of it and not repaired it. We drove around with it like that. We had an Oldsmobile Delta 88, a Lincoln Continental. But what we sang about was a classic 1968 Chevy, one of them beautiful old cars. It scanned, vocally: "Got a '68 Chevy with pipes on the side," which are sidewinder pipes, which custom shops in America would put on. What a great thing to sing: "I've got a '68 Chevy with pipes on the side." And then you've got the chorus: "she's got wheels, wheels of steel," So you've got your two bits.

Then you need a story to go in between it. So you just make things up that sing good. They don't make sense but they sing great. So all that: "she's doing a hundred and forty, she'll do even more," all that crap. It's just people throwing things in they like. That's how that came about. Great drumbeat, great guitar part, great guitar solo, memorable chorus. Job done. We were on our way with that.

BIFF BYFORD: Why did we write so many songs about transportation? It's just those songs seem to have landed on the hits. You have to remember I was a biker back then. I used to get on motorbikes and ride really fast. The other guys, I don't even think they were on a motorbike. Maybe Steve Dawson had a Lambretta, which doesn't really suit the image. I was the biker, so I was writing songs about motorcycle men.

STEVE DAWSON: We'd got the Motörhead tour, in 1979, which we didn't really want to do. Not because we had anything against Motörhead, but we were more UFO people. But it were the best thing ever. It was a good move from our manager. They were at the top of their career, more or less. Everything was sold out. It was just like the Beatles coming to town. We were right for that audience. And because we only had half an hour, we just went fucking crazy for half an hour. Absolutely crazy. And the way Motörhead sounded were an advantage to us because our music was slightly more subtle. We went straight off that on to our own headline tour.

*NWOBHM patron saint and
guiding light Lemmy Kilmister
of MOTÖRHEAD, Hammersmith
Odeon, November 26, 1980.
"It was just like the Beatles
coming to town."*
LAURENS VAN HOUTEN

They were brilliant people. Philthy Animal and Fast Eddie were so funny. Lemmy were Lemmy. He were a great bloke and he'd always give you the time of day. But he were a thinker, you know what I mean? The other two were just pure comedy and they were always fighting. It were like Pete and Dud. Philthy Animal had an empathy for us because he was from Bradford. And Fast Eddie were southern. They were like chalk and cheese. There were always banter going off between them.

We lived with them all that tour—same hotels, same tour bus—so we saw it all. This is what being in a big rock band's really like: sex, drugs, booze, you name it, twenty-four/seven. It's public knowledge that Lemmy appreciated a substance called sulphate. And so did everybody involved. We didn't take it, so we didn't realize the effect it were having on them, why they were constantly fucking talking. And no fucking rest at all. There were no concentration on anything: it were all flitting from one thing to another. We couldn't understand why they never ate anything. You'd go into a motorway services and their

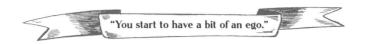

roadie'd bring 'em three big slap-up meals with a pint of milk. They'd have two gulps of milk and walk out, leaving food. And we'd think, "What's going on? Nobody's eating." And they never slept, either. We'd be fucking knackered, going to bed in their hotel, and we'd get up and they'd still be up. It eventually dawned on us what was going on.

KIM MCAULIFFE (vocals and guitar, Girlschool): Lemmy was quite quiet actually. He'd just sit there and read, keep himself to himself on the tour bus. The others would fight in hotels. They'd come out of the lift, the two of them, just rolling around the floor.

On that first tour, I remember knocking on Lemmy's door one morning. "Bloody hell, you're up early!" "I haven't been to bed yet." I don't think he ever went to bed. I don't know how they survived. That first tour, we had some wild times. We were no slouches in the partying. We used to try to get some sleep and look after ourselves a little bit, but it was three weeks of mayhem.

There was one time, Lemmy came to our dressing room to wish us well before we went on and he was hanging around a bit longer than usual, and we thought, "This is a bit weird. He's normally gone by now." I opened up my guitar case and screamed my head off. I thought there was a human hand in there. It was half a pig's head. All the insides were spilling out. That's why he'd been hanging around, to see the reaction. But he missed it. Tim [Warhurst, sound engineer] wrapped it up in towel. He knocked on their door and said, "I think this belongs to you."

They had all the journalists come up one night. They had them all on a coach, and they'd decorated the coach by going to the butcher's and getting a load of offal. Those poor people had to sit on a coach surrounded by offal. I can see Lemmy walking down the corridor in his underpants and sunglasses with a bin on his head. The poor maid. We were getting to leave one hotel and we heard screaming. This poor maid had gone in the room. God knows what she found in there; I don't think it was very nice. But we found our identity. It was a crossover thing, and finally audiences accepted us. Finally we were accepted. There we were.

DENISE DUFORT (drums, Girlschool): We just carried on like we always did. We never thought about fame. We just carried on gigging and recording and doing what we did. We never had conversations

about any of that sort of thing. We headlined the Electric Ballroom, the Lyceum, the Hammersmith Odeon. We looked over to our right and Led Zeppelin were standing there watching us. That freaked the shit out of me, I must say. And it really freaked the shit out of Kim as well. We were really, really into Led Zeppelin. And there they were standing there. That was our headline gig at the Hammersmith Odeon.

DOUG SMITH (manager, Motörhead and Girlschool): With Girlschool, getting them away had a lot to do with the fact that Motörhead were doing well and Gerry [Bron of Bronze Records] was really milking the Motörhead situation into Girlschool and the team was there at Bronze. Bronze were the only record company in the music business at that time to be connected to a computer. Gerry decided that was a business he wanted to get into.

Their offices were next to the Roundhouse in Camden, and that modern building there was all Gerry's. They moved in there from where they were previously, and they had a floor empty, so Gerry decided he wanted to go into computers. And in those days that meant a whole floor of tapes turning the whole time for computers. But of course they got the benefit downstairs, where every one of the staff was linked to a computer. And during the night, when they weren't making use of the computers, they were rented out to major corporations and accounting companies. So he made his money through those.

Same as starting the studio—he financed the studio for his own acts by letting it out the rest of the time for all the acts who paid for it. But he put his money behind his mouth. Nick Raymond [in A&R] was given responsibility for Girlschool, and so as things were going well with Motörhead, he got the budgets to really throw into the girls, and they got some great production and they got a lot of airplay out of it.

ENID WILLIAMS: Punk was three chords going back to the rock 'n' roll of the late fifties and how it started and that energy and that simplicity and that passion. The songs on those first two albums were very influenced by glam rock because we grew up with that, and some of that was very three-chord stuff, but there was also the post-punk element. Kim and Denise were very much into being a traditional rock band, and Kelly [Johnson, guitar] and I were much more into experimental music and punk. Kelly really loved Bill Nelson and XTC

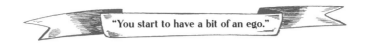

and that kind of slightly post-punk band. I think you can hear a little bit of that on *Demolition*.

KIM MCAULIFFE: Funny thing is, when we first met Vic [Maile, *Demolition* producer] we really didn't get on. He was trying to tell us what to do and how to play. And we thought we knew better, so we didn't have a very good start with him at all. Anyway, we got through it. We were being so difficult and such idiots, thinking that we knew best. We did that, and of course it got really good reviews, and from then on we loved him dearly.

When we first met him we did not get on at all, but then we realized that he knew what he was talking about and we didn't. He really liked the four/four bass drum. And we'd be going. "We want it this way!" He'd done "2-4-6-8 Motorway" [Tom Robinson Band] with the four/four beats. There were other bits we didn't think were as good as we thought we could do. But he knocked us into shape.

We were pleased with *Demolition*. Your first album is pretty easy because you've been playing those songs for a while by the time you record your first album. The most exciting thing was that it got in the charts, I think to number twenty-eight, and the record company sent us twenty-eight red roses each.

DENISE DUFORT: Reading '81 was a highlight. I remember thinking, "Oh my God, we're going to headline the Reading Festival." That was a big deal. A real big deal. We were with Doug Smith and for some reason they got us this Cadillac to turn up in to the festival. It turned out to be Jayne Mansfield's Cadillac—not the one she died in, though, not the one she was decapitated in. It was a big, pink Cadillac, and that's how we drove to Reading, with the top down, driving up the motorway to Reading. There was a bunch of bikers all beeping their horns at us. They escorted us to the gig because they were going and they seemed to know who we were. They were beeping their horns, and we were waving. And then they escorted us. Fantastic.

KIM MCAULIFFE: We'd been to Reading ourselves. So to do that, and be the first all-female act to headline, was amazing. And we had the biggest flash bombs as well, apparently. They could be heard about ten miles away when they went off. That was in the days before health and

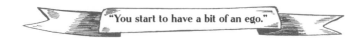

safety—you wouldn't have that now! They were like bloody bombs going off. That was a great night.

STEVE DAWSON: We played quite a lot with Iron Maiden. And we kept bumping into them—we'd go to a motorway rest stop and they'd be there. But it's like I said, the rivalry between southern bands and northern bands…there's a massive gap. Humor's different, accent's different. Without sounding elitist, I think the tunes we wrote were more catchy songs. Not just a riff with some twat fucking screaming.

A lot of the so-called NWOBHM bands wrote riffs with singing, and not songs—melodic tunes that you can whistle. Iron Maiden were sort of in that bracket to me. We couldn't get us heads round why they kept stopping and starting. There would be ten bits in one song. We used to think, "Why is there no groove?"

To me, they came into their own when they made *Number of the Beast*, because there were tunes on that. Actual tunes that were crafted. Not just riffs with singing and guitar playing for the sake of it. Like constant guitar soloing all the way through the song. It's something we could never write.

PAUL DI'ANNO (vocals, Iron Maiden): The sound was bloody horrible on our first album. That music was so powerful and it didn't come across that way because the overall production was pretty shit. I wasn't happy at all. We was excited making that first album because it was the first time we'd ever done it. We recorded down at Mutt Lange's studio, and I spent most of my time chatting my ex-missus up. I suppose the reason we let it carry on the way it was is that we didn't know any better. When you hear it later on, it's, "Blimey, great songs but shitty production."

DENNIS STRATTON (guitar, Iron Maiden): My favorite songs were "Remember Tomorrow," "Strange World." When you try and explain the punk side of Maiden on the first album, everything was played too fast. Even now they rush some of the stuff. The slower, more easy on the ears, less frantic songs I preferred. Things like "Charlotte the Harlot" were rush, rush, rush, so you never actually got into a groove when you played it. My personal favorite was "Phantom of the Opera"; even that's got slow parts to settle down in.

MALCOLM DOME: Wil Malone is a very diverse producer who has gone on to do a lot with different things from different areas. I'm not sure he was definitely a rock or metal producer. But what he allowed Maiden to do was to play. And I think he does a lot to enhance what's on that first Maiden album. I know that Steve Harris hates it. But what would he have done differently?

Obviously Martin Birch came in for the second album, very well established, and took them to a different area, in the same way Mutt Lange took Def Leppard into a different area. But they needed to do those first albums to get where they wanted to with the next album. They were good stepping stones, and they still sound really good.

DENNIS STRATTON: My first gig with Maiden would have been the first gig of the *Metal for Muthas* tour. We had to come off that because we had to make the album. Then the album had to be done because we were going on tour with Judas Priest. I remember being onstage for the first gig, it was a wall of noise. I'll never forget how loud it was.

When I first joined and we were rehearsing in Hollywood Studios, when we had a break we'd go down the pub for a pint, and Steve used to tell me about the gigs they were doing up in Middlesbrough and all that. They had the Green Goddess, up to Warrington, Burnley, Blackburn, doing the circuit. To be honest, I never ever believed the fan base they had until he told me how many people would go and see them in Middlesbrough. I remember a guy from EMI saying, "The album's going to go top ten with advanced orders from the fan base." That was when I realized they'd done their homework, they'd done their road miles in the transit van.

PAUL DI'ANNO: Apparently I said we were going to blow Judas Priest off the stage on the UK tour, but I don't think I did. I think it was somebody else who said that. I've had this row with Kenny Downing. I know we were bloody hungry, but I don't think I'm the one who actually said that. And if I did I apologize, because I'm a huge Judas Priest fan. I love that band. But I bet he was annoyed. We went on two tours together, so I bet he was well pissed off. You'd think you'd remember it if you came out with something stupid like that.

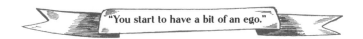

K. K. DOWNING: I can remember reading it in a magazine and we were still in the studio, the *British Steel* record was just being wrapped up, and I thought, "Who the fuck is this lot?" Because the thing is, I'm just there thinking there are so many bands that would be grateful for the tour, why should we give it to these bands if that's their attitude? That's a big statement to make. And it didn't happen, that's for sure. It didn't happen, it just created an atmosphere.

DENNIS STRATTON: Paul insulted K. K. Downing and said something about blowing them off the stage. And you don't really do that before you go on tour, because you're relying on that main band to let you use the PA and the lights. I don't know how much EMI paid to buy on to that tour, I imagine it wasn't a lot, because we sold a lot of seats. Judas Priest were having a little bit of a lull in their career and they felt threatened, which was right. We had a lot of support and it was growing. But they got the hump and they only let us use half the lights.

DAVE LIGHTS (lighting technician, Iron Maiden): Reading '80 felt like a triumph.

PAUL DI'ANNO: Me and Steve Harris was in a right old state. I was really frightened inside, but something happened. An old girlfriend I used to go to school with, I met up with her a couple of days before we played Reading, in a pub in Leytonstone. So I met her and I invited her up. She didn't have a fucking clue what I was doing—she was well taken aback. So I had something to occupy my mind a little bit. I just went on and did what I had to do, and she was, "Cor, fucking hell." She'd never seen anything like it, and that took the nerves away a little bit. It's only when you're thinking about it before you go onstage that it's horrendous.

DENNIS STRATTON: We were coheadlining with UFO, because they were another band that weren't really pulling their weight at the time, but Maiden were growing rapidly. Rod [Smallwood] went, "We don't want any special effects. We're just going to go on, do the show. We're better than them." I said, "Rod, we've got to have something on stage." My brother-in-law was there, and Loopy [Steve Newhouse, roadie] and Pete the guitar tech, and they had them rubber Eddie masks. I said, "Go and find some fire extinguishers." And that's all we had. But when

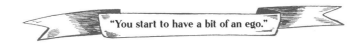

you see the photos with them fire extinguishers coming out of the side, it just makes a bit of difference.

We had no dressing room, just a little caravan to get changed in. Rod said, "We're not spending no money, we're not having a hospitality tent like everyone else. We'll use the normal bar." That's why everyone called him Tightrod.

DAVE LIGHTS: UFO were the headline band—in those days at Reading there were two stages. There was a lighting rig that was already there, but we wanted to be different from every other act so we brought our own lighting rig in as well, which caused a bit of an uproar. We had a load of pyro we brought in as well.

UFO had three guys jump out of an airplane with UFO on their parachutes. They came in late, and they came in as Maiden were going on, so it looked like it was part of our show. Phil Mogg [UFO's singer] was bent out of shape, to say the least. We were on a big high playing to that amount of people. And it was our show. Our gig. As far as we were concerned, we took it over.

DENNIS STRATTON: One hundred thousand people, and the crowd are in the palm of your hand, and Paul's not talking to them. For some reason he used to get shy and walk off. After about two or three songs they were going absolutely mad. You could hear them, but you couldn't see them. Dave Lights was mad on aircraft lights, and he used to have them all round the stage facing outwards. When he was on the lighting desk, he used to put the light from the desk under his chin, and all I'd see on the tower was a little face.

I think it was two or three songs in, the crowd were deafening, but you could only see the first two rows. And I went to the mic—if Paul's not going to talk to them, I'll do it. I went to the mic: "You alright? Dave, I can hear 'em but I can't see 'em. Light 'em up." All of a sudden, boom! Soon as you saw that, the people went miles back, as far as the eye could see.

PAUL DI'ANNO: It really dawned on me about three days after. I woke up shaking, and I think it was Reading coming out late. I was euphoric after the shaking finished. I'd just kicked another one off my bucket list. Brilliant.

The original TYGERS OF PAN TANG (from left: Robb Weir, Jess Cox, Brian Dick, and Rocky Laws) face down the mods of their hometown Whitley Bay. RIK WALTON | ARENAPAL

DANTE BONUTTO (writer, Record Mirror *and* Kerrang!*):* We always felt with Maiden they lived by a certain set of values and rules that needed to be respected. But we felt we shared those because we were rock fans as well. I think with rock music, if you love rock music, it doesn't just define who you are, it defines what you're not.

And I felt they were very much about this particular thing. It was about believing in something, being very down to earth about it, and sticking to your guns. And not being driven by trend or genre or fashion or media. It was about having that very blinkered, in a positive sense, view of the world. You were single-minded, shutting out bullshit. And they never veered from that.

MALCOLM DOME: MCA were thinking: "We've got to be part of this. We don't know which bands to go for. Let's just sign as many as possible. The ones that stick, we'll keep. The ones that don't, fine, we'll drop." Tygers of Pan Tang were the ones who stuck.

ROBB WEIR (guitar, Tygers of Pan Tang): It was a multi-album deal, depending on how the first one went, I suppose. As with any band, I

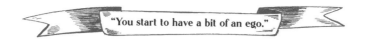

mean, if your first album bombs, the record companies aren't going to be interested. But *Wild Cat* very much didn't bomb: it actually made history for a hard rock band, entering the charts at eighteen.

JESS COX (vocals, Tygers of Pan Tang): On the Magnum support tour we went back to Newcastle City Hall. That was something else because as a kid all my life I'd gone there to see the great bands. And here was me, actually playing it. By then we were pretty confident, and it was this guy—not me—who got up on stage and did all that. So I could just do it. It's daunting playing your own town. You think, "Oh shit, they know me here. I can't pretend to be a rock star." But then again, "It's what I do now. It's what I am."

We played the City Hall quite quickly with two or three other bands. We played with Def Leppard one time, we played it with Saxon 'cause we did the *Wheels of Steel* tour. So we were coming around semi-regularly. But the first time we headlined the Mayfair, I remember that quite vividly, because that's where I spent my misspent youth. I first went there when I was fifteen years old—though I was probably only twenty when we played it. Other bands were very jealous of us because we'd come along from nowhere, basically, and been swept up and got this major deal. We were the first band in the area to get a major deal and all the old guys in the other bands were not very impressed. Especially when they decided they were magnificent musicians and we were just crap, and we were kids who didn't know what we were doing, kids who'd had all this stuff given to us and we didn't deserve it.

Some of the other bands came along to heckle us. Certainly Fist came along to heckle us. Or the bass player did, anyway. I think he threw a glass at us. It was quite outrageous. We knew it was going to happen—we had forewarning, so I came on in an American football helmet. But we got on with it and did our thing, and people seemed to enjoy it. But it was daunting to play your home town. When you go away you can be somebody else, but when you're on your home turf, every band is the same. Later it becomes nice, but in the early days it's like, "Oh shit."

ROBB WEIR: Your head grows and you start to have a bit of an ego. It's hard not to, really. You're writing songs, you're playing them, there's hundreds,sometimes thousands, of people standing in front of you, singing or playing air guitar along to some stuff that you've

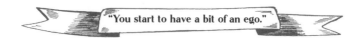

created, whether it be in your bedroom or in the lounge or in the bath or whatever, and all of a sudden, the masses are all joining in, kind of getting it. So you think to yourself, "Well, I must be doing something right," and then of course, afterwards, they all appear, they want your autograph and want to talk to you and have a pint with you and all this kind of stuff. So your brain naturally says to itself, "Crikey, I'm a bit of a celeb here, I'm wanted." So of course that in turn develops your ego, whether you want one or whether you don't. And egos are the undoing of people, unfortunately.

But we were having so much fun. Probably too much fun. Crikey: what's not to like? A few factors go into it. The fact that you're in a different place every day, you're on top of your game of your chosen profession, as it were, people come to see you as an artist, although that didn't really sink in as much as you're just wanting to play every night. In fact, you could play all day long. The thirty-minute, forty-five-minute support spot that you've got just wasn't enough. I guess it's adrenaline, but the juice running through your veins really turbocharged you.

And it's something which is difficult—and other artists will say this to you—it's difficult to quantify to somebody, to people, to anybody, that hasn't experienced it. It's a very unique experience, it's an absolutely amazing experience, and it's orgasmic. It's better than that. It depends what kind of orgasm you have, but oh, my goodness, it's almost beyond words, the feeling and the rush you get when you're stood behind the curtain, and when the curtain draws back, and your chosen intro plays the last nanosecond, and that's it; you're off, and you're searching for eyes, you're entertaining, you're looking for nods of approval, there's a thousand things going through your mind. How many people are there? Where are they standing? How are they reacting? Are they jumping about or bobbing their heads? Are they playing air guitar? Are they singing along? It's marvelous, it really, really is. So, yeah, we were having a fantastic time.

TOM NOBLE (comanager, Tygers of Pan Tang): The Saxon support was categorically very important, and it told us three things. It told us how good the Tygers could be, because Saxon were magnificent on that tour. They were ten times better than the Tygers. We used to watch them every night. It told us we needed another guitarist, because on

TYGERS OF PAN TANG prepare to let loose in Holland. COURTESY OF TOM NOBLE

the big stages the sound simply wasn't big enough. The main time we realized that was the band did five gigs with Scorpions, and on the stage at the Apollo in Glasgow, the band were dwarfed. That's when we said, "Guys, we're going to need another guitarist." The third thing was that it started to cast doubts about whether Jess was going to be the right singer for the band. He was the gruff-voiced heavy metaller, and I think the band had visions of being more than a heavy metal band.

ROBB WEIR: I knew I had to up my game when John Sykes joined. John was always a ten times better guitar player, so I was never going to match him for playing ability. But I thought to myself, I'm going to have to sharpen things up if they're not already sharp. And I think I did sharpen up, listening to live recordings. We used to record shows on the desk, and listen back to them on cassette player, for timings—whether we were playing fast or slow—and John and I would listen to our guitar solos, and just get a feel to make sure we were on the ball. It was the big time, and there were lots of bands out there in competition. And he

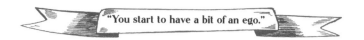

changed the songwriting. On *Wild Cat*, most of the musical ideas came from me, but *Spellbound* was half me and half John for music.

JESS COX: We were auditioning guitarists and John was one of the applicants—we'd seen this photo and he looked absolutely fantastic, like a rock god. Then we heard the tape and, "Fuck! God almighty! He's got the job!" John came and lived with me, and we hit it off big time. We were inseparable, all the time we were together.

Even after I'd gone from the Tygers we both still lived in the same flat. He lived with his uncle in Spain when he was a kid, didn't go to school, couldn't speak the lingo, but his uncle could play the guitar and he showed him. That's how John became so fantastic. Because that's all he could do. He didn't have any friends or go out—he just played his guitar. That's why he became so great.

TOM NOBLE: When we got him into the band, and I told MCA—you couldn't make this up—one of the guys at MCA said, "That's a foolish thing to do, Tom. Do you not realize that two-guitar bands are on the way out?" I said, "Like Def Leppard and Iron Maiden, you mean?" I couldn't believe this guy had said it to me, but it was because MCA wanted power.

ROBB WEIR: We did a club warm-up show in Wallsend [as Sykes's first show, before Reading 1980]. We did it under the pseudonym of the Wild Cats, which didn't really fool anybody. It was absolutely rammed, sold out. It was an upstairs community hall, and our road crew set off so many smoke bombs and explosives that we couldn't see the audience and the audience couldn't see us, for twenty-two minutes. We played absolutely blind for twenty-two minutes. Nobody could see anybody. It was ridiculous. *Spinal Tap* was alive and well long before *Spinal Tap* was thought of.

JESS COX: Everybody took their girlfriends to Reading—there was a big crew, must have been twenty or thirty of us. We went up in two or three nine-seater coaches to the show. We came through the backstage area and walked through. Once you were there, people were wanting your attention. You were backstage with a huge amount of press. Everybody was there—big stars, and the big bands on the show.

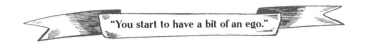

Coverdale and Whitesnake were there. They were funny because they were such rock stars. Everybody had little caravans to get changed in, and a time slot allotted to you to use it. I think they had their own one, but they had a roped area around it backstage. They had a silver Rolls-Royce to take them from their caravan to the backstage ramp so they didn't have to walk through the scum. Which was about a hundred yards. Britt Ekland was there, and me and John tried to chat her up at the bar. Nothing doing. She talked to us for a while, but she was with some big hairy guy.

As the time got nearer I got nervous, then, "It's your time," and my stomach turned. It was broad daylight. Walking up the ramp was like being taken to be shot. I'd never seen the crowd, and I thought, "Once I get on I'll be okay." But of course there was a big bloody delay. Robb had a bloody board of effects, and the impedances all fucked up the PA, so it went mad. It blew up and wouldn't work. It was a nightmare. His pedal board was like a coffin—it even had a lid on it. We'd sing the funeral march as we took it out of the car.

So I'm standing there with time on my hands, and I think, "I'll have a look." I made the big mistake of looking between the Marshall stacks, and I could see this utterly humongous crowd. I couldn't see the end of it. I could see white tents at the perimeter. I was, "Oh my God, I shouldn't have done that."

I remember going on, and once you get on you just got on with it. You hear guitars and they sound like a car starting up, and you're hearing it from both sides, and because they're rock guitarists they haven't got a clue about turning the bloody amp down. They have the damn thing blasting. Then you have drums behind you that sound like someone's building a house. You can't hear through the wedges because the guitars are so loud. You've got to be as calm as you possibly can and go out and sing. Hopefully you are coming in at the right time, you've counted the bars right. Then there was some girl onstage dancing behind me. Who the hell's this girl? And I looked over I could see Bob Harris in the DJ booth. Was this girl part of the show? And I couldn't hear myself, and there's this mad crowd, and it's hot as hell. That's what I remember. You just have to look like you're meant to be there, even if you feel like you're dying.

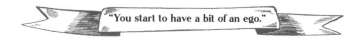

But we did it. We threw all the right shapes, did all the right songs, and I think it went okay. We went down really well. It was terrifying initially, but we got through. It was almost John's first gig, and he was standing in the corner with his head down. He was very shy. He didn't move. He stood in one spot. There was none of it being John Sykes throwing his guitar around and flicking his hair. He just stood there with his head down playing his guitar.

TOM NOBLE: There's a great picture of the band going onstage, and the picture on their faces says it all. They looked slightly haunted. Because here they are, they've got what they wanted. They are going on in front of sixty thousand people, and it's the first time they've ever done anything like that. And the looks on their faces say everything.

ROBB WEIR: We were the fourth act on, on the Saturday afternoon. It was huge. We'd never played in front of that amount of people. We'd played the Mayfair in Newcastle to two thousand people, but we'd never played to forty-six thousand people. And you couldn't see the back of the audience. It was absolutely mega. I remember standing side-stage and geeing everybody up: "Come on! Let's do this!" But secretly shitting myself. If they only knew how I really felt inside. It was tremendous.

Back then you could buy a plastic bottle that held a gallon of beer—like a plastic petrol can. It would have been quite a weight. And someone threw one of those at us half filled—not with beer, of course, but with the aftermath of what beer turned into. In those days, people did throw things with no rhyme or reason, apart from the fact they could. We didn't get anything else thrown at us, but this thing arrived on stage, and my immediate thought was, "Well done," because that must have been some feat to throw that a good eighty yards. They should have put him in the Olympics.

JESS COX: The head of MCA, Stuart Watson, had said to me, "Jess, the only reason we signed the band was because of you, because you looked so great." So everyone was telling me how wonderful I was. But Chris Tsangarides [producer] was more of a purist, and I think maybe he started saying, "You need to get a guy in who can break you in America—and in America you need someone who can do high harmonies." He saw the Tygers as a career as well. He wanted to be

The remade TYGERS OF PAN TANG circa 1982 (from left: Rocky Laws, Fred Purser, Jon Deverill, Brian Dick, Robb Weir). COURTESY OF TOM NOBLE

with them for ten albums. Everyone saw the way Def Leppard were going for America, even if they were despised in the UK and Europe for it. Ultimately they became superstars in the States by being this harmony American band. That's the way people saw it going.

Then all of a sudden, Stuart Watson was also in among it and I could hear these rumors going round about them wanting a high harmony guy. Nothing was ever said to me, but I could feel attitudes were getting a bit stinking towards me.

TOM NOBLE: After they had toured with Saxon and played at the Reading Festival, they went on a tour of their own, playing universities and ballrooms. And on the very last night, Rod MacSween [the band's booking agent] and his partner Barry Dickins came over to me and said, "We're not totally sure this band can go to America because it's not the right kind of sound." So the band, who were fiercely ambitious by this time, chatted it over with Jess, and said, "This doesn't seem to be working the way we want it to."

I got the job of sitting down with him at a magnificent building in Whitley Bay called the Spanish City, and we sat in the bar there and talked it through. The six of us and Grahame [Thompson, Tygers comanager] had been together for two years and didn't have any other

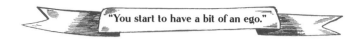

friends. We were all each other's friends, so it was very, very hard. But I had to think, is this going to work? And it was obvious it wasn't. And I don't think Jess was desperately happy at the time either. I think he felt slightly alienated from the band.

ROBB WEIR: It was clear in the bigger rooms that Jess's voice wasn't strong enough. And certainly our agent, who had the biggest agency in the UK, ITB—it still exists and Rod still runs it—he had an opinion, and shared it with our management. And things had to change. So Jess went his own way and did what he did. And we advertised once again. One hundred and twenty singers came over a period of two or three days to the rehearsal room and sang a song with us.

Rod was just expressing an opinion. As an agency, I guess they have to sell you, and they have to be confident in that fact—they're selling you to a promoter who's going to pay a lot of money, and you have to deliver the goods, in as much as you have to obviously perform, but you have to bring people in. Jess was a good front man. Unfortunately, not the greatest vocalist.

JESS COX: After I left, in late '80, the band didn't last that much longer as they were. Only two years, really, because there was more Chinese whispers and other band members had to leave. John Sykes was the first. He and I were so close that when I left, I think he said, "Stuff this for a game of soldiers." And he went. By the end of the band, there was only Brian Dick [drums] left in it who was an original member.

Still, NWOBHM made my life. Tygers of Pan Tang made my life. Every day is a Tygers of Pan Tang day. It's there somehow.

13

"The singer swallowed a bee. He carried on."

Monsters of Rock launched in August 1980
at Castle Donington. The scrappy first outing gave
few clues to how enormous the world's first music festival
dedicated entirely to metal would later become.

PHIL ALEXANDER (fan, Kerrang! editor): Another thing that is crucial about the impact of NWOBHM is the creation of hard rock festivals around the world. That show at Donington Park, that's the template, Paul Loasby putting that bill together. Yes, we know it's essentially a Rainbow show, but it isn't: it's a proper festival.

Of course, Reading has been there before, but Reading is not as puritanical as that. What you're getting at that point is the cream of hard rock in one place. Reading will give you some of that, but it will also give you some new wave, some esoteric stuff, and the Climax Blues Band. It's not as pure.

ROB HALFORD (vocals, Judas Priest): That first Monsters of Rock was an extraordinary day. It was the first metal festival. And it kicked off a whole experience, not just in the UK but in Europe.

PAUL LOASBY (promoter, Monsters of Rock): Bill Graham had used the name Monsters of Rock for his Day on the Green festival in Oakland. We spoke to Bill Graham, said, "Do you mind if we use that name?" He said no. I think he'd pinched it as well.

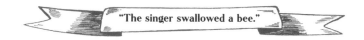

DANTE BONUTTO (writer, Record Mirror and Kerrang!):
One of the first gigs I ever reviewed was the first Monsters of Rock festival in 1980. I'd never been to a rock festival before. I was taken up in a coach to see seven bands play in a vast expanse. There was no second stage. Seven bands—that's what you watched. That was kind of groundbreaking at the time.

I'd never experienced that before, and to me that was really important—because you were in a field with lots of other people who loved what you loved, so it was very empowering and very defining. And you were celebrating with other people that you liked, and you were seeing all these bands who were right at the top of the game and defining their genre. It gave enormous impetus to the fact that rock was more than just a collection of individual bands. It was a whole movement, a whole scene, an international force.

Many people also picked sides: a lot of people hated that first festival. I was with some journalists from *Melody Maker*, who absolutely hated it, while I was absolutely loving it. I thought as well as representing the audience, I think it helped to define and grow the audience.

PAUL LOASBY: I was with Harvey Goldsmith [concert promoter] for four years, and there's always the itching belief you can make it on your own. I had been speaking to Neil Warnock, the agent, and he said, "I've always fancied someone doing a metal festival in the Midlands." Reading had moved more and more to hard rock, but it was still a mixture. It had lost its identity, and the audience drop-off was quite significant.

I got out a map, and went: Birmingham, M6 motorway, M1 motorway, and drew a triangle. This was in the back room of Harvey's offices. And the guy who did all of Harvey's site production work—the name was Mike Good, and he was good, because the basis was getting the toilets right happened to be in there. I said, "Do you know any sites near Birmingham, but near the motorways?" He said, "I do: Castle Donington racetrack." This was March 1980.

I looked at my map, and fuck me, it's next to an airport. I'd always dreamed that helicopters would fly into the airport and the artists would collect their cars to go backstage. I didn't think about airplanes taking off and drowning out the sound. In my mind metal would drown it out. I didn't realize the runway was just over the fence from the racetrack. I thought, "This looks good."

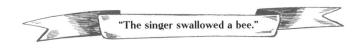

NEAL KAY (DJ, promoter, impresario): By then promoters had realized rock fans were never going to settle for a mixed bill. Not in this country. No bloody way. We're like that. Rock is a way of life. It is not just music.

PAUL LOASBY: I rang Bruce Payne, Rainbow's manager, and said, "Suppose I got a heavy metal festival together and made you an offer? I know Ritchie Blackmore hates open airs, but what do you think?" He said, "Yeah, we'll do it." It was obviously the money. I said it would be sometime in the summer, and he said that would be fine. It was really that easy. I'd got the headline act, I'd got an idea for the site.

On the Saturday we were going up. I had no money, but I had become very friendly with [promoter] Maurice Jones of MCP. I used to meet him in Birmingham when I did gigs at the Birmingham Odeon, and we'd get completely blattered and have a curry. I said, "Here's the idea: Rainbow, may have a site, summer, what do you think?" And he said, "I'm in, fifty-fifty." I thought, "Well, I've laid off half." So we all agreed to meet at Castle Donington.

There was a natural bowl on the site, and it was perfect. We drove round, saw the airport. We were told the farmers were amenable to helping out with car parking because they were used to it from the racing. So by the third week of March it looked as though everything was fine. We come out of there going, "This is doable, let's run." We did a deal with the site—it wasn't very much because we had so much work to do. It was five figures, but on the low side of five figures. It was very much seen as a one-off experiment.

The track only had one date available, August 16—the first day of the football season. And the following day was a vintage car race, but we thought they would just cry off. We had all these problems because we were so short of time. By the time we were three weeks in, we decided to announce it. At this point the bill came together. Bruce Payne wanted his other act Touch opening, and Judas Priest said yes pretty quickly, so did Scorpions. Maurice lived door to Rob Halford, so that made it pretty easy.

ROB HALFORD: Maurice was my next-door neighbor, but I don't think we only got on the bill because we were neighbors. He was our Midlands promoter, and we'd done a couple of UK tours with him.

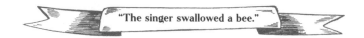
PAUL LOASBY: We all thought Scorpions was a good idea. Saxon had done support work with Rainbow on the previous tour. So that all made sense, and they were flying by this time. April Wine was considered to be a slightly different version of rock. And Riot...they were around. The key was Rainbow, Judas Priest, and Scorpions.

The whole bill took less than two weeks. There weren't other festivals competing for bands, of course. I think Judas Priest were the last to confirm. But it was pretty quick. For fees, the top figure would be so many thousands, the second one would be half of that, the third one would be half of the second, and that's how it went. So whoever was bottom would be getting a few hundred. But they were playing to the biggest heavy rock show.

STEVE DAWSON (bass, Saxon): I don't know, to this day, how much we got paid for that. Because, believe it or not, when someone offered us a gig—for instance, in the early days, if someone said "Will you play at Newcastle Mayfair?" we'd say, "How much will you pay?" "£800" So you knew how much you were getting. But once you move on to a different level, you don't know how much you're getting for a gig.

We played Sheffield City Hall—if it were under normal circumstances, you'd say, "Well, we want three thousand quid." But you don't know, and that's a scam, I think. If somebody said, "Do you want to do Donington? Will you do it for five hundred quid?" you'd say, "Fuck off, there's gonna be sixty thousand people there. We want more." But the negotiations weren't in conjunction with the band. It was the manager. So I don't know if any of the bands knew what they were going to get, apart from Blackmore. He were probably on a percentage.

JENNIE HALSALL (publicist, Samson, Rainbow, and Monsters of Rock): I started doing Rainbow's press in the late seventies. It was basically, "You know the band, they're going to be the headliners." The easy option is always to get the headliners' PR to do the gig. So I was pleased to do it because it meant extra money for me. For Castle Donington my fee was £700. For the whole of the Donington campaign. That was really hard work. My job was to promote this gig and to sell tickets. We sent out a press release to as wide an audience as we could. Then you start doing phone interviews with local papers— you hardly did anything live. Then the promoter would call you up

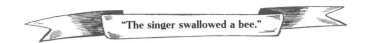

and say, "We haven't got enough tickets sold here, we haven't got enough tickets sold there." I would have been under a lot of pressure, because whenever you did a tour your responsibility was to do as much promotion to sell tickets as possible. National press was most important—*Melody Maker*, *NME*, and *Sounds*.

JUDY TOTTON (publicist, Monsters of Rock): In the very early days, one of the most important targets was the local media, because you couldn't survive without the support of local media and their readers. And the council in their part in it all was very important. So you're talking about the *Leicester Mercury*, the *Nottingham Evening Post*, the *Derby Evening Telegraph*, Radio Trent, BBC Nottingham. The local media were very, very important.

This was before emails or mobile phones, so everything was done through the mail. Once you knew where the pockets of rock fans and heavy metal lovers were based, you could always target that, so we always had quite a big contingent come in from Manchester and the north of England, particularly. Nottingham was always a good one.

JENNIE HALSALL: And reviews were important, as they knew they were going to do it again and they needed the reviews to get in the money, because they had to take out massive loans. They didn't have the thing they have now, which is concessions—now at those big gigs the concessions make a huge amount of money before they even start. But they didn't have that then.

PAUL LOASBY: Tickets went on sale in April at £7.50 and the first week of sales was eighteen hundred, so Maurice rang me and said, "Shall we cancel?" I said, "Well we can't, can we?" He said, "No, I was only joking." It was all very well trying to do budgets, but because we hadn't done it before we had no idea. We hoped we would get fifty thousand. If we had got fifty thousand it would have been a dream come true. We wanted to break even at thirty thousand.

However, because it was done the way it was, we were not in control of some of the aspects—like the cost of the police. That's always a difficult one. But also, the "fuck factor" as you'd call it, is the miscellaneous. It rained and it rained and it rained, so suddenly your trackway costs [temporary road] and your straw costs rise. Let's say you put down ten grand. Well, that's going to balloon to more like fifty grand. And that's what happened. Because it just didn't stop raining.

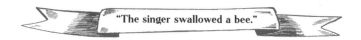

JENNIE HALSALL: It was so wet, it was disgusting.

PAUL LOASBY: I was up twenty-four hours a day getting ready. With two weeks to go we were on eighteen thousand ticket sales. I'm going, "This is the end. How am I going to get out of this one?" I'd borrowed money from people to put up my half. Not from banks. There were a couple of people who thought it could be good, three were friends, two were legitimate investors in the business. I hadn't bought a property, so there were no assets behind me other than these loans.

What I didn't know is that Maurice didn't have any money either. I'd laid it off, but he had borrowed money as well—but I didn't know that for years and years. With a week to go we crossed to about twenty. The week of the show we went up to twenty-seven. So we're opening with about twenty-seven thousand. And this became a pattern, for all the time that I was involved, that the walk-ups were staggering. They were thousands and thousands of people. On the day, we did eight or nine thousand on the door. We ended up with just under thirty-six thousand. A quick bit of math showed that we'd lost money, but it wasn't horrible.

ALLAN JONES (writer, Melody Maker): It turned out that the previous night Rainbow held a full-scale dress rehearsal, which included their pyrotechnics. They wanted to end their set with some huge explosion, so they'd brought a ton of fucking gelignite or something and it had accidentally gone off. It blew out Judas Priest's entire backline as I remember, buckled some of the lighting rigs, nearly killed a load of people who were sitting backstage.

So as we arrived we were given a document to sign, indemnifying Rainbow and the promoters in the event of injury or death, however caused. So that was a sobering start to the day.

GRAHAM BONNET (vocals, Rainbow): The pots were backstage. Fucking huge. They looked like garbage bins. During the drum sound check, Cozy Powell wanted to use gelignite for the explosions in his "1812" solo. They said, "You can't." He said, "Give it a shot." So they got this gelignite in and loaded the bins and it fucked up the whole PA. So they had to send out for a new PA. All the speakers had just ripped. This was a big explosion. It was like death. Bless his heart, he wanted it to be really spectacular.

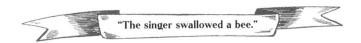
"The singer swallowed a bee."

K.K. DOWNING (guitar, Judas Priest): Rainbow blew all of our speakers in their sound check. So we had to replace all our speakers.

PAUL LOASBY: On the day I left the site maybe one, two in the morning and I joined everyone in the bar for a quick drink and went back to my room. I never touch Scotch normally, but for some reason I had some Scotch. At five o'clock I was back up and it was still raining. I was opening the doors. I tended to be doing more on site, whereas Maurice had taken over much of the administration. If it hadn't been for Maurice Jones the festival would never have reached the heights it did. I just happened to have come up with the idea for the act and the site.

So I go around with a policeman opening all the gates, one at a time. So where I started, those people got to the front of the stage quicker. The box office was open, and the queue had started and it just kept coming and coming. You open the site at six a.m., and the first act's not on till twelve, but you're always checking—have all the dressing rooms got the drinks and the deli trays and the ice?—but also the council needed to inspect the site, and you're checking in with the police and traffic and the car parking. There was never a spare minute.

JENNIE HALSALL: You're too exhausted to even think. You are so tired because you're running everywhere. You've got to get this person here, get that person interviewed there, or the local TV station wants to do something onstage. You're looking for your artist who's wandered off somewhere. But yes it was fun, because it was ridiculous.

NEAL KAY: It was a two-day thing for me. I had to go up there and do sound check and stuff the day before. Went up there in my Jag. No trouble with a Jaguar, you get backstage. That was something I learned from doing the Hammersmith Odeon. You turn up in a Ford and the old boy around the back never even raises the barrier. You drive up there in a Jaguar XJ6, no problem. "Good afternoon, sir. Nice to see you again." They think you're one of the band.

So I went up there and we got called at night to do a little sound check—back then I was right on the front of the stage at one side, not hidden away. When I went out there in the morning of the show—didn't sleep the night before, I watched Jimmy Bain [formerly of Rainbow], pissed out of his head, fall into the fireplace at the hotel.

ANDY COPPING (fan, Download booker/promoter): I was seventeen or eighteen, living in Lincolnshire. There was a group of friends from Lincoln, six of us. We were all huge rock music fans and we all decided to go to Monsters of Rock. We went in an open-topped jeep, all piling in the back. We had sandwiches, beer, we took everything with us.

We took the journey to Donington Park, and even that was an incredible experience because it felt like we were going to Vegas. We were going somewhere really special: all these amazing bands we all loved, all on one bill, all on one day. The weather was glorious sunshine, and when we were driving down, on one of the roads as we got close to the site, there was police directing traffic, and there was an AA sign that said "Pop festival." We were all freaking out, going, "This isn't a pop festival, this is a ROCK festival!" We were outraged by it.

BIFF BYFORD (vocals, Saxon): I rode around half the track on a bike, which was great. We had a great time—we had a few girls with us, too.

MARK MANGOLD (keyboards, Touch): It looked like Woodstock. The hill goes up. Cozy Powell [Rainbow drummer] rode motorcycles, and I know he took a couple of spins around the track before the gig. So there were a couple of people going very fast on the track.

PAUL LOASBY: Don't ask me why, but we forgot to put water on site. There weren't any bars because we weren't allowed to sell alcohol. All we had was orange juice, Coca-Cola, and whatever. We had to announce there was no alcohol on sale. But you could bring in plastic, so you could see huge plastic containers full of beer or wine or whatever. So nobody went short, it's just we weren't selling it.

ANDY COPPING: We walked up, went in through the gate, and then had to cross over the racetrack. That itself was an experience. We got over the racetrack and had just come to the brow of the hill, and we looked down—I'm getting shivers telling you this now—over the hill across this sea of people. Thousands upon thousands of people, and you could see the stage at the front with scrims either side with the Rainbow album cover covering the speakers. And I'm like, "Oh my God." Every single person there was me. Thousands of carbon copies

The staging of Monsters of Rock appears primitive today, but at the time the scrims covering the speaker stacks were the last word in production values. COURTESY OF NEAL KAY

of me. For a small-town boy from Lincoln, this was the most incredible experience.

People had band T-shirts on. I was talking to some guy from Bristol in a Judas Priest T-shirt, and he'd seen them at Bristol Colston Hall. You'd talk to someone else wearing a Saxon T-shirt, and they saw them in Manchester. And suddenly we were all talking to each other, and we were all talking about the experiences of gigs we went to, and then someone else would turn out to have been at a gig you'd been to at Stafford Bingley Hall or Leeds Queens Hall. And you'd be talking about the shows.

One of the things that resonated with me more than anything was that although this was tribalism, it was one tribe. It wasn't like football, where there's someone from another town and they ain't into your team. This was a total community. You wanted to hear each other's stories. The community spirit I bore witness to and was part of is so hard to describe.

PAUL FLOWER (fan): I'd not been to a racetrack prior to that, and it was quite exciting. You're getting off a coach with hundreds of other people, queuing with thousands of people, and you see the tire arch over the track, and the stage was the biggest I'd seen at that point. There was a vast number of people. The biggest shows I'd been to at that point were eight thousand people, and there must have been thirty-five thousand here.

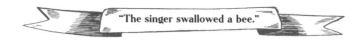
PAUL LOASBY: We had advertised no camping, but we had set up camping, too, because we knew it was going to happen. There's a hilarious piece of me being interviewed for the local news, where I'm talking and talking, and there are occasional campers walking by, one or two at a time. It's not a stream.

ANDY COPPING: When I walked over the hill and saw it, the stage looked like a palace. Now I look at photographs of it and I'm going, "Oh my God." It looked like you could have pulled the thing over with your bare hands. The other thing was the complete lack of toilet facilities, and the complete lack of food and beverages. I just remember the queue for the one burger van—it was just insane. In fairness, you could take food and drink in. Honest to God, I don't remember seeing a toilet. Everybody just went up against trees, or anywhere they could. There were people urinating wherever because there was nowhere else to go.

NEAL KAY: I think they paid me a hundred quid for the day. Eleven o'clock in the morning comes, my gear set up. It's all sound checked. "Good morning Castle Donington!" Whoa! And do you know what? The first four or five rows right down the front were all Soundhouse members. I knew them all. Now that produced a few tears. I never expected it.

I just looked down there and I thought, "Fuck, they're here." And I welcomed everyone to the first event. I was dead chatty, because I am an entertainer. I picked the right moment to play "Stairway to Heaven," just as the twilight hours were coming. It was a great day for me. I was having an immaculate day. The littlest nothing on the bill and I was really enjoying myself doing my job.

JENNIE HALSALL: It was definitely not luxurious. We used the raceway pit lane as dressing rooms, so each band had a pit stop and then they'd be ferried to the back of the stage where there were further caravans with bits and pieces on. But then I was ferrying the press backwards and forwards in my little Mini, with two walkie-talkies and trying to coordinate everybody. And my modus operandi was to get everyone as drunk as possible.

ALLAN JONES: The backstage area was so far from the stage that at one point we couldn't hear a band called Riot playing through eighty

thousand watts. They had to run a shuttle service from the backstage area to the stage, otherwise it was a thirty- to forty-minute walk. But the shuttle service was terrible. It was like a milk cart or something. And it was a very bumpy ride.

JENNIE HALSALL: The dressing rooms were half a mile away from the backstage area. They had given me a tent, and put a frilly flounce around it as the PR tent. I remember that quite distinctly. Maurice Jones hated paying money out. He was tight. He was so tight.

STEVE DAWSON: When you get to a big festival, you've always got things in your mind like Woodstock. That's what I thought a festival were like, and Donington were, really, in my eyes. It weren't as big, obviously, but you've got a massive backstage area with all these things going off. You could hear the other bands playing, and the roar of the crowd. And there were all these famous faces walking about—Judas Priest, Rainbow, Scorpions. And the dressing rooms were a long way away from the backstage, in the pit lane. The dressing rooms were all side by side, upstairs, above the pit lane. And we came out and had to walk there. You could hear the crowd. It were just fucking buzzing.

ALLAN JONES: The other thing that stood out from the early part of the day was that Arista Records had a mobile home on the site, with a bar serving drinks, and there was going to be a reception for Touch, who were kind of poodle-haired American rockers, who were the festival openers.

DANTE BONUTTO: They had a champagne reception at eleven in the morning, and I'd never been to a champagne reception. So I had to see that! I got there for that, and it was amazing. Then it was time to go and watch the band. But the backstage was a long way from the stage. We had to ride there, bouncing around in the back of a truck, being taken to the stage having had our Buck's fizzes.

GRAHAM BONNET: It seemed very groovy and posh and wonderful. It felt absolutely massive. And it almost didn't matter what the stage was like. It was the audience that made the show—and they always do. That day was probably the best day I've ever spent in music. Nothing went wrong.

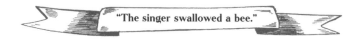

MARK MANGOLD: It was magical. There are pictures on the *Monsters of Rock* album sleeve where you see the policemen standing there as people are driving in. Being Americans, even the look of that with their bobby hats was very cool. We drove up and hung around the stage, and we in Touch were very well taken care of. You see people start to come in, and they go on as far as the eye can see, so it's just an amazing, mind-blowing experience.

We were tight. We were not worried about our music; we had played it so much and we knew what each other were going to do and we knew we would be musically doing our thing. So it wasn't a question of being nervous, it was a question of getting out there to the crowd. They don't turn up all the faders for an opening band, so I think we were a bit quieter than some of the other bands. I'm not sure how it translated out there to the huge meadow, but I think people close to the stage really got to hear it. Very often they'll put a piece of tape on the fader on the mixing board and say, "If you move it beyond this, you will die." Or something like that. But we did our best. We unfortunately had to cut a song—for various reasons we went on late so we had to cut one of the songs. But we got our point across.

ALLAN JONES: After their set, Adrian Boot [photographer] and I made our way back to the reception area to find all the girls from Arista weeping and wailing because of some catastrophe.

JENNIE HALSALL: A wasp flew into the mouth of the singer from Touch when they were onstage, and he had to be carted off. There was a lot of speculation about whether that was false or not, but it absolutely wasn't. It was mad. It was completely and utterly mad. Mad and memorable.

DANTE BONUTTO: The singer swallowed a bee. He carried on.

MARK MANGOLD: It was Doug Howard, our bassist. He had a beer and was going back to his amp, and took a chug, and there was a bee in there. I think the bee was drunk in the beer and Doug swigged it and that was it. I don't think it happened while we playing; I think it was after the gig.

ALLAN JONES: After enduring their set I was rather hoping it was the fucking singer.

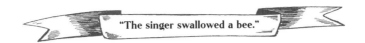

PAUL LOASBY: Donington didn't know this, but the drainage system for the bowl stopped halfway down. So all the water bubbled up about a hundred feet in front of the stage, where this river of mud started flowing, underneath the right PA stack. So the stage sank on the right. It was quite severe—something like a foot. On a stage a hundred-foot wide that's some decline. There was a wonderful book that came out a year or so later, of overhead Britain. Somebody took a photo and it ended up in the book—a wonderful shot of the crowd, and you can see this river of mud going through the right-hand side. It's really huge, and there's an enormous gap in the crowd. It really does look awful.

JENNIE HALSALL: First of all, they put the stage in the wrong place. Second of all, it absolutely pissed down. It was a Glastonbury, mud everywhere.

ANDY COPPING: When we got there, I was in trainers, and they got a little bit dirty. But I wouldn't say muddy. We were lying on the grass, at the top of the hill where you look down on to the main arena. We were lying there with shirts off, so it wasn't bad up there. But obviously all the water would have gone down the hill, and all the crew putting the stage up would have churned it up. But we didn't see any of that.

JENNIE HALSALL: The mud in front of the stage was about a foot deep. I had not experienced pee in plastic bottles before. That was the first time I had ever seen that. And seeing these bottles of yellow being thrown around in front of the stage and thinking, "Urgh, how disgusting," because the guys at the front of the stage were not going to move.

DANTE BONUTTO: It was no more a mud bath than we've come to expect. It was a rawer experience, but we had nothing to compare it to. There was massive excitement in the crowd, and because there were only seven bands, everyone played a reasonably long set, and there was pleasure from being in one spot watching everyone do their thing, rather than watching ten minutes here and ten minutes there. It was all bands you knew, had heard about. It made it feel more important, because it was selective.

PAUL FLOWER: We had large plastic bottles filled with lager. And I think it was a warm day. There were lots of bottles being thrown, as was

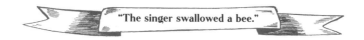

normal at the time. Not by me, God no. I was far too well behaved for that. Not hit by any either, thank God.

ANDY COPPING: The bottle fights. Oh my God, the bottle fights. We can laugh at it now, but it must have been horrific for anyone who got injured. But the sight of all these cans and bottles and apple cores and orange peel…anything was being thrown in the air between bands.

The bottle fights at Donington ran for years, but that was all part of the festive spirit. When you saw a bottle fight going off, anyone sane moved away. First, I don't want to get hit by a bottle with any kind of fluid in it. It's like being hit with a rock. And I certainly don't want to be hit by any container that's got piss in it. There was nowhere to go to get cleaned up, and you would be covered in it for the rest of the day, and you'd go home covered in it. Some people would feel, "If I get covered in mud, that means I've been to a festival. If I get covered in piss, then that means I've arrived." Good luck with that.

STEVE DAWSON: You go up the stairs to the stage, and you could fucking see 'em, as far as the eye could see. And there's only one thing crossing your mind: "Fucking hell, I hope I don't fuck up. I hope I can remember what I'm doing." They announce your name, you go on, there's a deafening roar, and it starts. And you go into automatic pilot then. It's like you're not there. It's like you're just doing something and it's over in a split second, and you come off, and everyone's patting you on the back, saying how great it were, you really killed it.

And you go back to the dressing room, and there at the top of them fucking stairs is Rob Halford in his full regalia. Hat, sunglasses, whip, studs from head to foot. And it were like, "FUCKING HELL!" Let's face it, we're fans. We're in a rock band and we've made records, but we're fans. And that's Rob Halford. He looked to me like he were twenty foot high. He were an iconic fucking figure. But then as soon as he opens his mouth it comes back to West Midlands. It's quite comical.

ROB HALFORD: I was looking at some of the backstage shots the other day, where I'm hanging out with Joe from Def Leppard and Michael Schenker.

BIFF BYFORD: We were obviously selling shitloads of albums, of *Wheels of Steel*. By the time we walked on stage, though, we were the

underdogs because all the other bands on there had at least three albums on us and maybe five, some of them. But it was a great day. I don't think anyone could have foreseen how well we went down. We only played thirty minutes and had to cram in our songs, and it's my job to get the audience going as well. But it was great—I remember every second. We did very fast, aggressive, songs, not like the other bands.

K. K. DOWNING: I was a bit disappointed we weren't headlining, really. And I thought Rainbow, with whatsit in the suit and all that, weren't what they were. I'd obviously enjoyed Purple, and Rainbow with Ronnie James Dio, but I thought this was—can I say?—a bit of a thrown-together band. If we didn't headline, Scorpions should have. Good lineup apart from Rainbow.

ROB HALFORD: I felt a little bit anxious before we went on: it was a big deal. We knew this was a very exciting opportunity to make a strong metal statement as Judas Priest, to the massive numbers of people who'd come from all over the UK and—we later found out—from all over the world. It was a very important show, not only for Priest but I think for everybody that took part in the event. It was the beginning of something that was going to exponentially grow and become part of the metal world.

NEAL KAY: I made one of the worst mistakes of my life. Very few mistakes I've made, but I made one that day. I can't remember the number Priest had played, but it was right at the end of their set. The next thing I see the stage crew moving in and moving all their backline away. I thought, "Fuck, they finished." So I said, "Right, you lot, round of applause for Judas Priest!" The place went absolutely nutty.

And before I realized what was going on their manager rushed up and said, "Hey, they're supposed to do an encore." I said, "But they're taking the backline away." He said, "You should have waited to be told." I said, "No one's told me anything all day long. I just saw what happened and reacted." But that was my fuck-up. That's why I never got back there. That was my fuck-up. I was made acutely aware of the fact and I felt very bad.

K. K. DOWNING: I don't remember that.

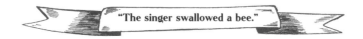

ANDY COPPING: For me, Saxon, Scorpions and Judas Priest totally got it. They went out there and just ripped the crowd apart from the minute they came on to the minute they went off. They delivered killer sets. Those three were incredible.

DANTE BONUTTO: Everyone went down really well, and Saxon wrote that song "And the Bands Played On" about it. The weather was reasonably kind, and everyone felt they were part of something special—we didn't know there would be another one the next year. It felt groundbreaking. We were all in it together, watching rock.

PAUL FLOWER: I'm pretty sure it was the first time I saw Judas Priest, who I was pretty unsure about, but the motorbike onstage made an impression: at least they were trying something a little different. Everyone else just brought their theater show—there was no scaling up. It didn't feel like anyone had put any extra effort in.

MARK MANGOLD: Judas Priest, when he rides out on his motorcycle: holy shit! And consummate performers.

NEAL KAY: Priest were great. I took my camera up there with me. I've got a picture of Rob and the crew bringing his Harley out of its flight case. You know, he couldn't ride it. He never had a license. It was a nice Harley and they had a bracket on the back near the exhaust and a microphone was fitted to it and they fired it up. But Rob himself couldn't ride it.

ALLAN JONES: I didn't really enjoy any of the music that day. The Scorpions were okay, and Judas Priest were amusing. Rob Halford rode a motorbike onstage, which for comic purposes I was hoping would go over the edge. But he stopped it in time.

PAUL LOASBY: There was a live album, for which we were on a minute percentage. Judas Priest weren't on it, and they weren't on the festival shirt either. I think that was a mistake. It's up to them, but these days you'd want to be on the festival shirt. I think it was more of a management decision. It's like Creedence Clearwater Revival, who didn't want to be filmed at Woodstock. Biggest mistake ever.

ANDY COPPING: As the night drew in, the bonfires started. People made lots of little bonfires. We had gone towards the front for Rainbow,

A wall of Marshalls, K. K. Downing of JUDAS PRIEST, and Rob Halford's great parking motorcycle spot at Monsters of Rock. COURTESY OF NEAL KAY

and my mate tapped me on the shoulder and said, "Look back." And there were all these bonfires everywhere. The smell was incredible. It's a smell you never forget, that smell of bonfires in the air, and the look of them as it got dark. It was like something out of *Game of Thrones*. And then people just running around—somebody found a pallet and smashed it up and then that was being burned, and the boxes they brought their food and beer in.

The other thing I remember is that there were vendors going round, selling these long strips of plastic which were necklaces. You would crack them and put them together and they would glow in the dark, So you would bend the ends together to put them around your neck and you'd have Day-Glo necklaces. That looked incredible. I don't think we'll ever see or feel anything like that again.

PAUL LOASBY: I had a hired car that got wrecked driving back and forward in the mud. I also had an accident in it, which didn't help. I came backstage for something about fifteen minutes before Rainbow were due on stage, and I skidded on the mud and went into a trailer, only to discover I'd just snapped the cables for the quad sound. So the show start was delayed while they repaired it. How could this happen?

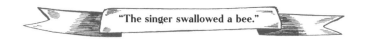

"The singer swallowed a bee."

GRAHAM BONNET: One person had told me there would be around eight thousand people there and when I walked out, I thought, "Oh my God, that's more than eight thousand people." I couldn't believe how many people were there—all their lighters lighting up. And I thought, "Somewhere out there are my mum and dad." And my brother and his wife, and my nieces and nephews, My whole bloody family was out there. They weren't at the front. They were near the soundboard.

But I saw this crowd and blocked it out so all I saw in my mind was four rows, so the other people behind those four rows weren't there. There was light coming from the stage for the first few rows. You see them. It's like you're playing in a rock club. Then you hear the rest of the audience, and it was like a jet plane coming in. It's fucking amazing. When I heard that, I thought, "Is that real?" I was very lucky to be part of that. When we went onstage, people were well fucking drunk, and they were louder than I could believe.

ANDY COPPING: Rainbow were my all-time favorite band. I loved Ritchie Blackmore. I went to see Rainbow in '78 at Stafford Bingley Hall. My mum drove me and my friend there. And when Ritchie smashed his guitar, my friend got half of it. He shoved it under his jumper. So I loved, loved, loved Rainbow, even though by then Graham Bonnet was the singer. Even that *Down to Earth* album they brought out was incredible.

There was no question I preferred the Ronnie James Dio era of Rainbow, but I was obsessed with Ritchie Blackmore and you would sometimes see great shows, and sometimes see poor shows, in comparison. I would put the Donington performance somewhere in the middle. My personal feeling was that I had seen them better. I don't think it helped, the way Graham Bonnet was dressed. Not that that should have any effect, but as a teenager, when you're seeing denim and leather and studs and long hair, and Graham Bonnet comes out dressed like he did, it was odd.

BIFF BYFORD: I wasn't very fucking enamored of their song choice, but that's Ritchie Blackmore. I like "Will You Still Love Me Tomorrow?" but it's nothing I would play at a rock festival. Definitely not.

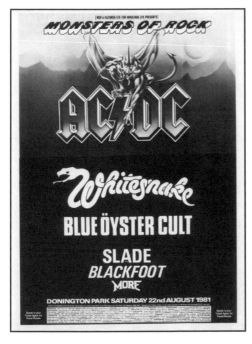

Graphic ad for the follow-up 1981 edition of Monsters of Rock at Castle Donington.

ANDY COPPING: There were a couple of songs—"Will You Still Love Me Tomorrow?"—that had me thinking: "You're headlining! You should be banging out some really big tunes!" But that's classic Ritchie Blackmore. He wants to cheese off an audience. I didn't go away disappointed, and you can't lose sight of the fact I was wrapped up in the whole event. The whole thing was a new experience, and you wanted to go away thinking it was fantastic, so you kind of made concessions. And I would say there was definitely a concession with Rainbow.

GRAHAM BONNET: The sound was fucking amazing—it was quadrophonic. Unbelievable.

ALLAN JONES: Anything like that, you try to see as much as possible because there's always the possibility there might be some startling fucking moment when you're least expecting it. But I don't think Ritchie Blackmore playing "Greensleeves" through an eighty-thousand-watt sound system much appealed to me.

PAUL LOASBY: At the end, I happened to be walking past Ritchie Blackmore's trailer, and he just came out. I said, "Congratulations,

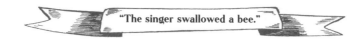
Ritchie, that was tremendous." He said, "The reviews will be terrible." I said, "That's as may be—did you see the power out there?" He said, "Yeah, it was good," and walked off with a smile on his face.

I'd worked with him since '76 and yes, he had a reputation, but you sort of knew what he wanted and that was delivered. And if it wasn't, you knew about it.

DANTE BONUTTO: There wasn't much lighting. So when it got dark you couldn't see where to go.

PAUL FLOWER: It was a bit chaotic getting out, finding your way out to bloody coaches that all looked the same wasn't the greatest thing in the world, especially when you're tired and hungry.

ANDY COPPING: I think we must have got lucky. There's no question about it. I'd gone with a group of guys—two of them, bizarrely, were farmers who were used to working in the dark. And one of them, it was his open-top Land Rover and he drove. We just followed the way we came in. We knew at the top of the hill we had to go over the racetrack, and there had to be an exit close by. But there were no lights, there were no stewards directing you.

We definitely got lucky, because when I went on my own to Reading, I couldn't find my car. On the first night I found a bin bag and slept in that by the entrance to the arena. It was horrific. But at Monsters of Rock we got lucky and found our vehicle and got out, despite there being literally no direction whatsoever.

DANTE BONUTTO: When I met up with the guy from *Melody Maker* who was taking me home, he was so upset about the whole event and hated it so much, he took off his shoes and threw them out of the window of the car. He said, "I want no more of that mud anywhere near me." He dropped me in the middle of nowhere.

ALLAN JONES: I don't remember us giving anybody a lift back.

JENNIE HALSALL: I couldn't read Allan Jones at all on the day, but when his review came out [in *Melody Maker*], I just about wet my knickers. It was just about the most hysterical thing I'd ever read in my life as a PR. He got the whole day and smashed it. And the manager made me read it to him on the phone.

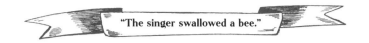

ALLAN JONES: I've had worse days than Castle Donington, just to be clear about it.

JENNIE HALSALL: I heard a click on the extension and I figured it was Ritchie. I never found out if it was. But Bruce [Payne, Rainbow's manager] said, "Right, Jennie, come to the hotel. I'm going to Heathrow, you're going to come with me." And I was just screaming with laughter: "You're going to fire me, aren't you?" I got to the hotel, got in a cab, and halfway there Bruce said, "You're fired." That was when my association with that client finished.

GRAHAM BONNET: Monsters of Rock was the last time I saw Ritchie. Cozy left Donington, and Don Airey [keyboards, Rainbow] and I were staying at a hotel in Leicestershire. Cozy was meant to be in the same hotel but he got in his car and drove away. He sort of flitted away.

Don said to me, "I don't like it any more. Cozy's gone and I can't do without Cozy." I said, "I feel the same way." He said, "He's a really important part of the band."

We tried till six in the morning begging him to stay, but he had work coming up he wanted to do more than Rainbow. We were saying, "Cozy, for Christ's sake, man, we're going to make another album." Anyway, he was gone and it was very disappointing. So Don said he was going to leave the band. Okay. I went back to LA. But he went back to the band. I didn't go back to the band.

PAUL LOASBY: We lost about ten grand each, but it didn't put me off.

STEVE DAWSON: It was summat to say: "We've just done Donington," or, "We're doing Donington." But it weren't, "This is a milestone that will be remembered for a long time." I don't think many people at the time realized it would become a regular thing, either. It were just thought it would be a one-off.

BIFF BYFORD: We had no idea what a big deal it would turn out to be.

PAUL LOASBY: And the classic car race on the Sunday—they decided to carry on. So a load of the campers and people who'd fallen asleep overnight stayed on, and they had a successful classic car race. The next year they did the same. Only by the third year of Monsters of Rock did they acknowledge it had become too big for that.

Biff Byford of SAXON, Monsters of Rock Festival, Castle Donington, August 21, 1982.
GEORGE BODNAR | ICONICPIX

14

"The daft bastards would be bound to set themselves on fire."

The rise and rise of Venom, who preached the gospel of Satan,
practiced the gospel of "everything bigger than everyone else,"
and left a blueprint for all cult underground metal to follow.

MANTAS (guitar, Venom): On May 23, 1979 I saw Judas Priest at
Newcastle City Hall. It was life-changing. That's all I can describe it
as—life-changing. How can I describe it? The early formation of Venom
was happening at that point and I said Right, "this is what I want to
do." And the guy who did it was K.K. Downing. At that point there was
no extreme metal, so this was as hard and as heavy as you were getting.

I remember walking out of Newcastle City Hall with excitement just
pounding in my ears. When the band came onstage I remember that
blond guitarist ran on and I was like, "Wow! That's what I want to do!"
He was the epitome of the English heavy metal guitarist. The leather,
the studs, the hair, the Flying V.

I have got no shame in admitting that days after that I went to the
local music store in Newcastle city center and I asked them to get
me a Flying V. No way could I afford a Gibson so I got a copy. It was
white and red, exactly the same as K.K.'s. And then I went to Boots
the Chemist and bought a bottle of bleach and that was it. So K.K.
Downing became not only a guitar hero to me but he also became a
distant mentor. Back in those days there was no internet, no social
media, no connection with these people, so they were gods. They
didn't take a dump in the morning and go to the shops to buy a jar of

coffee. God, 1979 is a long, long time ago, but it's still for me a life-changing event.

ABADDON (drums, Venom): I met Jeff [Mantas] through an advert on a wall in a music store. He was looking for a drummer. We'd been playing in the bedroom and getting stale with that, so I answered this message. We got together, and I wasn't very impressed with the other members of his band. I thought it needed a bit of a shake-up if we were going to do anything, or we were all going to be stuck back in the bedroom again, or in a church hall or school hall. I thought the whole thing needed a shake-up.

The stuff Jeff was playing was very much Judas Priest, that kind of ilk. It wasn't aggressive enough. I was listening to Motörhead and I'd seen some of the punk bands, and I thought we needed to be more aggressive. We needed to be faster, we needed to be more in your face, more vicious. The lyrics had to be something new. It was hard to drag Jeff through this, but when Conrad [Cronos] joined there were two of us of the same accord and it made that a little bit easier.

MANTAS: The initial lineup of Venom, the very first lineup of Venom, was myself, Dave Rutherford on rhythm guitar, Abaddon on drums, Clive Archer on vocals and a bass player whose name I can't remember. And his girlfriend always used to come to the rehearsals and sit there and look at us in disgust. The language was foul, we were foul, it was horrible and she'd just sit there and roll her eyes constantly until one day he turned up and went, "I'm sorry, I've got to fucking leave here."

ABADDON: Jeff met Conrad, and he thought he might be good on the bass-playing part. He knew Conrad worked at Impulse Studios, which was where Neat Records was. That was the reason Conrad was in the band. Jeff wanted him in because Jeff had already been to Neat Records to get a deal and he'd been sent away and told there was a price for recording in the studio.

MANTAS: I invited Conrad to come along just to have a look at the rehearsals. We were rehearsing in the West End of Newcastle in a church hall. So anyway he turned up this Saturday afternoon. Abaddon's first words when he saw him walk in were, "Oh fucking hell, who's she?" So this was late '79, early '80.

DENIM AND LEATHER 339

CRONOS (bass and vocals, Venom): My main music was punk. That was my generation. You had the metal stuff going along beside that, which was why I used to call myself a metal punk.

My first job leaving school was in a recording studio, Impulse Studios, which became Neat. I remember when I went for the job, thinking I'd be able to record my band, finding out the studio was really old-fashioned, didn't have any modern music. It was local comedians and things. My influences were really punk and bits of Black Sabbath and Status Quo. I wanted to merge the two together.

The NWOBHM had started, and you had bands like Iron Maiden and Saxon coming out, but I just saw that as a rehash of Purple and Zeppelin and bands like that. I wanted something different. Plus I had that punk element, which they didn't have. I had that snot and piss and shit element, which I wanted to put back into metal. I saw more and more bands shoving socks down their pants and putting lipstick on, and I just was disgusted by that, to tell you the truth. Fucking hell, if heavy metal was anything it had to be raw and dangerous and in your face.

ABADDON: Conrad's background wasn't with Motörhead or anything like that. Conrad was more into new romantics and Kate Bush and that sort of stuff. He talks as if he was a punk, but he really wasn't.

TOM NOBLE (comanager, Tygers of Pan Tang): When the Tygers were in there recording, I used to play pool with Conrad, and he would say to me, "I'm going to start a band, and we're going to be huge, and we're going to have more bombs going off than any other band." And he was a really nice guy. I used to think, "Dream on," because he was actually a Kate Bush fan.

MANTAS: We adopted the stage names because we just wanted to piss people off and be arrogant and fucking obnoxious. We all seemed to be of the same mind where we wanted to be the loudest, the fastest, the biggest, the baddest, the dirtiest, the nastiest.

That was the premise of the band, and I'm not going to go out as Jeffrey Dunn, he's not going to go out as Conrad Thomas Lant and you're not going to go out as fucking Tony fucking Bray or whatever your fucking name is, so we decided to change the names. And at that point I think we had one copy of the Satanic Bible between us that we'd bought in a fucking newsstand or something like that.

ABADDON: We were just walking one day, the three of us, and I think Jeff said he'd seen a Manta, which was a car. And he liked the Mantis thing because he was doing some taekwondo stuff at the time. I think he thought it sounded oriental when he added the "s." But he always wanted to keep the Jeff with it. I was reading a lot of Stephen King and that sort of stuff. I got turned on to some of the Bible stuff that was left out, and I wondered why you would have Matthew, Mark, Luke and John, but you wouldn't have Peter, who was more important in the story of Christ. So I went back to reread the Bible.

I got to Revelation and went "Holy hell, this is exactly what we're writing about." And Abaddon is named in the Bible, it's from the Hebrew, and I loved it. Cronos had somehow thought his name was something to do with the chromatic bass scale, but that would have an "h" in it. But he missed that out. Then he found out there was Kronos in Roman or Greek mythology, but that was spelled with a "k." So it was kind of a bastardization of that whole thought pattern.

CRONOS: Even when I joined and it was the other guy singing, Clive, and we changed the name to Venom, we all said "We need stage names! We can't go out as Jeff, Conrad, Tony and Clive, you know?" Jeff was first, he came up with Mantas, then I found Cronos. Clive was Jesus Christ. I thought that was a really cool stage name. But we wanted to create something larger than life. We loved what Priest did, the leather and the chains, that was the epitome of metal. There was no mistaking it. You wear that shit, you're metal. Simple as that.

We loved it. It was a great image. We even enjoyed wearing it. A lot of people go on about how uncomfortable it is, but I love that shit. I find it more comfortable than my day-to-day clothes.

MANTAS: Venom's very, very first gig with the four-piece lineup was my girlfriend's birthday party and I don't even think the other members would remember that.

ABADDON: It was in Wallsend, just a club. The thing I remember is getting all the gear set up and getting ready to play. And we started playing and the stage—it looked out on the double doors that opened at the bottom, and because it was a birthday party there were lots of parents in, all sitting down with their hands over their ears, thinking, "What the fuck is this?" But then the doors opened. I remember it as if

there was dry ice blowing in the doors. Obviously there was lights. We had all the lights turned off and a few lights on the stage. But the lights in the hallway behind on the stairs would have been on.

So the doors opened—and though there wasn't, I remember dry ice—and these five figures kind of bowled into the room, standing with their hands on their hips, and I couldn't see their faces. It looked like an album cover. And it was the guys from Tygers of Pan Tang. I'm sure it wasn't anything like that, but that's what I thought.

MANTAS: The next show we did was at the church hall where we used to rehearse, in Westgate Road. We played a couple social clubs on the south side of the Tyne, and we also played a place called the Meth, which was the Methodist Church on Station Road in Wallsend. And after that the next British gig we did was Hammersmith Odeon in 1984.

DAVID WOOD (founder, Neat Records): I went to the first Venom gig, in a church hall in Wallsend. They had the pyro and smoke machines and set it all off, and for the entire set no one could actually see the band. They were immersed in fog. It was exciting. It was really exciting. Too damn loud.

ABADDON: We did a couple of club gigs and we didn't have good experiences because the pyro used to blow the main fuse in the whole building. We did that a couple of times.

We weren't playing to anybody that particularly wanted to come to see us. We weren't garnering a crowd, like Raven were. We were playing to people who basically didn't want to be there. It wasn't like we were making any money at it. And everything else around us was going so right, we just thought, "What's the hurry? It'll happen when it happens."

David Wood was quite vociferous in asking us not to play live. He said the fact we were mysterious was what everyone was ringing him about: "Who's this fucking band? What are they playing at? What's the game? Can I get them? Are they real? Is it just one person? Are there really musicians behind the three of them?"

MANTAS: I don't think Clive was very appreciative of the overtly Satanic influence we were trying to have with the band. There was a bit of friction between him and Bray [Abaddon]. So Clive went and Conrad took over.

VENOM hittiing the bricks in Shad Thames, London, August 1984. FIN COSTELLO | REDFERNS

ABADDON: Clive was an odd guy. When I worked with him in the factory, if you had a bottle of pop at break time at work, he would ask you, "Are you going to open that?" And I'd say, "Yeah." "Well, are you going to offer me a drink?" And I'd say, "Yeah." "Can I have the first drink?" He predicted COVID and all that. He was very insulated.

He had to have his mam make his fried eggs in the morning, because only she made them the right way. He was a nice guy, but he was always a little bit weird. And when they said, "Clive doesn't want to do it any more," I don't think in my head, even though he was my friend, I even questioned the fact he wasn't going to do it. I just thought, "Yeah, okay. What do we do?" Conrad said, "I'm going to have a crack at it." And I thought, "Yeah, okay. Can you do that and play the bass?" And he said, "We'll go in the studio and we'll find out." And to be fair to him, Cronos has a recognizable voice. And he had a recognizable attack, that throaty, Lemmy sort of attack.

CRONOS: I used to see bands and think: "You're massively talented, but you're just sitting in this club getting your fifty quid," and I never understood it. I wanted to go the opposite way. I wanted to be the Kiss

of Newcastle. People said there was no way I could do that, so I wanted to do it. That was the reason behind the leather and the studs, and all the time spent sewing and putting in studs, and getting bleeding fingers. And all the time creating these big drum risers.

ABADDON: My drum riser was about ten-foot square, and it was made with a steel frame off a garage. At the time there were a lot of houses being pulled down. A lot of urban redevelopment. A lot of council houses were getting pulled down, and these new homes built that nobody could afford. And I nicked this frame off a garage. Now that I think about it, the stuff I pulled off it was probably asbestos, because a lot of the garages were flameproofed with that. It was the steel frame that was left. And I got some big four-by-eights, so it would have been eight-foot square. Two eight-foot boards.

Where my mam and dad lived was in a cul-de-sac, horseshoe shaped. But in the middle was a big field where we used to play football and whatnot. I took all this steelwork out and built this drum riser, to be sure it would work, in the middle of the field. And took my drum kit out there, and put my drum kit on it, and started playing. And all the neighbors were like, "What the fuck's going on with that kid?"

So the vans had to get bigger. We had to spend more money on the vans because of course I would throw a hissy fit if I couldn't have my drum riser at rehearsals. And then I painted the logo on a piece of cloth in front of the drum riser, so that would look good. And then we had smoke jets under the drum riser, that would come up through the drum stands—I drilled holes so they would come up through the drum riser—and all of that became part of the thing, even in rehearsals.

So when we were at the church hall, which is where all the bike shops are in Newcastle, part of the things people would do on a Saturday afternoon was go and see Venom rehearsing. Because we'd set all this pyro off. You might not like the music, but the daft bastards would be bound to set fire to themselves at some point, so let's go and have a laugh. That was part of the Saturday afternoon experience in Newcastle.

STEVE THOMPSON (house producer, Neat Records): Conrad used to tell us about his band, and in fact he didn't talk about the music so much. He'd talk about how they'd save up their dole money and go and spend it all on pyro. And then they'd go and do a gig and blow up

some village hall. And he'd do a full description of all these explosions. We were charmed by it all. It sounded fantastic.

And once this heavy metal thing started to happen, and we recorded Fist and White Spirit, and I got involved with Raven, Conrad seeing all this stuff pestered me and pestered me. I knew there was a free day, and I said to come in. The three of them came in, Tony, Conrad and Jeff. It was a favor to Conrad. We just had a whole lot of fun. There was no pressure. Nobody knew this band would become mega, with a big following. Tony said to me last year, "You know, Steve, when we did that session I hadn't actually learned to play drums yet." I said, "Gosh, Tony, I would never have noticed."

I saw something. I knew it was different. And I knew there were no constraints upon us, because I didn't even think it would be released. I showed them some things—I showed them a two-note musical interval that comes under the name the triad. It's also called a flattened fifth. But it's also colloquially called the devil's chord. So I like to say I introduced Venom to the devil. When you crank it up, it's really discordant. And they loved it. They used it here and there.

In all honesty, I had no vision of what that might become, and nor did they. They had hopes and dreams, and in their case they came true.

MANTAS: No! We didn't know what a fucking flattened fifth was! There is no flattened fifth on "Welcome to Hell," "In League with Satan," fucking whatever! I didn't know it was the fucking Black Sabbath note—I got no musical theory, I wasn't interested, I just wanted to make a noise. But there's a fucking fairy-dairy tale from fucking fairy-dairy land.

ABADDON: With "In League with Satan" [Venom's first single, 1981], I hadn't been playing all that long, and I hadn't got a drum kit. I had bought all these drums and all these toms. And I didn't realize the snare drum was as important to the makeup of the drum kit as it is. So I had all these toms and just started hammering out this war rhythm kind of thing, because they were there. And Steve Thompson said, "Yeah, that's great. Just keep playing that." And it was building this big rhythm without playing the central part of the kit, which is the snare drum. And people were just like, "That's insane." The guys from Sepultura, when they did the big tribal drum thing, they said that was the first thing they'd heard that made them think, "Fucking hell." It's a huge song to play, with that huge, building rhythm.

CRONOS: When [Steve Thompson] mixed it, we hated it and we didn't want it to come out. We were so stressed out and freaking out. The record label was saying it was okay and it was going to come out. We'd already given them the single sleeve that I'd drawn, with the pentagram on and everything, and we'd done the photo session on the beach, so I was kind of shitting myself. And then, I don't know, the Devil just came and helped us out. It was perfect.

I went into work one day and went into reception and said to the girl, Susan, "So who've we got in today?" and she said, "Oh, nobody's in today." Suddenly a light bulb went on in my head. I said, "I'm just going to go into the studio and put all the cables away, tidy all the microphones into their proper boxes and get the session ready for tomorrow." I ran upstairs, grabbed the master tapes, slapped them on the sixteen-track machine and I remixed all three songs. I think it took me three or four hours. I top and tailed it, mixed them down, put all the leader tapes in, re-marked the boxes, went into the record store, changed the master tapes over on the quarter-inch and then the next day they went off to Utopia Studios in London to be cut into the vinyl.

A week or two later, the test pressings come in and they are so radically different from the mix that this guy had done. I'm standing in the office, they put them on the record player and everybody's looking at each other and I'm thinking, "I'm gonna get fired here. I'm fucked. I've lost my job."

The producer guy's like "What the fucking hell's happened here?" He thought it was down to the pressing plant. He thought they'd re-EQ'd it or re-tweaked it or whatever, to make it sound like that. I had to put my hand up. I turned round and said, "Look, no disrespect, but this is my band, not yours. And you're shit. Your mix is shit and your production's shit and you don't understand Venom. This is Venom."

It was really bassy and over-the-top and boomy and the speakers were rattling on the shelves. I said, "This is Venom, and if you don't like it, fuck off." The record company, not wanting to spend any more money, they said, "Oh well, it'll have to go out the way it is, and if it all goes to shit then it'll all be on your shoulders, Conrad, and that'll teach you a lesson and you'll never work in this industry again." All the usual shit. It came out, everybody loved it, big middle finger to the producer, fuck off.

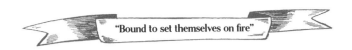
MANTAS: *Welcome to Hell* [Venom's first album, 1981] was supposed to be our second lot of demos. That's what it was, we went through the studio demos and I remember Dave Woods had said, "Have you got enough material for an album?" And we sort of smiled and went yep— "Okay then, get yourself upstairs and do it," and that was it.

CRONOS: Once the single did well, Neat wanted more. That's when they said, "Why don't you come in and record all the songs you've got? We can listen through them and see if there's an album there." Which we did. We recorded all the songs, then the label turned round and said, "Right, we've got an idea—we're going to take the single cover, we're gonna make it big, twelve inches, we're gonna turn it gold, put all the songs you recorded on it and call it your first album." I said, "Nah, we've got to record it properly! They're demos, mate!" But he [David Wood] wasn't prepared to spend any more money. That's it.

TOM GABRIEL WARRIOR (fan, founder of Hellhammer, Celtic Frost, and Triptykon): For me personally, for my career, the first Venom album was very important. I liked the second one too, but the first was absolutely crucial. They were extreme. Nowadays you find extreme music everywhere, in every shape or form, and it's accepted. It's part of the music industry, it's totally normal. At that time, the most extreme hard rock or metal band was probably Motörhead, and if you wanted something more extreme you had to go to Discharge, which was punk but had some metal touches about them. That was it. That was the limit.

And these bands were shunned. Even Motörhead were shunned by many metal fans as being unmusical and too primitive. And then the first Venom album came out and there was an immense wave of rejection by so-called normal metal fans, cultivated metal fans, who listened to Deep Purple or Black Sabbath. They wouldn't accept it. I remember having many discussions with many people about this. But to us, the absolute untamed nature of their music—the first album is also a hybrid between punk and metal, and it tore down any perceived limits or perceived borders, and that appealed to us. We felt the same way: we were always looking for something heavier and Venom gave us exactly this, without any fear. They released their music and it was like a punch in the face, and all the other bands didn't dare go so far.

BRIAN SLAGEL (fan, founder of Metal Blade Records): Look, they weren't the best musicians ever, but there was something magical about what they were doing around that time. It was the whole package. The imagery, the covers, the lyrics, the way they presented themselves. And then the music. It hit a lot of people. They were a massive influence on a band like Slayer.

GEOFF BARTON (reviewing Welcome to Hell in Sounds, December 26, 1981): This album is the musical equivalent to the earth splitting asunder, opening up and revealing a filthy, gaping maw to the Kingdom Below. It's the sound of sinners screaming in eternal hellfire and damnation, hellfire licking at their charred and blackened limbs. It's the sound of a succubus mating orgasmically with a mortal man. It's the sound of Lucifer's voice emanating from Linda Blair's luscious lips. It's the sound of a sacrificial knife slicing bloodily between a virgin's pert little breasts. And above all it's the sound of Old Nick himself, reclining on his red-hot throne, throwing his horny head back and just laughing...An epic of ugliness, a riotous noise, an appalling racket, this album brings new meaning to the word cataclysmic and is possibly the heaviest record ever allowed in the shops for public consumption.

PHIL ALEXANDER (fan, Kerrang! editor): Their lack of technical proficiency is pretty evident. So you're dealing with that idea of garage metal in a lot of ways, overlaid with that overtly Satanic lyricism. So it's doubly exciting. You just hadn't heard anything that sounds like that, and it feels almost made up on the spot, but there's definitely an energy on those records that you don't find on, for want of a better term, normal records.

Not to labor the point, but it's the same with the records Crass were making at that time. They are almost deliberately lo-fi. That whole sound and that atmosphere is incredible. Whether that's by design or by accident I'm not entirely sure. But I'm sitting there in my bedroom as a teenage kid with these albums, going, "Oh my God. This is just insane music."

ABADDON: I think the local bands probably resented us, the Ravens and Tygers and whatever. I think they thought that we were hardly honed musicians, whereas they'd struggled for years and they'd done

all the stuff where you take the pickups out of your guitar and you
have new ones put in and you restring it. We went and got four bits
of wood, put some strings on it and went in the studio. Literally, the
guitars and drum kit were just cobbled-together pieces of shit. And the
musicianship was pretty much non-existent. But the will to do it and
the strength of character was what it was about.

To do that, we didn't need a thousand gigs in working men's clubs.
You needed to just stand up and shout in the street and go out in
fucking spandex with a double-headed axe in the middle of the street
and let somebody take some photos of you.

SIMON PORTER (publicist, Venom, Girlschool, and Motörhead):
They were a publicist's dream in many respects, because they were
so loud and so terrible. People used to take the piss out of them, but
people used to like talking to them because they were good value.

I tried to take it to another level, and create ideas. So it's Venom—
we'll get some snakes involved. I had my photographer of choice who
I always used to use in those days, Fin Costello. At the time he had a
small studio in Bayswater, down in some basement. It was a really small
studio. So I said, "Let's try and get a shot of them and we'll bring in a
load of pythons, but the real obvious, best one would be if we could rig
up something so we could get a shot of Cronos face to face with a cobra,
flared up." So we worked out a way of doing it. In those days you could
just go through the *Yellow Pages* looking for animal trainers and hire a
load of snakes. We hired this guy. He had some very large pythons.

We set up a dinner banquet, with a table for the guys, did all these
python shots. But for the money shot it was planned to do the shot with
the cobra. Fin had built this glass cage, and the trainer—who'd brought
it in a shoe bag—said: "It'll rear up when it's let out, and it'll try to find
somewhere to escape to." The container didn't have a lid on it, and it
was three foot, three and a half foot off the ground. And because of all
the reflections and the glass, Fin had worked out a way of getting his
lens through this very, very small hole, so he could get the shot without
reflections. And it was a really small studio.

Cronos was on the floor, on his elbows, opposite it, face to the glass.
So we let this fucking cobra out, and straight away, within a second, it
finds the hole where the lens was and got out. We're in this very small
room. Fin had obviously lit the whole thing, and there were loads of

cables, and this blasted thing got out, and as it did, Fin's assistant—who was absolutely petrified of snakes—was stood behind me.

Everyone starts to yell and scream, including Venom, obviously. This assistant went into freeze mode, grabbed me round the throat, and was literally virtually throttling me. So I'm stood there, being strangled, and there's a fucking cobra on the loose in the studio. It was one of those surreal moments you can't forget. The trainer saw the cobra entwined in all the cables, pounced on it, put it back in and we got the shot.

ABADDON: We weren't self-conscious about our shoots. It was always a big production deal and it was always in London. So we had to get up and get on a train. It was like doing a gig. And that was how we prepared for it. Everybody who photographed us said we were the best band in the world for that, because we would just fall into poses.

MANTAS: I had a copy Les Paul and I had the bright idea, because it was coming up to Guy Fawkes Night, of nailing a Catherine wheel on to it. And you know those little screamer rockets? I had a couple of those attached to the headstock because I thought I was fucking Ace Frehley [guitarist with Kiss] at that point. So we're rehearsing on a Saturday afternoon and I set the whole thing away—fucking hell… You know those little screamer rockets are designed to go quite far and these two little fuckers did not give up, they bounced off every wall in that church hall. We were shitting ourselves. There's me still running around with a fucking Catherine wheel on my Les Paul and these little screamer rockets bouncing off everything. We're experimenting with lighter fluid, we used to put lighter fluid on the guitar and set that off. Methylated spirit I think we used at one point as well.

CRONOS: We used to make our own pyros. We had these steel pots that were about six inches. We got some wooden boxes made, put three steel pots in each box then filled the box with sand. We ran cables underneath. There was a local shop that used to sell Le Maitre effects and we would buy as many as we could afford. We'd open them up, pour the gunpowder into these pots. We'd make a fuse from a tiny piece of cable between the live and neutral wires, stripped back, plug it into the wall and then that goes in the bottom of the pot. When you flick the switch on the wall, it cracks the fuse and: boom!

There was a lot of trial and error. We brought the ceiling down in one rehearsal room. We had a couple of pots set up. We put a bit too much

gunpowder in. Flicked the switch, lights went out, the ceiling came down on top of us. We were rolling around laughing on the floor. But we could easily have killed ourselves.

ABADDON: We used to try everything. Well, I'd never be setting rockets off. It was always just buying the rockets to empty the powder out. We'd always use the black powder as best we could. Rehearsing in the church hall was always a laugh.

There was one time, absolutely brilliant. Conrad's brother—his elder brother—was a right dandy kind of a guy. He came down to one of the rehearsals at night-time, and I said, "I need to check these bomb pots I've just made." So instead of using all six of the boxes I just brought one box in to Spectra Arts, the rehearsal place [Venom moved to in central Newcastle, after the church hall]. Bear in mind it's the middle of the night. And Conrad's brother had these white loafers on. He was a right dandy. Really good-looking guy. Nice hair and everything.

We all got out of the van, we rehearsed, and at the end of the rehearsal we put all our gear back in the van. And I said, "Right, I'm going to set this bomb off, are youse ready?" "Yeah." "You all stand by the door." This is while I'm still plugging it in to the wall, so I had to stand by the sockets. So we put this thing down the bottom of the room, this box. I said, "Okay, three-two-one." Boom!

All the lights went out, so it was pitch black. I blew the ceiling down. The ceiling came down along with all the muck and the shit that was up there. It all crashed on the floor. And I think it's like an adrenaline buzz, because I could hardly get up for laughing. I was laughing so much I didn't even think about the damage we'd done and how we were going to pay for it. But the last thing I remember was seeing Graham, Conrad's brother, on his hands and knees covered in shit, and his beautiful white loafers covered in crap, trying to get to the back. I couldn't stop laughing.

We'd played these couple of gigs, and we'd blown all the sockets. I'd wire all these things into the board and it would be into a thirteen-amp socket. I was sitting there having a couple of beers, and I thought, "I'm sure you only need a battery to set it off." And instead of just getting a little cap and setting it off with a battery in the house and going, "That's alright," I thought, "I know what I'll do."

MANTAS: There was just me and Bray and we'd had several cans of beer and it must have been two, two-thirty, maybe even three o'clock in the morning and we had the bright idea of testing one of these pots out. So we took this pot and we put it into his backyard, and he had put terminals into this pot and we attached a fuse wire between the terminals and then ran a two-core cable up the stairs, wired it to a three-pin plug and then filled the canister with this bomb powder that we'd got from somewhere. Where the fuck did we get that stuff? It must have been one of these sound and lighting companies that we used to go into. So anyway, we put a good few spoonfuls of this stuff in. Bearing in mind this stuff is quite easily set off by a nine-volt battery.

ABADDON: It was an upstairs flat in a terrace, which backed on to the next terrace, so you had the back lane. It didn't have a garden. It wasn't a flame pot, it was an explosion. I hung the explosion in a bag, put the little firing cap in it, and put wires on to the back of a frying pan, and hung it out the window and set it off with a battery. I was really just checking that a battery would work, instead of thirteen amps, so we wouldn't blow the mains. That was the whole thing.

MANTAS: These two fucking brain surgeons plugged it into the wall, switched it on. My God.

ABADDON: Because it was an explosion, and because it was the middle of the night, and because the streets were back to back, it was gigantic. The actual explosion was fucking huge.

MANTAS At three o'clock in the morning the resulting flash and the bang was fucking colossal, I'm not kidding you. Every light in the neighborhood went on, the fucking curtains were open, fucking hell! Me and Bray ran down the fucking stairs and out of his house and legged it up the fucking street. One guy came out in his fucking dressing gown screaming that the gas mains had gone up and, fucking hell, we ran! Then we thought, "Where the fuck are we gonna run to?"

ABADDON: We went right up the terrace, came back round and came down again as if we were coming from the Mayfair. So we were just whistling, as if we'd had a great night. All the lights were coming on, and everyone else was jumping out of bed, saying, "What the fuck?" And as we got down, the guy next door was out, and me and Jeff

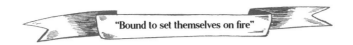

were just walking in, like, "Eh, we've just been to the Mayfair, what's happened, like?" "But it's your house with a big fucking burn mark up the wall!"

CRONOS: I always used to call the band power metal, but I had all these other phrases, like death metal, black metal, power metal. And what made me put my foot down was when Michael Jackson got in the bloody heavy metal charts in *Kerrang!* with Eddie Van Halen doing a solo on "Beat It." Number one in the heavy metal charts? Michael Jackson? I saw red. I just couldn't believe it. I've got no problem with Michael Jackson, but he's not fucking heavy metal. Come on.

So we were doing an interview with Garry Bushell for *Sounds*. And when he said, "So about this heavy metal . . ." I was like, "WE ARE FUCKING NOT HEAVY FUCKING METAL!" I said, "We're black metal, speed metal, power metal." I just spat all these phrases at him. That's where the black metal stuck. So we called the [second] album *Black Metal* and thought, "Right, we're going to shove this down people's throats." [Note: *Black Metal* was released on November 1, 1982; "Beat It" was released on February 14, 1983.]

ABADDON: He's mixing two stories up. We were being interviewed by Garry Bushell, and Garry was a big name on the punk scene. He wasn't interviewing us like other people had. He was interviewing us about being different, and what made us different and why did we think anybody should bother with us. It wasn't a kiss-arse kind of an interview that he did.

He had a copy of *Kerrang!*, and it was actually Bon Jovi on the front cover. And Garry said, "Let me ask you, so it's clear. Are you a heavy metal band?" And I picked *Kerrang!* up and said, "No, if this is heavy metal, if this represents heavy metal today," because it was all the hair metal stuff that was around at the time, "then, no, we're not a heavy metal band."

He said, "Then what the hell are you?" And then Conrad piped up with, "We're power metal, we're speed metal, we're thrash metal, we're black metal." We just came up with this whole plethora of anger with the word metal attached to it. Everything we could say with the word metal on it. And he went on, "Hang on a minute." And he started writing them all down. "What was that last one?" "Power metal." "What was the one before that?" "Black metal." And he wrote them all down.

And those genres became genres of their own. It was only us in one interview being angry because the front cover happened to have fucking Bon Jovi on it. That was all it was. [Note: Bon Jovi first appeared on the cover of *Kerrang!* for issue 92, April 19–May 1, 1985; Garry Bushell does not recall the specifics of the incident.]

CRONOS: We couldn't get a gig. Agents would say they wanted to see us before they'd book us into decent-sized venues. We said, "We're not coming to play the clubs. Why would we play in a club with no effects for you to then see whether we were capable of playing in a big venue?"

So what we did was, we took the first royalties we got and made a video of "Witching Hour" and "Bloodlust," where we hired a theater in Newcastle and brought the lighting rig in, brought everything in. It was money out the window. But it was a speculate-to-accumulate situation: if we record a couple of songs the way we see the band live, all the stage gear, the drum riser going up in the air, the big banks of lights, the effects going off, dry ice everywhere, we can send that to promoters and say: "Do you want that in your country?" And it worked a treat. Because that's how the Seven Dates of Hell tour came about.

ABADDON: We were very aware of wanting to do big gigs. And if we did one gig a year that was huge, that was more what we were about. Because then the press would be talking about it for months. We didn't feel we needed to be a touring band.

MANTAS: We felt that Britain was ignoring us. We didn't feel we had the support from our home country. It seemed that if you were an American band Britain loved you or if you were a nice British band everybody loved you, but we weren't a nice British band, they didn't like us, we didn't like them and that's why we fucked off.

ABADDON: Eric [Cook, manager] had the foresight to ring Nick Peel, who was an agent, and said, "I've got a band on in London. Why don't you come and see them? I want you to be the agent." He said, "Great. Who is it?" "It's Venom." He said, "Okay, I've heard of them but not very much. Where are they playing?" "Hammersmith Odeon." And Nick was like, "Great, who are they supporting?" "It's their own gig. We've booked it." And Nick just started laughing. He put Eric on hold

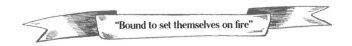

and came back. "Fuck me, you've practically sold out." Eric says, "Yeah, I know, we're looking at booking a second date." "Mate, you haven't played anywhere. What the fuck are you doing with Hammersmith Odeon?" "Well, Motörhead did it, so that's what we're going to do." I think everyone in London was just laughing at this Geordie kid on the phone.

CRONOS: We hired Hammersmith ourselves: we took the risk of putting the money down. And within a week we had sold out.

PHIL ALEXANDER: That's complete bollocks. It was half-empty. Absolutely categorically half-empty. There is no way that was full. I don't even know if the balcony was open.

SIMON PORTER: They didn't sell it out. We made out it was a sell-out, but it wasn't sold out.

TOM GABRIEL WARRIOR: We went to see Venom on the Seven Dates of Hell tour in Zurich in February 1984. And that concert was a massive disappointment. They had brought tons of stage effects, but we wanted to see extremity. We wanted to hear extreme music. And it had become a circus. There were tons of explosions and colors, but we had come for a live representation of the first two albums. And their opening act was Metallica, and Metallica were given hardly any stage. They had to have flight cases in front of the stage to give them room to move, because Venom gave them so little stage, and yet Metallica blew them away. That really shows that Venom weren't able to translate the magic of their first two albums on to the stage. And also, from the third album on they had really lost that bite, that untamed attitude. They had become an act.

PHIL ALEXANDER: Tom's point is really valid, and it's really the contradiction that lies at the heart of Venom. This is the thing: as an audience member you receive this music and go, "They're evil and scary." But in their own minds they're going, "We want to be the biggest band in the world." If that is the case, why are you making music like this? There is no doubt it creates the underground scene; people do latch on to what they do, immediately.

I can understand Tom's disappointment, but I don't remember feeling that at all. I just thought they were magnificent. They smashed

up so much gear. At least three guitars got smashed, two basses. Obviously, Abaddon smashed up the drum kit at the end. But it was a pretty short, sharp set. They were everything I wanted them to be. I could have done without the bass and guitar solos, but I think that was just them going, "We don't really know what else to do, so give it a bit of that."

ABADDON: The show centered around the moving drum riser. We had it built in Wallsend, in the shipyards. It was a ridiculous thing. It started off about three or four feet high, and it was a scissor lift, a gigantic riser, about fifteen feet wide. And the scissor lift went up to about fifteen feet in the air. It had huge spark-firing things. We put a load of gerbs along the front of it, firing down, so when the thing took off and started going up, it would look like the drum kit was taking off.

But the problem was that it all had to be balanced properly. It all had to be correct in the way it would go up, and the hydraulic pistons had to be coordinated properly. What I didn't allow for was the fact that when we filmed the show that night, the camera guy and his grip, the guy who had control of all his cables, they both jumped up on the back of it. Which made it tip backwards.

So if you look at the Hammersmith Odeon video, you can see a part where the kit starts going up and then it stops, and then it carries on. Where it stopped you can see me screaming at the camera guy to get the fuck off the riser, but the camera guy just thinks it looks heavy metal to have me screaming at the camera, so he just stays there. This thing had cost us three grand or something. It was all nicely engineered, but in the end there were drum roadies underneath jamming bits of wood under it to try and keep it from tipping over.

And my kit was absolutely gigantic. Absolutely weighed a ton. It was a Ludwig kit we had made with twenty-six-inch bass drums. Normal drum kits are twenty-twos, or twenty-fours at most. But we had two twenty-six-inch bass drums. So if it had tipped over backwards and gone off the back it would have been quite a mess.

MANTAS: No matter what you call it these days it's still the Hammersmith Odeon. And every time I see a show on TV like a comedy road show or something like that and it says "Live from the Hammersmith Apollo," it's "Fuck, I've played that place!"

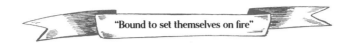
GEOFF BARTON (reviewing the Seventh Date of Hell in Kerrang!, June 14–27, 1984): The biggest drum kit I've ever seen, giant ramps bearing the legend "666," immense backline and bank-upon-bank of lights drew gasps of genuine admiration; this was unexpected class from such a relatively small-time band. You couldn't exactly apply the term "class" to Venom's music, though. The band patently can't play, and while most songs sounded like road drills and were completely unrecognizable, each was permeated with awesome amounts of sheer, staggering, senses-shattering total noise power…We were consistently confronted with less of a wall of sound and more of an unassailable fortress hewn from sonic granite, its drawbridge down, decibel demons howling from within.

MANTAS: By the time of *Possessed* [the fourth Venom album, 1985] it was over. It was fucking over. We got overtaken rather quickly. I think we dropped the ball and I think the band that picked it up really fast after us was fucking Slayer.

I remember when Slayer supported us on the World Possession tour. There was a balcony in this fucking venue and part of the balcony was closed off for VIPs. So Slayer had opened the show and I had never seen them live so I thought, "Oh I'm going to go up into the balcony and watch a bit of the band before I get changed and ready for our show." I went up into the balcony and I was right above Dave Lombardo [Slayer drummer] and I just stood there just looking just thinking, "Fuck me, we've got to follow this." Jesus Christ they were raging, they were fucking raging.

ABADDON: I think the fact Jeff thinks that is indicative of where his head was at that point, because I see a band being faster or heavier than us as a gauntlet being thrown down to get back in the studio and make something heavier or faster or louder. I don't see it as: "They're louder and faster than us, so I better stop." I don't take that point of view at all.

That was the tour Jeff didn't want to go on. He didn't turn up. And when he did turn up and we finally got him there, as soon as Jeff got onstage he said, "I want to go home." I was like, "Fuck you, you just got here." "Yeah, and I just want to go back." It was all negativity from then on.

MANTAS: At the end of the day, you had a job to do. You had to get up there and give it what for. You can tell when someone who's got a day job is sitting there fucking hating it watching the clock all day, but when you're on tour and you've got to go back into the same bus and you've got to go back to the same hotel and you can't get away from your workmates, there's a massive strain there.

CRONOS: From the highs of the *At War with Satan* [third album] thing to the crushing lows of the *Possessed* album, it was just a band that came to the end of the line. We all got out of perspective and it's not about any one person. We all lost it. It took three people to fucking tango in the first place, so if the three of us can't fucking get it together then it isn't going to work. So I think we should all shake hands and part company.

I remember Jeff saying once, "We're all trying to get to Newcastle, but we're all taking a different route." I said, "I'm not heading to Newcastle, I'm aiming for Madison Square Garden, so we're not even heading to the same place."

KEITH KAHN-HARRIS (fan, sociologist, and writer): As much as anything, it's the creative rereading of Venom that is vital in the history of metal. The central conceit through which the black metal genre was born was, "Okay, what would happen if we took that seriously?"

I think the wider influence is very important in thrash. They're sort of like your slightly embarrassing uncle. You love them, they've inspired you; you wouldn't be the same person without them. But you wouldn't want to be like that. That seems to be the place Venom has in metal. It is the iconography but also they were the first people to say, "What if we played metal incredibly fast? What if we took things to the next level?" It's like an experiment that you really honor them for doing, but ultimately people who came after could do it better. You still honor that history.

PHIL ALEXANDER: I started writing for a French magazine called *Enfer*, which means "Hell," when I was sixteen. They didn't know I was sixteen; I just wrote to them. I did an interview with the guys in Venom in 1984 for a feature where you played music to other artists and they would offer an opinion up without knowing who it was. At that time there was a lot of bog-standard hard rock, and I remember playing

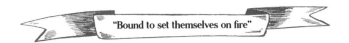

them a Y&T song or something like that, and they hated them because they were a "girl's band" or something like that. But I remember playing them an EP by an Italian band called Bulldozer. I'd bought it on import. It was a piece of extreme metal. Just a simple, primal piece of extreme metal. But what does it sound like? It sounds exactly like Venom. And basically they turned around and went, "Who is this? Is this us?" The point is: by 1984 extreme metal is properly alive and well, and a global concern. It completely stems back to Venom.

15

"It could be pretty vile."

The NWOBHM was overwhelmingly male. For the men, the onset of rock stardom brought sexual opportunities as never before. For the women of Girlschool, the macho metal world presented problems none of the men had to deal with.

JENNIE HALSALL (publicist for Samson, Rainbow, and Monsters of Rock): Most of the record business was all blokes. It was hard because you got treated really badly. That's the way it was. You just shut up and got on with it.

Being at a record company at the beginning of my career, I got so used to it. It was normal. It was normal that the boys earned more money than the girls did. It was normal that the boys got expenses and often the girls didn't. It was normal that as a woman you often got passed over for something and a man would get it. It was just normal. It's when you look back later on that you think, "Oh, that wasn't very nice." But that's the way it was.

JODY TURNER (vocals and guitar, Rock Goddess): There were a few arseholes, but arsehole men are often arseholes to other men. There were occasions when we were treated differently for being women, but not as much as people would think. But I'm quite a hard-nosed cow. Maybe I just didn't want to see it.

KIM MCAULIFFE (vocals and guitar, Girlschool): We used to get patronized quite a lot in the early days, but we didn't take any notice. We had Tim Warhurst, who went on to be a brilliant sound engineer,

GIRLSCHOOL (From left: Enid Williams, Denise Dufort, Kelly Johnson, Kim McAuliffe).

PETER NOBLE | REDFERNS

looking after our sound. And our mates helping us with gear. And along the way we gathered a little fan base, the Barmy Army. And we went down okay. Through the punk movement there were quite a few girls in bands then. There weren't many female bands, but there were a lot more women playing live. So it was a bit anything goes.

ENID WILLIAMS (bass and vocals, Girlschool): We were women going, "We want to play music. We want to travel the world. Fuck you, we're going to do it anyway." And so from that point of view, there was a feminist impulse in that we weren't going to have our lives limited by our gender. So we were living as feminists in a sense. We were women doing what we wanted to do. That in itself was feminist. But I tended to look at the whole issue of feminism in a much broader sense.

MALCOLM DOME (writer, Record Mirror and Kerrang!): In this modern era, there has thankfully been a movement to condemn sexism in rock and metal. But when NWOBHM was in full swing, it was sadly very much in evidence. There were very few female musicians involved with the genre. Those who were, such as Girlschool and Rock Goddess, received very little respect. They were dismissed

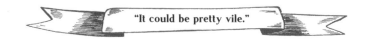

with the somewhat patronizing description as being "good all-girl bands." Patronizing? Of course. Because Iron Maiden or Saxon were never depicted as "good all-boy bands."

The problem was that NWOBHM facilitated the ongoing belief that females did not belong in metal. And on many occasions, Girlschool and Rock Goddess were subjected to moronic chants from those at the front of the stage. Is it any wonder that women weren't comfortable at shows or being in bands? While NWOBHM offered a lot, the role of women was downplayed and ignored.

DENISE DUFORT (drums, Girlschool): In the very early days, when we did pubs and clubs, we'd get catcalled. The crowds would be shouting "Get 'em off!" Kim used to shout back, "You fucking get 'em off!" We always used to get stuff like that. But the more we gigged, people started to respect us.

Kelly [Johnson, guitar] looked incredible on stage. She had this incredible swagger. It was natural. She would swagger across the stage. None of us would dress up in all that other crap, at least in the early days. Later on, we did start kind of dressing up a bit more. To look a bit more presentable on stage for bigger audiences. But basically we used to go on in jeans. We wore what we wore anyway, and that's what people liked about us. We weren't false. We weren't fake. We weren't put together. We were just friends doing what we loved and wearing what we wanted.

ENID WILLIAMS: Early '79 we did our first tour with Motörhead. And the volume suddenly went up. It was a big boost for us. Motörhead weren't huge at that time. They were playing theaters and there were enough people to be respectable, but they weren't sell-outs. There was a bit of "Get your tits out, love."

Lemmy treated women really well on one level, in so much as he liked women that had brains, and he appreciated women's brains, but he liked them to have a pair of tits and a short skirt as well. It was almost like having a group of courtesans around him. It's a complex scenario: he respected women for their brains, but he also like women to behave in a particular way. And I don't think he particularly liked me very much in the beginning because I went to bed early and I wouldn't take speed. I wanted to go to bed early because I wanted to get up early and go around the local museum.

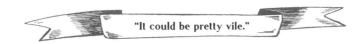

I always believed that when a woman in a band gets involved in any way, shape or form with a man in a band, it's bad news for the woman for the simple reason that she will then be seen as his girlfriend. And I was very disappointed that forty years later, when Lemmy died, there was an eighteen-page article in one magazine. There were a few little bits by different people commenting and I had a little piece there. But there were only a couple of sentences about Girlschool. There was one sentence about Motörhead's biggest hit, "Please Don't Touch" [with Girlschool].

One of the worst examples was when Courtney Love did *Celebrity Skin*. Now I'm no Courtney Love fan, but *Celebrity Skin* was a brilliant album. Fantastic. Then people turn around and go, "Kurt Cobain must have written that before he died." Oh, fuck off. I'm sure you can come up with all sorts of criticisms about the woman. Maybe some of them are justified, but that's a damn good album.

KIM MCAULIFFE: We were compared to them all the time: "Motörhead's little sisters." "Motörhead with tits," was another one, which was lovely. But there you go. It gets a bit wearing after a while, but whereas some of the others would get a bit fed up of the fact we were always associated with Motörhead, I never forgot the fact that we started off with them. That meant a lot.

ENID WILLIAMS: I'm very proud of our association with Motörhead— having toured with them, having done the *St Valentines Day Massacre* single, and I love Motörhead. I love the innovation of Lemmy's bass playing. I love their attitude. The way that Phil [Taylor] played drums, Eddie [Clarke] had some beautiful melodies, like a haiku, just stripped down and beautiful. They were magic. But there's always another side.

When I brought this point up, Kim said, "Without Motörhead, we would have been nothing." And I said, "No, I don't agree with you. Even when we were playing covers, we got a lot of publicity, we're a decent band, we can play quite well. We've got a few things that are quite original." There weren't many female bands around at the time, and we could hold our own as a band. Something would have happened. It would have happened later. We might not have been on *Top of the Pops* at that point. But actually, I think we would have sustained our success longer. And we would have had more respect.

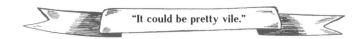
DOUG SMITH (manager, Motörhead and Girlschool):
I think the association with Motörhead did them no favors. I really seriously do think it did them no favors.

ENID WILLIAMS: When it came to doing our own tours, when we were getting a bit bigger, we'd meet fans and sign autographs. We were twenty, twenty-one, twenty-two and they'd be like seventeen. So we were treated a bit like goddesses. A seventeen-year-old who hasn't got a lot of experience with women, which covers most seventeen-year-olds, is slightly in awe of an older woman.

DOUG SMITH: At the time, you had an audience that wasn't really into females. Because they were pubescent. My wife Eve saw it all: she saw these kids, whereas I just saw punters paying to get in.

STEVE DAWSON (bass, Saxon): We were getting a young crowd. Young lads. All sweaty, pimply, long-haired, leather-jacketed, bullet-belted guys. With similarly clad women interspersed. It must have been like when Beatles attracted screaming women—but we attracted screaming boys. Young kids who were mainly at school.

I lived in a council house in Swinton, next to Swinton Comprehensive School, and at dinner time there'd be a hundred lads outside my house, all in school uniforms. And if they could see you through the window they'd all be shouting. That was the audience. They were all young. That was ninety percent of the audience.

DAVID COVERDALE (vocals, Deep Purple and Whitesnake):
Some of the ridiculous criticisms levelled at [Whitesnake] were inexcusable. So the cover of *Lovehunter* [which depicted a naked woman writhing astride a giant white snake] was in response to all the "sexist" rubbish. I thought, "Fuck it," and asked Chris Achilleos, who designed for men's scantily clad magazines, to design something naughty to stick it to the critics. You'd be surprised how successful that image still is, and with the ladies, too.

BERNIE MARSDEN (guitar, Whitesnake): The artist had appeared in *Penthouse* magazine, a feature on him, Chris Achilleos. There was this fantastic picture of a snake's head and somebody must have said, "Look at this, it's great." Next thing, the guy was commissioned to do the artwork. But none of us knew or were that bothered, apart from David. But put it this way: it's not something I'm going to defend.

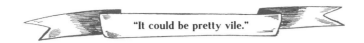

NEIL MURRAY (bass, Whitesnake): I remember being shown it by John Coletta, the manager, and not thinking it was suitable for the music and pretty crass. But the rationale was that people were criticizing the band for being sexist and tasteless, so let's take it to the nth degree. In a sense, they had gone out and put some effort into finding something that was actually a design, whereas some of the album covers were done very much on the cheap. For me, as an ex-graphic design student,there was a lot of grinding of teeth, but not much you could do about it unless you come up with something better yourself.

I guess if it had proved to be incredibly unpopular with fans, then he would have disowned it. But in a sense it's almost like these young bands are doing slightly shocking, tasteless, juvenile artwork, so let's beat them at their own game. But obviously some people think it's a "classic" and it's just accepted in the iconography of the genre.

BERNIE MARSDEN: Do you know what, I've had this conversation with several guys over several years. The first time I saw that cover was when it came out. Coverdale did all that stuff. That's alright—he was the one who was interested in it. We weren't interested in it. Is that bad? I was interested in playing guitar, writing songs, and playing live.

Now, I have two daughters, and yes, the cover isn't the greatest thing. But it was always tongue in cheek, excuse the pun. Just take the music seriously. Don't worry about that too much. David liked to play a game with the journalists with the sexism stuff, and the more they tried to rev him up, the more he played them along. But the rest of us didn't get too involved with it.

I had an altercation with him over "Would I Lie to You?" because at the end of it, at the end of the outro, he says, "Just to get in your pants, I think so." I said, "Do we have to have that on?" And he said, "Well, I think so." The compromise with that was that it was taken off the single version, because I think Ian Paice [drummer] agreed with me and said, "They won't play that on the BBC. Surely we want to have a hit record?" But it stayed on the album. I don't think David's ever forgiven me for that.

NEIL MURRAY: It's hard to rationalize [the sexism] away. The problem is that to a fair amount of women, David was the ultimate sex symbol. There wasn't any getting away from it. There was this big, muscly guy

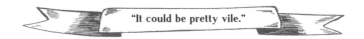

with very long hair and good looks who was well aware that to a lot of women he was sex personified, and if he played up to it, that wasn't putting most of them off. In fact, it was attracting them.

If you have an anonymous front man, who doesn't have that kind of charisma and sex appeal, you play the same songs and it's not the same. He projected an image of himself that was the image of the band by proxy. It definitely wasn't my image, but you could say it benefitted us.

And there was no incentive for him to change. If the women he meets who find him attractive are reinforcing his idea of himself as being a sex symbol and nobody's throwing anything at him onstage apart from knickers, and he's rubbing his willy and swearing and making single entendres and not being pulled up, except by humorless journalists, he's just going to keep on doing it.

K.K. DOWNING (guitar, Judas Priest): We were in our prime really, weren't we? We were able to do a lot of things. Very fulfilling, the whole thing really. There were literally no holds barred—any time, any place. It was part and parcel of the gig, really. I've never married, I'm still single, I've got no kids or whatever. It was part and parcel of the whole thing, and it was…interesting.

Obviously, I've had a lot of girlfriends, Playboy bunnies and those sort of things, so I said to my mum—'cause she always worries about me—I said to her years ago, "Look, Mum, I've lived three lives in one, trust me! You don't have to worry about a thing." And life's still good today, you know? I still have girls calling me up. I've got one now pestering me that I met in the Bahamas.

STEVE DAWSON: There were a lot of women. That's why I'm divorced. That's why I was a regular at the Department of Urology in Sheffield. It's a license for what you want, and as many as you want. So being as we were, not young lads, but knew what the craic was, we went for it. There was plenty of willing participants. It's all been said and it's all been done. It's just what any bloke would do. I've been in places where there's been stag nights going off and there's just as much debauchery going off there.

BIFF BYFORD (vocals, Saxon): We were debauching quite a lot, but you would do, wouldn't you? Though Steve Dawson was married, so I don't know how that went on. There were the odd orgy here and then.

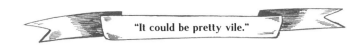
A lot of that is down to the girls, if they're into it. Nobody was forcing anybody. Some women are into that. That's how it goes. It was fantastic fun. It's what bands do, what bands like to do.

It got a bit crazy at one point, with too much going on. But that's what it was like. We were having too much sex basically, and all getting really knackered. Tired out from it, from being up all night partying and then another gig, another gig, another party. The tour manager had to curtail us a bit.

STEVE DAWSON: The gangbanging in rock bands is par for the course. That happened even before we were signed up. You get a certain amount of women who are just liberated and not bothered. And if you're sharing everything, and living like animals, then there's no hang-ups. There's none at all. It gets to the point where it's not an issue, no matter what you do and where you do it. There's no shock to it. It's a shock to some people, but not if you're in on it.

I can imagine it's hard to understand if you haven't lived it. If you walked into the middle of Sainsbury's supermarket and got your cock out, there'd be shock and awe. But you walk into a dressing room full of birds and just drop your trousers, somebody'll fucking perform a sex act on you. Without being prompted. So you get to a point where you do it because you can. "What will somebody do if I do this?" It's hedonism. You can do what you want, so you do.

But the more you do it, the less you want to do it. You do it because you can. The women who are goers not just for us, but for everybody, you tend to steer clear of them. What you've got to realize is this: how come they got into the gig for nothing? They'd usually done a few dodgy things to the road crew to get in. It was sloppy seconds. You tended to steer clear of them once you knew, because you'd be going to the fucking doctor's two days later. And once you'd been a few times, you know what's coming, and it's not nice. This is all pre-nasty diseases, before AIDS. If that had been around it wouldn't have happened. But you got a course of tablets or an injection in your arse, and it were gone in a week. It could have become a badge of honor—"I've had the pox twenty-five thousand times!"—but it's not summat you could be proud of, it's summat that just happened.

One of the places you're more likely to get involved with a woman is checking in a hotel. "What are you doing here?" "Oh, we're playing a

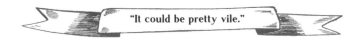

concert tonight. Do you want to come?" They get a pass, and you meet them, and it's more normal rather than someone throwing themselves at you. You might go to a radio station and there's a nice girl on reception. It's like normal life, but you've got an advantage that you are famous to them. And that attracts certain people to you. Because let's face it, we weren't the prettiest band you've ever seen. Two of us were bald.

ENID WILLIAMS: I would suggest that when you've got a bunch of guys in their twenties who go on the road, especially when they're not stunningly handsome, and suddenly they can have as many women as they want, most of them are going to go for it. There's a certain point where they might think, "Actually, I want something different in my life," but maybe not in their twenties.

DENISE DUFORT: It could be pretty vile. We were still quite young, and we'd never seen anything like it before. They had so many groupies, all these bands. I don't just mean Motörhead. Other bands had all kinds of groupies. The roadies had groupies. Everybody had groupies. Sometimes they would treat them like shit. Well, not shit. Like a piece of meat. Kim was horrified, well, we all were. In the beginning, I'm talking about. Luckily nobody treated us that way. If they had have done we'd have told them where to go.

KIM MCAULIFFE: We saw a lot [on support tours]. It was awful. Especially big long tours in America. But these girls, a lot of them would come back for more. I couldn't understand it. It was abuse. Of course it was. I saw one band who had abused a girl chain her to a radiator and then go off to the next gig. She was there at the next gig. I said to her, "Why are you here?"

Not all blokes were like that, but we did see some stuff that wasn't great. As a support band you have to look the other way. And a lot of the time it was the crew. It wasn't like we saw it all happen, but you knew it was happening, especially talking to the girls.

ENID WILLIAMS: Was sexual assault an occupational hazard? It could be. As a band, when we toured with other bands, they treated us with respect because we could play, because we put the work in, we paid our dues to get to where we were. However, there were a lot of things that went on that, from the perspective of today, would be considered

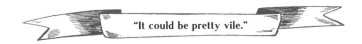

outrageous. And like today, very often alcohol would play a part. If a woman, for example, is utterly paralytic, there are some men that will take advantage of that. The attitude towards women and the attitude towards any kind of rape or sexual assault was a lot more laissez-faire then it is now; it was a very, very different world.

Sometimes certain lines were crossed. Not within the professional situation, but outside, within the socializing situation, some things happened with other musicians. And within the professional situation sometimes, with people in the business, there were some quite horrific incidents on a couple of occasions, which never did come out.

KIM MCAULIFFE: The way the press wrote about us got on our nerves a little bit [music press features often concentrated on Kelly Johnson's looks]. But, of course, Kelly was a star. Even now, if I see a video of her on stage, I can't take my eyes off her. I suppose the press was to be expected, but that's how things were. God, things have changed a hell of a lot since those days, thank goodness. But that's how it was.

ENID WILLIAMS: We didn't sit down and talk about an image as such, but it seemed to work quite well because Kelly had such an androgynous look and people found her generally very attractive, without her trying. She had a certain quality about her. I feel she underestimated me, and likewise I don't think I recognized a certain charisma that she had until I stood in the audience and watched her. When somebody is burping and farting, and you see them first thing in the morning, it's hard to think of them as a sex symbol, or that other people perceive them that way.

The *NME* didn't do anything on Girlschool until we'd done "Hit and Run" and been on *Top of the Pops*, but they couldn't ignore us at that point. Paul Morley did a four-page piece with us. And there was a picture of Kelly on the front of the *NME*. Not the whole band, just Kelly by herself. The picture of Kelly that was on the front cover, she was in bed but with a sheet over. You didn't see anything, but she was in bed. Not cool.

It's hard for me to be objective sometimes because I have to take a step back and go, "Alright. Is this my ego getting in the way here?" In the piece, Denise and I were left out to a very large extent. But the really offensive thing was the amount of space he gave to interviewing Kim's father.

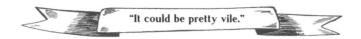

I hated the *NME* because they were so up their own arses. That was disgraceful, to put only one member of the band on the front cover, and without clothes, even though you didn't see anything, and then to have the article centered around, "Oh, but it was a man that put it all together." Despicable. They acted as though they were so PC and so forward-thinking compared to *Melody Maker* and *Sounds*, and yet they were the most misogynistic of the lot. This was utterly despicable.

DENISE DUFORT: There was the Runaways in America, and then we came along in the UK. And for years we were the only female rock band. We were really proud of it, and it was significant. But we were really upset there weren't more female bands. Maybe it was harder for women. Maybe they just weren't picking up instruments. I don't know. I don't have any idea why.

But nowadays when you look on YouTube or Facebook there are so many female drummers on there. It's brilliant. And female guitarists and female rock bands. But back in the day it was just us and the Runaways and we couldn't believe it. We wondered why.

KIM MCAULIFFE: Being the first successful, British, all-woman rock band was something to be proud of. But once we had a bit of success, we were expecting loads of bands to come up. But it didn't happen. Rock Goddess came behind us. And one interesting thing about them is that they came from literally a mile and a half away from where we were. It was so weird. There must have been something in the water in Wandsworth. But it didn't happen.

We were on *Top of the Pops* and everything, and you would expect girls at home to go, "Bloody hell, I'll have a bit of that!" But it didn't happen. It didn't happen till years later. I've no idea why it didn't happen. We thought, "There'll be a load of girl bands coming up now." But there weren't. No idea why.

JODY TURNER: People have been pitching Rock Goddess and Girlschool against each other for years. But they've given up now. They can't deny we're mates. But we were the only two women bands that really were around at that point. I don't know why, because we sound different, but people did try and make us out to be mortal enemies. We've always supported each other so much. And we're even closer now after all these years.

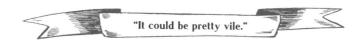

ENID WILLIAMS: I was very passionately feminist in a quite traditional way. The others were less bothered about it really. They would perhaps call themselves feminists but have a different interpretation of that word. As a teenager, I read *The Female Eunuch*, I read Betty Friedan, Kate Millett, and Simone de Beauvoir, and Colette. I was interested in a broad range of culture. Kim's idea of feminism was that, yeah, women stand up for themselves. The thing that I found very disappointing is that the whole audience pretty much would be male.

DENISE DUFORT: It was always young guys coming, and occasionally they'd come with their girlfriends. And their girlfriends hated us. They absolutely hated us. Some of the females in the audience didn't like that their boyfriends were cheering girls onstage. So we had a lot of that. It was basically all guys in the audience. But we didn't give a shit. I didn't care who was in the audience, as long as there was an audience.

It might have mattered more to Kim and Enid. Enid was a big feminist. It might have mattered to her, and it might have mattered to Kim even. But I don't think it mattered to me one way or the other, you know.

ENID WILLIAMS: I'd go, "Well, aren't we encouraging any other women to play?" I've met some since, decades later, who've said, "I started playing because of you." And so from a feminist point of view, I did think, "It's a shame that we're not getting more women in the audience." But on the other hand I think some of those guys changed their perspective on what women could be, perhaps because of us.

KIM MCAULIFFE: I'm proudest of the fact we had some sort of success, and we paved the way for other females. Not that it seems to have made a lot of difference. We sometimes got asked if we have any advice for any other girls out there: yeah, if you want to do it, give it a go, because it's fun. We've been all round the world—we've even toured India. I've met my heroes and gone out with a few of them. Things I would never have dreamed of doing when I was in the audience for Deep Purple and Black Sabbath. Me and Enid queued up all night to get tickets for Led Zeppelin in 1975. Little did I know I'd end up meeting them. I've been very lucky.

"Sometimes it was a good education. Sometimes it was a bad one."

Most NWOBHM bands never made it to America, or failed to make inroads. But those who impressed the U.S. cast an aura around British metal. Def Leppard became the first to break in the States, while Raven and Venom showed independent bands could also make an impact.

JOE ELLIOTT (vocals, Def Leppard): America was something we'd only ever seen on *Cannon*, or *Starsky and Hutch*, or *Charlie's Angels*. You'd occasionally see the opening of some detective show after the football results on a Saturday night, where there'd be a guy in roller skates playing electric guitar on Santa Monica beach. You'd see palm trees everywhere. You thought the whole of America was like that, not realizing it's just a tiny part of California. I didn't even realize it snowed in California.

We didn't have passports. We all had to apply for passports to go and do this tour. And the visas. And that's where [managers] Mensch and Burnstein were really good, because they had connections to get all that stuff done. So we headed out on May 18, 1980, from Heathrow to LAX.

RICK SAVAGE (bass, Def Leppard): Obviously, the weather was fantastic because it was that time of year. And just to listen to radio. Every city had a rock station, or maybe two or three. And just to be

Steve Clark, Rick Savage, Joe Elliott, and Rick Allen of DEF LEPPARD at The Fabulous Fox Theater, Atlanta, September 4, 1981. TOM HILL | GETTY IMAGES

exposed to that was fantastic. Because at that time in England, it was Radio 1 and the *Friday Rock Show* and the one on the Saturday afternoon. That was it. It was twenty-four/seven over there. If you wanted to listen to that type of music you could. It was just heaven. It was absolutely heaven.

JOE ELLIOTT: It was the beginning of the end for certain things, because when we landed, Pete [Willis, guitarist] had to be carried off the plane because he was paralytic. So, that was leading to one particular story of this band. But other than the airport, our first steps in America were on Sunset Boulevard. Come on!

We were staying at the Chateau Marmont, right, which didn't mean anything to us at that time, but as we walked up the steps going to reception, it was like, "Ooh, these steps are steep." And we get all the way up there, and as we get to reception, there's a picture behind the guy of Led Zeppelin sat on the steps we just walked up.

Me, and Steve [Clark, guitar]—definitely Steve—and somebody else ate in a famous deli on Sunset, with that classic *American Graffiti* look,

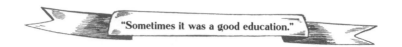

like a Cadillac. We had summat to eat, and then we headed up to the
Rainbow Bar and Grill, which we'd only ever read about in *Sounds*.

CLIFF BURNSTEIN (comanager, Def Leppard): There's this seedy
heavy metal club called the Rainbow, right next to the Roxy in Los
Angeles. The first night Def Leppard got to town, somehow a couple
of them made it to the Rainbow, as if guided by radar. And I swear they
were back with chicks that night. So I knew these guys could pull. And
if they could pull, they could sell.

JOE ELLIOTT: It was really early. It was maybe seven-thirty, so there
was nobody in. And we went up to the upstairs bar, and it was empty,
apart from four girls in the far corner. And we walked up to the bar—
this is where the Hollywood Vampires used to meet, and there were
these steps that looked like they were going up into a galleon, with
marine netting behind these three or four wooden steps, and it's like a
VIP area I guess, and back in the early seventies it was Lennon, Alice,
Nilsson, Ringo, a couple of others who used to get fucked up in there,
and they'd be left alone.

So we walked up to the bar, and the guy behind the counter says,
"Can I get you guys anything?" And either me or Steve said, "Can
we get two vodka oranges please, mate?" And he says, "Y'all mean a
screwdriver?" And I said, "No, if I wanted a screwdriver I'd go to a
fucking hardware store. I want two vodka and oranges, please." "Over
here, boy, we call these things screwdrivers." "Alright, two screwdrivers
it is, then."

So of course, this little kind of comedy kerfuffle attracts the attention
of these four girls. Who look like four girls from California. And they
come marching over and say the immortal words, "Are you guys in a
band? Oh my God, I love your accents." Now, nothing has ever been
said to a Yorkshireman's ears like that. That did not happen at West
Runton Pavilion. We were all flat caps and whippets, according to
everyone from south of Luton, but these girls kinda liked it. I won't
get into any gory details.

RICK ALLEN (drums, Def Leppard): I went nuts over there, women
left, right and center. It was great being the support band because you
had time to stand at the side of the stage and pick out all the best birds.
I ended up getting a few undesirable diseases, but I had a good laugh
over it.

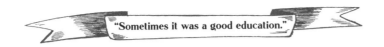

RICK SAVAGE: That was all part of the education. Sometimes it was a good education. Sometimes it was a bad one. And very often there was phone calls home trying to explain what somebody was saying you were doing. We were twenty years old and we had just been let loose in a supermarket full of candy. It was like, "Wow, this is incredible."

JOE ELLIOTT: The next day was a day off, and then we were opening for Pat Travers at the Santa Monica Civic. Again, I had this Bowie bootleg from 1972 from the Santa Monica Civic, so I'm like, "I'm about to stand on the same stage as David Bowie did just after he'd released *Ziggy Stardust*," you know? So I had all this going through my head.

It was crazy. The house lights go down and there's always a bit of noise coming out of the audience, but we started hearing people shouting, "'Wasted'! 'Hello America'!" Fucking hell, they've heard of us. What had happened was KLOS, a massively important station in Los Angeles, had also been playing the album, a track or two off it. So there was a few people out there among Pat Travers's fans that knew who we were.

BRIAN SLAGEL (fan, founder of Metal Blade Records): I did the first ever American heavy metal fanzine, and I reviewed Def Leppard when they came over and played in the US the first time, and it was a very negative review. Mostly because they were wearing clothes that shouldn't be worn in metal. That was the one thing I was very snobbish about: if you're a metal person you wear jeans, a T-shirt, a leather or denim jacket, some wristbands and that's it. Anything else isn't metal. So musically I was okay, but fashion-wise, it was a whole different story.

JOE ELLIOTT: In America the first album started to get a bit of traction. We were very fortunate that Cliff Burnstein had great contacts, with being in A&R so long, and he'd made friends. There was a lady in Portland, Oregon, called Gloria Johnson, and she was this late-night, deep-voiced DJ, like the Annie Nightingale of Portland. She was the first person ever to play a Def Leppard song on American radio.

We get to Portland, Oregon—eleven thousand people. And we are the fucking headline band as far as I'm concerned. They are going ballistic because she has been playing the one song over and over, but that's leaked over into requests coming in on the phone. "Is there anything else on that record you can play?" And people were buying it. So when

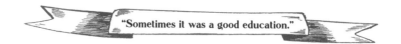

we went on, all the lighters were out. That became a thing to do with ballads, but it began as soon as we went on stage, we were just stood there gobsmacked. We went down an absolute storm. Two days later we were starting with Judas Priest, working our way east. So we'd gone all the way up the West Coast, and little by little, each day, the popularity of the band was becoming more apparent.

RICK SAVAGE: Then along came MTV at the end of '81 and changed everything because they picked up on "Bringin' on the Heartbreak." And from then it just went nuclear, out of control.

ROBERT JOHN "MUTT" LANGE (producer, Def Leppard): We really worked on the dynamics [on second album *High 'n' Dry*]. They had the riffs, but they would start loud and just get louder. That was one area where they were not experienced. So we'd break a riff into parts, take it down as well as up. That was the one thing the band learned from that album—the dynamics of songwriting. Because the song structures were pretty much there already.

They had learned their craft off bands like AC/DC before I'd met them. The style was similar, but Def Leppard's was more expansive in the sense that their songs had these little modal sections, which AC/DC would never have had. There was a possibility in those songs for an orchestral sound…The choruses in their songs deserved a real big sound, sort of like Queen, not just a straight guitar sound.

JOE ELLIOTT: Whitesnake were recording [in the next-door studio]. I was trying to sing "Bringin' on the Heartbreak" and Mutt was like, "No, do it again. That's wrong. Sing it like this." What the fuck do you want from me? And I stormed off. I went next door and watched David Coverdale sing a song in one take. I'm leaning on the piano with Jon Lord—which in itself was, "Fuck, this is Jon Lord from Deep Purple!"—and David Coverdale is like, "Joseph, dear boy, what's the matter?" I told him, "Oh, it's this fucking guy . . ." And he says, "We've all been there. Have a brandy." That one brandy led to two bottles of Scotch. I got so fucking ill. Mutt came looking for me, and David was going, "I'm sorry." Mutt said it was fine. I was staying at Mensch's house, and threw up all over the fucking pavement and went to bed.

I got up the next day and I heard what my inner self was saying: "Stop feeling fucking sorry for yourself; get in there and fucking do

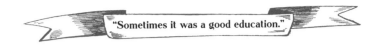

it." I went back in, and Mensch came down to the studio about six hours after I got there, just to check in, and Mutt said, "Listen to this." Mensch just looked at him and said, "Is this the same guy that tried to do this yesterday?" That's what Mutt did. I'd listen back to it and go, "That doesn't even sound like me. It sounds fucking amazing."

And then I realized the techniques I wasn't aware of. I wouldn't have got that from any other producer. So from that moment onwards I was much more of an attentive student. I still had my musical opinions and differences, but I would listen more because I realized what we were getting out of it was better than we would have done under our own direction.

CLIFF BURNSTEIN: The *High 'n' Dry* album was already history on the charts. But then MTV started playing "Bringin' on the Heartbreak." Slowly but surely we started getting sales reports on the record and it started selling about five thousand copies a week, which was enough to get it back on the charts. This was a whole new ball game. Before *Pyromania* came out, *High 'n' Dry* had gone gold.

JOE ELLIOTT: Mutt saw this as a huge FM radio hit, which it turns out it wasn't. But we worked the song really, really hard. It was one of three songs we thought were very important to us collectively—the title track, "Let It Go" and "Bringin' on the Heartbreak." When we were on the British tour and played Liverpool in 1981, we shot videos for those three songs with rent-a-crowd down the front. What was really important was that on August 1, 1981, my birthday, MTV launched in America. .

Nineteen eighty-one had been a very barren year. We had a six-week tour with Blackfoot. I mean, talk about a bad pairing—there's us dressed up like fucking Sweet in front of Lynyrd Skynyrd's crowd. Then we had a month with Ozzy, which was fucking brilliant, in very mixed venues—everything from theaters to big sheds. We did the tour and we didn't play that song live because we didn't think we could. But August '81, MTV launches in three or four cities and eventually starts to build and build and build.

And while we were making *Pyromania*, Peter Mensch had this massive thing in his basement, size of a washing machine. It was a Telex machine. And it would spew out stuff Cliff was sending over

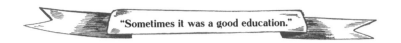
about the *High 'n' Dry* album. Six months after we finished touring it, and it's a dead record and we're making the third album, all of a sudden it's starting to sell. What the hell's going on? Well, there's this thing called MTV and they're playing all three of those songs we shot videos for, but they're specifically playing, five or six times a day, "Bringin' on the Heartbreak."

The great advantage was nobody else had videos. There was only a few because people weren't making videos the way they would come to, so they were playing ours all the time. And then they were starting to get requests for them, so they were playing them even more. And then radio stations were getting requests from people who'd been watching MTV: "Will you play that Def Leppard song, 'Bringin' on the Heartbreak'?" And they'd start playing it.

Long story short, while we were making *Pyromania*, *High 'n' Dry* goes gold: five hundred thousand copies. By the time we were ready to release *Pyromania*, it was getting towards platinum. It was really going through the roof. So when we did release *Pyromania* and release these videos that were so much more superior—"Rock of Ages," "Foolin'" and specifically "Photograph"—and they started playing "Photograph" in January of '83, it went fucking nuts. It was that moment over here, like it was for Bon Jovi in 1986 when they released "You Give Love a Bad Name." When that kicked in people just went boom, even though it was his third album. With us it was the same thing. Those who knew knew, but all of a sudden there was all this: "Have you heard this band Def Leppard?"

JONNY Z (record store owner, promoter, founder of Megaforce Records): I brought Raven over [in 1982] because they blew my mind. I still listen to *Rock Until You Drop* and *Wiped Out* today, like it's current listening. They're the most played band I have in my collection, I'm that much of a Raven fanatic.

JOHN GALLAGHER (vocals and bass, Raven): Jonny Z ran a small record stall in a flea market in New Jersey. He was selling all these imports, and lots of Raven. He said, "I'm putting together a couple of shows, a show called the Halloween Headbangers' Ball with Anvil and Riot and I'd love Raven to play. How about we bring them over?" It was a week's worth of dates, and I was, "Yeah, absolutely." We got over

RAVEN at Jon and Marsha Zazula's Rock 'n' Roll Heaven, New Brunswick, NJ, 1982. KEVIN HODAPP

there. We were staying in New Jersey. We'd been watching TV with America in it all our life. To get to actually go over there and see it was a very big deal.

We got to the St. George Theatre in Staten Island, and Riot were sound checking, and sound checking, and sound checking. Not really doing anything, just standing around, wasting time so nobody else gets to sound check. We set up and I find out long, long after that they had got the stage box where all the microphones go into and unplugged them and replugged them, so the bass guitar turns up on the snare drum channel, and the snare drum shows up on the microphone channel, and that kind of sabotage. Didn't matter. We still went down an absolute storm.

JONNY Z: The St. George Theatre was a condemned building and they were restoring it when we rented it. That's how we got it so cheap. We couldn't afford a real established theater. And no one would allow a metal show in one. We wanted to do things proper when it started. The hardest thing was, I couldn't afford security. Fortunately, I knew

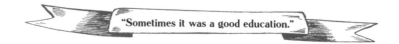

from the store almost every person in the place. There were a lot of fights that broke out, and in those days people wore real big, spiky, armbands and stuff. So when you got in fights you saw real perforations on people's faces, with blood just flying out of them, you know? I walked in the middle of five fights that night and broke them up. There was nobody else to do it. I had to say, "If you want to hit a guy, hit me. If you want to kill metal in the northeast, hit me in the face, motherfucker."

But the crowd was that crazy. It's like Bob Marley going to Africa, and people hearing the low end for the first time, and hearing that kind of music for the first time. You go through a whole catharsis mentally and through your nervous system, and these people were feeling things they never felt before. And seeing music they never saw before, because it wasn't just four/four beat and E progressions. The Europeans and the British brought a whole revolution of music scales and arrangements to the metal world.

JOHN GALLAGHER: That show was a big deal, an independently promoted show in Staten Island, with three thousand five hundred people there. That's crazy. So that was big, then all the club shows we played were packed out. It was amazing. People knew the words, they knew the songs. How? But they'd licensed the stuff, and there was a hungry core following of people who were going to these import stores and they saw an album cover that they liked and buy the record and love it, and freak out about it. Word of mouth, best advertising there ever was. We did another four or five shows with Anvil round the New York/New Jersey area.

JONNY Z: Wacko [Rob Hunter, Raven drummer] borrowed a kit from a fellow in New Jersey because we couldn't rent drums, we couldn't afford that. So we had people in our shop volunteer their instruments to play on. They brought their guitars, but they didn't bring their amps and drums.

I said to Wacko, "Whatever you do, please don't ruin the drums. Please don't destroy the drums. Please, he'll be right in the front." The guy comes, he sits right in the front row. Wacko plays the drums, and at the end of the set, which was the most brilliant rock 'n' roll set since the Who *Live at Leeds*, just a great set, Wacko takes the drum set and destroys it on the floor of the club in Brooklyn. He just demolished the

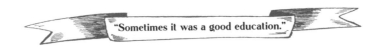

kid's drums. And at the end I went to the kid and said, "I'm so sorry, there's nothing I can do to control that guy, he's an animal." The kid said, "What an honor to have my drums destroyed by Wacko!"

JOHN GALLAGHER: Things were just so good. It was like: "Let's do it again next year and do it bigger and better."

JONNY Z: Then they headlined the Kill 'Em All for One tour [in summer 1983, with Metallica]. At the time, Raven were a much bigger band on Megaforce than Metallica.

JOHN GALLAGHER: It just seemed America was where the action was, and you have to go where the action is. So they wanted to do a full tour, and we needed an opening band. They said, "What do you think of this band? We've got the biggest band in San Francisco to open for you." We said, "Y&T? They're not going to open for us!" "No, Metallica!" "Who? Never heard of them." So we got a tape, played it. Sounded like Motörhead at the wrong speed. At seventy-eight rpm.

I said, "Alright, this sounds great. It'll be fine. We'll do that." So we flew over, stayed at Jonny's house. They came in and they were obnoxious little brats. It was pretty funny. You could tell right off the bat that Lars was the mover and shaker and the wheeler dealer. James Hetfield was just smiling and drinking. Kirk Hammett was just drinking. And Cliff Burton was the old soul on young shoulders. He was the most mature one of the whole lot of them.

We got on with them great, and off we went—two trucks, a six-berth Winnebago and seventeen people. Eventually we got mattresses and put them in the back of the trucks and took turns sleeping there, basically, because Cliff did the unmentionable in the toilet that you're never supposed to do on a tour bus, and then ripped the door off. So everyone could smell that for the next fucking month. We preferred to be in the back of the truck.

JONNY Z: The whole joke of the tour was the places they were booked into. They played a lot of the right places. In fact, they played all the right places. The problem was getting from one right place to the next right place. There was a crazy, crazy promoter in the Midwest, who told me he had a big, giant metal scene going on over there, and he came to my agent and offered me money like you couldn't believe to

RAVEN doing it "bigger and better" in the USA, November 1982. KEVIN HODAPP

get them to do these venues. I swore up and down they were the wrong venues. So did my agent, but this guy said he would do it and he'd pay up front.

We had to play Bald Knob, Arkansas. One of the venues we went to, they didn't have lights, they expected us to bring in staging and lights. It was a big amphitheater. So they went to a farm down the road and got two forklifts and put a truss of lights up above the band as their lighting. There was some crazy, ridiculous gigs on the Kill 'Em All for One tour, but it's the ones that weren't ridiculous that broke the band. You couldn't have one without the other.

LARS ULRICH (fan, drums, Metallica): It was very surreal. I had travelled a little bit in America and knew New York and San Francisco and LA and a few other places. But being in Bald Knob, Arkansas, and some of the other places off the map were experiences that we had no idea were going to happen. It was part of the unpredictability of it all.

Waking up that morning in that field out in Bald Knob, Arkansas, with the mosquitoes and the moths and whatever else was buzzing around us, that was a pretty surreal day. There was nothing in the playbook to prepare you for that. "But okay, let's have some fun and make the most of it—anybody got a beer?"

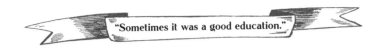

I grew up in a very athletic family. I'd hear stories from my dad about how he would turn up at a tennis tournament and the tennis court was made of cow shit, and then we had to play on that. So I guess my attitude was, "Okay, I guess tonight we'll be playing to sixty thousand mosquitoes and twenty-two people from Arkansas and we'll make the best of it and have a beer afterwards." I could put blinders on and just do it more than some other people could. There were some pretty surreal days out there in the summer of '83.

JOHN GALLAGHER: Bald Knob Amphitheatre. It was a natural bowl, with a stage built in the middle of nowhere with totem poles, insects as big as helicopters flying around, and cooks making catfish, and a whole bunch of redneck people, who just loved it. Then they booked us in Little Rock, Arkansas, at the Tarrant County Convention Center, which is a ten-thousand-seat arena. And in comes Raven and Metallica with our little club gear, playing for three hundred people in a ten-thousand-seat arena. Ouch. That was not fun. I said, "What about food?" And the guy said, "You guys just sold out Madison Square Garden, right?" "Who told you that? We need food!" He throws a couple of hundred dollars at my brother, "Go to McDonald's. Buy for the stage crew, for everyone."

But you do it the same as any other gig—you play to the people who are there and do your thing. After Arkansas we went to Oklahoma, and played a gig that was almost identical to the scene in *The Blues Brothers* with chicken wire. But there was no chicken wire. So everything they threw hit the bands. Metallica's up there, getting pints thrown at them, and beer coasters, and they're just freaking out and getting closer and closer to the drums and further and further away from the front of the stage. Just dying. We'd seen stuff like that, so we went out there and danced on the tables and kicked their beers over, and throw things back, and they continued to throw stuff, just like the Blues Brothers, but they loved it.

I remember Kirk coming on and saying, "How did you guys do that?" I said, "Don't you believe in what you do?" "Yeah." "Then just go and do it. Screw these guys. And if you can't win 'em over, piss 'em off." It's always worked.

JONNY Z: The great shows were Arizona and California. San Francisco and LA were really great. Chicago was the best show.

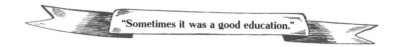

JOHN GALLAGHER: We played LA, the Country Club, which was great, and a whole bunch of people turned up for that—the Armored Saint guys were there. Then we went up to the Bay Area, to Palo Alto, Berkeley and then San Fran. I think all three were with Exodus opening. Definitely two of them.

They were crazy crowds. The slam dance and stagediving craziness which we hadn't seen before threw us for a loop. We'd seen wild crowds before. We hadn't seen them doing that. That's what was different about it. It was like sharks in the water, that kind of feeding frenzy.

LARS ULRICH: "Don't Need Your Money" was the first Raven song I heard, and it was so unpredictable, so different and so unique. They had a very unique sound—starts and stops. The song would go here, and then it would change, and the tempos changed. It was very unpredictable—it was quite progressive. And John's voice—he would sing and then hit a falsetto that only three dogs on the planet could hear. So there was a very unpredictable and wild thing to their music that we all fell in love with instantly. Later in the movement, as more and more bands started sounding the same, Raven definitely had their own sound and their own unique element. To me it was amazing.

There is nothing about any of these experiences that was anything less than amazing and I just get a little wearied because some things get taken out of context. I never want to say anything bad about anybody. There was nothing about any of that that wasn't the super funnest thing that can happen to an eighteen-year-old, disenfranchised Danish kid, who was trying to figure out what was up, down, and sideways. All of it was crazy cool.

Hanging out with the Gallagher brothers and Rob Hunter, that was the greatest thing in the world. Thirty-seven years later you can tell the stories of the camper wagons breaking down and how the whole thing was super-chaotic. Of course, it's easy to sensationalize it in that way. Other people can do that.

Jonny Z did an amazing thing. Jonny Z had a vision. Jonny Z had daring. Jonny Z was passionate and was drinking the same kind of Kool Aid that we all were drinking, that this was something that connected us, that this was something we believed in. This wasn't a business. This wasn't something anyone was doing for money. No one was thinking, "One day I'm going to buy a house." There were no ulterior motives.

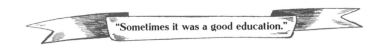

We were all just fucking swept up and in it for the music and what it felt like, that we belonged to something much bigger than ourselves, and to a movement, a fraternal—I don't know, it sounds corny—a brotherhood. And so, yeah, okay, it was a little chaotic. But the chaos at that time didn't necessarily seem like a negative thing. It was part of the path.

The obstacles were there, but no one thought, "I don't know if I can do this any more. I don't know if I can take this." For me and the rest of the guys in our band, we had won the lottery. So whether the camper wagon had air conditioning or not, or whether we broke down every fifty miles on the freeway, or whether twenty people showed up at a gig in Arkansas, none of that meant anything at the time.

JONNY Z: Venom didn't have the players. I thought Venom sucked, let's be honest, but they had an energy and something special about them, and I wanted to see what they would be like. I was curious to see it. So I tried to bring it here. But they wanted nine people to come over—they wanted to bring their crew. It was insane. It cost me $7,000 to fly Venom here and back in April 1983. That's not including the rental of the gear, the rental of the venue, or feeding them for two weeks, because I had them doing shows with Metallica. It probably was about a $20,000 expense in the end.

And the shows did very poorly, by the way. They weren't as popular as I thought. This was the Paramount Theater on Staten Island, where they'd just had Billy Idol for three nights.

MANTAS (guitar, Venom): I think Jon was a bit surprised by Venom when we turned up. We turned up there with a fucking homemade flight case which was about eight foot by three foot, full of pyrotechnics and explosives which had come over on the airplane. You look back at it and think, "How the fuck did that happen?"

JONNY Z: One guy came with a bomb board. On an airplane. This was like a board used by the IRA to set off bombs. Right through customs, right to my house. They had dynamite. They blew holes in the stage. They blew holes in the floor.

MANTAS: The first show, that first explosion took fucking everything out. There were these metal canisters Tony Bray [Abaddon] had made—three canisters in a box of sand. There must have been eight or ten of these boxes along the front of the stage so we're easy talking twenty to thirty of these canisters, all wired up ready to go with fucking bomb powder in them. Right at the last minute the pyro guy ran round and put a second dose in because he didn't think they had been filled. So homemade pyros, fucking boxes filled with sand, and a homemade pyrotechnics board with a fucking key in it. First explosion goes off, it took all of Cronos's bass out of the backline, it blew a hole in the stage, there was sand and bits of wood everywhere.

JONNY Z: When the first bombs went off, they were smoke pots, and the whole front row of the audience went blackface. It was unbelievable to see that. I had my hands over my head, going, "What a fucking disaster."

ABADDON (drums, Venom): The hole in the stage was the first thing we saw when we realized things had gone drastically wrong. The whole bomb box—the wooden thing with three steel pots in—had exploded. And it had gone down with the thrust, and bust the stage. Bust a hole in the stage. But it had also gone through a water pipe, so there was water pissing up out of the stage, going everywhere. There was smoke everywhere. It was absolute fucking mayhem.

We had these speakers for Conrad in the backline, and the explosion blew two four by fifteens, and it blew all the speakers in the backline. But Conrad was playing through direct input [DI] out of the front of house, so he couldn't hear his backline, but the bass was still coming out at front of house. But he didn't think it was because he couldn't hear his backline. All this mayhem had gone off, water flying everywhere, and all of a sudden Conrad takes his guitar off and just throws it to one side. We played the rest of the gig with just me and Jeff and Conrad's vocals. Insane.

JONNY Z: We didn't know at the time that we needed transformers to change the current for their amps and heads to the American voltage. We blew out the twelve giant bass bins on stage while they were playing, and the Marshalls went. We managed to fix it up, but Cronos didn't know. He was playing DI, but he couldn't hear himself onstage. He didn't know people were still hearing the show. So he went crazy. It was total inexperience as to what was going on onstage around him. It was an evil vibe.

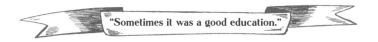

Hell comes to Staten Island, April 22–24, 1984…and causes $666 of damages. The fine print reads: "The U.S. Spirit of Kerrang! Magazine."

CRONOS: One of the pots we'd loaded full of explosives flew up and buried itself in the wall beside the balcony seats. Luckily there weren't many people in the balcony—they were all downstairs going mental. It was buried in the wall: it flew off the stage into the balcony. If there'd been someone sitting there, or had the pot been a bit to the left, it could have killed somebody.

JONNY Z: It was in a seat, not the wall. It blew up like a satellite, like a flying saucer. Flew over the audience, embedded itself in a chair at the back. Let me tell you something. The bill for the damages was not so bad, but it came out to $666.

ABADDON: Jonny Z would be being a businessman, talking to the promoter and the guy who owned the building about how he hasn't got any insurance to cover this. So Jonny Z would have a go at Eric [Cook, Venom manager], and Eric would say, "Well, that the fuck did you expect when you booked fucking Venom? This is what you get."

So of course we have to come down and back that up: "Yeah, you get what you fucking get, mate, that's us. You've just had one of the most talked-about gigs of your entire fucking life. You'll be talking about this when you're fucking eighty."

MANTAS: The second night, explosion goes off, we run on stage, the curtains come up, but the curtain was so old and full of holes it took half the stage mics up with it as well.

ABADDON: The best thing about that gig was that it was in an old vaudeville theater, and it had these curtains at the front, these huge, heavy, red velvet ones with tassels on the bottom. And the whole thing had to lift up into the ceiling. The curtains were closed, so I climbed up on to this drum riser. I think it was about fifteen feet high. I'm standing waiting for them to come on. I'm already up there, and the intro tape's playing. The two mic stands are out there—one for Jeff and one for Conrad—and the mic stands were those boom stands, with the bit coming out the back.

I climbed up on the bass drum, my arms in the air, waiting for this big reveal. And these curtains lifted, and the tassels on the bottom caught the back of the mic stands and lifted them both into the air. Both mic stands up in the air. So Conrad and Jeff came on from stage right and stage left, ran on like fucking maniacs. Crossed over each other, getting the crowd going. Conrad then went back to start the vocals—we're already playing—and there's no fucking mic stand there. They were looking at each other, going, "What the fuck?" And I'm playing away, and they've stopped. And then the curtains came down again. The explosions had gone off. All the pyro had worked. And both mic stands were forty feet in the fucking air.

LARS ULRICH: What do you compare it to? It's ultimately about where do you set the bar. For us, for me, playing a show with Venom was literally the greatest thing on the planet. When Venom came out, it was like, "Fucking hell!" A lot of attitude, more of a punky, garagey sound. And definitely a lot of swagger, very driven and very ambitious. But even doing away with all that, some of the songs on that first album and some of the songs on the demo were very inspiring to us—it was that grey area between metal and punk, just high energy and a crazy, over-the-top attitude.

So when we got a chance to play with Venom, that was a huge fucking thing. We got a chance to meet them, we got a chance to hang out with

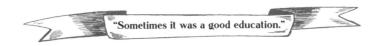

them, we got a chance to be on the same side as them. It was huge. I don't have anything other than good memories of any of that. It was great. Being completely truthful to you, my recollection of what happened in April of '83 with those shows was nothing but great. It was, "Holy fuck! Here we are playing with these guys! I can't believe we're doing this! I can't believe this is happening to us!"

JONNY Z: Venom and Metallica stayed with me. I don't remember how long, but everything seemed like months.

LARS ULRICH: We were all staying with Jonny Z and his wife Marsha. We were down in the basement. They were very gracious in terms of opening the doors to their homes, and we would all sit round the same dinner table and eat. They fed us and they gave us shelter. It was a lot, all of these people showing up and they were very generous. Of course it was pretty crazy to have a bunch of twenty-year-olds in the house, but it was fun. Good times. We were young and we were drinking a lot and we were delinquent, but my main memory is the fraternal element of it, that you were in this with like-minded souls.

ABADDON: Jeff went and left and stayed in a hotel because it was getting a bit too much a party place for him.

MANTAS: Me and my roadie and the drum roadie fucked off and walked out because it was fucking party central, it was twenty-four/ seven. It was the fucking lads sitting watching Cronos eating glass the night before the fucking show: "Look what I can do!" Yeah, that's fucking intelligent, you're the singer and you're eating glass, well done.

JONNY Z: Cronos is out of his fucking bird. He was eating my water glasses in my bathroom. He ate it down to nothing and spat the glass into a bag. Blood and everything coming out of his mouth.

LARS ULRICH: It was the greatest, coolest thing. I couldn't imagine it could happen. I had no analytical view of it. It was just: "Give me six beers and put Venom on a stage in front of me and I'm the happiest guy on the planet." Was there a lot of, "We're going to come in and set off more pyro than anybody else"? Of course. That goes back to that swagger: 'We're going to blow up more shit than the other guys!' Yeah! Cool! No shit! They blew a hole in the stage! That's fun!

Lars Ulrich and James
Hetfield of METALLICA
with Abaddon and Mantas
of VENOM, backstage at
Breaking Sound Festival,
France, August 29, 1984.
PG BRUNELLI | ICONICPIX

It wasn't so much our thing; we didn't sit there and say, 'Jonny, we want to blow up a bunch of shit, too.' We were happy with whatever we were doing. But watching Venom, watching Raven, watching Diamond Head at the Woolwich Odeon, the fact that the dream came to life was so surreal in itself, and you were so in the moment the whole time, tapping into the energy of the moment, and the surrealism of how this is really happening.

"The shock was how good that record sounded. It was like nothing else around."

Def Leppard's slick *Pyromania* signaled the beginning of the end of the NWOBHM. The kids from Sheffield created a commercial smash that other bands could not match— even as their record labels forced them to try.

LARS ULRICH (fan, drums, Metallica): What caused NWOBHM to fade? In one word: America. That may be a little too black and white, but when a lot of the bands started becoming successful in England and got a taste of that, a number of them set their sights on America, and in order to become successful in America, they had to take what made NWOBHM into NWOBHM out of it. Especially the Britishness.

There were very few bands that were able to navigate chasing any kind of success in America and still retain their NWOBHM roots. The distance from the first Def Leppard album to *Pyromania* is not as long as some bands' from their debut to their attempt to crack America. Def Leppard started much closer to where they ended up than some other bands did. Their transformation was much more organic than some other bands.

There were a couple of other bands where they really turned their backs on where they started. Yes, Def Leppard were the one band that really became big in America, but they always had that spirit, even in Sheffield in 1979. They seemed much more like they ended up being in '83 when *Pyromania* came out. There were already traces of that in '78, but you can't say that about five or ten other bands I could name.

STEVE DAWSON (bass, Saxon): Def Leppard had to be successful. They were made to be successful. Def Leppard, I think, caused a lot of trouble for a lot of our type of band, apart from Iron Maiden, who stuck to it. It happened to Tygers of Pan Tang. Leppard were the pretty girl walking down the street.

JON DEVERILL (vocals, Persian Risk and Tygers of Pan Tang): *Pyromania* destroyed the New Wave of British Heavy Metal. It would have petered out anyway, but this total obsession with commercial success at the expense of your artistic aspirations…Def Leppard were never a band I liked—not on any personal level; they're great guys— but I don't like their music. I find it soulless and contrived. You can't argue with that kind of success, but it's not for me.

DENISE DUFORT (drums, Girlschool): *Pyromania* was the sound we were going for on *Play Dirty*, and the fans hated it. We lost quite a lot of fans over that album.

BRIAN TATLER (guitar, Diamond Head): Once you've got one Leppard you don't want another one. Our budget for *Canterbury* was fifty grand or something, whereas Leppard spent £700,000 making *Pyromania* and none of the other bands would have been allowed that budget. I don't know how they got away with it. I think it was just a case of "We're in too deep, let's just carry on."

They apparently had three weeks to make that album—'cause *Highway to Hell* was done in three weeks with Mutt Lange—and it ended up taking nine months and costing seven hundred thousand quid. And back then, that's a lot of money.

PHIL COLLEN (guitar, Girl and Def Leppard): A lot of the rock stuff—unless you're a Zeppelin or a Hendrix or a Beatles or something—was fairly cheap. It was cheaply done, cheaply assembled and quick. This wasn't. Time had been taken.

PHIL ALEXANDER (fan, Kerrang! editor): People are always bandwaggoning and chasing success. So the success of Leppard in America and around the world changed the way record companies looked at hard rock. And there is no doubt there were a bunch of bands who lost themselves in that. But by the same token, there were a lot of bands who did not have the wherewithal. Leppard always had a vision of what they should be and how to move forward. They were never afraid of commerciality. In a number of respects they were atypical of NWOBHM, and so they were able to do what they did.

All the people who tried to become like Leppard never wanted to be that, didn't have an understanding of what they were meant to be, and were made to make records that were commercial for no apparent reason. They didn't have the songs, they didn't have the vision, they didn't have the ambition. In a number of ways, *Pyromania* is a watershed moment for NWOBHM.

JOE ELLIOTT (vocals, Def Leppard): We wanted to make a great rock record that changed the way rock music was thought of. We wanted this record to be heard by people who wouldn't normally like rock music. And you know what? It worked.

In 1984 I went to an Elton John gig at Wembley, because Elton wanted me to get up and sing with a bunch of other people on the old Marvin Gaye song "Can I Get a Witness?," or—as they had it on the setlist—"Can I Get to Widnes?" And when it got to the end of the show I was whisked backstage into Elton's hospitality suite, and the next person who walks in is George Michael and he goes, "Hey, I bought your single 'Photograph.' Amazing song!" Then I read that Kate Bush adored *Pyromania.* Elton comes in and he goes, "Congratulations. What an album." All that kind of stuff. Rod Stewart same thing, Gary Kemp, all these people. It basically crossed over to all these people that would never in a million years listen to a Maiden album or a Saxon record.

We wanted a crossover record. There's no shame and no guilt in that. We were taking everything, not just rock.

RICK SAVAGE (bass, Def Leppard): The impetus [for *Pyromania*] came from us. We saw what [second album] *High 'n' Dry* was—we were really proud of it, and we thought [producer] Mutt Lange did a great job. It didn't take that long to record, and it gave us a platform to create our own sound. We always wanted to be a little more wide-ranging in our appeal, and I think *High 'n' Dry* was probably our most metal album in its strictest sense. We didn't want to lose too much of that, but moving forward we wanted to add to it. We wanted to have more vocals, more orchestrations—we wanted it to be more of a production. It was round about the time of the Indiana Jones films, where just about every scene there was detail in it, something that grabbed you. The attention to detail was phenomenal, and we wanted to make an album like that. You've still got to have the songs and the melodies, but how you portrayed them was key.

We wanted to make an album that was still hard rock, but similar to Queen. If there was one band that was universally liked within the group, it was Queen, and to a lesser extent AC/DC. And really that's all we've ever tried to be—a mixture of Queen and AC/DC. We're still trying, even now.

When we went in to make *Pyromania*, that was our mandate: keep elements of *High 'n' Dry* but make it more appealing, with a wider range of sounds, make the production bigger, have loads of vocals, overdub more guitars. In fairness, Mutt went: "Absolutely. That's where I hear you guys, that's the type of album we're going to make." From then it just took off.

DAVID BATES (A&R at Phonogram for Def Leppard):
I never saw them as a heavy metal band. I saw them as a rock band. A rock band who could cross over to pop audiences. Did I see *Pyromania* coming? No. No, I didn't. But at that point there's a combination of Mutt and his songwriting ability and the band and their songwriting ability and the creativity that they came together with.

PHIL COLLEN: I've never met anyone like Mutt. He really believed in what he was doing. It was like a jigsaw puzzle. I remember once, we'd been sitting there for hours in the studio playing guitar. We woke up and it was five o'clock and we'd all fallen asleep on the floor. He would keep your attention and keep you grounded. He wouldn't make you feel insecure. A lot of artists are very insecure. It's like being around a shrink. He liked country music, and we could never understand why. He said it was about the stories in the lyrics. And he listened to everything. Everything. Wide open, with no blinkers. That's what I loved about him.

You can absolutely fuck a song up by doing the wrong solo or not listening, by injecting ego into the situation. You get that a lot. If you look at the song, there's a narration going on. It doesn't matter what the

Her majesty's ambassadors DEF LEPPARD, US tour, February 1984. JOE BANGAY | ARENAPAL

lyrics are, they could be inane, but the song has to respect the narration, and it has to respect the melody and the rhythms and that was all Mutt Lange. He taught us how to do that. You give way to the greater good of this thing, which is the song, and you actually move within and around and enhance all the great qualities of it.

I know it's kind of hard when we're talking about songs like "Rock of Ages" or "Pour Some Sugar on Me," but it exists in every single song. With a lot of great pop songs and great pop songwriters, they do that from the get-go. When you do it with production as well, it's a win–win.

RICK SAVAGE: That idea of songs respecting narrations came absolutely naturally to us. The great thing for us was that Mutt could put that into something you could hear. He had the ability to take what you were trying to do, take what's in your mind and get it on to the tape. Every single thing—whether it was a bass drum beat or a hi-hat count—had its own space sonically, and it had to work for what the song was doing. There were no passengers as regards instruments: no, everything has to be right.

And we were very detailed in everything we did. Everything worked towards the song. We were slaves to the song. The song was key. We're very fortunate that the ego within the band is big enough to have a confidence, but never so big to stop people realizing the song is bigger than them.

PHIL COLLEN: Mutt's always the best singer in the room—he sang on all of our stuff. You hear his voice on all of it. He would say, "We'll sing it like this," and he would hit it on the first take. Same with guitar playing: "No, play this," and he'd pick a guitar up and just play it.

It's not that he sat down and practiced for years, it just flowed out of him. He's one of the rare people with that gift, and a great way of putting it over so you don't feel like a useless dick. That would be really easy, because it's easy for him to do it.

JOE ELLIOTT: The first two albums we were still feeling our way. The first album was just a collection of songs we'd been playing live for eighteen months. They were never going to change, so we recorded them and that was the first album. It showed potential, let's put it that way. With the second album, the first we did with Mutt, we were starting to develop.

RICK SAVAGE: When we went in to record the first album with Tom Allom, we were familiar with the songs. We'd played them numerous times. We'd lived with them for eighteen months. Me and Rick did all the songs, all the backing tracks to every song, in two days. It was that straightforward. With Mutt, we were literally starting from ground zero and building every single song. We were writing the songs together, we were constructing them, we were working on them from nothing, so Mutt did become the sixth member. He was part of just about everything we were doing. He became our guru, our mentor, our inspirational figure.

JOE ELLIOTT: The songwriting was getting better. It was still essentially very hard rock, but we always had this inner demon of pop wanting to come out, especially me and Rick Savage—his love of bands like Queen and T. Rex and my love of T. Rex and Bowie and Sweet and Slade—three-minute songs with big choruses. We were always aiming to do something like that but we could never really pull it together until "Photograph."

BRIAN TATLER: We worked with Mike Shipley [on the *Canterbury* album], and he had worked on *Pyromania* [as an engineer]. He said they spent two weeks on the first four lines of "Photograph," just getting the vocal. Whereas most bands could do an album in that time.

JOE ELLIOTT: I remember the first time I heard the riff through the wall in the studio: they were trying to come up with a guitar lick for the beginning of the song, and me and a couple of the crew all kind of went, "What?" When that happens collectively, you know somebody's hit on something. It's magic. And as that developed, and we started putting melodies together, and defining the idea…it's not about Marilyn Monroe, but it's based on the idea of her.

I had a poster on my bathroom wall when I was living in Isleworth, but it was only up to cover a hole in the wall—it was like a scene out of *The Shawshank Redemption*—because some previous tenant had punched a hole through it. I remember saying to Mutt: the idea of a song where the ultimate I-want-what-I-can't-have because she's dead—Jayne Mansfield, etc.—and that's what the song was based around. Lust for the impossible. But from a musical point of view, a melody point of view, it was like leaving for where we were more than happy to go.

PHIL COLLEN: It's all fine and dandy saying "We are hardcore," or "We are death metal," or black metal or whatever, but you're gonna limit your audience. Reaching as many people as possible is exactly what we were trying to do. But keeping your integrity at the same time is the tough bit right there, because you don't feel like you're trying too hard or come over like you're trying too hard.

JOE ELLIOTT: When we came to doing *Pyromania*, it's 1982 and there had been the Human League and a ton of stuff where you can hear drum machines and sequencers. Sequencers had been going on for ever—you think back to "I Feel Love" by Donna Summer, and then think of "Rock of Ages." It's kind of the same. What we were, as kids and fans of that Donna Summer record—we thought Giorgio Moroder was a great producer—was not wanting to limit ourselves to being the band that set up in the corner.

Mutt used to have cassettes sent over from America that had the top forty pop and the top forty rock songs on, and we'd scoot through listening to them, laughing at some, worshipping others,and clap at some and boo some. We were listening to all sorts of stuff that was going off. Our plan was to make an album that nobody else had ever made. We wanted to embrace all the techniques of Joy Division, or the Human League, or Kraftwerk, or Bowie, or any of the people that had pushed the envelope, but we wanted to do that while making a rock record.

Because we did the drums last, we played all the instruments to a rhythm box—slightly better than the one that opens "In the Air Tonight" by Phil Collins—but you can imagine how difficult that was for the guitar players. The reason we did that was that when a drummer—bless 'em all—when a drummer plays, they tend to want to get their licks in, and sometimes their licks come right where there's supposed to be a really cool vocal and the drums are blocking it. You can't go in and change that if you do the drums first.

So Mutt, being a song structuralist, said, "That's why we're gonna do the drums last," which didn't make any sense to Rick Allen. He was like, "Fuck that. I'm just gonna have to wait around?" I said, "Yeah, that's what I have to do. I can't sing till there's a fucking song to sing on." And for six months we didn't know what we were doing, even Mutt. I was thinking, "I don't know if this is working. I hope it does. I've got a feeling this is going to be great."

So we were all floundering in the dark. But eventually, we got all the melodies and lyrics written. And then we started programming the rhythm box so it sounded a little better, so when Rick came to do the drums, he had the structure of how it was supposed to be in his head, so he could actually follow the lead of what it was. Which is not normally what a drummer does. But it gave us song structures, so the lyrics and the guitar hooks weren't cluttered by things underneath getting in the way. We were constructing backwards. It was really weird.

DAVID BATES: I have a history of making records that take a long time. I've been around records that take a long time. You also have to remember that in that period of time it was indulged. They did have royalties coming through, which would have offset. Yes, they did go into the red. Yes, it wasn't the norm. But with any of these things you have to believe that it's going to be fine, it's going to be good. If at the beginning you think, "Oh, not sure about this band, not sure about the songs, not sure about the producer, not sure about anything, oh God, we're six months in and we haven't got anything," yeah, you would be shitting yourself. But they had got a track record.

I didn't even hear demos. By this point I wasn't dealing with them day to day, and they weren't dealing with anybody from the label day to day. They were out on their own.

RICK SAVAGE: Everything had to be larger than life. Who cares whether that snare drum sounds like a real snare drum? We're not interested. Does it sound good? Yeah, it sounds bloody amazing. Then it works. That's how we were. And through the way you heard your own songs, or how you felt they should be portrayed, it just happened that it became an arena rock blueprint.

PHIL COLLEN: When I joined all the rhythm guitars on *Pyromania* had been done [by original guitarist Pete Willis]. And I just came in and played solos and lead guitar and sang, so I had fun. It was just pure fun. Even Mutt said, "Okay, do whatever you want over the top, do a solo, play some lead guitar, do some vibes," and I was like, "Fuck, this is great." I remember it sounding very different to anything I'd ever heard. They'd spent so much time and it was very precise and just different. Rock bands didn't really do that.

Mutt Lange is amazing. He really is an incredible musician, an incredible person, and he just approached it differently. He didn't say it had to be hard rock, or that we had to belong to this club or anything like that. That's the great thing. It knocked down all those barriers and you hear that. So for me to just play over the top of that…and then when he found out I could sing, then I was singing on everything, doing backing vocals. It had a different sound to it, a different texture all of a sudden. It was amazing and it was really fun.

JOE ELLIOTT: The final straw with Pete was the fact that he started to behave in the studio the way he behaved on tour. We'd always heard about Keith Moon and Keith Richards and people like that doing crazy things, throwing TVs out of the window, but they'd get up on stage and do the job. So it was acceptable to do that kind of stuff, and there always seemed to be a sense of humor to it. Keith Moon was portrayed as a lovable cheeky chappy, though if you talk to Pete Townshend he was a pain in the arse. There was nothing mean about it, just pushing the boundaries of good taste a little far.

DENIM AND LEATHER 399

But Pete just used to be an angry drunk. He was an angry drunk, probably because he's five foot two. He couldn't have a drink and tell a dirty joke a little louder. He'd just get violent. He was not pleasant to be around. The amount of times we had fights about his drinking. He'd be drunk on stage so he couldn't play. He said, "I'm just really nervous." Then why are you in a band if you can't fucking do it? Why are you even here? I had so many of these fucking fights with him.

One day in 1981 it got so bad I phoned up Phil, who I'd got to know by then. I met him in 1980, when Girl opened for UFO and him and Phil Lewis [Girl's singer] stayed at my mum and dad's house instead of going back to Buxton. Their hotel was in Buxton for some strange reason. My mum woke up the next morning and said, "Who's that who stayed in the spare room? There's mascara on the pillowcase!" Yes, that's my friends from the band Girl.

PHIL COLLEN: Then Steve [Clark, guitarist] and Joe and I think maybe Sav [Rick Savage] had come down to London and slept on my mom's couch in Walthamstow a few times, so we totally knew each other.

JOE ELLIOTT: Pete turned up so bollocks drunk one morning that Mutt was actually laughing, going, "You've got to hear this," as Pete attempted to play a guitar solo. Just hand a guitar to somebody who can't play. That's what it sounded like. I was really scared Mutt was going to walk off this project with this thing unfinished. I wasn't prepared to let that happen, so I called a band meeting without Pete and said, "I'm not doing this if he stays in the band." And [manager Peter] Mensch backed me up. Mensch spoke to Mutt, and Mutt said he was a liability. He was letting our side down.

He'd gone back to Sheffield for a couple of days and we had this meeting at Mensch's house, and we asked—poor guy—Russell [Major], our then drum tech, to drive Pete down the M1 motorway to Mensch's house, when we all knew what was going to happen. You can imagine that drive for Russell must have been extremely awkward.

We brought him in, middle of the afternoon, July 1982, and said, "I'm sorry, mate, but this has gone too far." "Well, I'll go and see a shrink." "Pete, you should have done that already. You have a problem, and it's not our problem any more." He didn't say anything for about two minutes, then he went, "You know what? This is a fantastic relief for me. I'm actually glad you said this because I wasn't enjoying it at all."

We already had Phil lined up. It was a Sunday, I believe, because it was the World Cup final. Pete left, we started watching the game. Phil came in within an hour of Pete leaving. Mensch said, "I want Mutt to be part of this decision." I said, "Fine, but Mutt's not going to go out on the road with us for the next thirty years." Everybody agreed. The whole band. Steve was a little unsure at first—he thought we should get a keyboard player like Paul Raymond from UFO. But Steve and Phil became inseparable.

Anyway, Phil got invited down to the studio the next day to listen to what we were doing, and he was just blown away by what he heard of *Pyromania*. In fairness, credit where credit's due, Pete Willis's rhythm playing is fucking phenomenal on that record. It's really, really good. So there was a bed there and it was easy for him to just wang bar over top.

Phil played on five tracks and sang on a couple, but on the others he didn't play anything. On the five tracks that Steve played the solo on, Phil didn't play, but the five tracks that were set aside for Pete to solo on, we gave them to Phil. He listened to all the songs and we gave him a cassette of "Stagefright" to go and work out a solo. So he got in his twenty-five-quid Ford Consul, drove back to Walthamstow, came back the next day, and we left him and Mutt alone for a little while.

I swear it was only twenty minutes before Mutt came charging out of the control room going, "You've got to come and hear this." And he played us the solo of "Stagefright" and it was, "Wow!" It was one of the historic moments in this band, internally, a private moment nobody could witness. That cemented the deal. Mutt's words were: "Sign him up." But as Phil will testify, I don't think we actually asked him to join the band until about ten years ago. He just kept turning up.

PETE WILLIS (guitar, Def Leppard): It had to be done. I didn't like it, but it was necessary. I don't hold any grudges at all about it. Actually, the guys were pretty nice about it, saying things like, "Don't think of it as an end. Think of it as the start of something new."

DAVID BATES: It was a shock when I heard the album because it was a real pop-rock record. But in real terms it was led by America, not by us. The success in America was feeding back. It was catching fire in

America big time, and that vibe was coming back. And "Photograph" was the song, the video. In America it was going through the roof. The shock was how good that record sounded. It was like nothing else around.

PHIL COLLEN: Video was just coming to fruition as the album was coming out. [Managers Peter] Mensch and Cliff Burnstein were like, "Fuck, you know, everyone's doing videos. We've got to do that now." A lot of bands were going, "Well, we're artistic and we don't need the visual." We were like, "Fuck that." It's Bowie. Me and Joe were jumping at it. "Oh, God, fuck, great. Pictures of us playing live? Wow, this is great." It was Bowie. It was Marc Bolan. It was all of that stuff. So us and Duran Duran really, really adapted and adopted this new way. We were really ecstatic about it, especially being a rock band. "A rock band that's gonna be on TV? Fucking great."

We weren't like Bad News and I think a lot of other bands were. They'd be, "Nah, we want to be rock, bacon and eggs down a greasy café afterwards." And we didn't. We wanted to be Duran Duran. We wanted to be international. We had this record that sounded very open-minded for a rock band and you just needed the visual to go with it. MTV was everything. The biggest rock album the year before had sold two million, I think. I think it was John Cougar Mellencamp. And then we had this album that ended up doing ten. It sold six million copies while we were on tour, purely because of MTV. So if you say, okay, we sold three times more than the biggest rock album of the year before, that was all because of MTV, without a doubt.

MALCOLM DOME (reviewing Pyromania in Kerrang!, February 10–23, 1983): Have no doubts about the true worth of *Pyromania*. This is an awesome turn in the career of arguably the best band to come out of the NWOBHM. Their policy of pursuing excellence whatever the cost (financially, critically and timewise) has often led to them being seen as inferior to bands more regularly in the public spotlight. But at the end of the day, I'd rather possess the true blinding power of *Pyromania* than myriad copies of *Number of the Beast* or *Denim and Leather*. Those LPs might stun—this one slays…Whereas even a year ago, these Sheffield city snouters were simply a potential top-class unit, these days they've become a GREAT band, capable of taking full advantage of all-proffered production goodies.

Guitars and stripes...Iron Maiden's front line in America, Madison Square Garden, New York City, October 8, 1983. FRANK WHITE

TOM GABRIEL WARRIOR (fan, founder of Hellhammer, Celtic Frost, and Triptykon): *High 'n' Dry* and *Pyromania* are phenomenal albums, and they are rightly placed in the New Wave of British Heavy Metal, even if Def Leppard don't like that. But they had a very detrimental influence and they basically killed off the essence of the wave. And the essence of the wave was underground, and do-it-yourself, being untamed, wiping away the seventies dinosaurs.

Pyromania was already going that way again: it sounded like the commercial albums of the late seventies, as phenomenal as it is. It was taking that turn of pleasing the record company, pleasing the larger commercial audience. That's exactly what the NWOBHM was not about.

Sometimes I have the suspicion that bands who destroyed their own career use record-company influence as a cheap excuse. On the other hand I myself know how infinitely powerful record companies were in the 1980s, especially if you were a small band without any muscle or major management. But as NWOBHM began to fizzle out in '82, '83, '84, there were a whole bunch of very melodic, commercial albums from established bands that were incredibly disappointing because they had just lost the underground values that had made them.

PAUL SUTER (writer, Sounds and Kerrang!): What you have
to bear in mind is that most of the record companies in Britain were
subsidiaries of American record companies. So success in Britain was
fine in the short term, but the parent company was looking at what was
going on in the international subsidiaries—Britain being one of them—
and going, "That's working quite well. What would it do here?" And in
some cases, like Def Leppard, it was hugely successful. So the record
companies were happy because the parent company would now be
making a shitload of money. The bands were happy because they were
also making a shitload of money. Everyone wanted the same thing. But
it wasn't a case of the bands getting greedy, it was a case of the record
companies themselves wanting American success.

BRIAN SLAGEL (fan, founder of Metal Blade Records):
You get these cool underground scenes that start to do really well, and
then record company and business people get involved and say, "If
you had a radio song it would work really well." And that ruins them. It
really kind of killed the New Wave of British Heavy Metal. Countless
bands either broke up because there wasn't much going on, or they got
that push and they went in the wrong direction: Tygers of Pan Tang is a
good example of that. They went from being this really great, cool band
and just tried to be commercial and it didn't work.

ROBB WEIR (guitar, Tygers of Pan Tang): The record company said:
"We want you to be more like Def Leppard." Because Def Leppard
were just breaking the States then. They said, "We want you to be like
them and have a softer, more commercial edge." Hmm. I thought to
myself, "That's not the Tygers. You're asking us to change." It was like
asking Motörhead to play Spandau Ballet songs. It's not what the fans
would be used to. There were all sorts of emotions running around, but
we went along with it.

Def Leppard were still writing their own songs, albeit on their
big albums they were writing with Mutt Lange. That was the big
difference. Had MCA said to us: "We want you to be a bit more like
Def Leppard; will you write songs with Desmond Child?" that would
have been a whole different ball game. We would still be writing songs,
albeit with someone else, so it would be a collective. Rather than:
"Will you just record a Steve Thompson [former Neat Records house
producer] song? Just go off and do that." There's no creativity there

for an artist. What goes against the grain is that the *Wild Cat* album came out, charted at eighteen. *Spellbound* was in the top twenty as well—and they were self-penned albums. So we had a track record of charting albums written by us. So why would we want to spend the time learning the chords of some pop songs by outside writers? It just doesn't add up.

JON DEVERILL: Back then, it was the rise of the rock single. Suddenly you had to have a hit single. Every rock band had to have a hit single. To break rock bands, instead of touring, you had a hit single and went on *Top of the Pops*. There's a lot to be said for that. The producer on *The Cage* [the fourth Tygers album] was Peter Collins, who was a brilliant producer. And his partner at the time was Pete Waterman.

TOM NOBLE (comanager, Tygers of Pan Tang): We had a giant row over "Love Potion No. 9." I had the version by the Searchers, and when MCA rang me and said, "Pete Waterman tells us you're going to record 'Love Potion No. 9,'" I said, "Over my dead body." So MCA bought me a plane ticket, flew me down to London, and at Heathrow I met with Pete Waterman and the producer. Again, they talked to me for two hours. When I came back I gave my vinyl *Best of the Searchers* album to John [Sykes, guitarist] and Robb, and said, "They want you to record this song 'Love Potion No. 9,' guys, but it's not gonna work."

ROBB WEIR: John Sykes and I were sat down in Tom's lounge, and Tom said, "What do you think to this?" John and I looked at each other and Tom said, "Before you say anything, the record company want you to record it." We nodded our heads and said, "We'll try and do something with it." I wrote the opening gambit, and John came up with the rock 'n' roll middle bit, and there we have it. We had made it ours.

TOM NOBLE: They routined it, they structured it, they arranged it. That was John and Robb. And they made a fantastic version of it. But the rest of the album was not great.

PETE WATERMAN (impresario, producer, songwriter): I've always seen it as a real rock song. Not dressed up to be a rock song. It is a rock song. I thought that if you were going to be a rock band, do a rock song, so the people that buy it understand what it is. We all look back and say, "What worked once upon a time for other people?" So in a way I guess that's where it came from. To me the influence was: I had seen this band that reminded me very much of what I was into when I was sixteen, seventeen, the excitement they had generated. I thought of bands I had seen in Coventry, like the Mighty Avengers and the Matadors, and the one song that stood out to me like a sore thumb from those guys was "Love Potion No. 9."

JON DEVERILL: The success of "Love Potion No. 9" was purely the Tygers of Pan Tang. Okay, it was his idea to do the song, but we turned it into what it was. He had no influence on the arrangement and recording of it. The arrangement is totally ours—one hundred percent. And "Love Potion No. 9" was the closest thing we had to a hit single. It reached number thirty-two. We were number thirty-two in the charts. Toyah was fifty-something with "It's a Mystery," and she got *Top of the Pops*. Why? Why did these things happen to us? We were high in the bloody charts but she got *Top of the Pops*. [Note: "Love Potion No. 9" actually reached number forty-five. It was not in the chart at the same time as "It's a Mystery."]

ROBB WEIR: We were recording *The Cage*, and Peter Waterman came in. We'd never met him. He said, "I've got it! This is going to be your next hit single." And we were all looking around at each other, going, "Who the fuck's this fella?" But he seemed to know Peter Collins, which was strange. We didn't know he was his manager.

He said, "We're going to record this song 'Paris by Air' [written by Steve Thompson]. The cover is going to be the Eiffel Tower, and here's the killer—we're going to give away an earring in the shape of the Eiffel Tower!" This was Peter Waterman saying this. We looked at each other, put our heads in our hands and thought, "Oh my God." He didn't get that right. It charted, but not anything like "Love Potion No. 9."

JON DEVERILL: The covers we did on that album were songs that had already been rejected by all the other rock bands. We did a John Parr song, "Danger in Paradise," which we never should have done. Why did we record that song? At the time we must have liked it, but for me that's one of the worst songs on the album. And "Rendezvous." Oh my God. But I liked what Peter Collins did with them. We were one of the earliest heavy rock bands to use an electronic Simmons kit,

Reading Rock '82 promotion—at this point, the heavy metal takeover of the world's oldest pop music festival was complete, but things were starting to go wrong for Tygers of Pan Tang and several others on the bill.

which was very big in the new romantics. That big electronic sound, a combination of electric and acoustic drums, we were one of the first rock bands to do that. *The Cage*, there's something about the album that's really quite groundbreaking. You take a song like "Rendezvous." It wasn't given that standard AOR treatment. It's got these electronic drums in the background, and interesting sounds.

[After *The Cage* tour], we started demoing songs for a new album. MCA liked it, and Peter Waterman did too. But again they wanted us to do so many covers. "Very nice, lads, a couple of good songs, but this is a real song." That was the attitude, and it was so insulting to us. And especially when we had good material—we totally believed in these songs and wanted to record them.

MCA was still in the mindset that we had to have a hit single. "You haven't had a hit single, so we'll find one for you." And the person doing the finding was Pete Waterman. It was truly artistic differences. We wanted to go in a completely different direction from the one the record company wanted us to go in. We'd just had our most successful album, so that gave us a certain amount of kudos, we felt. But it didn't.

It didn't mean a thing to MCA. It didn't mean anything that we were selling records. It's so bizarre the way they treated us. If *The Cage* had flopped, I'd understand it. But it sold a shitload of records.

TOM NOBLE: It started to go wrong with the 1982 Reading festival. I was in Greece, and I got a note pushed under my hotel door that said, "Please ring MCA Records urgently." I was flying home the next day, so I waited until I got to Gatwick airport, and I rang MCA. They said, "The band are about to pull out of the Reading festival, stop them."

So instead of going home, I went to Birmingham, where they were rehearsing. I said, "What's all this about pulling out of Reading?" They said, "It's where they've put us on the bill—they've put us between Gary Moore and Iron Maiden, and we're being used as a buffer."

I thought they had a point, but I said, "Guys, Adrian Hopkins, who's promoting your tour of city halls, will pull out of that tour if you don't do Reading, and you'll lose a lot of credibility." We had a vote on it, and they voted three-two to play there. And they went down really well. Following Gary Moore and before Iron Maiden is not a great spot, if you're the pretty boys of heavy metal, but it worked.

They played their UK tour, I went to the MCA conference, and on the last date of the tour, in Edinburgh, I said to them, "Guys, I'm going to have to resign. I can't get MCA to do what I want. I don't have the clout I need. You need a manager who can exert the amount of pressure you need to get to America, so I'm doing what I think is the right thing and I'm going to resign."

ROBB WEIR: It got to the middle of '83. I went on holiday to Spain for a fortnight, came back. First job was to ring Rocky [Richard Laws], the bass player, asking him what had been going on while I was away. And he said, "I've got some bad news." I said, "Oh. What's going on?" He said, "You and Brian [Dick, drummer] are not in the band any more." And I said, "Really?" And he said, "Yeah." And I said, "Okay, great joke. What are we doing? What's happening? When am I coming round?"

And he said, "No, Robb. I'm being serious." I could hear the hurt in his voice, telling me this. Rocky and I were so solid. He had answered my original ad and we went down the road together. I said, "What do you mean? What's going on?" And he said, "When you were away we had a meeting with Rod MacSween."

JON DEVERILL: The final disastrous decision was myself and Fred [Purser, replacement guitarist for John Sykes] getting involved with Rod MacSween, who ran ITB, a very, very big touring agency. Rod had always been involved with us. We liked him on a personal level. We took our demos, the ones MCA had more or less rejected, to Rod. He loved them. And he became our manager. But then he wanted to change the lineup of the band, which was very wrong in hindsight. It was wrong. We should have broken away and formed a new band, not retained the name Tygers of Pan Tang.

ROBB WEIR: Rocky told me, "Rod said the band didn't look right and you and Brian were the ones that didn't look right. So we're carrying on." What started out as a nice, happy conversation, just got difficult and uneasy. Rocky and I are still friends, and he says it was a horrible phone call, and he didn't understand why he was making it, or why he agreed to it.

I put the phone down, picked it up, put in another ten pence and rang Brian and said, "Brian, apparently we're not in our band any more." And he went, "Yeah." And I said, "Shall we start a new band?" He said, "Yeah." I said, "I'll ring you back in ten minutes. I've got an idea." And I rang a singer, and he said he knew a bass player, and I rang Brian back in ten minutes and said, "Can you make it to a rehearsal next Friday night?" He went. "Yeah." I said, "We've got a new band then." And off we went. That's a whole 'nother story.

BIFF BYFORD (vocals, Saxon): I think as you become a musician and artist, you tend to become a bit more sophisticated as time goes on. Whether that's a great thing or not, you're striving to do something better than you've done before and sometimes you can confuse that and lose the plot and get concerned with the sound of the songs and how they are being recorded. For instance, we changed slightly from [the album] *Power and the Glory* to *Crusader*. We were still writing great metal songs, but sprinkled in that is something a little bit less heavy. The record company was seeing NWOBHM slipping away and thought we should enter the American market.

STEVE DAWSON: My argument was that we should have got heavier. But I must admit, by this time there were a lot of personal things happening in people's lives. I'd got divorced. I weren't living in a stable environment. I just rented places. All I did all day was sit about at home fucking around with tunes. I wrote a load of tunes. Some of them were great. But some of them weren't as hard. Poppy tunes, but with an edge. And when you see the great success of *Pyromania*...Maiden were big, but they weren't big like they are now. Not massive. Def Leppard, from town next door to where I was, had made this innovative album, and it was an influence.

We drifted to not writing the same sorts of songs. If somebody said, "You need to write harder, heavier songs," we might have done. But because we were left to our own devices, we didn't. *The Power and the Glory* were quite a good-sounding album, but there are a lot of weak songs on it. But things like "Sailing to America" were just weak. They're not heavy. They're not what our fans wanted.

DAVID BATES: *Pyromania* was a great rock album and a great pop album. You could say the same about *Thriller*. Any great album that crosses over to everybody you can say was made to appeal to everyone. It's just a great album. Some scuzz band can resent that and say they've sold out. It's just because you haven't come up with that and written songs as good as that and you haven't recorded it as well as that.

MALCOLM DOME (writer, Record Mirror *and* Kerrang!*)*:
In one respect *Pyromania* probably was the end of NWOBHM, because it took production to a new level. It took the whole ethos of making a rock album to a new level, and every label looked at it and said, "That's the way we have to do things like that now." Except without the producer and without the budget.

By that time NWOBHM was limping along. Thrash was coming through, glam was coming through. Realistically, Leppard finished it off, and *Pyromania* took things to a new level.

JOE ELLIOTT: We were young and spitting venom, and we wanted to stand on our own two feet. We always said: if a movement dies, everyone within it dies, so don't put us in it. Being in the press was useful, but the term NWOBHM has if anything been detrimental. People get the impression I have this vitriol and hatred towards it. I really don't care. I'm just sick of talking about it. Musically we're closer to Duran Duran.

PHIL COLLEN: When we finished our *Pyromania* world tour, and we were starting to write *Hysteria* in Dublin, Mutt sat down and the first thing out of his mouth was "Okay, we can't make *Pyromania* part two, because everyone else has just made that." The Def Leppard albums had been works in progress and when *Pyromania* came out it was, "Okay, this is how we sound."

The early stuff didn't sound uniquely Def Leppard: *High 'n' Dry* sounds a little bit like AC/DC; the first album is trying to find itself, it's trying to find its thing. Back then you could do that. Record companies would nurture artists and bands to do exactly that. There's that identity that you crave, and I think it started really on *Pyromania* and that's why it sounds drastically different. But when Mutt came in and said everyone was trying to copy that album, and we don't want to sound like that again, we went left field and just opened it up even more. The canvas was wide open.

Afterword

I f *Pyromania* was the flame that finally destroyed NWOBHM, leaving nothing but scorched earth behind it, the signs of its demise had been visible for some time. As early as October 1980, Geoff Barton had surveyed the slew of cash-in compilation albums, the bands hastily repositioning themselves as heavy metal, and written in *Sounds*: "The movement known as the New Wave of British Heavy Metal—and that's positively the last time I use the term—has peaked and is currently and irrevocably locked into a slow downward spiral into ignominy. Amidst a welter of hastily assembled albums, cash-ins and trash-ins, it becomes increasingly difficult to discern the difference between good and bad, between genuine, committed HM exponents and freshly smelted bandwagon jumpers."

Nevertheless, while 1980 was the movement's high-water mark, it remained a commercial force through 1981 and 1982. In 1981, Girlschool reached the top ten with their second album, *Hit and Run*. In 1982, Tygers of Pan Tang had both their biggest hit album (*The Cage*, number thirteen) and single ("Love Potion No. 9"). But there was a sense of constant instability, which couldn't have helped the bands. While Def Leppard remained reasonably stable, aside from swapping out Pete Willis for Phil Collen, almost all the other major bands were discarding and recruiting members with unseemly haste. While it worked for Iron Maiden—who, one by one, dispensed with Dennis Stratton, Paul Di'Anno and finally Clive Burr between the recording of their first and fourth albums—it crippled others, notably Samson, who lost Bruce Dickinson to Maiden. Tygers of Pan Tang had just one original member by the time they folded. But these were very young men, making mistakes as they went along, and not having the wisdom or the time to rectify them. "You've got to remember how young we all were," says Jon Deverill of Tygers of Pan Tang. "I was immature in many ways, but hindsight lets you realize your mistakes. If only I'd been a bit more mature, but I was only a kid, with a kid's mentality. One of my biggest regrets was when me and Fred Purser broke away. That was very wrong. The three members we broke away from had more claim to the name Tygers of Pan Tang than me and Fred."

In truth, too, most of the NWOBHM bands were simply not good enough to thrive on their own, away from the security of the movement that birthed them. It wasn't just good management that meant Def Leppard and Iron Maiden were able to transcend NWOBHM and establish themselves as stadium rock bands, it was having songs that appealed to more people than anything Mythra or Silverwing could come up with. In many ways, NWOBHM is reminiscent of the US garage-punk explosion of the mid-1960s: scores of bands with maybe one or two songs that simply needed to be heard, to explode out of speakers in someone's bedroom. Like garage punk, many of the NWOBHM bands were simply unsuited to albums; they couldn't build a career on two good songs, but tried to—with the result they get remembered not for the six minutes of brilliance they had, but for the other thirty-four that filled up their albums.

Of course, the bands were not helped by the things that continually plague young groups: inexperienced managements, record labels who had no idea how to develop the groups they had signed, industry figures who steered the bands towards terrible decision making. Almost every band in this book has a complaint about either their management or their record label, and it was ever thus.

Nevertheless, the importance of *Pyromania* cannot be overstated. It wasn't just that Def Leppard changed the direction of hard rock, they did so in a way that could not be emulated. They were granted the resources to make an album that could break America, whereas the other bands who tried to make radio-friendly rock were not. They also, of course, had a management who knew what they were doing, and a record label who let both management and band get on with it. David Bates might have been Def Leppard's A&R man, but the reality of the situation was that Mensch and Burnstein were doing the job that most

other managers—without their experience at the top end of the music industry—were unable to do for their bands.

Mensch and Burnstein went on to become two of the most powerful and successful management pairings of the last 40 years. Q Prime, the company they set up in 1982, has offices in London, Nashville and New York. Mensch and Burnstein still personally manage 12 acts, including the stadium-filling Metallica and Muse, though Def Leppard left Q Prime in 2005. Nevertheless, Mensch and Burnstein were, as Joe Elliott says, "massively important. Every musician that's made it will look back and realize, if they're honest with themselves, that it's not just about how talented they are and the music. It's all down to what decade their music came out in, how fortunate they were that certain things happened at certain times in their career that made them bigger. Why the Rolling Stones and not the Pretty Things? Is it all down to the songs? There was a time when the two of them were like that. And us and Diamond Head were like that. There was more ambition in Jagger and Richards than in the Pretty Things, I would say, for a start. And for us there was definitely more ambition. Not that Diamond Head weren't ambitious. I went to see them at Sheffield City Hall, and you could see they were trying really hard to be somebody. They were probably no better or worse than us. But the difference was, we always had a poppier edge than any of the other NWOBHM bands. There was a pop band waiting to burst out. That was always going to win over any manager, because we wanted to be more like Fleetwood Mac or the Eagles than we wanted to be like Hawkwind."

As *Pyromania* was smashing the US charts wide open through 1983, metal was undergoing a schism, as if the fading of NWOBHM had left a vacuum, waiting to be filled by some new, dominant form of metal. On the one hand, Los Angeles produced what came to be known as hair metal, bands for whom the rock-star lifestyle was the reason to make music; on the other came the significantly harder thrash scene. By the mid-1980s, the "big four" of thrash—Metallica, Anthrax, Slayer and Megadeth—were all established, and while the hair bands might have been the ones in the singles charts, the conversation around the future of metal was centered on thrash (albeit that, on this side of the Atlantic, *Kerrang!* was distinctly sniffy about it at first). By 1988, when Metallica released the landmark...*And Justice for All*, Saxon, once a byword for heaviness, were releasing a tepid cover of Christopher Cross's yacht-rock staple "Ride Like the Wind." Six years earlier, Metallica had opened for Saxon. Years later, Biff Byford would join them on stage to sing "Motorcycle Man." But the American dream had consumed so many NWOBHM bands so completely there was no way to recover.

Hindsight is a wonderful thing, of course, and the bands who dyed their hair and added a bit of mascara in 1983 weren't to know they were choosing the wrong fork in the road. But maybe Tygers and Saxon and Girlschool and the others who tried to become more American might have had different careers had they stuck to their guns—perhaps they would have suffered a couple of years of famine before harder-edged metal started having commercial success, but equally, perhaps they would have been able to capitalize on the success of thrash. That it might have been possible is proven by Judas Priest and Iron Maiden. In 1981, Priest made their own attempt at a radio-friendly record, *Point of Entry*, arguably the least beloved record of their golden age. In 1982 they followed that with *Screaming for Vengeance*, perhaps the most viscerally metallic album released on a major label to that point, and the one that took them into the arenas of America. *Screaming for Vengeance*, especially with "Riding on the Wind" and the title track, that's pretty intense," Rob Halford says. "There were some very, very strong statements in that album." Even its lead single, "You've Got Another Thing Coming," sounds like Venom compared to anything from *Pyromania*. Maiden, meanwhile, simply refused to change. They did what Maiden do: long songs with lots of sections, making no concession to radio, and by summer 1983 they, too, were on the American arena circuit.

Still, NWOBHM never died, and one of the most delightful things is that almost everyone in this book is still playing heavy metal music. They're doing it for fun these days, to supplement their day jobs, but they're still doing it. Because they love it. Sometimes they are still playing in the bands named in this book (albeit often featuring one original member), sometimes under different band names. The venues aren't as big these days, and the crowds have aged along with the musicians. But they still play their music, and people still come to see them, sometimes from unusual places.

A few years ago, I was on the 134 bus from central London to my home, and realized the top deck was filled with people speaking French and wearing battle jackets. On every single one of those battle

jackets was a Tygers of Pan Tang patch. A quick Google search revealed Tygers were headlining a mini-metal festival at the Dome in Tufnell Park that day. And while it's possible the French fans were émigrés who already lived in London, it seems geographically and statistically more likely that a bunch of people had crossed the channel to see a band they viewed as legends of metal.

Robb Weir of the Tygers—whose presence in *Denim and Leather* does not reflect the vast amount of time he spent talking to me—explains well why he still takes annual leave from his job to make records and tour. Yes, he admits, there are times when he looks at Maiden or Leppard and feels jealousy that they are the ones who fill stadiums. But, still, he has no regrets.

"In 2017 we were touring out in South America, and we were playing São Paulo. The venue held just under two thousand, I guess. Standing, but there was a balcony upstairs as well. It was a big old place. And the guy who owned it owned a TV and radio station as well. So he had been advertising that we were coming and doing his bit. I looked out the curtain—and I never do, because when the curtain's open, whoever's there is whoever's there. And that's that. It doesn't matter if it's one man and his dog or it's full. You still have to give the same one hundred and ten percent, because they've paid their money and they expect to be entertained. And I looked out the curtain and there were about two hundred people in, I suppose, at the front of the stage, and along the big, huge long bar along the full length of the room. And I thought, 'Oh well, okay, two hundred people is better than twenty.' And then another forty-five minutes pass. It's showtime. Lights go out, intro goes on, curtains open, off we go and the place is packed to the back wall. Your mindset is that there's two hundred people, but the curtain opens and it's full. Towards two thousand people in. And you think, 'Shit. Where have they come from?' It's a revelation. And a big part of the Tygers world is after the show. We give ourselves fifteen, twenty minutes, and we're straight out, talking to people, having a drink with people, signing things. It doesn't matter where. It's great, I absolutely love it."

If anyone embodies all the good things that came out of NWOBHM—the love of playing for whoever turns up, and the determination to do it even if no one does turn up—it's Robb Weir. He was one of the ones Biff Byford was singing about. It was him—and those like him—who set the spirit free.

Where Are They Now?

Both *DEF LEPPARD* and *IRON MAIDEN* went on to establish themselves among the most popular rock bands in the world, and they each still fill arenas and stadiums. Joe Elliott, Rick Savage, Rick Allen and Phil Collen remain in Def Leppard. Dennis Stratton and Paul Di'Anno were sacked from Iron Maiden, in 1980 and 1981 respectively, replaced by Bruce Dickinson and Adrian Smith. Dennis Stratton, up until the COVID-19 pandemic, played a regular residency at the Woodbine pub in Waltham Forest. He also plays with Lionheart, the group he formed immediately after leaving Maiden. Paul Di'Anno has had a more troubled time, with drug and alcohol addictions and severe health problems. The pandemic forced the cancellation of his appearance with the band Ides of March, composed of early members of Iron Maiden—including Doug Sampson, and with lighting by Dave Lights—at the Beermageddon festival in 2020.

JUDAS PRIEST remain a hugely popular live draw and recording band, and Rob Halford remains their front man—after a spell out of the group when he was replaced by the singer of a Priest tribute band. K. K. Downing left Priest in 2011. Relations between him and the rest of the band are rancorous.

Cronos continues to front a lineup of **VENOM** who tour the world. Mantas plays guitar in Venom Inc., who also play Venom songs and also tour the world. In the fall of 2022, they released the album *There's Only Black*. Abaddon drummed with Venom Inc. until 2018. It would be fair to say Mantas and Abaddon were not, at the time of writing, speaking fondly of each other.

Thanks to the royalties from Metallica's cover versions, Brian Tatler has never had to take a day job and continues to play guitar in **DIAMOND HEAD**, in which he is the only original member. Late in 2020, Diamond Head released a rerecorded version of the *Lightning to the Nations* album. Sean Harris writes songs, but he has no interest in either recording them or performing them. He still lives in the same house in Stourbridge that was Diamond Head HQ when Lars Ulrich went to stay with him.

After being sacked from his own band in 1983, Robb Weir formed a new version of **TYGERS OF PAN TANG** in 2000, since when the band have released six albums, the most recent being *Ritual* in 2019. Jess Cox went behind the scenes in music, and has run several metal labels, including several years as owner of Neat Records, before selling it to Rod Smallwood's Sanctuary Group in 2001. Jon Deverill became Jon De Ville and took up musical theater, in which guise he has appeared in *The Sound of Music* at the London Palladium.

John Gallagher and his brother Mark continue to tour and record with **RAVEN**. Though their dalliance with Atlantic Records in the 1980s proved to be a bit of a disaster, the only thing that has ever interrupted them was a collapsing wall crushing Mark's legs in 2001, forcing them to take a four-year hiatus while he recovered. Raven's 2020 album *Metal Nation* received rave reviews from the metal press.

Biff Byford and Steve Dawson parted ways in 1986, when Dawson was fired from **SAXON**. In 1999, however, Dawson and his fellow former Saxon member Graham Oliver registered the band's name as a trademark. A subsequent court case found that Byford was entitled to keep the name. Saxon still tour and record (and Byford also released his first solo album in 2020), putting out a new album of original material, *Carpe Diem*, in 2022. Since being interviewed, Steve Dawson has left

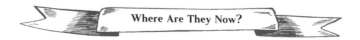

Oliver/Dawson Saxon, who toured playing Saxon material, but Oliver continues alone as Graham Oliver's Army.

ANGEL WITCH continue to tour and record, though not with Kevin Riddles, who left the band in 1981. He formed the band Tytan on leaving Angel Witch, and revived that band in 2012.

After leaving Samson in 1981, **THUNDERSTICK** formed his own band, named after himself. He re-joined various lineups of Samson, then brought back the Thunderstick name in 2016. Thunderstick continue to write and record.

Tino Troy and his brother Chris continue to lead **PRAYING MANTIS**, who are now in their third spell of existence, having split between 1985 and 1990 and then again from 2003 to 2008. Dennis Stratton has, on occasion, also been a member of Praying Mantis.

Andro Coulton recorded just one album with **WITCHFYNDE**, *Friends of Hell* (regarded as their classic, though its follow-up, *Stagefright*, is compellingly peculiar). These days, he has his own band playing the songs he played between 1975 and 1980, called Andro Coulton's Witchfynde. Montalo himself, a thoughtful and quietly spoken man who asked me not to reveal his real name, ended Witchfynde in 1984, but reconvened a lineup of the band in 2000 and they have continued to play and record intermittently since then. Andro Coulton's website notes that his own version of the band has Montalo's approval.

WITCHFINDER GENERAL split after two albums, but their influence persists. Phil Cope returned to the building trade and never left it. He still lives in Stourbridge and sometimes meets Brian Tatler of Diamond Head for a drink. Labels continue to make offers to repackage and reissue his band's slim output.

David Coverdale is still the front man of **WHITESNAKE**, and still changing the lineup: late in 2021 he announced the band had its first ever woman member. Neil Murray and Bernie Marsden have continued to have productive musical careers, with many and varied bands.

Ian Gillan, after dissolving **GILLAN**, was briefly and disastrously the front man of Black Sabbath, but has spent much of the time since 1985

fronting various lineups of the re-formed Deep Purple, sometimes with Ritchie Blackmore. Blackmore had joined the re-formed Purple, but finally left in 1993. He has spent much of the intervening time playing renaissance music in Blackmore's Night, though he revived the **RAINBOW** name for three shows in 2017. He was the only member from any of the first era of Rainbow lineups to appear. John McCoy formed a band called Mammoth after Gillan, largely because all of its members were large. He has mainly been a producer since the 1980s.

GIRLSCHOOL continue to tour and record, with both Kim McAuliffe and Denise Dufort in the band. Though they had sacked Enid Williams in 1982, they brought her back in 2000. They sacked her again in 2019. Their most recent album, *Guilty as Sin*, was released in 2015.

The many writers quoted remain writers, by and large, though some are not as prolific as they once were (Dante Bonutto now runs Spinefarm, a rock label that is part of the Universal Music Group). It was saddening to learn that Ian Ravendale—whose real name was Ian Penman, but who wrote under a pseudonym to avoid confusion with another writer of the same name—died in March 2021, not long after the completion of this book. Malcolm Dome, too, passed away in October 2021. His status within the world of metal could be judged from the enormous number of musicians who paid tribute to him. He will be missed. Neal Kay is now officially retired as a DJ, but he continues to champion hard rock and heavy metal whenever he is given the opportunity to do so.

Acknowledgements

This book originated in a piece commissioned by Ben Beaumont-Thomas for the *Guardian* in 2019, to mark the fortieth anniversary of Geoff Barton's review from the Music Machine. Without Ben, this book would not have happened. He also allowed me to use my interviews for a long piece for the *Quietus*, which proved there was scope for more, and my thanks go to John Doran and Luke Turner of the *Quietus* for running that. My agent, Matthew Hamilton, persuaded me there was a book to be written (and later, being unexpectedly well connected in the world of metal, provided me with useful introductions), and Andreas Campomar of Little, Brown decided to publish it. Then Ian Christe of Bazillion Points decided U.S. readers should not be denied the minutiae of Tygers of Pan Tang's catering habits

It was my original interviewees who provided all the material that got people interested in the first place, and I thank Robb Weir (whom I think of as the hero of this book, even if his is not the most dramatic story, and even if it is not told in full), Cronos, David Wood, Tony Wilson, Jody Turner (Rock Goddess felt too late a band to be included properly in this book), Biff Byford and Brian Tatler. Special thanks to two of those original interviewees: Neal Kay, who put me in contact with several other people I spoke to; and to Joe Elliott. Joe, Phil Collen and Rick Savage each agreed to several interviews for this book, when they had not the slightest need to, for which I am truly grateful.

Steve Hammonds, Malcolm Dome and Jerry Ewing each provided me with invaluable help tracking down some of the more elusive and obscure musicians. On the PR side, Andy Turner, Duff Battye, and Sharon Chevin were helpful to an extent I had no right to even hope for. Adam Sagir, Simon Glacken, Barbara Charone and Ant Giannaccini arranged interviews with those musicians who were not even primary parts of the story, but who I felt needed to be heard. Dom Lawson helped me out with additional material when Cronos decided he didn't want to speak to me again. My deepest thanks to David Fricke for allowing me to quote from interviews in his book *Def Leppard: Animal Instinct*.

Back issues of music papers came from three sources: the Humanities Reading Room at the British Library, where the staff are ever helpful and the resources boundless. And, when that closed owing to the COVID-19 pandemic, the personal collection of Mark Wagstaff of *Mojo* magazine, who loaned me his run of the first couple of years of *Kerrang!* And finally, James Hyman of HYMAG, the world's largest magazine collection, gave me access to his repository in Woolwich to track down the final missing articles.

Along the way I needed to do some journalism, so thank you to those editors—Ben and Laura Snapes at the *Guardian*, John and Luke at the *Quietus*, and Jan Dalley at the *Financial Times*—who let me turn some of my ongoing interviews into features for them.

Thanks to anyone who ever replied to a Twitter or Facebook appeal for help and information. And to the whole metal community: in recent years I've travelled to Nepal and India to write about metal, and without fail the people I have encountered on those trips have been completely delightful in their love of metal music and metal culture.

The same holds true for every single person I interviewed for this book, who—let's not forget—actually changed music. So my sincere thanks to every person who spent time talking to me, be it for twenty minutes or four hours. I transcribed almost all of this myself, but there were a couple of times when the backlog of recordings got too much. Thanks to Liz Dexter, Johnny Sharp and Martha Bird for their transcription services. More personally, long afternoons in the Social in Little Portland Street in London with Robin Turner and Julian Stockton (Robin once wearing a Saxon bandana throughout) were often based around conversations about NWOBHM, which made me realize how fun it all was. Because almost all the work on the book was done during the pandemic, when it was impossible to meet people face to face, there wasn't a lot of discussing it during its construction, but one

Acknowledgements

friend who has constantly encouraged and supported my writing over the years has been Laura Barton. Others saw parts of the manuscript as it was written, and I'm grateful for the encouragement of Robin and Julian, as well as Steven Adams and Craig Finn.

And my apologies to my family: my brilliant and wonderful wife Isabel Berwick, and our children Freya and Gabe, for putting them through a year of non-stop metal. Gabe brought a girlfriend home one evening, and before I could even speak, he told her: "Just tell him you like Diamond Head." I promise we can now also listen to different music in the car—sometimes.

Additional Sources

Where material has been taken from contemporary publications, it is credited in the text. All other material comes from author interviews, except the below.

The Cronos quotes listed below come from an interview by Dom Lawson, for the booklet of the Venom box set *In Nomine Satanas*.

The remaining quotes all come from *Def Leppard: Animal Instinct* by David Fricke (Zomba Publishing, 1987).

All are reprinted with kind permission of the authors.

CHAPTER 6

Cliff Burnstein: "I said to them, 'Hey, it wasn't a great show ...'"
Peter Mensch: "I was getting friendly with the group ..."

CHAPTER 7

Peter Mensch: "When the first tomato and beer can hit the stage ..."

CHAPTER 11

Cronos: "The guy who ran the place was a bit of an Arthur Daley, you know? ..."

CHAPTER 14

Cronos: "Even when I joined and it was the other guy singing ..."
Cronos: "Once the single did well, Neat wanted more ..."

Cronos: "From the highs of the *At War with Satan* thing to the crushing lows of the *Possessed* album . . ."

CHAPTER 16

Cliff Burnstein: "There's this seedy heavy metal club called the Rainbow . . ." Rick Allen: "I went nuts over there, women left, right and center . . ." Robert John "Mutt" Lange: "We really worked on the dynamics . . ."

Cliff Burnstein: "The *High 'n' Dry* album was already history on the charts . . ."

NWOBHM Playlists

EARLY NWOBHM

Early recordings from the groups who began releasing in 1979 and 1980:

Girlschool – "Take It All Away"

Diamond Head –
  "Shoot Out the Lights"

Saxon – "Stallions of the Highway"

Samson – "Mr. Rock 'n' Roll"

Def Leppard – "Getcha Rocks Off"

Iron Maiden – "Running Free"

Vardis – "If I Were King"

Tygers of Pan Tang –
  "Don't Touch Me There"

Angel Witch – "Baphomet"

Fist – "Name, Rank and
  Serial Number"

Witchfynde – "Give 'Em Hell"

White Spirit – "Backs to the Grind"

Girl – "My Number"

Blitzkrieg – "Blitzkrieg"

The Handsome Beasts –
  "All Riot Now"

THE SOUNDHOUSE TAPES

The Soundhouse was the CBGB of British hard rock. This was the first ever Soundhouse metal chart, published in Sounds *on August 12, 1978 (minus "Motorcyle Dream" by Slack Alice and "Earache My Eye" by Cheech and Chong):*

AC/DC – "Kicked in the Teeth"

Deep Purple – "Child in Time"

Pat Travers – "Statesboro Blues"

ZZ Top – "Tush"

Foreigner – "Long, Long Way
  from Home"

Angel – "Got Love If You Want It"

Boston – "More Than a Feeling"

Thin Lizzy – "Rosalie"

Meat Loaf – "Bat Out of Hell"

Montrose – "Space Station #5"

Robin Trower –
  "Too Rolling Stoned"

Joe Walsh – "Rocky Mountain Way"

Status Quo – "Bye Bye Johnny"

UFO – "Love to Love"

Led Zeppelin – "Heartbreaker"

Lynyrd Skynyrd – "Free Bird"

Rainbow – "Starstruck"

Jethro Tull – "Aqualung"

THE NWOBHM EXPLODES

The banner year 1980 saw a rash of debut albums and defining NWOBHM anthems:

Saxon – "Wheels of Steel"
Iron Maiden – "Iron Maiden"
Tygers of Pan Tang – "Euthanasia"
Def Leppard – "Wasted"
White Spirit – "Midnight Chaser"
Raven – "Don't Need Your Money"
Diamond Head – "Am I Evil?"
Angel Witch – "Angel Witch"
Girlschool – "Emergency"
Samson – "Take It Like a Man"
Motörhead – "Ace of Spades"
Judas Priest – "Breaking the Law"
Holocaust – "Heavy Metal Mania"
Spider – "College Luv"
A II Z – "No Fun After Midnight"
Quartz – "Stand Up and Fight"
Vardis – "100 MPH"
Girl – "Hollywood Tease"
Aragorn – "Black Ice"
Chevy – "The Taker"

POST-PURPLE

The NWOBHM activities of the former principals of Deep Purple:

Ian Gillan Band – "Scarabus"
Ian Gillan Band –
   "Smoke on the Water"
Gillan – "Vengeance"
Gillan – "Unchain Your Brain"
Gillan – "Trouble"
Gillan – "Born to Kill"
Gillan – "Living for the City"
Rainbow –
   "Man on the Silver Mountain"
Rainbow – "Sixteenth
   Century Greensleeves"
Rainbow – "Stargazer"
Rainbow –
   "Long Live Rock 'n' Roll"
Rainbow – "All Night Long"
Rainbow –
   "Since You Been Gone"
Rainbow – "Lost in Hollywood"
Whitesnake – "Ain't No Love
   in the Heart of the City"
Whitesnake – "Take Me With You"
Whitesnake – "Walking in
   the Shadow of the Blues"
Whitesnake –
   "Fool For Your Loving"
Whitesnake –
   "Don't Break My Heart Again"
Whitesnake – "Crying in the Rain"
Whitesnake – "Here I Go Again"

DENIM AND LEATHER: 1981

The first wave of bands were on to follow-up records, while new groups kept emerging:

Saxon – "Denim and Leather"
Samson – "Riding With the Angels"
Iron Maiden – Drifter"
Rage – "Money"
Raven – "Rock Until You Drop"
Blitzkrieg – "Buried Alive"
Holocaust – "Death or Glory"
Def Leppard – "Bringin' on
 the Heartbreak"
Praying Mantis – "Cheated"
Judas Priest – "Desert Plains"
Girlschool – "C'mon Let's Go"
Motörhead/Girlschool –
 "Please Don't Touch"
Motörhead – "Overkill" (from
 No Sleep Til Hammersmith)
Vardis – "Silver Machine"
Bitches Sin – "Always Ready"
Jaguar – "Backstreet Woman"
Buffalo – "Battle Torn Heroes"
The Handsome Beasts –
 "Local Heroes"
Demon – "Night of the Demon"
Witchfinder General –
 "Burning a Sinner"
Venom – "In League With Satan"

DENIM AND LEATHER: 1982

The last of the NWOBHM's great years, before Pyromania *brought down the curtain:*

Tygers of Pan Tang –
 "Love Potion No 9"
Girlschool –
 "Screaming Blue Murder"
Judas Priest –
 "Screaming for Vengeance"
Diamond Head – "Borrowed Time"
Demon – "Total Possession"
Girl – "Ice in the Blood"
Rage – "Long Way from Home"
Witchfinder General –
 "Free Country"
More – "Blood and Thunder"
Raven – "Crash, Bang, Wallop"
Cloven Hoof – "Back in the USA"
Heavy Pettin – "Roll the Dice"
Samson – "Life on the Run"
Vardis – "Gary Glitter Part One"
Ded Ringer – "Hot Lady"
Tank – "Turn Your Head Around"
Fist – "The Wanderer"
Legend – "Anthrax Attack"
Iron Maiden –
 "The Number of the Beast"

DENIM AND LEATHER:
THE HIGH-GLOSS YEARS

Def Leppard's Pyromania *was the biggest US smash, but plenty of groups tidied up their sound in hopes of commercial success:*

Def Leppard – "Photograph"
Saxon – "Sailing to America"
Girlschool – "Going Under"
Diamond Head – "Makin' Music"
Tygers of Pan Tang – "Paris by Air"
Heavy Pettin – "In and Out of Love"
Raven – "Gimme Some Lovin'"
Nightwing – "Searching"
Terraplane – "I Survive"
Persian Risk – "Too Different"
Wrathchild –
   "(Na Na) Nukklear Rokket"
Samson –
   "Can't Live Without Your Love"
Cloven Hoof –
   "Could This Be Love"
Def Leppard – "Too Late for Love"

The preceding playlists are also accessible when searched by title on major streaming services including Spotify and at this location:

youtube.com/bazillionpoints

About the Author

Michael Hann's work has appeared in *The Guardian*, the *Financial Times*, *The Times* of London, the *Independent*, *The Spectator*, *The Economist*, *The New Statesman*, *The Quietus*, and *Uncut*, among others.

He is the former music editor of *The Guardian*, and a former editor of *FourFourTwo* magazine.

The first band he saw was Samson, opening for Whitesnake at Hammersmith Odeon in January 1983. He believes Witchfinder General's *Death Penalty* to be the best NWOBHM album.

Denim and Leather is his first book. He lives in London.